Practical Strategies to Reduce Childhood Trauma and Mitigate Exposure to the School-to-Prison Pipeline

Belinda M. Alexander-Ashley
Independent Researcher, USA

A volume in the Advances in Early Childhood and K-12 Education (AECKE) Book Series

Published in the United States of America by
IGI Global
Information Science Reference (an imprint of IGI Global)
701 E. Chocolate Avenue
Hershey PA, USA 17033
Tel: 717-533-8845
Fax: 717-533-8661
E-mail: cust@igi-global.com
Web site: http://www.igi-global.com

Copyright © 2023 by IGI Global. All rights reserved. No part of this publication may be reproduced, stored or distributed in any form or by any means, electronic or mechanical, including photocopying, without written permission from the publisher.
Product or company names used in this set are for identification purposes only. Inclusion of the names of the products or companies does not indicate a claim of ownership by IGI Global of the trademark or registered trademark.

Library of Congress Cataloging-in-Publication Data

Names: Alexander-Ashley, Belinda, 1963- editor.
Title: Practical strategies to reduce childhood trauma and mitigate
   exposure to the school-to-prison pipeline / Belinda Alexander-Ashley,
   Editor.
Description: Hershey, PA : Information Science Reference, [2022] | Includes
   bibliographical references and index. | Summary: "This book presents
   holistic evidence-based strategies and practices supporting multiple
   educational levels of leaders, professors/teachers, educators, trauma
   survivors, youth and government administrators in both in-class and
   remote learning environments focused on reducing trauma and mitigating
   exposure to the school-to-prison pipeline"-- Provided by publisher.
Identifiers: LCCN 2022034098 (print) | LCCN 2022034099 (ebook) | ISBN
   9781668457139 (Hardcover) | ISBN 9781668457177 (Paperback) | ISBN
   9781668457146 (eBook)
Subjects: LCSH: Problem children--Education--United States--Case studies. |
   Psychic trauma in children--United States--Prevention. | Psychic trauma
   in adolescence--United States--Prevention. | School
   environment--Psychological aspects. | Discrimination in school
   discipline--United States--Case studies. | School-to-prison
   pipeline--United States. | At-risk youth--Behavior modification. |
   Teachers--Training of--United States.
Classification: LCC LC4802 .P73 2022 (print) | LCC LC4802 (ebook) | DDC
   371.93--dc23/eng/20220902
LC record available at https://lccn.loc.gov/2022034098
LC ebook record available at https://lccn.loc.gov/2022034099

This book is published in the IGI Global book series Advances in Early Childhood and K-12 Education (AECKE) (ISSN: 2329-5929; eISSN: 2329-5937)

British Cataloguing in Publication Data
A Cataloguing in Publication record for this book is available from the British Library.

All work contributed to this book is new, previously-unpublished material.
The views expressed in this book are those of the authors, but not necessarily of the publisher.

For electronic access to this publication, please contact: eresources@igi-global.com.

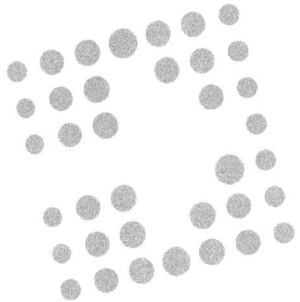

Advances in Early Childhood and K-12 Education (AECKE) Book Series

ISSN:2329-5929
EISSN:2329-5937

Editor-in-Chief: Jared Keengwe, University of North Dakota, USA

MISSION

Early childhood and K-12 education is always evolving as new methods and tools are developed through which to shape the minds of today's youth. Globally, educational approaches vary allowing for new discussions on the best methods to not only educate, but also measure and analyze the learning process as well as an individual's intellectual development. New research in these fields is necessary to improve the current state of education and ensure that future generations are presented with quality learning opportunities.

The **Advances in Early Childhood and K-12 Education (AECKE)** series aims to present the latest research on trends, pedagogies, tools, and methodologies regarding all facets of early childhood and K-12 education.

COVERAGE

- Reading and Writing
- Learning Outcomes
- Diverse Learners
- Performance Assessment
- Curriculum Development
- Bullying in the Classroom
- Urban K-12 Education
- Special Education
- Early Childhood Education
- Common Core State Standards

IGI Global is currently accepting manuscripts for publication within this series. To submit a proposal for a volume in this series, please contact our Acquisition Editors at Acquisitions@igi-global.com or visit: http://www.igi-global.com/publish/.

The Advances in Early Childhood and K-12 Education (AECKE) Book Series (ISSN 2329-5929) is published by IGI Global, 701 E. Chocolate Avenue, Hershey, PA 17033-1240, USA, www.igi-global.com. This series is composed of titles available for purchase individually; each title is edited to be contextually exclusive from any other title within the series. For pricing and ordering information please visit http://www.igi-global.com/book-series/advances-early-childhood-education/76699. Postmaster: Send all address changes to above address. © © 2023 IGI Global. All rights, including translation in other languages reserved by the publisher. No part of this series may be reproduced or used in any form or by any means – graphics, electronic, or mechanical, including photocopying, recording, taping, or information and retrieval systems – without written permission from the publisher, except for non commercial, educational use, including classroom teaching purposes. The views expressed in this series are those of the authors, but not necessarily of IGI Global.

Titles in this Series

For a list of additional titles in this series, please visit:
http://www.igi-global.com/book-series/advances-early-childhood-education/76699

Preparing Pre-Service Teachers to Integrate Technology in K-12 Classrooms Standards and Best Practices
C. Lorraine Webb (Texas A&M University, San Antonio, USA) and Amanda L. Lindner (Texas A&M University, San Antonio, USA)
Information Science Reference • © 2022 • 340pp • H/C (ISBN: 9781668454787) • US $215.00

Cutting-Edge Language and Literacy Tools for Students on the Autism Spectrum
Katharine P. Beals (Drexel University, USA)
Information Science Reference • © 2022 • 298pp • H/C (ISBN: 9781799894421) • US $215.00

Handbook of Research on Family Literacy Practices and Home-School Connections
Kathy R. Fox (University of North Carolina Wilmington, USA) and Laura E. Szech (University of North Carolina Wilmington, USA)
Information Science Reference • © 2022 • 353pp • H/C (ISBN: 9781668445693) • US $270.00

Rethinking Inclusion and Transformation in Special Education
Maria Efstratopoulou (United Arab Emirates University, UAE)
Information Science Reference • © 2022 • 348pp • H/C (ISBN: 9781668446805) • US $215.00

Best Practices for Trauma-Informed School Counseling
Angela M. Powell (Lone Star College, USA)
Information Science Reference • © 2022 • 331pp • H/C (ISBN: 9781799897859) • US $215.00

For an entire list of titles in this series, please visit:
http://www.igi-global.com/book-series/advances-early-childhood-education/76699

701 East Chocolate Avenue, Hershey, PA 17033, USA
Tel: 717-533-8845 x100 • Fax: 717-533-8661
E-Mail: cust@igi-global.com • www.igi-global.com

This book is dedicated to the educators, administrators, school personnel and supporters who committed to creating a brighter future for the next generation.

Table of Contents

Preface xv

Acknowledgment xxvii

Chapter 1
Spaces of Healing and Empowerment: Creating Safe, Trauma-Free Schools for All Youth 1
    Joe Lewis, Hamline University, USA
    Letitia Basford, Hamline University, USA

Chapter 2
When They See Us: Implications for Anti-Racist School Leadership Through Examining the Experiences of Black Boys 20
    Jennifer Grace, University of Houston-Clear Lake, USA

Chapter 3
Culturally-Responsive Disciplinary Strategies After Returning to the In-Person Learning Environment in the Era of the COVID-19 Pandemic 48
    Wei-Ling Sun, University of Texas at El Paso, USA

Chapter 4
Using Trauma-Informed Care and Horticulture Therapy With College Students: A Counseling Approach Modeled After a Refugee Resettlement Community 66
    Jon N. Trauth, Central State University, USA
    Karleah Harris, University of Arkansas at Pine Bluff, USA
    Nikkita Jackson, Central State University, USA

Chapter 5
Emotional Coaching: A Technique to Regulate School Bullying 83
    Sruthi Suresh, CHRIST University (Deemed), India
    R. Vijaya, CHRIST University (Deemed), India

Chapter 6
Leveraging Literacy Instruction to Support Learners Who Have Experienced Compounded Trauma 111
    Karyn A. Allee, Mercer University, USA
    Annemarie Bazzo Kaczmarczyk, Mercer University, USA

Chapter 7
Practical Strategies for Higher Hope Learning Spaces: Reducing Childhood Trauma in a Post-Pandemic Era 141
    Belinda M. Alexander-Ashley, Independent Researcher, USA

Chapter 8
Integrating Family History Into the Post-Pandemic Elementary Learning Space: Reducing Childhood Trauma 168
    Belinda M. Alexander-Ashley, Independent Researcher, USA

Chapter 9
Teachers as Disruptors of the School-to-Prison Pipeline: Creating Trauma-Sensitive Spaces in Classrooms 194
    Michele McMahon Nobel, Ohio Wesleyan University, USA

Chapter 10
Increasing Readiness for Cultural Responsiveness and Trauma-Informed Practice: Collective and Individual Readiness 229
    Jerica Knox, National Center for School Mental Health, USA
    Adam Alvarez, Rowan University, USA
    Alexandrea Golden, University of Memphis, USA
    Elan C. Hope, Policy Research Associates, USA

Chapter 11
Using Positive Behavioral Interventions and Supports to Disrupt the School-to-Prison Pipeline: Decriminalizing Childhood Adversity 261
    Erin E. Neuman-Boone, Robert Morris University, USA
    Patricia Kardambikis, Robert Morris University, USA
    Vicki J. Donne, Robert Morris University, USA

Compilation of References 289

About the Contributors 341

Index 347

Detailed Table of Contents

Preface xv

Acknowledgment xxvii

Chapter 1
Spaces of Healing and Empowerment: Creating Safe, Trauma-Free Schools
for All Youth 1
    Joe Lewis, Hamline University, USA
    Letitia Basford, Hamline University, USA

In this chapter, the authors begin by describing the experiences of one family with the school-to-prison pipeline, seeking to elucidate its causes and illustrate its damaging effects on real people. Next, they analyze the success of two dropout recovery programs that are dismantling the school-to-prison pipeline. They identify and describe five key qualities that explain the success of these programs, including: a casual, family-like atmosphere with a close-knit community; creative responses to chronic absenteeism; extreme patience and flexibility in the classroom; innovative programs that hook student interest and provide a means for students to heal from past trauma; and wrap-around services, including heavy advising, for all students. Finally, the authors share their theory of pedagogical and institutional plasticity, an overarching philosophy and practice that provides a framework for creating safe, trauma free schools that serve all youth with spaces of healing and empowerment.

Chapter 2
When They See Us: Implications for Anti-Racist School Leadership Through
Examining the Experiences of Black Boys 20
    Jennifer Grace, University of Houston-Clear Lake, USA

This chapter examines the experiences of Black males and their description of race-based trauma encountered at school and its impact. The author conducted semi-structured interviews with Black males who had been expelled from school. Participants describe school as a hostile environment for Black males, citing microaggressions, isolation, and verbal abuse as indicators. This is in additional to environment stressors such as racism, violence, and criminalization. The participants narrate their emotional responses to this repeated trauma. Based on the findings, the authors make practical recommendations for anti-racist school leadership to reduce the trauma inflicted by schools due to racial bias and racist policy and practices, thus mitigating exposure to the school to prison pipeline.

Chapter 3
Culturally-Responsive Disciplinary Strategies After Returning to the In-Person Learning Environment in the Era of the COVID-19 Pandemic 48
    Wei-Ling Sun, University of Texas at El Paso, USA

In this chapter, the researcher provides in-depth discussions regarding the commonly used disciplinary strategies in schools before the COVID-19 pandemic, and the implementation of social-emotional learning initiatives after returning to in-person learning that is intentionally selected to address the increasing exposure of home violence, abuse, homelessness, and isolation among students during the pandemic in a predominately Latina/o population community located in a Texas borderland area. This research uses critical race theory and culturally responsive school leaders as a theoretical framework to analyze leadership strategies to address students' behavioral issues due to trauma and prevent exposure to the school-to-prison pipeline. With the elementary and secondary school emergency relief (ESSER) fund and the education disruption due to the pandemic, a paradigm shift pushes school leaders to adapt culturally responsive disciplinary strategies when addressing students' behavioral issues. Policy implications of the findings are discussed.

Chapter 4
Using Trauma-Informed Care and Horticulture Therapy With College Students: A Counseling Approach Modeled After a Refugee Resettlement Community 66
    Jon N. Trauth, Central State University, USA
    Karleah Harris, University of Arkansas at Pine Bluff, USA
    Nikkita Jackson, Central State University, USA

Trauma-informed care has been considered for high schools since 2010. Both teachers and support staff realize that it is important to make sure to meet students' basic needs for any learning to occur. This information rings true for all college students, especially since the pandemic. The trauma-informed care model has been presented to faculty and staff at Central State University to engage them and allow them to learn new strategies that will help them work with a traumatized student population. This chapter addresses how the model of trauma-informed care training on the website starr.org will help students to complete their college courses more effectively. The small mid-western college in the United States pulls from a few models that were used at the lighthouse community school and the St Leo Burundi refugee resettlement programs. School challenges can be from, according to previous research, being bored with school programs, missing too many days, and being unable to catch up. The chapter will consider how these issues can be combated using the TIC model.

Chapter 5
Emotional Coaching: A Technique to Regulate School Bullying........................83
    Sruthi Suresh, CHRIST University (Deemed), India
    R. Vijaya, CHRIST University (Deemed), India

The present chapter aims to address school bullying as a source of childhood trauma and recommends the use of emotional coaching as a regulatory strategy. The chapter will begin with an introduction to the concept, types, occurrence, and impact of school bullying. Next, the authors will outline the role of school bullying in pushing students to enter the school-to-prison pipeline and the challenges involved in identifying and supporting these students. The chapter will then explore the process of emotional coaching, the steps involved, the role of teachers, and the challenges they could face during this process. Finally, the chapter will end by providing practical strategies to incorporate emotional coaching in traditional and virtual classrooms as well as provide a sample template script for the same. The summary and key points section will briefly review the content and highlight the key takeaways for the readers to keep in mind.

Chapter 6
Leveraging Literacy Instruction to Support Learners Who Have Experienced Compounded Trauma..111
    Karyn A. Allee, Mercer University, USA
    Annemarie Bazzo Kaczmarczyk, Mercer University, USA

Children can experience trauma in multiple ways and spaces which can have profound effects on their development and impact student engagement, approaches to learning, and student outcomes. In this chapter, the authors break down various types of trauma, adversity, and stress that can contribute to delays in children's development. Schools can impact children's pre-existing trauma (or cause new trauma), even unintentionally, and children's classroom behaviors can signal that trauma may be affecting them. Teachers can use instructional strategies that both buffer students to potentially mitigate the harmful effects of systemic and compounded trauma, and also meet academic learning goals. The authors provide some suggestions on how to use literacy learning strategies in elementary school to support learners, especially those who may be historically marginalized due to systemic conditions like racism. They conclude by providing their thoughts on how future research can continue to identify evidence-based ways to support vulnerable learners.

Chapter 7
Practical Strategies for Higher Hope Learning Spaces: Reducing Childhood Trauma in a Post-Pandemic Era 141
    Belinda M. Alexander-Ashley, Independent Researcher, USA

Childhood trauma was found to increase the risk of aggression and disruptive behavior in classrooms. The disruptive behavior risks exposure to the school-to-prison nexus, a result of inequities in zero tolerance and exclusionary policies. The coronavirus disease (COVID-19) pandemic disrupted the world's learning systems leaving in its wake feelings of anxiety, depression, fear, uncertainty, and hopelessness. This exacerbated the existing trauma experienced by students. Thousands of studies involving hope theory advanced to a science with predictable outcomes and progressively more benefits for dealing with childhood trauma. The eight recommended practical strategies for higher hope include acknowledging that hope takes work, understanding the tenets of hope theory, emphasizing a personal approach to student needs, protecting educators from vicarious trauma, listening more and talking less, developing ambassadors of hope, and creating partnerships of hope focused on positive experiences, effective communication, and resilience to reduce the effects of childhood trauma.

Chapter 8
Integrating Family History Into the Post-Pandemic Elementary Learning Space: Reducing Childhood Trauma 168
    Belinda M. Alexander-Ashley, Independent Researcher, USA

The COVID-19 pandemic highlighted existing inequities as a result of zero tolerance and exclusionary policies that disproportionately impacted the world's learners living in poverty, people of color, and those experiencing special challenges. Under the existing educational system, marginalized students often feel devalued and without a voice. Integrating family history and genealogy into the elementary school learning space provides a methodology and framework that focuses on the historical conditions that promote healthy dialogues and sustain discourses connecting to other historical events. The process of creating positive experiences with family history, improving the classroom environment, effectively communicating, rapport and trust building, and strengthened socio-emotional skills reduce childhood trauma. The six recommended strategies include introspection and reflection, navigating parallel time periods, valuing genealogical tools, encouraging an environment of hope, normalizing authenticity, and transforming the learning environment.

Chapter 9
Teachers as Disruptors of the School-to-Prison Pipeline: Creating Trauma-Sensitive Spaces in Classrooms 194
Michele McMahon Nobel, Ohio Wesleyan University, USA

This chapter seeks to provide context for teachers' overreliance on punitive discipline practices and how these practices contribute to the school-to-prison pipeline. If preservice teachers course content can be enhanced, it may help teachers learn about their own bias, more proactive responses to challenging behavior, trauma and its manifestations, and trauma-informed alternatives to challenging behavior. These changes may lead to classrooms that are more trauma-sensitive and culturally relevant, which will allow teachers to disrupt punitive discipline systems that are contributing to the school-to-prison pipeline. This chapter provides an overview of relevant literature and suggestions for ways that teacher training programs can prepare teachers to be more trauma-sensitive. Topics include positive behavioral interventions and supports, social-emotional learning, and trauma-informed approaches. Specific classroom practices will be described.

Chapter 10
Increasing Readiness for Cultural Responsiveness and Trauma-Informed Practice: Collective and Individual Readiness 229
Jerica Knox, National Center for School Mental Health, USA
Adam Alvarez, Rowan University, USA
Alexandrea Golden, University of Memphis, USA
Elan C. Hope, Policy Research Associates, USA

For years, the most prominent approaches to addressing youth trauma have been heavily influenced by whiteness and hegemonic systems of dominance. Rather than universal designs meant to address the needs of "all" children, it is imperative that trauma-informed practices be more culturally responsive. A major challenge, however, is that educators may be at various starting places when it comes to understanding and enacting culturally responsive practices that are also trauma-informed. In short, educators need learning opportunities that can increase their level of readiness—their attitudes and self-reported beliefs about their capacity—to implement culturally responsive, trauma-informed practices. The chapter has two overarching goals: (1) to contextualize trauma-informed practices within a culturally responsive framework and (2) to provide practical strategies and insights for promoting educators' readiness to engage in culturally responsive, trauma-informed professional learning.

Chapter 11
Using Positive Behavioral Interventions and Supports to Disrupt the School-to-Prison Pipeline: Decriminalizing Childhood Adversity 261
  Erin E. Neuman-Boone, Robert Morris University, USA
  Patricia Kardambikis, Robert Morris University, USA
  Vicki J. Donne, Robert Morris University, USA

Poverty and trauma risks need not create a criminal pathway or pipeline to prison. As the number of adverse childhood experiences (ACEs) increase, so does the risk of dropping out of school. The more often students are suspended, the more likely they are to be referred to the juvenile justice system and face jail or prison time. Once in the system, the likelihood of recidivism is great. One multifaceted intervention to disrupt the school-to-prison pipeline (STPP) is positive behavioral interventions and supports (PBIS). The aim of this model is to alter the school environment by creating improved systems involving discipline, reinforcement, and data management. These systematic changes may disrupt the STPP for students living in poverty and experiencing ACEs.

Compilation of References 289

About the Contributors 341

Index 347

Preface

Nearly 1.6 billion learners in more than 190 countries have been interrupted by the COVID-19 pandemic creating the world's largest disruption to the educational system (Chaturvedi et al., 2021). To minimize the spread of COVID-19, schools and other learning spaces closed impacting 94 percent of the world's student population, approximately 99% in low and lower-middle income countries (United Nations, 2020). The pandemic exacerbated existing educational disparities by reducing learning opportunities for many of the most vulnerable children, youth and adults which include those living in poor or rural areas, girls, refugees, children and young adults with special needs, and forcibly displaced persons (United Nations, 2020). Beyond education, school closures hampered essential services to children and communities including access to nutritious food, parents' ability to work, and increased risks of violence against women and girls (United Nations, 2020).

Racial disparities resulting from inequities in discipline and exclusionary policies in the education system left poor and disadvantaged students, especially Black and Brown students, exposed to the school-to-prison pipeline (Basford et al., 2020), more recently known as the school-to-prison nexus (Goldman & Rodriguez, 2021). In its aftermath, students, their families, and educators were left feeling anxious, depressed, scared, and overwhelmed. This exacerbated existing trauma experienced by students and their teachers. While not caused by the pandemic, childhood trauma was found to increase the risk of violent and aggressive behavior in adulthood that often leads to criminality (Kalmuss, 1984; Straus et al., 1980; Widom, 1989).

Because similar patterns exist within both the criminal justice and educational systems, their linkages are difficult to ignore (Wald & Losen, 2003). The rates of childhood and adult trauma are high among the incarcerated (Wolff & Shi, 2012). Research has shown that putting a high percentage of a nation's population in prison has a negative impact on society as a whole, perpetuating a cycle of crime and violence that may extend to future generations (Simpson 2020). The elevated rates of trauma necessitate a need to reduce childhood trauma within the education system and disciplinary referrals that increase exposure to the school-to-prison pipeline. While the pandemic not only offered challenges, it offered opportunities to interrupt these upheavals and reshape the future educational system.

THE CHALLENGES

The educational system involves many contributors including students, parents, guardians, teachers, administrative staff, cafeteria works, assistants, technical staff, and bus drivers, among others. For the system to work properly, all facets of the system must be valued for the contributions made in fulfilling the needs of each student. Oftentimes, cafeteria workers are overlooked because they do not teach or create policies. However, cafeteria staff are responsible for fulfilling the basic nutritional needs of the students. Without their services or contributions, many students may be unfocused and distracted because they are hungry. Bus drivers, too, are often overlooked for their contributions including transporting students to and from school and/or other activities. If students are unable to attend class, the system breaks down. Therefore, it is imperative to celebrate and value all the everyday heroes of the educational system that help it to operate successfully.

Equity is giving everyone what they need to be successful (Horner, 2019). Equity presents a challenge to disadvantaged learners, especially challenges brought about by emergency online education including insufficient access to reliable devices such as computers, laptops, tablets or other smart or mobile devices. Additionally, other challenges include limited or poor connectivity, the inability to afford connectivity costs, and/or lack of digital skills, all of which are essential to successful online learning (Xiao, 2021). Understanding the individual needs of each learner makes personalized learning and effective communication with the student and their families imperative.

Best practices for educators necessitate that they create a safe, secure environment where students' physical and emotional needs are met (Education Staffing Space, n.d.). In reshaping the educational system, it must be acknowledged that teachers, too, have needs that must be met. An estimated 17% of public-school teachers reported leaving the teaching profession before their fifth year due to low salary and insufficient resources as major reasons for departure (Gray & Taie, 2015). Since the onset of the pandemic, the departure of teachers has risen to 44% (Jagannathan, 2021). This rise indicates a disconnect or disparity that exists between teachers and the educational system that must be bridged if the exodus is to be halted. Teachers must not be forgotten in the educational process and provided a voice and platform to shape the educational system of the future. Otherwise, the exodus from the teaching profession that began before the pandemic will continue on its accelerated course following the pandemic.

Preface

If the world is to continue to attract the best and brightest in the educational profession, some things must change about the way our educational system operates. Communication and compassion will be important in modeling the priority that should be placed on the teaching and the educational community. Finger pointing or finding blame for the state of affairs will not solve this crisis. Even with the knowledge of who or what is to blame for educational challenges, the problem will still need resolution if every student is to reach their highest potential. Therefore, a more global approach incorporating the needs of all in the educational system is recommended to reflect the diversity required to understand and respond to the needs of the educational system.

SEARCHING FOR A SOLUTION

School closures due to the COVID-19 pandemic, racial violence, injustice, and resource inequities highlight the need for multi-disciplinary strategies and practices that support evidence-based practices across a range of educational levels for leaders, professors/teachers, educational professionals, trauma survivors, youth and government programs for both in-class and remote learning environments. In the face of these complex disparities, this book provides an array of practical strategies and tools focused on reducing childhood trauma while mitigating exposure to the school-to-prison pipeline for multiple grade levels and multiple learning environments. There is no one size fits all for every district or learning space.

There are practical solutions that can be accomplished at all grade levels and environments to move the educational system toward the greater goal of preventing a learning crisis from becoming a generational catastrophe (United Nations, 2020). Within the educational system, all learners must be valued including students with special needs who often have little or no voice or representation in the educational community. Simply acknowledging the value of each student and members of the learning community and committing to reconciling their place in the future may prove essential in reshaping the interconnected global educational system. The world will not rise to its highest potential unless everyone is offered an opportunity and access to a quality education.

Additionally, this book unites amazing authors with a vision for strategies to move successfully into the post-pandemic learning space. There is no one right strategy for all situations, grade levels or learning spaces. This book offers a three-pronged approach that includes the voices of students and specific nontraditional programs targeting the needs of students and lessons learned, student/teacher classroom strategies, and preservice training and leadership development. The chapters work together to present cohesive strategies, but do not require that chapters be read in chronological order to achieve positive results. Each school system is unique and operates with both strengths and weaknesses. It is important to encourage and reinforce the strengths of each person within the school system regardless of their title while minimizing their weaknesses.

The heart of the educational system are the students and their ability to learn and mature to reach their potentials and contribute to the global economy. However, to reach their potential, student voices must be heard, educators' views must be included in the conversation, input processed and their needs met. Any solutions must be inclusive of the most vulnerable if we are truly to improve equity in our educational system.

ORGANIZATION OF THE BOOK

The book is organized into three sections, (1) voices of impacted students, the traumatic echoes that reverberate from those impacted from one generation to the next, and lessons learned from those most impacted in nontraditional programs and their responses following the pandemic; (2) interactive strategies to connect and communicate with students and teachers; and (3) preservice training and leadership development. The sections are important in creating evidence-based knowledge and facilitate access to required information seamlessly. Section 1 includes four chapters encompassing individual student voices impacted by the school-to-prison pipeline, two drop out recovery and nontraditional school programs that present their lessons learned and disciplinary modifications representing shifts in the post-pandemic leadership. The final chapter of Section 1 presents one university's responses to its student needs in the wake of the pandemic using sensory-based therapies including horticulture therapy with college students.

It is critical that the educational community hear and understand the voices of those impacted by trauma and the school-to-prison pipeline. The voices of those impacted create waves of trauma that echo in waves from one generation to the next. Section 2 provides creative classroom strategies utilizing four different approaches supported by evidence-based practices. Finally, Section 3 encompasses a trio of preservice training and leadership development from various facets and roles within the educational system.

The authors provided vision for the future educational system that differ in their approach, but captures common threads that bind their research into cohesive multifaceted strategies to achieve common goals. There are four major themes that reverberate throughout the book. First, each chapter seeks to reduce trauma and/or mitigate student exposure to the student-to-prison pipeline by focusing on cultural responsiveness, creating positive experiences, dialogues, and best practices within their subject matter. Second, flexibility and adaptability were encouraged to create connectedness with all stakeholders through introspection, reflection, and social and emotional safety. Third, each seeks to value the personalized experiences of students and educators capitalizing on their uniqueness to become a blended, more inclusive safe cultural learning environments. Fourth, the voices of all the stakeholders at every level are valued for their contribution to the success of the entire educational system. For these reasons, listening and learning to be open to hearing what is being conveyed is critical to transformation of the school system.

SECTION 1: STUDENT VOICES, ECHOES, AND SHARED LESSONS LEARNED

Section 1 contains four chapters that present the voices of those impacted by trauma and the school-to-prison nexus. Listening and understanding the experiences of those negatively impacted help to understand the magnitude of the problem, the traumatic echoes that permeate one generation to the next, and the imperative need to respond quickly. Readers are provided a glimpse into the lives of the students impacted by trauma and the school-to-prison pipeline which serve to inspire and create a more informed learning environment for students. The goal is to inspire interest in not just hearing, but listening and acting with purpose to reshape the educational system.

Chapter 1: Spaces of Healing and Empowerment – Creating Safe, Trauma-Free Schools for All Youth

Chapter one is segmented into three distinct parts that capture the voices of a family impacted by the school-to-prison pipeline, the echoes left behind, followed by lessons learned from two drop out recovery programs in the Upper Midwest within the United States, and finally presents recommendations gleaned from the researchers gathering the data. The authors allow the readers to glimpse first-hand the impact of trauma and the school-to-prison nexus has on individuals and their families. Success for the students and the programs hinged on their ability to adapt and change to address the needs of students. This personalized approach to student experiences undergirded the recommendations provided by the researchers in helping to reshape the educational system, reduce trauma and mitigate further exposure to the school-to-prison nexus.

Chapter 2: When They See Us – Implications for Anti-Racist School Leadership Through Examining the Experiences of Black Boys

Chapter two presents the race-based traumatic experiences of ten high school students in New Orleans in the United States of America. The authors' research provided in-depth day-to-day experiences of young people caught in a cycle that they neither wanted nor controlled. By providing this platform for them to share their truths, it is hoped that readers will gain a deeper understanding of their experiences, connect with common situations, and pursue alternative paths to dealing with trauma more effectively. By creating positive experiences, effective communications, and open dialogues, childhood trauma is reduced (International Schooling, n.d.).

Chapter 3: Culturally-Responsive Disciplinary Strategies After Returning In-Person Learning Environment in the Era of the COVID-19 Pandemic

Chapter three discusses disciplinary strategies in a Texas school and provides culturally responsive recommendations to school leaders that reduce trauma and exposure to the school-to-prison pipeline. In relation to culturally responsive learning spaces, four elements are discussed including self-reflection, development of culturally responsive teachers, promotion of inclusive school environments, and engagement of students, parents and indigenous contexts. It is important that the voices of all stakeholders are heard to create trusting relationships and an open honest dialogue where they are heard. Findings show that school leaders prioritized mental health services to replace the use of exclusionary practices.

Chapter 4: Using Trauma-Informed Care and Horticulture Therapy With College Students – A Counseling Approach Modeled After a Refugee Resettlement Community

Chapter four discusses sensory-based therapies including a horticulture therapy with trauma-informed care that were used in a college counseling center to reduce trauma following the pandemic. Their approach is modeled after a refugee resettlement community in Ohio. Horticulture was used as a method of treatment for a wide range of ages in a variety of environments to promote health, well-being and social cohesion (Harris & Trauth, 2020).

Preface

SECTION TWO: INTERACTIVE STRATEGIES FOR STUDENTS AND TEACHERS – CONNECTING AND COMMUNICATING EFFECTIVELY

Section two chapters encapsulate classroom strategies and best practices that encourage flexibility, adaptability, and creativity in reducing trauma and mitigating exposure to the school-to-prison pipeline. The approaches include emotional coaching, school-based meditation, creating higher hope in elementary learning spaces, leveraging literacy where students are seen, and integrating family history into the elementary school environment. The authors present evidence-based strategies that target multiple grade levels for educators and school personnel that may be used to address the unique student needs.

Chapter 5: Emotional Coaching – A Technique to Regulate the Traumatic Experience of School Bullying

In chapter five, the authors begin by discussing bullying, a common cause of childhood trauma, its impact and connection to the school-to-prison pipeline. Research has indicated that children involved in bullying are more likely to have delinquent thoughts and engage in violent and criminal behavior, such as dating and domestic violence, thereby contributing to the school-to-prison pipeline (Bender & Lösel, 2011). Finally, the chapter focuses on the role of bullying as a childhood traumatic experience and explore emotional coaching as a strategy to break the school-to-prison pipeline by building resilience and regulating bullying more among children.

Chapter 6: Leveraging Literacy Instruction to Support Learners Who Have Experienced Compounded Trauma

Chapter six leverages literacy to increase self-awareness using strong stories. Establishing social and emotional safety is important to create a more positive learning environment. The authors present strategies that create learning spaces where children feel "seen" and heard. Promoting a more inclusive school learning environment helps with engagement with students, teachers, and all personnel within the school system. By creating positive experiences, effective communications, and open dialogues, childhood trauma is reduced (International Schooling, n.d.).

Chapter 7: Practical Strategies for Higher Hope Learning Spaces – Reducing Childhood Trauma in a Post-Pandemic Era

Chapter seven provides a methodical approach to creating an elementary higher hope learning space that encourages positive experiences and effective communication to reduce trauma and mitigate exposure to the school-to-prison pipeline. Positive experiences, rapport building, effective communication, and increased resilience reduce risk of childhood trauma (International Schooling, n.d.) and subsequently reduces exposure to the school-to-prison pipeline. The higher the hope of a child, the higher the daily attendance, the lower the tardiness rate, the higher the grades, and better the test scores (Gwinn & Hellman, 2019).

Chapter 8: Integrating Family History Into the Post-Pandemic Elementary Learning Space – Reducing Childhood Trauma

Chapter eight serves as a transformational tool to encourage deeper understanding of experiences, connectedness and empathy. Genealogy and family history provide critical methodology which focuses on the historical conditions that produce dialogue, how individuals have been shaped in a given time and space, as well as the mechanisms of power that produce and sustain such dialogues (Arribas-Ayllon & Walkerdine, 2008, p. 91). Research indicates young people who possess a positive racial identity are more likely to perform better in school and possess a higher level of assuredness and confidence in their social relationships (Sellers et al., 2006). Creating effective communication reduces childhood trauma and mitigates risk to the school-to-prison pipeline (International Schooling, n.d.).

SECTION THREE: PRESERVICE TRAINING AND LEADERSHIP DEVELOPMENT

Section three contains three chapters encompassing multi-faceted preservice training and leadership development for teachers, leaders and other school personnel. This section focuses on the benefits of training new teachers to be more trauma-sensitive and providing on-going training to other school personnel. Approaching development from both individual and collective approaches focus on the importance of each individual contributing to the success of the entire educational system, reducing trauma and exposure to the school-to-prison pipeline.

Chapter 9: Teachers as Disrupters of the School-to-Prison Pipeline – Creating Trauma-Sensitive Spaces in Classrooms

Chapter nine champions teachers as disruptors of the school-to-prison pipeline in secondary schools. The realization is that teachers while helping children who have experienced trauma, they too may experience secondary trauma. Protecting them is very important in promoting the health of the entire educational system. The Substance Abuse and Mental Health Services Administration (2014) framework's methodology is used including (1) realizing the prevalence and impact of trauma, (2) recognizing the signs of trauma, (3) systematically responding with best practices, and (4) resisting re-traumatization. This methodical approach assists teachers in understanding their role and importance in reducing childhood trauma.

Chapter 10: Increasing Readiness for Cultural Responsiveness and Trauma-Informed Practice – Collective and Individual Readiness

Chapter ten increases readiness to better prepare educators and schools to implement cultural responsiveness and trauma-informed practices more effectively and cohesively. The authors use a collective and individual framework for professional development. Collective readiness seeks outside sources, increases the color consciousness perspective, and increases collective thought. Individual development focuses on personal identity through such things as family trees. Self-reflection and awareness are important in creating trusting environments where students feel safe to share their voices, where trauma's impact may be reduced and exposure to the school-to-prison pipeline mitigated.

Chapter 11: Using Positive Behavior Intervention and Supports to Disrupt the School-to-Prison Pipeline – Decriminalizing Childhood Adversity

Chapter eleven examines using positive behavioral interventions and support to decriminalize childhood adversity and disrupt the school-to-prison pipeline. By acquiring the voices of various stakeholders and considering the school's culture, Positive Behavioral Interventions and Supports (PBIS) can be customized to represent and meet the specific needs of the school's demographics and community (Goodman-Scott et al., 2018). An individualized response to the needs of students is critical to reshaping a system where their needs are met. If there is no acknowledgement of a problem, there can be no response to the problem.

Belinda Alexander-Ashley
Independent Researcher, USA

REFERENCES

Arribas-Ayllon, M., & Walkerdine, V. (2008). Foucauldian discourse analysis. In C. Willig & W. Stainton-Rogers (Eds.), The Sage Handbook of Qualitative Research in Psychology (pp. 91-108). Sage Publications. doi:10.4135/9781848607927.n6

Basford, L., Lewis, J., & Trout, M. (2020, May 22). It can be done: How one charter school combats the school-to-prison pipeline. *The Urban Review*. Advance online publication. doi:10.100711256-020-00583-x

Chaturvedi, S., Purohit, S., & Verma, M. (2021). Effective teaching practices for success during Covid-19 pandemic: Toward phygital learning. *Frontiers in Education*, 6, 1–10. doi:10.3389/feduc.2021.646557

Education Staffing Space. (n.d.). *Best practices in teaching and learning elementary education*. https://ess.com/blog/articles-best-practices-in-teaching-and-learning-in-elementary-school/

Goldman, M., & Rodriguez, N. (2021). Juvenile court in the school-prison nexus: Youth punishment, schooling and structures of inequity. *Journal of Crime and Justice*, 45(3), 270–284. doi:10.1080/0735648X.2021.1950562

Goodman-Scott, E., Hayes, D., & Cholewa, B. (2018). It takes a village: A case study of positive behavioral interventions and supports implementation in an exemplary urban middle school. *The Urban Review*, 50(1), 97–122. doi:10.100711256-017-0431-z

Gray, L., & Taie, S. (2015). *Public school teacher attrition and mobility in the first five years: Results from the first through fifth waves of the 2007-08 beginning teacher longitudinal study*. U.S. Department of Education. https://nces.ed.gov/pubs2015/2015337.pdf

Gwinn, C., & Hellman, C. (2019). *Hope rising: How the science of hope can change your life*. Morgan James Publishing.

Harris, K., & Trauth, J. (2020). Horticulture therapy benefits: A report. *International Journal of Current Science and Multidisciplinary Research*, 3(4), 61–65.

Horner, J. (2019, May 1). *Let's think about equity, equality and justice*. https://psychology.wisheights.org/2019/05/01/lets-think-about-equity-equality-justice/

International Schooling. (n.d.). *Six ways to minimize the effect of childhood trauma.* Retrieved August 15, 2022, from https://internationalschooling.org/blog/6-ways-to-minimize-the-effect-of-childhood-trauma/

Jagannathan, M. (2021, February 22). *Teachers were already leaving the profession due to stress then covid-19 hit.* https://www.marketwatch.com/story/teachers-were-already-leaving-the-profession-due-to-stress-then-covid-19-hit-11614025213

Kalmuss, D. S. (1984). The intergenerational transmission of marital aggression. *Journal of Marriage and Family, 46*(1), 11–19. doi:10.2307/351858

Sellers, R. M., Copeland-Linder, N., Martin, P. P., & Lewis, R. H. (2006). Racial identity matters: The relationship between racial discrimination and psychological functioning in African American adolescents. *Journal of Research on Adolescence, 16*(2), 187–216. doi:10.1111/j.1532-7795.2006.00128.x

Simpson, V. (2020, September 14). *Incarceration rates by country.* World Atlas. https://www.worldatlas.com/articles/largest-prison-population-rates-in-the-world.html

Straus, M. A., Gelles, R. J., & Steinmetz, S. (1980). Behind closed doors: Violence in the American family. Anchor Press.

Substance Abuse and Mental Health Services Administration. (2014). *SAMHSA's concept of trauma and guidance for a trauma-informed approach.* Substance Abuse and Mental Health Services Administration. https://store.samhsa.gov/sites/default/files/d7/priv/sma14-4884.pdf

United Nations. (2020, August 22). *Policy brief: Education during covid-19 and beyond.* https://unsdg.un.org/resources/policy-brief-education-during-covid-19-and-beyond

Wald, J., & Losen, D. (2003, November 5). Defining and redirecting a school-to-prison pipeline. *New Directions for Youth Development, 99*(99), 9–15. doi:10.1002/yd.51 PMID:14635431

Widom, C. S. (1989). Child abuse, neglect, and violent criminal behavior. *Criminology, 27*(2), 251–271. doi:10.1111/j.1745-9125.1989.tb01032.x

Wolff, N., & Shi, J. (2012). Childhood and adult trauma experiences of incarcerated persons and their relationship to adult behavioral health problems and treatment. *International Journal of Environmental Research and Public Health, 9*(5), 1908–1926. doi:10.3390/ijerph9051908 PMID:22754481

Xiao, J. (2021). From equality to justice: Should online education be the new normal in education? In A. Bozkurt (Ed.), *Emerging pedagogies for the future of education: Trauma-informed, care, and pandemic pedagogy* (pp. 1–15). IGI Global. doi:10.4018/978-1-7998-7275-7.ch001

Acknowledgment

Great thanks and gratitude to the committed, visionary authors who contributed to the book to expand the voices and expertise available to educators and those seeking to transform the educational landscape following the pandemic. It has been my honor and pleasure working with you.

Thank you to IGI Global for their willingness to expand the wealth of knowledge available to the educational community. It has been my great honor serving with your company.

Thank you to my Board of Advisors who contributed their expertise to making this book the best that it can be. Special thanks to Dr. Georgia Pavlic-Roseberry for her endless support!

Thank you to the readers who ultimately benefit from the knowledge provided by the authors, Board of Advisors, and IGI Global Publishers.

Finally, thank you to my wonderful husband, Joey, my children, Olajuwon and Joy Ashley, who have supported and encouraged me along this journey. Special thanks to my parents, Thomas and Gladys Alexander, and my ceaseless cheerleaders, Bruce Alexander Sr., and Larry Abernathy!

Chapter 1
Spaces of Healing and Empowerment:
Creating Safe, Trauma-Free Schools for All Youth

Joe Lewis
Hamline University, USA

Letitia Basford
Hamline University, USA

ABSTRACT

In this chapter, the authors begin by describing the experiences of one family with the school-to-prison pipeline, seeking to elucidate its causes and illustrate its damaging effects on real people. Next, they analyze the success of two dropout recovery programs that are dismantling the school-to-prison pipeline. They identify and describe five key qualities that explain the success of these programs, including: a casual, family-like atmosphere with a close-knit community; creative responses to chronic absenteeism; extreme patience and flexibility in the classroom; innovative programs that hook student interest and provide a means for students to heal from past trauma; and wrap-around services, including heavy advising, for all students. Finally, the authors share their theory of pedagogical and institutional plasticity, an overarching philosophy and practice that provides a framework for creating safe, trauma free schools that serve all youth with spaces of healing and empowerment.

DOI: 10.4018/978-1-6684-5713-9.ch001

INTRODUCTION

We dedicate this chapter to Philip Borer Nelson, who was tragically shot and killed in 2017. Philip and his family inspired our initial interest in understanding and seeking to dismantle the school-to-prison pipeline. After sharing his story openly and honestly with us, Philip also began to speak in our classes, at other universities, at K-12 schools, conferences, and public events. His goal was to share his own school-to-prison pipeline story with as many people as possible, particularly future teachers, so that other young people would never have to experience it. Philip became a fierce advocate for change, as well as a talented advisor and mentor for youth at a local charter school. We miss him dearly and will always cherish his friendship. We also wish to thank Bridget and Jordan for openly sharing their family's story.

This chapter proceeds in three steps. First, we describe the experiences of one family with the school-to-prison pipeline, seeking to elucidate its causes and illustrate its damaging effects on real people. Next, we share the success stories of two dropout recovery programs that are dismantling the school-to-prison pipeline with innovative, culturally sustaining, student-centered programs. We analyze and describe the key qualities that explain the success of these two schools. Finally, we share our own theory of pedagogical and institutional plasticity, an overarching philosophy and practice that provides a framework for creating the safe, trauma free schools that all youth deserve – spaces of healing and empowerment.

BACKGROUND

Letitia (one of the authors) first met Bridget Borer in 2012 as a graduate student in a "Diversity and Education" course. Bridget was a white woman in her mid-40s with two bi-racial sons, both of whom identified as Black. At the time, Bridget's sons, Philip and Jordan, were incarcerated. In class, Bridget often spoke with exasperation about how her sons had been mistreated in schools and how this experience had pushed them toward prison. For example, Bridget shared (in a later interview):

I was a young, single mother on welfare and not very confident. I was pretty trusting of the school system when my sons first entered. I thought it would be good for my kids to be in school and be guided by people better educated and more mature than myself...After both of my boys had been in school for a few years, I was already getting the sense that boys in general, and especially black boys, were being treated more harshly than other kids. I saw it in the way teachers talked to the boys. I saw it in the way the boys came home angry...Teachers and school administrators think they have to keep a closer eye on boys, especially black boys, and crack down on them sooner to prevent them from becoming bigger menaces...Unfortunately, this tendency to regulate black boys more frequently and harshly only contributes to the problems these boys already face.

We felt it would be extremely powerful for Bridget to share her story with a wider audience to illustrate the damaging effects of the school-to-prison pipeline on real people. Bridget agreed and soon Philip and Jordan joined the project, sharing their memories of school. For example, Philip shared:

I probably have been suspended from school close to 40 times ... I remember being suspended for three days for sticking up my middle finger...I've been suspended for smelling like marijuana but was never offered chemical dependency [treatment] ...I've been suspended for fighting and cursing but never offered anger management... Going on and off suspension for kids is like going in and out of jail for adults. It becomes acceptable in one's life and leads kids to believe that they are a part of the trouble, so they should just stay that way.

As Philip's example illustrates, school systems have tended to punish and push away those students who are most in need of social services and steady, reliable guidance. A disproportionate number of students who receive the most severe punishments in school are students who come from single-parent households, qualify for free-or-reduced-price lunch, have learning disabilities, are in foster care, or are homeless (Noguera, 2008). A disturbing percentage are also black or brown boys and young men. Ironically, schools dole out the most severe discipline to those kids who are most in need of support.

Why does this happen? We contend that the school-to-prison pipeline has directly mirrored a larger societal trend of mass incarceration. Over the last 40 years, the U.S. prison population has exploded from 300,000 to more than 2 million, a figure that is six to ten times higher than any other industrialized nation. These arrests and convictions have overwhelmingly targeted low-income communities of color (Alexander, 2012). In what follows, we outline three trends that have occurred in schools that have contributed significantly to the growth of the school-to-prison pipeline, all of them outgrowths of the larger societal trend of mass incarceration.

CAUSES OF THE SCHOOL-TO-PRISON PIPELINE

Zero-Tolerance Policies: Zero-tolerance policies became widespread in the mid-90s after federal legislation required states to expel students who brought firearms and drugs to school. After the Columbine shooting, schools also began to crack down on minor violations to prevent more serious crimes from occurring in the future. These policies were intended to prevent drug abuse and violence in schools. Unfortunately, their enforcement led to several negative outcomes, most significantly an overzealous policing of students of color.

Jordan first experienced "zero tolerance" when he was eight. Bridget shared:

One day in Mrs. Johnson's classroom, they were celebrating birthdays and some of the kids joked about giving birthday spankings. Apparently, this kind of talk concerned Mrs. Johnson, so she reminded them that the school had zero tolerance for hitting, and if you hit someone you would be sent to the principal's office and could be suspended or expelled. To Jordan, her words seemed hypocritical. He had seen Mrs. Johnson show favoritism toward the girls in his class. The girls had repeatedly hit, pinched, and poked him without any consequence. So, in response to her lecture, he proceeded to get out of his seat, walk up to Mrs. Johnson, and slug her in the arm. He then said, "Can I go to the office now?" Since she had just given the class a lecture on zero tolerance for hitting, she had to follow through.

For this incident, Jordan was suspended for ten days and transferred to a new school because he had acted in a "threatening" and "violent" manner. Bridget was never consulted on the transfer, though by law she should have been. She recalled feeling "powerless" as her son's future was irrevocably altered. Jordan had been categorized as a "violent black male" at the age of eight. He was never given the opportunity to share his perspective on what happened. He was never asked how he felt about his class or his teacher. He was given no opportunity to learn about making amends, reconciliation, or forgiveness. This was simply an open and shut case of zero tolerance (though it is important to ask if the situation would have progressed differently with a white, middle-class student).

Bridget's son Philip followed a similar trajectory. He was suspended more than 40 times during a three-year time frame for things like smelling like marijuana or cursing. Philip reflected:

Once my teachers characterized me as a 'troubled kid,' I felt I had to continue to be that way, upholding an image I thought was cool, but an image I did not create by myself. I began to go to school to start trouble and came to be known as a 'troubled kid.' I won't pretend that I was an easy kid. I had a lot of issues. But isn't it up to the schools to support students in all aspects of life?

Zero tolerance made it much easier for schools to dismiss and ignore students like Jordan and Philip.

An Increasing Police Presence in Schools: Zero tolerance policies paved the way for an increased police presence in schools, often in the form of School Resource Officers (SROs). An SRO is a sworn law-enforcement officer who works either full or part-time in a school. Most SROs are uniformed, armed, and carry restraints like handcuffs. They also have the power to arrest students. In theory, SROs have some training in working with youth, though a 2018 study found that one in five had received no training and high percentages of SROs felt underprepared to work with special education populations and/or students who had experienced childhood trauma (Education Week, 2018).

Though incidents of violence have certainly occurred in suburban and rural schools, a higher police presence became more common in low-income, urban settings that have greater percentages of students of color. Again, this trend in schools has paralleled an over-policing of communities of color, encouraging racial profiling and leading to an atmosphere of mistrust and suspicion.

Jordan shared his experiences with police in his high school, saying:

The police presence was very strong in my high school. The police had their own office and officers would take you there and threaten you. They would even arrange drug busts. I was taken to the office one time for an altercation and the police threatened me.

Since the murder of George Floyd in 2020, urban school districts like Minneapolis and St. Paul have opted to remove or reduce the police presence in schools. This decision has been controversial, with several principals pushing back. In an open letter to policymakers in October of 2020, several Twin Cities principals of color described their SROs as important and beloved members of the community (Abdullah et al., 2020). When trained and carefully selected, a school resource officer can serve as a person that supports at-risk youth. Meanwhile, more than 30,000 children under the age of 10 have been arrested in the U.S. since 2013, and kids as young as 6 years old have been zip-tied and shoved into police cars (Ball et al, 2022). A sense of "safety" for some students and staff results in other students feeling marginalized, over-monitored, and criminalized.

Racial Bias: In the same way that low-income communities of color are targeted for arrest and incarceration, low-income students of color like Jordan and Philip have been targeted as "problem kids" or "bad boys" early on in their school experience. As the years went by, Bridget watched as teachers and administrators kept a closer eye on her sons, cracking down on them sooner and more harshly. Jordan and Philip became aware that the lowest-tracked classrooms, as well as those reserved for students labeled with Emotional and Behavioral Disorders, were filled with mostly black or brown youth. They became keenly aware that most of the kids suspended or expelled were black or brown.

When educators view children of color from a deficit perspective and identify them as "problem students," this can lead to premature disciplinary referrals. When they view children of color as having inferior intelligence or academic skill, it can lead to an overrepresentation in lower-track placements. Bridget saw this deficit perspective in the way teachers talked to and about her sons. And ultimately, she saw it in the way her boys came home from school angry and frustrated.

Study after study has documented the overuse of suspensions and expulsions on young men of color (Christle et al., 2005; Fenning & Rose, 2007; Rashid, 2009; Solomon, 2004). The most obvious problem that can result is the disruption of student learning. This disruption can be especially detrimental if it occurs frequently or over a long period of time. Students who miss a lot of class time fall behind and have difficulty catching up. If students are frequently suspended and not in school, they may also have greater periods of unsupervised free time, increasing the likelihood of getting in further trouble. Equally damaging is the stigma created by multiple experiences of suspension and/or expulsion. Feelings of shame, humiliation, and anger may set off an irreversible downward trajectory like the one Philip describes above. Students may begin to distrust their teachers and school. They may feel rejected and unwanted, resulting in a much higher risk of dropping out and/or landing in prison.

SCHOOL DISCIPLINE RESEARCH / ALTERNATIVES TO EXCLUSIONARY DISCIPLINE

In their comprehensive review of school discipline research, Welsh and Little (2018) provide a detailed analysis of the factors contributing to discipline disparities, as well as the effectiveness of emerging alternatives to exclusionary discipline. Their meta-analysis highlights the well-documented racial, gender and income disparities in discipline outcomes, emphasizing that "race trumps other student characteristics in explaining discipline disparities" (p. 757). Race is a significant predictor of exclusionary discipline even after accounting for socio-economic status. They conclude that "Black students are disciplined more ... and the vast majority of disciplinary infractions for which students receive a disciplinary consequence are subjective" (p. 780), behaviors such as: being disrespectful, loitering, or excessive noise. This suggests that teacher and principal *perceptions* of behavior (which may include significant implicit bias) contribute significantly to exclusionary discipline.

Meanwhile, some school practices appear to have a greater impact on mitigating behavior challenges and improving student success than others. For example, discipline approaches designed to assist students with "assimilating to the school culture" are less effective than approaches that attempt to create a school culture that "fits the social, emotional, and cultural needs of students" (Welsh and Little 2018, p 773). Again, this seems to suggest that reforms should focus more on the dispositions and implicit biases of teachers and school leaders, rather than on student behavior.

Welsh and Little (2018) found that Restorative Practices often led to a decrease in office referrals, as well as improvements in student achievement. Similarly, culturally responsive interventions led to improvements in school attendance, student perception of the school climate, academic achievement, and feelings of belonging and self-efficacy. They conclude that "interventions that target school climate and teacher-student interactions in a culturally responsive manner … have the potential to reduce discipline disparities" (Welsh and Little, 2018, p. 780).

Restorative Practices: As Welsh and Little (2018) note in their meta-analysis, Restorative Practices (RP) can positively imfluence school climate, student behavior, and relations between and among students, teachers, and school leaders (Gregory and Evans 2020; Gonzalez 2015; Richmond 2015). A central tenet of an RP model is to repair harm, as opposed to simply getting rid of so-called problem kids (like Philip and Jordan). In this model, students reflect on their responses to challenges that arise and build skills at controlling anger, communicating their needs to others, and repairing mistakes. RP programs have been shown to reduce racial disparities in discipline referrals (Gregory and Evans, 2020; Wastvedt 2017), though they require ongoing professional development and critical reflection on the part of teachers and school leaders (Gregory and Evans 2020).

Culturally Sustaining Pedagogies: Culturally sustaining learning environments can also positively influence discipline outcomes and student achievement (Welsh and Little 2018). Building on the work of Gloria Ladson-Billings (1995) and Moll et al. (1992), Paris and Alim argue that schools and classrooms should be "relevant and responsive to the languages, literacies, and cultural practices of students across categories of difference and (in)equality" (Paris 2012, p. 93). Central to Paris and Alim's (2017) Culturally Sustain Pedagogy is a critique of White-dominated traditional school spaces that are inherently less welcoming to youth of color and tend to emphasize a deficit framework for teaching. Similarly, Emdin (2016) describes how traditional schools tend to judge students of color on how well they have assimilated to a dominant White culture, rather than incorporating students' cultural identities into their instruction. Emdin argues for a version of CSP called reality pedagogy.

Alternative Education: In her sweeping study of the alternative school movement, Conley (2002) examines the wide range of philosophies, curricula, and pedagogical practices that now fall under the broad term of Alternative Education. For the purposes of the studies in this chapter, we were specifically interested in alternative programs that targeted high school dropouts and served students through innovative, flexible programming, restorative practices, and culturally sustaining pedagogies. These approaches stand in stark contrast to the more compliance-oriented, authoritarian model of the so-called "no excuses schools," which Stahl (2019) has critiqued for their tendency to regulate and surveil the behaviors and bodies of low-income students of color.

Vander Ark (2019) describes a series of alternative high school programs explicitly designed to serve students who have not succeeded in the traditional system. For example, Da Vinci Rise High in Los Angeles helps students to address life challenges such as foster care, housing instability, and probation. They use a flex-schedule for classes, allowing students to recover credits while honoring the importance of family needs. They also work with youth development agencies to provide services such as counseling, tutoring, and job training. Bronx Arena High School in New York City serves students who are over-aged and under-credited. They focus on relationship building and pairing students with advocate counselors to design a self-paced personalized plan. They also partner with local non-profits to provide social services to students and families. Health Leadership High School in Albuquerque, New Mexico emphasizes hands-on, project-based learning for small groups of students. They have particularly strong programs leading to employment in the healthcare industry.

The studies presented in this chapter highlight schools with similar approaches to the ones described above. We describe the key qualities that lead to success, providing further evidence that such programs are essential to mitigating the school-to-prison pipeline.

MITIGATING THE SCHOOL-TO-PRISON PIPELINE

In this next section, we draw on two research studies conducted at charter high schools in a large metropolitan area in the upper Midwest that self-identify as "dropout recovery" programs. Though each school is distinct in its specific program and learning environment, our research indicates that they are both successfully mitigating the school-to-prison pipeline by guiding young men and women toward graduation and a personal plan for their future (Basford, Lewis & Trout, 2020; Lewis & Basford, 2020).

We identify and describe five key qualities that have allowed these schools to succeed at creating trauma free, restorative, and culturally sustaining learning environments. These qualities include: a casual, family-like atmosphere with a close-knit community; creative responses to chronic absenteeism; extreme patience and flexibility in the classroom; innovative programs that hook student interest and provide a means for students to heal from past trauma; and wrap-around services, including heavy advising, for all students.

Quality #1: School As Family – A Close-Knit, Casual Community

In our interviews with students and teachers at both high schools, we heard one word repeatedly: family. Both staff and students described an environment that is close-knit, highly respectful of individuals, and encourages a culture of acceptance and support. For example, school staff said:

The environment here is very accepting. It's a family. We care about each other and respect each other. If someone decides not to go along with that, we don't just kick them out. We talk about it and try to work it out.

We listen to each other and respect where people come from and what they have to say. A lot of our students came from schools where they did not feel connected, so we really try to have a warm, friendly atmosphere. We eat together. We joke together.

We have young people here from different groups that don't get along outside of school. At night, they're on opposite sides of the street. But when they're here at school or on the work site, they're supporting each other, laughing, shaking hands.

Students also emphasized the importance of a casual, close-knit atmosphere where youth are seen as individuals with gifts and potential:

Teachers at this school see you as a human being and as an artist, rather than a number or just a pain in their ass.

The teachers and advisors make you want to stay here and make you feel welcome... They show you more possibilities...If I ever have kids, I would want them to come to this school. I know that they would be supported here.

A friend of mine here was having a bad problem with drugs. Every day, her advisor would take her to recovery meetings [or] her probation officer. Whatever she needed, he was there. She said that her advisor is the reason why she don't do drugs anymore. I got no words for that. I wouldn't expect that from a school. I'd expect that from your family.

At one school, students and faculty participate in a communal lunch. With rare exceptions, everyone in the building gathers at lunch time to sit at small, circular tables and share a homemade meal, served family-style. The school chef, a former student known for his skill at making pizza and maintaining a fresh salad bar, tries to keep the menu healthy and local. Every table has at least one teacher and four or five students chatting quietly. People linger after they have finished eating, bus tables together and sweep the floor, then wander off to afternoon classes without a formal reminder. This stands in stark contrast to larger traditional schools with long lunch lines, institutionalized food, and adults whose primary function is crowd control, an atmosphere which can contribute to feelings of stress and anxiety, particularly for students with some history of trauma.

This same school also emphasized its small size as a key component of its identity and success. Class sizes are capped at twelve and are often as small as five or ten, making it possible for teachers to build close relationships with students and individualize instruction. The other school has chosen to grow bigger (not wanting to turn students away) and has had to contend with the challenge of maintaining a family-like atmosphere with a larger population. Both schools place a high value on creating a close-knit, personalized environment, with school functioning as a kind of family for students.

Quality #2: Creative Responses To Chronic Absenteeism

Chronic absenteeism is a major barrier to success for students in these studies. For a variety of reasons, students are unable or unwilling to attend class every day. Some have a history of school-related trauma and have developed a pattern of truancy over time that is difficult to interrupt. Others face serious personal challenges (such as homelessness, parental responsibilities, or a need to earn a paycheck) that make consistent attendance almost impossible. Instead of addressing absenteeism with punishment and dismissal, a typical response in a more traditional setting, the schools in this study have purposely designed unique approaches that make it possible for students to work toward their diploma even when attendance is inconsistent. One school leader explains:

Of course we want students to come to school every day, but we're never going to say, 'You can't come back or you've already failed because you didn't show up before.' When you learn a little about what some of these kids are dealing with, you just realize that you have to be somewhat flexible ... A lot of traditional schools have policies in place where students get pushed out if they don't show up on time or have a lot of absences...We don't have those kinds of ultimatums.

The following strategies appear to be successful in mitigating the challenge of chronic absenteeism.

Competencies, Not Credits: Traditional schools use credits to represent progress toward graduation, with time in class serving as a primary means for earning that credit.

These two schools focused instead on competencies, where students demonstrate proficiency with particular skills by designing individualized projects (working with teachers and advisors). "In our system," explains an advisor at one school, "it's not a matter of seat time. It's about the quality of the project. A particular project may take a week or a year [to complete], depending on the student." Often, students come to realize over time that they can complete more competencies by attending regularly (though it may take a year or more for them to reach this realization). To graduate, students complete a range of competencies, most of them rooted in state graduation standards. Both schools also require students to explore post-secondary options and develop a plan-of-action, which may involve college, a technical program, or a job.

Short Sessions, Not Semesters: Instead of traditional semesters, these schools use shorter sessions, ranging from three to six weeks, making it possible for students to dip in and out of school, depending on their needs and preferences. Rather than using a zero-sum game (where students fail and must begin again), the short sessions can help create momentum and a sense of continual progress. If students do not complete a project or competency in a particular session, the work can automatically carry over into the next session.

Use of Technology: More recently, teachers have begun to use online technologies to keep students connected, even when they miss class. This was occurring prior to the Covid-19 pandemic, though the pandemic has pushed all schools to put online technologies to use. As noted above, school staff and leadership feel strongly about maintaining that close-knit, in-person community, but they also see online technologies as an important tool for keeping students connected when they cannot attend in-person.

Innovative, Popular Offerings Linked To Attendance And Progress: Below we discuss the use of innovative programs as a strategy to hook student interest and draw them to the school. Both schools also try to link participation in these programs to attendance and progress toward graduation.

For example, one school offers popular trade programs in carpentry and landscaping. In addition to building real world skills and providing hands-on learning, these programs also provide a stipend, making it possible for students to support their families or save money. The school has made a conscious decision to link participation in these programs to attendance. Before students can begin a trade program, they must demonstrate an ability to attend class regularly. Program stipends are also linked to attendance. The leader of the carpentry program explains:

We have the best attendance because the kids really enjoy the hands-on, physical work. The stipend is also a major incentive. We tie their stipends to attendance and being on time, so they learn quickly to have good attendance.

The other school has a programmatic focus on hip-hop and the recording arts, boasting several studios with state-of-the-art equipment for performing, recording, and mixing music of all kinds. School leaders believe it is important to give students some immediate access to the recording studios, as a way to "hook" them, but they also try to tie this access to progress in other areas, such as developing a personal education plan and completing competencies toward graduation. One student explains:

I came to this school because I saw it as a great opportunity for music, to have an outlet that I didn't have in other schools, a place to record and make music. That brought me back to school and got me working on other things.

Absenteeism continues to be a challenge at both schools and is still the major barrier for students who do not graduate, but there is clear evidence that these schools are implementing innovative strategies to address this challenge. Impressive graduation rates provide evidence that it is working.

Quality #3: Extreme Patience And Flexibility In The Classroom

Teachers and advisors at both schools are highly committed to building relationships with students as an essential first step in guiding them toward success. That personal investment in each student, and the uncertainty that can go with it, is a central part of the job, requiring emotional stability, perseverance, and extreme patience over time. One teacher explains:

Sometimes you think it's not working, that nothing's happening. You want to give up, because it feels like they have. But if you just stick with them and sort of wait them out, a light turns on and they get to work. Most of them want to graduate, they want to accomplish something. That diploma gives them a sense of accomplishment and they know it's a steppingstone to something better.

Whether they have been formally trained in trauma informed practices or not, teachers understand that a respectful and caring relationship forms the basis for student's re-engaging with school. For some students, developing that sense of belonging must take precedence over academic progress.

Building on those individual relationships, teachers at both schools also seek to individualize their teaching, practicing an extreme form of pedagogical flexibility. "You really can't do a traditional lesson plan," explains one teacher, "since you often don't know who will be in class. I tend to plan my sessions as a 'to do' list for each student. When students come in, I'm trying to move each one forward on their list."

Effective teaching in this setting requires at least two forms of flexibility: a willingness and ability to respond to fluctuating groups of students (due to inconsistent attendance); and differentiation of the curriculum and instruction based on student interest and ability. This often results in individualized, project-based forms of learning. Another common practice is co-taught classes, providing opportunities for teachers and students to design cross-curricular projects and field trips. For example, a course called "A Closer Look," combines science and art. Teachers and students meet at a local park and use drawing as a strategy to help students observe nature closely and make inferences about what they are observing.

While every teacher spoke to the importance of flexibility and creativity, they each had different methods of putting it into action, depending on their area of teaching and the specific students. Discussing the importance of curricular flexibility, teachers simultaneously praised the freedom they have and admitted to the challenge of the work:

It's very empowering as a teacher to have the autonomy to design and teach classes that really speak to my students ... You have to think of each student as a work of art. It's highly individualized instruction, but in a group setting, so students get that social interaction piece. Doing it well is difficult.

Quality #4: Innovative Programs That Hook Student Interest And Help Students Heal From Past Trauma

As noted, one school has maintained a programmatic focus on hip-hop and the recording arts. Students have direct access to several state-of-the art recording studios and local recording professionals who volunteer their time at the school. Opportunities to engage in the recording arts and other forms of creative expression are used as hooks to get students in the door and participating in some form of learning. For many students, an initial interest in the recording arts has led them to discover other areas of interest or avenues for creative expression. For example, an extensive photography and videography program has developed based initially on the interests of one teacher and a group of students. Such innovative programs, and the flexibility to develop new programs based on student interest, are examples of Paris and Alim's (2017) Culturally Sustaining Pedagogy.

Creative expression can also become a form of healing for students who have experienced trauma (at home, on the streets, or at previous schools). For many students, artistic expression provides a means of recovery and restoration. A staff social worker explains:

Music, and really any art form, can serve as a kind of therapy. That's an important part of our program. They're empowered by their words, their songs, their pictures, and by that creative process. It's also really helpful for me to wander around the building and see what they are doing, to witness their creativity as a way to learn more about them.

The other school uses extremely popular trade programs as their primary hook for students. A prime example is the Youth Build carpentry program, where students spend half of their day working at a building site that will eventually be a single-family home (the site is managed by a community housing organization that supports low-income families). The crew works for an hourly stipend, building practical skills while earning a diploma that can lead to a formal apprenticeship in carpentry. The leader of the youth build program makes a strong argument for a return to trades education in general, pointing out that students don't need a four-year degree to make a good living. He is also an excellent advocate for hands-on, experiential learning: "It doesn't mean that you're dumb or lazy," he tells his crew. "It means that you learn best by doing." Youth Build students have the best attendance records and highest rates of graduation at the school. Students enjoy the work and are highly incentivized to succeed, both financially and in terms of future job prospects. Meanwhile, they are also expected to complete their academic competencies, so participation in the program does not preclude education in more traditional areas.

Though the specific innovative programs are quite different at these two schools, both function as essential motivational hooks, garnering that initial student interest and keeping them coming back for more. These innovative programs also provide meaningful hands-on learning opportunities that may help students heal from trauma, through artistic exploration, and develop practical skills for future employment.

Quality #5: Wrap-Around Services And Heavy Advising For All Students

In more traditional settings, "wrap-around services" are often reserved for students who qualify for special education services and have a legally mandated Individualized Education Program (IEP). These two schools make every effort to provide that same level of support for every student in the building. Wrap-around services may refer to an array of possibilities, depending on student need. This includes (but is not limited to): access to financial services, childcare, drug rehabilitation, sexual disease prevention, housing opportunities, therapy, internships, and job opportunities. The process begins with truly getting to know each student and building a solid relationship.

At one school, a central component of wrap-around services is an advisory system that functions independently from classroom teaching. In this setting, advisors are not licensed teachers, but they become the true experts at building relationships with students. Once that trusting relationship is established, they can also connect students to a wide array of support services, in the building and in the community.

Freed from the many responsibilities of teaching, the advisors focus on making daily, personal connections with each of their advisees. For students who are in the building, this may involve a check-in about the students' needs, goals, and progress toward graduation. The advisors are also constantly making connections with students who are not in the building (through phone calls, text messages, and even personal visits to the student's home), since absenteeism is a key inhibitor to student progress.

The director of advising describes the ideal advisor in this way:

Operating at its highest level, this will be that person you can always go to, confide in, someone who knows your parent or guardian, someone who is in touch with you every day. This is the advisor's only job—touching base with each individual student and helping in whatever way they can. We call it targeted engagement.

In this system, many of the advisors also come from similar backgrounds to the students. Some have personally experienced incarceration, drug abuse, homelessness, or other hardships. These experiences appear to bring the advisors a degree of respect and credibility with students, helping them to connect and build trust. Many of the advisors are also linked into the same communities as students, making it easier for them to find missing students, connect with and influence family members, and build community relationships.

Teaching staff at this school believe that the independent advising system is vital to the school's success, and they seek to honor the essential daily work that advisors do. One teacher explains:

I have huge respect for my colleagues who work so hard to get students in the building...Not only transportation, but in some cases, have they eaten? Where did they sleep last night? We have advisors who are calling and texting and using social media every day: 'Come to school! We really want to see you today! Let us know if we can do anything to help you get here.'

With a smaller student body, the other school uses its teaching staff to provide similar levels of advising support for students. A typical teacher has 10 to 15 advisees and really works hard to build a solid relationship and provide whatever kind of support the student needs.

AN OVERARCHING PHILOSOPHY: INSTITUTIONAL AND PEDAGOGICAL PLASTICITY

Ultimately, our research has revealed an overarching philosophy and practice that appears to guide these two schools and others like them, an approach that we have termed "institutional and pedagogical plasticity."

Schools which practice institutional and pedagogical plasticity are willing and able to adapt and change in response to student need. Classrooms are student-centered spaces, with flexible curricula, project-based learning, and differentiated instructional approaches. Culturally sustaining pedagogies promote critical awareness and link learning to real world problems (Ladson-Billings, 1995; Gonzalez & Amanti, 2005; Paris & Alim, 2017). Individualized care also extends to advising, with students receiving the specific attention they need, first to establish trust and build a relationship, then to ensure that students have the resources they need to develop a personal education plan and work toward graduation.

At the institutional level, a philosophy of plasticity avoids rigid discipline policies, such as zero tolerance, and leans heavily toward restorative practices, where student voice is valued and consequences focus on repairing injustice, re-establishing healthy relationships, and building a strong community (Davis, 2013; Smith 2015). Consequences are always context-specific and individualized. Institutional plasticity also refers to school-wide programming, which ideally provides motivational hooks for students, as well as opportunities to heal from past trauma. School programs are malleable and highly responsive to student needs and interests. School leaders are open to trying, and encouraging, new programmatic ideas as they arise. School leaders also plan for multiple points of entry throughout the year and have creative responses to chronic absenteeism.

CONCLUSION

In this chapter, we have shared the story of one family's experience with the school-to-prison pipeline, in the hopes of elucidating its causes and illustrating its damaging impact on real people. We have also examined the success story of two dropout recovery programs that are dismantling the school-to-prison pipeline with five key qualities. Finally, we have presented our own theory of pedagogical and institutional plasticity, a framework for creating the safe, trauma-free schools that all youth deserve.

We end where we began, with Philip. Working with Philip and his family was a transformational experience in our careers as educators. We have especially vivid memories of Philip's impact on our students. As Philip shared his stories of experiencing the school-to-prison pipeline and described the various ways that kids like him can get marginalized and pushed out of schools, we watched our students lean in and truly listen. These future teachers wanted and needed to hear from Philip, as he humanized the experience for them (much more profoundly than their privileged white professors could do). Though he might not have described it using these terms, Philip was a fierce advocate for culturally-sustaining, student-centered teaching. He reminded future teachers that they would play a central role in modeling respect and motivating kids to want to learn. He advocated for loving all kids, especially those who might seem difficult at first. And he practiced that love himself as an advisor and mentor for youth at one of the schools described in this study. We hope this chapter continues Philip's important work of advocating for safe, trauma-free schools – spaces of healing and empowerment for all students.

REFERENCES

Abdullah, Y., Fruestleben, M., & Hampton, N. (2020). Open letter from Northside principals to MPS & MPD policymakers. *North News*.

Alexander, M. (2012). *The new Jim Crow: Mass incarceration in the age of color blindness*. The New Press.

Ball, A., Zhang, D., & Molloy, M. (2022). *'She looks like a baby': Why do kids as young as 5 or 6 still get arrested at schools?* The Center for Public Integrity. https://publicintegrity.org/education/criminalizing-kids/young-kids-arrested-at-schools/

Basford, L., Lewis, J., & Trout, M. (2020). It can be done: How one charter school combats the school to prison pipeline. *The Urban Review*. doi:10.100711256-020-00583-x

Christle, C., Jolivette, K., & Nelson, C. (2005). Breaking the school to prison pipeline: Identifying school risk and protective factors for youth delinquency. *Exceptionality*, *13*(2), 69–88. doi:10.120715327035ex1302_2

Conley, B. (2002). *Alternative schools: A reference book*. American Bibliographical Center and CLIO Press.

Davis, M. (2013). Restorative justice: Resources for schools. *Edutopia*. https://www.edutopia.org/blog/restorative-justice-resources-matt-davis

Education Week Research Center. (2018). *School Policing: Results of a National Survey of School Resource Officers*. Editorial Projects in Education Inc.

Emdin, C. (2016). *For white folks who teach in the hood...and the rest of y'all too*. Beacon Press.

Fenning, P., & Rose, J. (2007). Overrepresentation of African American students in exclusionary discipline: The role of school policy. *Urban Education, 42*(6), 536–559. doi:10.1177/0042085907305039

Gonzalez, N., Moll, L., & Amanti, C. (2005). *Funds of knowledge: Theorizing practice in households, communities and classrooms*. Lawrence Erlbaum Associates.

Gonzalez, T. (2015). Socializing schools: Addressing racial disparities in discipline through restorative justice. In D. J. Losen (Ed.), *Closing the school discipline gap: Equitable remedies for excessive exclusion* (pp. 151–165). Teachers College Press.

Gregory, A., & Evans, K. (2020). The starts and stumbles of restorative justice in education: Where do we go from here? *Boulder, CO: National Education Policy Center*. https://nepc.colorado.edu/publication/restorative-justice

Ladson-Billings, G. (1995). But that's just good teaching! The case for culturally relevant pedagogy. *Theory into Practice, 34*(3), 159–165. doi:10.1080/00405849509543675

Lewis, J., & Basford, L. (2020). One student at a time: How an innovative charter school succeeds with dropout recovery. *National Youth-at-Risk Journal, 4*(1). doi:10.20429/nyarj.2020.040104

Moll, L., Amanti, C., Nef, D., & Gonzalez, N. (1992). Funds of knowledge for teaching: Using a qualitative approach to connect homes and classrooms. *Theory into Practice, 31*(2), 132–141. doi:10.1080/00405849209543534

Noguera, P. (2008). What discipline is for: Connecting students to the benefits of learning. In M. Pollock (Ed.), *Everyday antiracism* (pp. 132–137). The New Press.

Paris, D. (2012). Culturally sustaining pedagogy: A needed change in stance, terminology, and practice. *Educational Researcher, 41*(3), 93–97. doi:10.3102/0013189X12441244

Paris, D., & Alim, H. S. (2017). *Culturally sustaining pedagogies: Teaching and learning for justice in a changing world*. Teachers College Press.

Rashid, H. (2009). From brilliant baby to child placed at risk: The perilous path of African American boys in early childhood education. *The Journal of Negro Education, 78*(3), 347–358.

Richmond, E. (2015). What happens when instead of suspensions, kids talk out their mistakes? *The Hechinger Report.* https://hechingerreport.org/happens-instead-suspensions-kids-talk-mistakes/

Smith, D. (2015). *Better Than carrots or sticks: Restorative practices for positive classroom management.* Association for Supervision and Curriculum Development.

Solomon, R. (2004). Schooling in Babylon, Babylon in school: When racial profiling and zero tolerance converge. *Canadian Journal of Educational Administration and Policy, 33,* http://search.proquest.com/docview/61859546?accountid=28109

Stahl, G. (2019). Critiquing the corporeal curriculum: Body pedagies in 'no excuses' charter schools. *Journal of Youth Studies, 7,* 1–17.

Vander Ark, T. (2019). Eleven alternative schools that are real alternatives. *Forbes.* https://www.forbes.com/sites/tomvanderark/2019/10/07/11-alternative-schools-thatare-real-alternatives/#5d7fa6351c1c

Wastvedt, S. (2017). St. Paul schools see hope in 'restorative' discipline. *MPR News.* https://www.mprnews.org/story/2017/11/20/stpaul-schools-see-hope-in-restorative-discipline

Welsh, R., & Little, S. (2018). The School Discipline Dilemma: A Comprehensive Review of Disparities and Alternative Approaches. *Review of Educational Research, 88*(5), 752–794. doi:10.3102/0034654318791582

Chapter 2
When They See Us:
Implications for Anti-Racist School Leadership Through Examining the Experiences of Black Boys

Jennifer Grace
University of Houston-Clear Lake, USA

ABSTRACT

This chapter examines the experiences of Black males and their description of race-based trauma encountered at school and its impact. The author conducted semi-structured interviews with Black males who had been expelled from school. Participants describe school as a hostile environment for Black males, citing microaggressions, isolation, and verbal abuse as indicators. This is in additional to environment stressors such as racism, violence, and criminalization. The participants narrate their emotional responses to this repeated trauma. Based on the findings, the authors make practical recommendations for anti-racist school leadership to reduce the trauma inflicted by schools due to racial bias and racist policy and practices, thus mitigating exposure to the school to prison pipeline.

INTRODUCTION

Race matters. In an educational system in which the academic achievement scores and graduation rates of Black males continue to lag behind that of their peers, yet Black males lead their peers in suspension and expulsion rates, there must be a call to action. Acknowledging that race matters and racism exists is central to tackling persistent achievement disparities and opportunity gaps and dismantling oppressive

DOI: 10.4018/978-1-6684-5713-9.ch002

Copyright © 2023, IGI Global. Copying or distributing in print or electronic forms without written permission of IGI Global is prohibited.

school systems that work together to relegate Black males to second-class citizenship. Current educational policy and practice send a strong message that Black males have no worth and do not matter based on the rate at which they are discarded. This research aims to provide an in-depth description of how Black males encounter anti-Black racism and trauma within their day-to-day school experiences.

Boutte and Bryan (2021) conceptualize the everyday anti-Black violence and trauma experienced by Black students in U.S. schools. Specifically, Boutte and Bryan (2021) describe symbolic or metaphorical anti-Black violence as rejecting the lived experiences of Black youth, silencing their voices, and misreading their culture. Additionally, systemic anti-Black violence is explained as structures, processes, discourses, customs, policies, and practices rooted in racist ideology or racial bias, which result in lack of access to highly qualified teachers, lack of funded resources, and disproportionality in special education representation, gifted and advanced placement, and exclusionary discipline (Boutte & Bryan, 2021). This chapter aims to elevate the voices of those most marginalized by the U.S. educational system. The young men interviewed in this study cite examples of how they have encountered symbolic and systemic anti-Black violence in every aspect of their education, resulting in race-based traumatic stress. Furthermore, this chapter aims to provide educational leaders, teacher, support staff, and anyone who serves Black males with practical research-based strategies to reduce racial bias and disrupt racist policies, structures, and practices that perpetuate the school-to-prison pipeline. In this chapter, readers will be presented with background-concerning disparities in educational outcomes and the impact of race-based trauma on Black males, a description of the research methodology, findings derived from the research and research-based strategies to disrupt systemic racism in schools.

BACKGROUND

The writings of Gillborn (2005) and Ladson-Billings (1998) suggest that the concept of systemic racism is demonstrated by the outcomes of policy and practice in education. Policy and practice become a function of systemic racism when there is a disproportionately adverse impact on members of a given social group (Ladson-Bilings, 1998). The school-to-prison pipeline (SPP) is a conceptual framework to understand how policy and practice in the educational system work together to manifest negative outcomes resulting in Black students, in particular, being disproportionately pushed out of school and into the criminal justice system (Rocque & Snellings, 2018). Kim et al. (2010) state that at its core, the SPP results from a failed K-12 public education system that does not meet the needs of many students it serves. Specifically, Rocque and Snellings (2018) note that failing schools with low graduation/high dropout rates, zero-tolerance disciplinary policies, and student disengagement are an impetus for the connection between the education and criminal justice systems. These schools are more likely to be attended by Black students (Grace & Nelson, 2019).

It is essential to note the detrimental academic experiences of Black students that contribute to school pushout. The opportunity gap persists for Black students as it relates to access to resources, advanced curriculum, quality instruction, and opportunities. (Flores, 2007; Grace, 2020; Noguera, 2017; Paschall et al., 2018). Black students are more likely to experience run-down school facilities, less experienced and underqualified teachers, and low teacher expectations (Day-Vines & Day-Hairston, 2005; Grace, 2020; Tsoi-A & Bryant, 2015). Additionally, they are more likely to be overrepresented in high-incidence categories related to special education and less likely to be identified as gifted or take advanced placement courses (Crabtree et al., 2019; Rynders, 2019). These are all factors in graduation and dropout rates.

Furthermore, exclusionary discipline practices often coincide with academic stratification, exacerbating disparate outcomes for Black children (Gregory et al., 2010). Excessive out-of-school suspension and expulsion rates for Black students result from zero-tolerance policies, which come with automatic consequences, even for minor offenses, and contribute significantly to the school-to-prison pipeline (Grace & Nelson, 2019). Losen and Martinez (2020) reported that Black boys lost 132 days, and Black girls lost 77 days of instruction due to out-of-school suspension. Moreover, Riddle and Sinclair (2019) report that Black students account for 28% of school-based arrests and 91% of referrals to law enforcement compared to their White peers, who account for 8% and 34%, respectively. Riddle and Sinclair (2019) explain exclusionary discipline practices as a result of racial bias, providing further evidence of the link between racism and school pushout. Underlying racism embedded in day-to-day schooling experiences significantly impact students exposed to constant subjugation.

The Role of Race-Based Trauma in the School-To-Prison Pipeline

It is important to understand the ways in which encounters with racism are a form of trauma, and ultimately, how it impacts Black male students. Common examples of trauma include experiencing physical, emotional, or sexual abuse, neglect, exposure to violence, life-threatening situations, experiencing natural disasters, or the death of a loved one (McInerney & McKlindon, 2014). Motley and Banks (2018) report that trauma has been identified as a significant public health issue, with Black males at higher risk for exposure to trauma. In their study, Motley and Banks (2014) reported the following rates for trauma exposure among Black males: physical abuse/assault (52%), sexual abuse (37%), serious accident/injury (52%), death of a loved one (59%), domestic abuse (24%), emotional abuse (62%), and witnessing trauma (39%). In addition to being at a higher risk for exposure to trauma typically recognized by mental health and medical professionals, Black males face a myriad of racial trauma daily. Racial trauma comes in the form of repeated environmental and social microaggressions (Sue et al., 2007).

Roberson and Carter (2021) report that race-based traumatic stress (RBTS) has been defined in terms of the emotional and psychological stress responses resulting from experiences of racial discrimination. Bryant-Davis and Ocampo (2005) likened the response of victims of racism to the response of victims of sexual assault, including shock, dissociation, and self-damaging behaviors. Roberson and Carter (2021) also note that Black men who reported hostile racial encounters such as verbal assault, being profiled, stereotyped, and denied access were more likely to experience hypervigilance in some cases, depression, anxiety, low self-esteem based on internalized racism, and anger.

This chapter is based on research about Black males who had been expelled from school. The participants recall school as a hostile environment for Black males, affecting their sense of belonging and engagement in schooling. Specifically, being subjected to practices like harsher discipline, inequitable access to quality instruction, microaggressions, labeling, and ostracization were race-based traumatic events that contributed to pushing the young men out of school. These findings are significant because, together with experiencing the day-to-day stress of encountering microaggressions within society, Black males must contend with institutionalized racism in their schooling systems, further perpetuating the school-to-prison pipeline.

METHODOLOGY

This section details steps taken to engage in this research and methods used to perform analysis and derive meaning. I employed a phenomenological approach to this research. As such, interviews with 10 Black males, who had been expelled from school, were conducted and analyzed for this study. After obtaining Institutional Review Board (IRB) approval, I contacted the principals of several alternative schools in New Orleans for permission to conduct research at their sites. One principal allowed me to do so.

Participants

Participants who met the following criteria were chosen to be a part of this study: Black, male, expelled from a public school within the last one to three years, and currently enrolled in a disciplinary alternative educational setting. The participants' ages ranged from 15 to 18 years old. Five of the young men were considered seniors in high school, one was a junior, and four were considered sophomores. Eight of the young men were expelled from public charter schools in New Orleans, while two were expelled from the remaining traditional public schools at the time. Eight of the young men also participated in football and basketball at their previous school setting and the current setting. All of the young men had post-secondary goals beyond completing high school. Two of the young men aspired to join the military immediately following graduation; one young man planned to attend a technical or community college. Seven of the young men aspired to attend a four-year college or university upon completing high school. To gain a deeper understanding of how these young men perceived their educational experiences, they were interviewed individually.

Data Collection and Analysis

After working with the principal and counselor to identify potential participants, I obtained consent and assent from the participants. As outlined by Moustakas (1994), the procedures for data collection consist of identifying a phenomenon to study, bracketing out one's experiences, and collecting data from several persons who have experienced the phenomenon. The participants' descriptions of their K-12 schooling experiences were obtained through in-depth interviews. I scheduled at least one meeting with each participant and conducted one-hour individual interviews at their school sites during extracurricular classes. An interview guide was developed, adapted, and utilized to gather data from participants. The interview guide was used to ensure a standard interview process for each participant. The semi-structured interviews lasted one hour in the participants' school setting. It is important to note that only one formal interview took place with participants due to the transient nature of the alternative environment. Participants could be enrolled anywhere from 10 days to one year. These interviews were audiotaped, transcribed verbatim by me, the researcher, and analyzed for categories that further illustrated the research problem.

Data analysis in a phenomenological study focuses on the crux of an experience (Creswell, 2013). Data were analyzed using modified methods described by Moustakas (1994) in his guidelines for analysis of phenomenological interview data, which includes coding for statements of significance, clustering for units of meaning, and then writing a composite description that provides the essence of the phenomenon in its entirety. Transcripts were manually coded using the open coding method, which consisted of a line-by-line analysis of each transcription and focused on patterns that yielded codes (Saldaña, 2021). Next, I used the codes to search for themes, followed by a review of themes generated. Lastly, I worked to define the themes or explain the phenomenon (Saldaña, 2021). All transcriptions and coding were done manually to avoid errors that coding software might cause. Coding and themes were validated by having the analysis reviewed by an independent researcher and member checking (Lincoln & Guba, 1985; Saldaña, 2021).

Positionality

Phenomenologists are concerned with showing how complex meaning is built out of simple units of direct experience (Merriam & Grenier, 2019). To accomplish this, Merriam and Grenier (2019) propose that the researcher must bracket their previous experiences to analyze and understand the crux of the experience from the participants' perspective. I engaged in bracketing to remove "my experiences" from the analysis process, which enabled me to focus on the participants' authentic lived experiences and their interpretations of those experiences. I employed the use of a journal to further explore the memos or notes about my feelings that surfaced during data analysis.

As a Black woman, and former K-12 educational leader, I too, am affected by daily occurrences of racism within my profession and in society. I too have experienced secondary trauma in witnessing how racism has impacted Black male students I have worked with in the past. The participants' stories did affect me emotionally and the journal was an important way to acknowledge my bias and attempt to minimize it as much as possible. My positionality as a racialized being no doubt influenced research design and decisions from the topic to the research questions. Furthermore, I acknowledge the interpretation of data was undeniably influenced by my understanding of myself as a racial being and my observations of how race affects the world around me. Nevertheless, the complexity in my lived experience and inherent positionality provided for a rich and complex analysis of the findings from the perceptions shared by participants.

SCHOOLING EXPERIENCES OF BLACK BOYS

This section contains themes that emerged from this research and emphasizes the voices and lived experiences of the participants.

On Being Black and Male

Racial oppression and discrimination are entrenched in the day-to-day experiences of Black males (Bailey et al., 2021). During this research on Black males who had been expelled from school in New Orleans, participants were asked to describe some of the challenges that Black males in society face. Malik's response was,

I don't know, like we face challenges everywhere. It's just a lot like I don't wanna talk about it like it probably bring tears to my eyes. Imma tell you, like a couple of years ago like my best friend got killed by the police. They dragged him down the street, calling him out his name, and shot him ... People calling you Black niggas and all kind of stuff, that's on my mind every day.

In one breath, Malik had summed up his experiences with complex, racial, and historical trauma as challenges associated with being Black and male. Theron added to this discussion by sharing his experiences,

It's like I'm always being stereotyped. Just the other day, I was riding my bike past Wendy's, and I stopped my bike to catch some Wi-Fi, but I stopped near a White lady, and she ran off looking like I was gonna do her something. Like she was terrified. Really and truly, I felt like cussing her out because it angered me like I wasn't there to harm her in no type of way. I shouldn't be feared walking down the street. That's something I never understood. And it's funny because I actually like other races, like White people, Asian people, Mexicans, but I always get looked at different.

Theron described his day-to-day encounter with microaggressions and being othered as hurtful and unjust. Malcolm described feeling like he is constantly under threat of being criminalized,

Black men have their own space, their own time. They are building jails for Black people, not for White people or women. They are building them for Black males.

Participants describe grief, anger, and hopelessness while discussing their experiences with racism. Bailey et al. (2021) report that Black male youth in America experience more than five encounters with racism daily, affecting how they internalize racism, their health and mental health, and their schooling experiences. Specifically, English et al. (2020) explain that Black males are exposed to preconceived notions of criminality, intellectual inferiority, and second-class citizenship daily. Bailey et al. (2021) suggest programs in education that thwart anti-Black racism to decrease the possibility of racial trauma for Black males.

The Single Story of Black Males in School

Participants described being bounded by a cloud of low expectations and anticipation of failure related to their academic achievements and survival. Clifford expressed the constant pressure of low expectations. He stated,

For me? Well, it feel like, well, I have to prove everybody wrong. Like it's so many people who said I couldn't do it ... go to school, finish school, go to college and do what I gotta do and take care of my family.

Brandon shared his perceptions of what others believe about him when they see him. He surmised, "Like people be like he's not gonna graduate, he's gonna drop out. Like stuff like that." He gathered that this was the perception of Black males because of the things people have said to him, including teachers. He added,

There's nobody to tell em good things. Somebody always doubting em. You ain't gon live to see this age you gon die tomorrow such and such. I been told you ain't gon be shit. This was my seventh-grade year.

Most participants explained that they received those messages right in the classroom of people who were supposed to nurture them. For example, Malik said, "Sometimes teachers will have something negative to say about you. You get a lot of people, teachers and students, talking down to you growing up in New Orleans you get that a lot."

Robert stated that sometimes low expectations are also evident in actions. He added, "You deal with teachers not really wanting to deal with you ... stuff like that. Like they might not want to get you to where you want to be like they are." Roland agreed with this sentiment. He reflected,

Some teachers don't really care about the students. Some of the teachers want me to succeed, but not all of em. If you ask them for help and they don't help you, or they ignore you when they don't care about your education. I just kind of read their actions.

Malcolm explained that many young Black males begin to internalize the constant weight of low expectations, which is often an antecedent to disengaging in the schooling process for Black males. He elaborated,

A lot of teachers feel like they won't be anything. Certain teachers be like they not gon live long. They feel as though there's no future for em. So they feel I'm not

gonna do nothing. I can't go to college, or even if I can go, I can't pay for it. This is a waste of my time.

Participants lamented the constant messaging they have received throughout their lives from people laced with the expectancy of failure. In her TED Talk in 2009, Chimamanda Ngozi Adichie said, "Show a people as one thing, as only one thing, over and over again, and that is what they become." The single story and expectations of failure underscore the experiences of Black males in schooling environments.

Criminalization and Policing in Schools

In addition to school being a place associated with violence, participants describe their encounters with policing in schools. Police were often used as a regular disciplinary strategy even once school administrators had already given consequences. For example, Dylan remembers when he got into a fight at school. He said, "I didn't think I was gonna get arrested because they gave me a suspension and let me go home. Then they called the police. I knew I was gonna have to find me another school." In some cases, the participants recall jail being threatened even in cases of suspicion. Brandon described being searched based on a suspicious look and being intimidated and removed from school. He voiced,

They put me in handcuffs and was like, you got two choices: call your mama or you going to jail. So, they had called my mom, and she came picked me up because they was like, come get him off this campus right now, or he goes to jail, and you get him from there. I was like am I going to jail for something I didn't do? He was like, shut up. Shut up; you wait here until your mom comes. First of all, you didn't find nothing on me to put handcuffs on me.

Brandon described his experience in a traditional public school before being placed at a Disciplinary Alternative Education Program (DAEP). When I questioned him about the DAEP setting, he explained behavioral consequences, including jail or permanent exclusion from school. He added,

You go home for the rest of the year. It's either that or they give you more time here. Like, say, if I'm caught with something right now (like weed), I'm probably gonna go to jail or get my time extended here til the end of high school. I ain't tryna do that.

Other participants like Darvell expressed a lack of due process when being disciplined, arrested, and placed at a DAEP. Darvell explained, "They just took me into custody and didn't ask me no questions about my side, and they just sent me here." Similar to being under a constant cloud of low expectations, Theron described how Black males are criminalized daily. He reflected,

We also get looked at by like police offers watching you while you on your way to school, thinking you have something on you just because you Black and you a male. So like, if I'm late to school and running to catch the bus, they probably think I did something, but if a White male do the same thing, it's like, oh, he going to school.

Participants describe criminalization as a regular part of their schooling experiences.

Disciplinary Practices

As with school-based arrests, participants describe due process with disciplinary decisions as nonexistent. For example, Malik reported,

One of the security guards said she saw marijuana and a cigar when she went through my bag while I was playing a basketball game. Like she claim she saw all that, but they still let me play in the game and didn't address it until like the next day. I think that was really like down bad. Well, by them not really knowing anything about it and addressing it the next day and not wanting to listen to me after I've done all this for y'all school. Like I was a basketball star for them, they wouldn't hear me out. I felt like they could have at least addressed the security guard because she had a role to play in it, too, by mishandling everything. It wasn't fair to me. I say that every day.

Malik not only expressed his feelings towards the lack of due process but also felt used by the school when they let him compete in a sports event to help their image and then expelled him. Malcolm also described playing a prank, along with some of his peers who were athletes, however, the prank resulted in another student getting injured. He explained,

I didn't play football at [names school]. Me and the other guys who didn't play football got expelled. The two football players did not get expelled. That's not equal to me. That's not fair to me.

Malcolm felt unappreciated by his school since he was not an athlete. Theron described his perception of school discipline practices as a form of control and a popularity contest rather than a consistent, unbiased policy. He said,

Rules are there to create structure, but half of em are just because they wanna control you. And I feel like how you get treated for breaking a rule really just depends. It's not the same for everybody.

He also perceived DAEP settings as a dumping ground for "bad kids" versus a quality educational setting. Shakur added to this by sharing his story. He lamented,

Like I been in an alternative school since sixth grade. Really, I didn't have no fights at school. It was like getting in trouble, walking out of class, that was it. People apply rules to people differently. To this day, I still don't know what I got expelled for. I don't see what's the reason that I got expelled. Here people bring guns to school and smoke weed ... I ain't do none of that. I was just one of those kids who got in trouble like once every two weeks, and I got expelled.

Shakur also saw DAEP settings as a dumping ground because there were plenty of students there like himself, who had not done anything extreme like fighting or possessing a weapon or drugs.

Emotional Dissonance

Participants describe a roller coaster of emotions while navigating the space of being Black and male. For example, Malik describes the stress associated with trying to relate or communicate with teachers. He stated,

Like sometimes, teachers will have something negative to say about you. Sometimes things get out of line. I like to talk to teachers on the side, but that don't work for everybody. Sometimes it escalates if they say something negative to you. Like you not gon play on me in front other students.

In this instance, being humiliated and belittled by a teacher increases stress and can trigger an aggressive response. Dylan agreed with this by expressing,

Teachers don't be thinking 'bout what people be going through at home and talkin' to people wrong. If you let them mess over you, they will, but if you go off, they not. I know that. So that's what I do.

In Theron's opinion, misplaced emotions are the root cause of why many Black males end up in DAEP settings. He reflected,

Really and truly, for me and most Black males, it's like getting caught up and having to show you who they are like they somebody when in actuality, you're nothing yet because you still in school, ya feel me. I don't know. That's crazy to me. I guess they get here through aggression and not knowing other ways to show emotion.

In other words, Theron theorized that Black males use aggression as a defense mechanism against constant surveillance, criminalization, microaggressions, low expectations, and abuse encountered in and outside school. Malcolm had a lot to say about the emotional toll of trying to navigate being Black and male. He explained,

Many of times, I felt like I didn't know who I was because, like I wanted to be this person, I wanted to be that person. I didn't have no strong knowledge of who I am myself. Like, Malcolm, this is you. Over time I learned that it's nothing wrong with trying to be like someone but make sure that it's a positive person. And what teachers say matters. We already don been through something—half of us seen a lot and done a lot. So for you to even say negative things to me would be like, well, I always knew I wasn't nothing anyway, so I could walk out. I wasn't gon learn nothing anyway. It's hard. It's been a mixed emotional experience. A lot of times, I've been angry. A lot of times, I've been happy. A lot of times, I've wanted to push myself. A lot of times, I didn't want to do anything. It's always going to be mixed emotions. Um, you know, and also being judged. I don't like to be judged. I can't stand it. It's a lot of mixed emotions with that. If you looking at the record or report card and you treating me some type of way because of that report card, I don't respect you. You're going to have a problem out of me. I don't like that. I don't respect it.

Malcolm's stream of consciousness revealed feelings of having no identity and experiencing mixed emotions due to his day-to-day experiences in and out of school.

The Audacity of Hope

It is worth noting that despite the barrage of challenges and trauma faced by the participants, they remained hopeful of fulfilling their dreams. For some, those dreams included college; for others, it was obtaining successful trade careers. In all cases, finishing high school was the first obstacle. Theron reflected,

Like I shoulda been out of school. I should really be getting a GED, but who wants a GED, ya feel me, so I'm still here tryna graduate this year finally (laughs). I want to be an electrician or contractor.

Similarly, Brandon felt he never belonged at any school he had attended. However, he remains determined to complete school. He exclaimed, "But I ain't dropping out. To me, it's a good thing because I'm Black, and if I graduate, they gon be like oh, there's not too many of him that graduate." To Brandon, graduating high school would be proving a point and making a statement to everyone who views him through a negative lens.

Malcolm also described graduating and becoming successful as proving a point. He stated, "Really when I get out of school I want to go to the military then go to college to prove a point to my family and friends that I don't want to be like the next man." He saw the military and college as a means of breaking free of the stereotypes associated with being Black and male. Other participants had college on their radar too. Malik expressed,

That's what I'm really happy about. I can still try to get the chance to graduate— that's why I'm trying to keep my GPA up so I can do something with myself. I just wanna go to college, Delgado, if I have to. I just wanna learn. I always liked that part of school.

Post-secondary education was still on the radar for Malik, even if it was a community college instead of a four-year institution. Clifford had similar aspirations. He shared, "But me personally? That's a goal I have for myself to go to college for engineering and then minor in band." Hauntingly, Shakur expressed college as a means to "get out" and clung to this idea with fervent hope. Almost as if he was not present with me in this interview, he stared up towards the ceiling, and he trailed off,

If that's the last thing I do, Imma go to college. I hope I'm successful in life so I can give back to the Black community because they really ain't got nothing. I wanna get out this. I really hope I get out ... I hope so ... I hope so.

I included this section to counter deficit narratives that may say Black males are unmotivated or don't want to learn. This single story could not be further from the truth. Deep in the hearts of those ostracized the most, there is motivation and a desire to learn and become productive members of society. Jenkins (2021) asserts that school is a place where Black children are subjected to "Spirit Murder," in which they are humiliated, erased, dehumanized, and devastated. Williams (1991) describes spirit-murdering as the personal, psychological, and spiritual injuries to people of color through the fixed and fluid yet fluid structures of racism. Love (2014) adds that spirit-murdering, in an educational context, denies inclusion, protection, safety, nurturance, and acceptance—all things a person needs to be human and educated.

Consequently, school leaders must address the anti-Black spatial imagination that indicates Black children do not belong (Jenkins, 2021). School leaders should take steps to interrogate exclusionary discipline policies and collaborate with families and communities to promote self-determination, self-actualization, and self-efficacy for Black students (Jenkins, 2021). The question then becomes what do educational leaders need to do to create inclusive, equitable, welcoming, and empowering environments, ultimately dismantling the school-to-prison pipeline.

RECOMMENDED STRATEGIES FOR ANTI-RACIST SCHOOL LEADERSHIP

Given the detailed descriptions of schooling experienced provided by the participants, it is imperative that any educational stakeholder serving underserved populations, particularly Black males, employ strategies that mitigate the pervasive effect of racism. This section provides research-based strategies that support the intersection of anti-racism and school leadership. Consequently, it should be noted that while this may focus on the educational leadership role, there are practical strategies to be implemented by teachers, teacher leaders, support staff, district personnel, school-community partners, and other stakeholders when planning services for students.

Developing Racial Literacy

As highlighted in the description of the participants in the present study, Sealey-Ruiz and Greene (2015) contend that Black males are conscious of their marginalization based on race and gender. Black males are acutely aware of how they are perceived in society and how those perceptions infiltrate the practices of their teachers and administrators (Sealey-Ruiz & Greene, 2015). This hyper-awareness lends itself to feelings of powerlessness which can strike at the core of young Black males in schools (Sealey-Ruiz & Greene, 2015). Resistance to this sense of powerlessness is often interpreted as oppositional, aggression, and conscious volition (Sealey-Ruiz & Greene, 2015). Given how racism and racial trauma affect Black males, this presents an opportunity for educational leaders to consider how they might interrogate race and racism and their role in their students' lives.

To begin to interrogate race and racism, one must develop racial literacy. Sealey-Ruiz and Greene (2015) define racial literacy as a skill in which people are able to discuss the social construction of race and examine the existence of racism and its harmful effects. As it relates to educators, racial literacy allows for examining institutionalized racism in schools concerning the experiences and outcomes of BIPOC students (Sealey-Ruiz & Greene, 2015). Examining the effects of race allows for meaningful discussion and action to dismantle racist structures (Sealey-Ruiz & Greene, 2015).

Similarly, Nash et al. (2018) conceptualize racial literacy as "a humanizing epistemology requiring parents and educators to recognize, refute, critique, and synthesize the structure of race in daily living, moving toward actions, curricula, communication, and restructuring of oppressive structures that allow us to realize equity." (p. 260). Nash et al. (2018) assert several framing ideas for the development of racial literacy. The first idea is that racial identity and racial (dys)consciousness are learned over time. Thus, critical racial literacy requires reflection over time (Nash et al., 2018). Another notion is that critical racial literacy is a multifaceted and cyclical process that may require the support of critical communities working together to resist structures that perpetuate racism (Nash et al., 2018). Lastly, Nash et al. (2018) emphasize that critical racial literacy requires recognizing and addressing blind spots relative to racial socialization.

Strategies for Developing Racial Literacy

- Engage in reading critical texts to acquire language to facilitate reflection and discussion about race, racism, and anti-Blackness.
- Keep a journal for critical reactions to your readings and new ideas.
- Interrogate the limits of our own world views and ideologies.
- Examine the historical implications of race and racism that shape our communities and society.
- Join critical communities to share experiences and new learnings.
- Diversify your personal and professional circles.
- Engage with authors of selected texts.
- Attend workshops or seminars on topics of interest that expand racial literacy.

Critical Self Reflection and Awareness

Some implications of developing racial literacy are cultivating critical self-awareness, recognizing one's own implicit and explicit biases, and working towards understanding where those biases come from and reducing them. Diem and Welton (2021) emphasize the importance of intentionality in addressing anti-Blackness and implicit bias as educators. Critical self-awareness, or critical self-reflection, referred to by Khalifa et al. (2016), supports personal and professional growth in leaders by allowing them to interrogate their positionality and excavate their biases, assumptions, and values. Khalifa et al. (2016) assert that critical reflection and awareness about biases are vital to transformative, anti-racist educational leadership.

Furthermore, Zarate and Mendoza (2020) assert that critical self-reflection is a vital tool in the praxis of transformative social justice leadership. Critical self-reflection encompasses the interrogation of one's history, values, assumptions, biases, and positionality in relation to professional roles (Zarate & Mendoza, 2020). Reflection is an essential step if educational leaders are to be able to disrupt practices that perpetuate systemic racism (Zarate & Mendoza, 2020). Zarate and Mendoza (2020) note that the essential aspects of critical self-reflection are that educational leaders question, critique, and thoroughly examine their privileges, assumptions, and biases.

Critical self-awareness, in this context, is to develop a heightened sense of oneself as a racialized being, to understand what that means in relation to the community being served, and how it influences critical decisions and actions within the leadership role. As indicated by researchers (Diem and Welton, 2021; Khalifa et al., 2016; Zarate and Mendoza, 2020), this is done by deep reflection. Educational leaders may want to reflect on the following questions: What are my implicit biases? How have they informed my decisions regarding discipline, curriculum and instructions, and resources? How have they impacted important relationships with teachers, students, and their families? What understanding gaps might I have about the educational experiences of my students?

Strategies for Cultivating Critical Self-reflection and Awareness

- Assess your commitment to critical self-reflection and determine what commitment looks like for you when reflection becomes challenging.
- Identify your implicit and explicit biases.
- Unpack your implicit and explicit bias take time to understand how you came to hold these biases.
- Keep a journal to reflect on and critique personal experiences with race and racism.
- Have a plan for coping with and healing from potentially painful realizations based on the exploration and unpacking of your biases.
- Build your racial literacy.
- Be intentional. Learn more about people from different racial and ethnic backgrounds by interacting with them and become exposed to experiences that counter those previous beliefs and stereotypes.

ENGAGING IN COURAGEOUS CONVERSATIONS

Naming racism and calling it out is essential to integrate anti-racism into school leadership. Being able to name and call it out requires a specific skill set in facilitating what Singleton (2021) refers to as courageous conversations. Educational leaders must be able to engage in and promote dialogue centering on race with faculty, staff, students, and community members. Singleton (2021) describes four agreements for engaging in courageous conversations: Stay engaged, Experience discomfort, Speak your truth, and Expect and accept non-closure. Anti-racist work and courageous conversations require ongoing dialogue. The participants' experiences in this study determine it necessary for educational leaders to embrace intentional race-centered conversations as opportunities to unearth the root causes of racial disparities.

Several factors can contribute to the hesitancy of educational leaders to engage in courageous conversations about race. Oftentimes, there is a genuine fear of being labeled, ostracized, or saying the wrong thing due to a lack of knowledge about racism (Diem et al., 2019; Diem & Welton, 2021). Emotional safety is an area of consideration for districts and leader preparation programs to foster safe environments where conversations about race are normalized and function as an integral part of problem-solving and leadership (Diem et al., 2019). To that extent, building-level leaders should consider how they cultivate safe environments for faculty, staff, students, and their families to engage in courageous conversations about race and racism.

Palmer and Louis (2017) determined that focused conversations about race help educators manage their fears. Other strategies to facilitate dispelling fear of courageous conversations include building racial literacy, critical self-reflection, and structured professional development (Palmer & Louis, 2017). Palmer and Louis (2017) emphasize that it is vital that principals model these characteristics, in addition to being consistent and intentional in their leadership practices toward racial equity. Palmer and Louis (2017) gave additional recommendations for principals to facilitate courageous conversations amongst staff, including smaller groups, modeling vulnerability, creating a safe space to experience discomfort and speak truth, and remain persistent in the face of exhaustion with a complex topic.

Strategies for Engaging in Courageous Conversations

- Develop your own racial literacy and critical awareness.
- Model vulnerability in courageous conversations.
- Use data and critical texts as talking points. Be able to articulate why the conversations are needed and their impact.
- Have an intended goal for the conversations.

- Create a safe space for speaking truths.
- Establish and enforce group norms or rules of engagement.
- Give attention to process over content.
- Acknowledge and validate the feelings and lived experiences of others.
- Show encouragement and appreciation for those who speak their truths.
- Create a strategy to avoid the conversation getting sidetracked.
- Expect and accept non-closure. Issues of race and racism will not be resolved in one sitting. Exchanges must be ongoing and should leave room for continued thought and growth.
- End with a call to action.
- Embrace community partnerships. Don't be afraid to bring in university faculty or community agencies to support this work.

Elevating Student Voice in Policy and Decision-Making

Welton et al. (2022) conceptualize students as citizens in their communities (schools). Democratic society is built on the premise that constituents have a voice in policies that affect them (Welton et al., 2022). Welton et al. (2022) note that despite the promise and premise of a democratic society, students have little to no voice in policy making. Welton et al. (2022) explain, "Moreover, for youth from politically marginalized groups (people of color, members of the LGBTQI communities, members of immigrant communities, individuals receiving special education services), objectification through policy writing, interpretation, and enactment is even more severe." (p. 4). Political marginalization is particularly grave for students of color who do not mirror typical policymakers despite evidence of their invaluable insight in educational policy discussions (Welton et al., 2022). Welton et al. (2022) argue that movements like Black Lives Matter are indicative of the power of youth to advance policy issues in the fight for justice.

Bertrand (2014) highlights possibilities and hindrances in centering the voices of students of color in decision-making. Educational decision-makers are teachers, administrators, and relevant policy makers (Bertrand, 2014). The author explains how educational decision-makers responding to student viewpoints can help or hurt ongoing dialogue efforts (Bertrand, 2014). Actions that promote critical dialogue between educational leaders and students of color include openness and a focus on the content of what students say rather than their delivery (Bertrand, 2014). Conversely, when students feel as though their concerns are being dismissed, this dramatically hinders ongoing dialogue that can significantly impact policy in a positive way for students (Bertrand, 2014). Educational leaders should consider creating spaces that amplify student voices to address systemic racism through the lens of students' own experiences (Bertrand, 2014). Bertrand (2014) argues that centering student voice in decision-making is a form of distributed leadership crucial to actualizing systemic change.

Moreover, Mansfield and Lambrinou (2022) examined how student voices were elevated alongside board members to create anti-racist policy changes in a Virginia school district. The authors describe how students were promoted as stewards of change by planning and leading forums, defining policy problems, and calling for action (Mansfield & Lambrinou, 2022). While the particular issue at hand was the naming of their schools, students indicated that to be a first step in addressing more system issues such as racial disparities in student achievement and discipline, teacher cultural competency, and representation in the curriculum (Mansfield & Lambrinou, 2022). Not only were students able to readily identify these issues, but they also proposed solutions for which the board can continue to work towards (Mansfield & Lambrinou, 2022). This study recommends including students, families, and other community members in critical decisions and policymaking and amplifying the voices of students most impacted by systemic racism in schools (Mansfield & Lambrinou, 2022). Lastly, Mansfield and Lambrinou (2022) assert that centering student voices validates changes in social power structures and unequal hierarchies in schools.

Strategies for Elevating Student Voice in Policy and Decision-Making

- Distribute student surveys.
- Create student advisory committees for educational governing bodies.
- Revise policy to include student representation on school boards.
- Facilitate student focus groups for root cause analysis and policy feedback.
- Form student government or council and involve them in initiative development.
- Provide opportunities for youth participatory action research.
- Ensure student voice opportunities are open to all students, not just high-performing ones.

Fostering Educational Equity and Institutional Anti-Racist Change

The work of Galloway and Ishimaru (2015) suggests that a radical re-centering of equity in national standards for educational leadership creates a sense of urgency to develop the capacity of leaders to address racial inequity in schools. About the same time as this publication, the Professional Standards for Educational Leaders (PSEL) now included a standard on Equity and Cultural Responsiveness (NPBEA,

2015). Standard 3 of the PSEL standards contains language about ensuring equity in access, critically examining policies, and addressing racial bias (NPBEA, 2015). Standard 3 of the PSEL standards reads as:

Effective educational leaders strive for equity of educational opportunity and culturally responsive practices to promote each student's academic success and well-being. Effective leaders:

a) Ensure that each student is treated fairly, respectfully, and with an understanding of each student's culture and context.
b) Recognize, respect, and employ each student's strengths, diversity, and culture as assets for teaching and learning.
c) Ensure that each student has equitable access to effective teachers, learning opportunities, academic and social support, and other resources necessary for success.
d) Develop student policies and address student misconduct in a positive, fair, and unbiased manner.
e) Confront and alter institutional biases of student marginalization, deficit-based schooling, and low expectations associated with race, class, culture and language, gender and sexual orientation, and disability or special status.
f) Promote the preparation of students to live productively in and contribute to the diverse cultural contexts of a global society.
g) Act with cultural competence and responsiveness in their interactions, decision-making, and practice.
h) Address matters of equity and cultural responsiveness in all aspects of leadership. (NPBEA, 2015, p. 11)

Examples of striving for equity of educational opportunity include being willing to conduct racial equity audits and root cause analyses for issues such as disproportionate exclusionary discipline, special education referrals, and underrepresentation in gifted and advanced placement. Another example may be completing a needs assessment of your faculty and staff to determine the best approaches to building their capacity related to cultural responsiveness and reducing implicit bias. Another critical aspect of this is analyzing policies that create infrastructure for inequitable practices.

In addition, Welton et al. (2018) merge the concepts of anti-racism and organizational change to provide a framework for institutional anti-racist change. The first aspect to consider in organizational change is context and conditions (Welton et al., 2018). Paired with the Pedagogy, Individual Learning and Resistance, and Systemic Level Commitment of anti-racist change, K-12 educational leaders should start with assessing student experiences and teacher belief systems and audit relevant data such as discipline, special education versus gifted and advanced placement, and assessment data disaggregated by race (Skrla et al., 2004; Welton et al., 2018). Next, educational leaders should focus on structures and processes perpetuating systemic racism (Welton et al., 2018). This focus may look like reviewing and critiquing policy conducting an equity audit of student outcomes, instructional practices, and referral processes, and eliminating and restructuring operations to dismantle racist policy and practice and promote racial equity (Welton et al., 2018).

Furthermore, Welton et al. (2018) note that for institutional change to occur, leaders must address change at multiple levels. Implications for scale and degree considerations are that in addition to equity audits of student outcomes and policy analysis, there must be intentional efforts to develop better relationships with Black students and their families, as well as intentionality in changing the perceptions of Black students and creating new narratives on a systemic level (Welton et al., 2018). Still, leadership is vital in facilitating anti-racist change (Welton et al., 2018). School and district leaders set nonnegotiable vision and goals and support other educators in taking responsibility and ownership in mitigating racial disparities for Black students (Welton et al., 2018). Lastly, the continuous improvement cycle is crucial in fostering change and consists of ongoing race-centered dialogues, professional development, equity-focused inquiry, and recalibration of policy and practice (Welton et al., 2018).

Strategies for Fostering Educational Equity and Institutional Anti-racist Change

- Assess student experiences through surveys and focus groups.
- Assess faculty and staff attitudes, beliefs, and perceptions of Black students.
- Conduct programmatic, teacher quality, and student achievement equity audits.
- Set a clear vision and goals for institutional anti-racist change.
- Critique and reconstruct school and district-level policies and standard operating procedures.
- Create and implement a strategic plan for ongoing professional development for administrators, faculty and staff, race-centered dialogue with stakeholders, and program evaluation and monitoring.
- Partner with relevant community agencies and organizations to facilitate this work.

FUTURE RESEARCH DIRECTIONS

Future research should consider discourse analysis on federal, state, and local policies that impact educational stakeholders including students, teachers, support staff, and leaders. Leading to dismantle racist structures also requires that educational leaders undergo intentional and ongoing professional development to address their own biases, build their capacity to facilitate courageous conversations, and center race in decision-making. To that end, researchers should also further examine the process and challenges of school districts and educator preparation programs that are currently addressing racial equity to provide valuable guidance for improvement in implementation. Lastly, the stories of the participants indicate a need for more social and emotional learning support in schools, especially for those with large diverse student populations. Researchers should interrogate current practices for supporting student mental health, and race-based trauma informed practices.

CONCLUSION

Racial disparities in student achievement and discipline practices for Black students, particularly Black males, result in the detrimental exclusion and pushout of these students from school. Noting these disparities is significant given that there is a 70 percent chance that a Black male who does not graduate high school will be incarcerated by his mid-thirties (Kearney et al., 2014). Furthermore, the ACLU cites expulsion and DAEP placement as a stop on the pathway to prison (Grace, 2016). Dunning-Lozano (2018) asserts that children sent to DAEPs were referred there for nonviolent, discretionary referrals, such as violating student codes of conduct at their regular schools. More often than not, Black males end up being pushed out of school for many reasons rooted in systemic racism and racial bias (Grace & Nelson, 2019).

Because the institutionalized devastation of Black males known as the school-to-prison pipeline is rooted in racial bias and systemic racism, that must be the starting point for educational leaders and stakeholders to reroute the trajectory of Black males. Educators are urged to cultivate racial literacy and engage in deep critical reflection on themselves as racialized beings and how that influences their beliefs, actions, and decision-making. Next, educators must embrace the value of centering race in critical dialogue with stakeholders and are intentional about elevating the voices of their most marginalized students. Lastly, rerouting the school-to-prison pipeline requires an approach to leadership that fosters educational equity and institutional anti-racist change. Educational leaders are responsible for setting a clear vision, cultivating conditions, and restructuring policy and processes for change. Ultimately, these steps may prove arduous, but they are long overdue, and our children are worth every effort. We owe them the right to the audacity of hope without the weight of what it has meant historically to be Black and male.

REFERENCES

Adichie, C. N. (2009, October 7). *The danger of a single story*. [Video] TED.

Bailey, T. K. M., Yeh, C. J., & Madu, K. (2022). Exploring Black adolescent males' experiences with racism and internalized racial oppression. *Journal of Counseling Psychology, 69*(4), 375–388. https://psycnet.apa.org/doi/10.1037/cou0000591. doi:10.1037/cou0000591 PMID:34807669

Bertrand, M. (2014). Reciprocal dialogue between educational decision makers and students of color: Opportunities and obstacles. *Educational Administration Quarterly, 50*(5), 812–843. doi:10.1177/0013161X14542582

Boutte, G., & Bryan, N. (2021). When will Black children be well? Interrupting anti-Black violence in early childhood classrooms and schools. *Contemporary Issues in Early Childhood, 22*(3), 232–243. doi:10.1177/1463949119890598

Bryant-Davis, T., & Ocampo, C. (2005). The trauma of racism: Implications for counseling, research, and education. *The Counseling Psychologist, 33*(4), 574–578. doi:10.1177/0011000005276581

Crabtree, L. M., Richardson, S. C., & Lewis, C. W. (2019). The gifted gap, STEM education, and economic immobility. *Journal of Advanced Academics, 30*(2), 203–231. doi:10.1177/1932202X19829749

Creswell, J. W. (2013). *Qualitative inquiry and research design: Choosing among five traditions* (3rd ed.). Sage.

Day-Vines, N. L., & Day-Hairston, B. O. (2005). Culturally congruent strategies for addressing the behavioral needs of urban, African American male adolescents. *Professional School Counseling, 8*(3), 236–243.

Delgado, R., & Stefancic, J. (2017). *Critical race theory: An introduction* (Vol. 20). NYU Press.

Diem, S., Carpenter, B. W., & Lewis-Durham, T. (2019). Preparing antiracist school leaders in a school choice context. *Urban Education, 54*(5), 706–731. doi:10.1177/0042085918783812

Diem, S., & Welton, A. D. (2021). *Anti-racist educational leadership and policy: Addressing racism in public education*. Routledge.

Dunning-Lozano, J. L. (2018). School discipline, race, and the discursive construction of the "deficient" student. *Sociological Spectrum*, *38*(5), 326–345. doi:10.1080/02732173.2018.1532364

English, D., Lambert, S. F., Tynes, B. M., Bowleg, L., Zea, M. C., & Howard, L. C. (2020). Daily multidimensional racial discrimination among Black U.S. American adolescents. *Journal of Applied Developmental Psychology*, *66*, 101068. Advance online publication. doi:10.1016/j.appdev.2019.101068 PMID:33994610

Flores, A. (2007). Examining disparities in mathematics education: Achievement gap or opportunity gap? *High School Journal*, *91*(1), 29–42. https://www.jstor.org/stable/40367921. doi:10.1353/hsj.2007.0022

Galloway, M. K., & Ishimaru, A. M. (2015). Radical recentering: Equity in educational leadership standards. *Educational Administration Quarterly*, *51*(3), 372–408. doi:10.1177/0013161X15590658

Gillborn, D. (2005). Education policy as an act of white supremacy: Whiteness, critical race theory and education reform. *Journal of Education Policy*, *20*(4), 485–505. doi:10.1080/02680930500132346

Grace, J. (2016). *Rerouting the school to prison pipeline: A phenomenological study of the educational experiences of African American males who have been expelled from public schools* [Doctoral dissertation, University of New Orleans, USA].

Grace, J. (2020). "They are scared of me": Black male perceptions of sense of belonging in U.S. public schools. *Journal of Contemporary Issues in Education*, *15*(2), 36–49. doi:10.20355/jcie29402

Grace, J. E., & Nelson, S. L. (2019). "Tryin' to survive": Black male students' understandings of the role of race and racism in the school-to-prison pipeline. *Leadership and Policy in Schools*, *18*(4), 664–680. doi:10.1080/15700763.2018.1513154

Gregory, A., Skiba, R. J., & Noguera, P. (2010). The achievement gap and the discipline gap: Two sides of the same coin? *Educational Researcher*, *39*(1), 59–68. doi:10.3102/0013189X09357621

Jenkins, D. A. (2021). Unspoken grammar of place: Anti-Blackness as a spatial imaginary in education. *Journal of School Leadership*, *31*(1-2), 107–126. doi:10.1177/1052684621992768

Kearney, M. H., Harris, B. H., Jácome, E., & Parker, L. (2014). *Ten economic facts about crime and incarceration in the United States.* The Hamilton Project. https://www.brookings.edu/wp-content/uploads/2016/06/v8_THP_10CrimeFacts.pdf

Khalifa, M. A., Gooden, M. A., & Davis, J. E. (2016). Culturally responsive school leadership: A synthesis of the literature. *Review of Educational Research, 86*(4), 1272–1311. doi:10.3102/0034654316630383

Kim, C. Y., Losen, D. J., & Hewitt, D. T. (2010). *The school-to-prison pipeline: Structuring legal reform.* NYU Press.

Ladson-Billings, G. (1998). Just what is critical race theory and what's it doing in a nice field like education? *International Journal of Qualitative Studies in Education: QSE, 11*(1), 7–24. doi:10.1080/095183998236863

Lincoln, Y. S., & Guba, E. G. (1985). *Naturalistic inquiry.* Sage Publications. doi:10.1016/0147-1767(85)90062-8

Losen, D. J., & Martinez, P. (2020). *Lost opportunities: How disparate school discipline continues to drive differences in the opportunity to learn.* Learning Policy Institute; Center for Civil Rights Remedies at the Civil Rights Project. https://learningpolicyinstitute.org/product/crdc-school-discipline-report

Love, B. L. (2014). "I *See* Trayvon Martin": What teachers can learn from the tragic death of a young Black male. *The Urban Review, 46*(2), 292–306. doi:10.100711256-013-0260-7

Mansfield, K. C., & Lambrinou, M. (2022). "This is Not Who We Are": Students Leading for Anti-Racist Policy Changes in Alexandria City Public Schools, Virginia. *Educational Policy, 36*(1), 19–56. doi:10.1177/08959048211059214

McInerney, M., & McKlindon, A. (2014). Unlocking the door to learning: Trauma-informed classrooms & transformational schools. *Education law center,* 1-24.

Merriam, S. B., & Grenier, R. S. (Eds.). (2019). *Qualitative research in practice: Examples for discussion and analysis.* John Wiley & Sons.

Motley, R., & Banks, A. (2018). Black males, trauma, and mental health service use: A systematic review. *Perspectives on social work: the journal of the doctoral students of the University of Houston Graduate School of Social Work, 14*(1), 3-19.

Moustakas, C. (1994). Phenomenological research methods. Sage.

Nash, K., Howard, J., Miller, E., Boutte, G., Johnson, G., & Reid, L. (2018). Critical racial literacy in homes, schools, and communities: Propositions for early childhood contexts. *Contemporary Issues in Early Childhood*, *19*(3), 256–273. doi:10.1177/1463949117717293

Noguera, P. A. (2017, April). Introduction to "racial inequality and education: Patterns and prospects for the future". []. Routledge.]. *The Educational Forum*, *81*(2), 129–135.

Palmer, E. L., & Louis, K. S. (2017). Talking about race: Overcoming fear in the process of change. *Journal of School Leadership*, *27*(4), 581–610. doi:10.1177/105268461702700405

Paschall, K. W., Gershoff, E. T., & Kuhfeld, M. (2018). A Two Decade Examination of Historical Race/Ethnicity Disparities in Academic Achievement by Poverty Status. *Journal of Youth and Adolescence*, *47*(6), 1164–1177. doi:10.100710964-017-0800-7 PMID:29313249

Riddle, T., & Sinclair, S. (2019). Racial disparities in school-based disciplinary actions are associated with county-level rates of racial bias. *Proceedings of the National Academy of Sciences of the United States of America*, *116*(17), 8255–8260. doi:10.1073/pnas.1808307116 PMID:30940747

Roberson, K., & Carter, R. T. (2021). The relationship between race-based traumatic stress and the Trauma Symptom Checklist: Does racial trauma differ in symptom presentation? *Traumatology*, *28*(1), 120–128. doi:10.1037/trm0000306

Rocque, M., & Snellings, Q. (2018). The new disciplinology: Research, theory, and remaining puzzles on the school-to-prison pipeline. *Journal of Criminal Justice*, *59*, 3–11. doi:10.1016/j.jcrimjus.2017.05.002

Rynders, D. (2019). Battling implicit bias in the idea to advocate for African American students with disabilities. *Touro Law Review*, *35*, 461.

Saldaña, J. (2021). The Coding Manual for Qualitative Researchers. *Sage (Atlanta, Ga.)*.

Sealey-Ruiz, Y., & Greene, P. (2015). Popular visual images and the (mis) reading of black male youth: A case for racial literacy in urban preservice teacher education. *Teaching Education*, *26*(1), 55–76. doi:10.1080/10476210.2014.997702

Singleton, G. E. (2021). *Courageous Conversations About Race: A Field Guide for Achieving Equity in Schools and Beyond*. Corwin Press.

Skiba, R. J., Horner, R. H., Chung, C. G., Rausch, M. K., May, S. L., & Tobin, T. (2011). Race is not neutral: A national investigation of African American and Latino disproportionality in school discipline. *School Psychology Review, 40*(1), 85–107. doi:10.1080/02796015.2011.12087730

Skrla, L., Scheurich, J. J., Garcia, J., & Nolly, G. (2004). Equity audits: A practical leadership tool for developing equitable and excellent schools. *Educational Administration Quarterly, 40*(1), 133–161. doi:10.1177/0013161X03259148

Sue, D. W., Capodilupo, C. M., Torino, G. C., Bucceri, J. M., Holder, A. M. B., Nadal, K. L., & Esquilin, M. (2007). Racial microaggressions in everyday life: Implications for clinical practice. *The American Psychologist, 62*(4), 271–286. doi:10.1037/0003-066X.62.4.271 PMID:17516773

Tsoi-A-Fatt Bryant, R. (2015). *College preparation for African American students: Gaps in the high school educational experience.* CLASP. https://vtechworks.lib.vt.edu/handle/10919/83649

Welton, A. D., Mansfield, K. C., & Salisbury, J. D. (2022). The Politics of Student Voice: The Power and Potential of Students as Policy Actors. *Educational Policy, 36*(1), 3–18. doi:10.1177/08959048211059718

Welton, A. D., Owens, D. R., & Zamani-Gallaher, E. M. (2018). Anti-racist change: A conceptual framework for educational institutions to take systemic action. *Teachers College Record, 120*(14), 1–22. doi:10.1177/016146811812001402

Williams, P. J. (1991). *The alchemy of race and rights.* Harvard University Press.

Zarate, M. E., & Mendoza, Y. (2020). Reflections on race and privilege in an educational leadership course. *Journal of research on leadership education, 15*(1), 56-80. doi:10.1177/1942775118771666

KEY TERMS AND DEFINITIONS

Anti-Racism: Active efforts to disrupt beliefs, change behaviors, and revise policies that perpetuate systemic racism.

DAEP: Disciplinary Alternative Education Program. An alternative school setting for students who have been given long term suspensions, expulsion, or court adjudicated consequences for behavioral infractions in the traditional school setting.

Educational Equity: Ensuring every student has equitable and access to opportunities, recourses, and high-quality educational experiences needed to reach their full potential.

Institutional Anti-Racist Change: Organizations facilitate a paradigm shift which centers racial equity utilizing needs assessments, equity audits, ongoing capacity development, resource allocation, and policy evaluations to eliminate instructional racism. Organizations must take into consideration the role of people, processes, programs, and policy in facilitating instructional change for racial equity.

Opportunity Gap: Students from underserved communities, particularly Black, Indigenous, and People of color, have unequal access to high quality educational opportunities and experiences.

Race-Based Trauma: An emotional response to racist events at a micro or macro level.

School Pushout: Exclusionary discipline practices such as excessive out of school suspension, expulsion, or "counseling out" in which students end up permanently removed from school.

Chapter 3
Culturally-Responsive Disciplinary Strategies After Returning to the In-Person Learning Environment in the Era of the COVID-19 Pandemic

Wei-Ling Sun
University of Texas at El Paso, USA

ABSTRACT

In this chapter, the researcher provides in-depth discussions regarding the commonly used disciplinary strategies in schools before the COVID-19 pandemic, and the implementation of social-emotional learning initiatives after returning to in-person learning that is intentionally selected to address the increasing exposure of home violence, abuse, homelessness, and isolation among students during the pandemic in a predominately Latina/o population community located in a Texas borderland area. This research uses critical race theory and culturally responsive school leaders as a theoretical framework to analyze leadership strategies to address students' behavioral issues due to trauma and prevent exposure to the school-to-prison pipeline. With the elementary and secondary school emergency relief (ESSER) fund and the education disruption due to the pandemic, a paradigm shift pushes school leaders to adapt culturally responsive disciplinary strategies when addressing students' behavioral issues. Policy implications of the findings are discussed.

DOI: 10.4018/978-1-6684-5713-9.ch003

INTRODUCTION AND LITERATURE REVIEW

Before the COVID-19 pandemic, conversations regarding issues related to the school-to-prison pipeline are primarily focusing on racial disparities of the use of exclusionary disciplinary practices (Muñiz, 2021; Welsh & Little, 2018) and the debate on abolishing school resource officers (SROs; Mann et al., 2019; Muñiz, 2021). As research shows, the use of out-of-school suspensions increases students' risk of an exposure to juvenile justice system (Heitzeg, 2009; Skiba, Arredondo, & Williams, 2014; Novak, 2019), suspending students due to their misbehaviors does not address the root cause of student behavioral issues (Mann et al., 2019) and puts students at risk of exposure to the school-to-prison pipeline. Mann et al. (2019) proposed decreasing the funding for SROs and increasing the number of social workers or school counselors in schools to address student behavioral issues to mitigate a troubling trend of the school-to-prison pipeline. Although Sun (2022) found disciplinary practices in school leaders' everyday disciplinary decisions—some strategies are racialized, the COVID-19 pandemic has drastically interrupted the disciplinary practices meant for an in-person learning environment. During the pandemic, students experienced school closures, and issues related to remote learning, loss of jobs or housing, social isolation, traumatic loss or grief, and domestic violence intensified (Evans et al., 2020; Swedo et al., 2020; Usher et al., 2020). Addressing behavioral issues triggered by trauma has become one of the top priorities in supporting back-to-school efforts.

School Districts in a Texas Borderland

According to 2018–2019 school year data, school districts in the borderland area, which are mostly Title I schools, had more than 60% of the students who were labeled as at risk of dropping out of school, on average; 25% of the students were enrolled in bilingual and English language learning programs; 75% of the students were economically disadvantaged; 1% were African American students, 0.4% Asian American students, 90% Latina/o students, and 3% White students, with 80% Latina/o teachers. Meanwhile, school districts in the same area have more Latina/o students and teachers, fewer African American, Asian, and White students, and fewer experienced teachers than the state average.

Texas public schools also face rapid policy changes due to the recent passing of HB 4545—a school accountability bill[1], SB 3—a critical race theory ban bill, the ban of mask mandate in public schools, and school reopening in the fall 2021 semester. After more than a yearlong school closure, schools in Texas not only have to assist students in readjusting their routines but also must quickly adapt to all the new policy changes during the continuing COVID-19 pandemic. Receiving federal and state funding has become even more critical to the schools located in the borderland area.

Education Crisis, Pandemic, and Student Behaviors

Education crisis is not a normal experience in schools. Research on how education crisis impacts student behaviors is relatively limited. Although we have very little knowledge of how the nationwide interruption of the education system due to the pandemic impacted student behaviors and learning experiences. To date, literature regarding changes in student behaviors due to education crisis is mostly concerned with natural disasters, including Hurricane Katrina or Hurricane Sandy (Schwarz et al., 2015; Ward et al., 2008). Students experience increased risk for anxiety, depression, and PTSD after a crisis and are more likely to experience behavioral issues (Schwartz et al., 2015; Ward et al., 2008). Gross et al. (2016) found that school leaders shifted priorities to address the emotional needs of students in response to catastrophe. In this unsettling and unprecedented time, remote learning increased the exposure to domestic abuse in student homes (Taub, 2020) with very limited access to social workers. Black and Brown communities also have to grieve for the passing of loved ones due to the highest COVID-19 death rates (Ford et al., 2020). With all these traumatic events that devastated the marginalized and minoritized communities in borderland communities, we can see the parallel trends of challenges and priorities schools are facing during the pandemic and the literature on the education crisis.

Although the need for increasing numbers of social workers and school counselors to address behavioral issues is not a new concept, receiving enough funding to hire mental health personnel and programs has been a significant challenge to schools (Gagnon & Mattingly, 2016). The nationwide school closures and the online learning experiences during the pandemic have brought issues of childhood trauma among students to light. Federal lawmakers passed the American Rescue Plan (ARP) Act establishing the Elementary and Secondary School Emergency Relief Fund (ESSER Fund) on March 11, 2021, to provide funding to implement mental health services and support, including hiring counselors and implementing evidence-based mental health programs in schools. School leaders now have recourses to address the root cause of behavioral issues with the ESSER Fund. This research seeks to explore research questions, including:

1. What are disciplinary strategies used during the COVID-19 pandemic in predominately Latina/o student schools?
2. How does the ESSER Fund support school efforts to address behavioral issues triggered by trauma?

THEORETICAL FRAMEWORK

In this research, the researcher combine concepts from critical race theories and culturally responsive school leadership framework to examine the use of disciplinary strategies during the COVID-19 pandemic and the rationale for using the ESSER Fund. Critical race theory (CRT) lens serves to challenge notions of objectivity, racial neutrality, and deficient perspective of students of color (Solórzano & Delgado Bernal, 2001; Solórzano & Yosso, 2001). CRT also serves as a tool for centering experiential knowledge through counter-stories and narratives (Delgado, 1989; DeCuir & Dixon, 2004). Counter-storytelling allows individuals to share their voices, experiences, and expertise as "valid, legitimate and intellectual" contributions toward academic and social discourse (Rodríguez & Greer, 2017). The study site is located in a majority Latina/o population Mexico–U.S. border area, where the majority of school administrators are Latina/o. The voice and the experiential knowledge of Latina/o school leaders position the participants as knowledge holders and producers of knowledge (Bell, 1987; Solórzano & Delgado Bernal, 2001). CRT lays the foundation to center the narratives of leaders of color.

The culturally responsive school leadership (CRSL) framework is defined as a liberatory practice that resists various forms of oppression in the education system while institutionalizing or normalizing cultural practices of students and local communities (Khalifa et al., 2016). The CRSL framework includes four elements: (1) critical self-reflection on leadership behaviors, (2) development of culturally responsive teachers, (3) promotion of a culturally responsive or inclusive school environment, and (4) engagements of students, parents, and indigenous contexts. A CRSL framework centers on inclusion, equity, advocacy, and social justice in schools (Khalifa et al., 2016) and offers a lens to understand race-conscious sensemaking discourse that reveals invisible marginalization and highlights conversations about critical self-awareness of color-blind ideologies. Promoting or implementing disciplinary practices or disciplinary policy reforms to address racial disparities, decrease the use of exclusionary disciplinary practices, or create an inclusive learning environment is part of the CRSL practice (Khalifa, 2019). Bringing the two theoretical lenses together creates an opportunity to have a more in-depth understanding of the rationale for implementing culturally responsive disciplinary strategies that can mitigate exposure to the school-to-prison pipeline in a borderland area in the era of the COVID-19 pandemic.

METHODOLOGY

This chapter is drawn from a larger mixed-method case study. The section analyzed here is a qualitative piece examining in-depth interviews through the CRT and CRSL lenses. Focus groups (n = 7) and interviews with high school principals, central office administrators, and a director of school counselors ($n = 46$) from a school district were administered during the 2021–2022 school year during the pandemic. The school district is in a Mexico–U.S. border area. The school district has a majority Latina/o student population.

The Border Land School District (BISD, pseudonym) is selected using purposeful sampling. BISD, a Title I and majority Latina/o student district located in a rural borderland area, started a series of instructional technology reforms in the 2018–2019 school year prior to the pandemic. When the school closure began in the spring 2020 semester, BISD had already initiated the implementation of innovative instructional technology initiatives. BISD was in a unique position to experience a nationwide instructional technology crisis during the pandemic while the district leadership had already begun the advancement of technology use district-wide.

BISD is considered a unique case (Yin, 2017 in understanding school efforts and the use of the ESSER Fund to address student behavioral issues and trauma after returning to in-person learning during the pandemic. Using a single case study (Yin, 2017), the researcher conducted seven focus groups[2] (Nyumba et al., 2018) with school leaders, teachers, and students to understand general school experiences during the COVID-19 pandemic in spring 2021. The researcher used Google Sheets to document three steps of empowerment evaluation (Fetterman et al., 2014) during the focus group sessions (Billups, 2020) to gain a general understanding of what has been done district-wide and at the campus level during the online learning phase to address student behavioral issues. Each focus group session had 5–6 participants and lasted about 1.5 hours. The researcher then conducted a total of 46 one-hour, in-depth, semi-structural interviews with individuals, including central office administrators, principals, assistant principals, teachers, school counselors, and high school students[3] in fall 2021, to inquire about their individual experiences of the impact of COVID-19 pandemic, including school administrator and teacher experiences addressing student behavioral issues and student experiences of trauma. All focus groups and interviews were audio- and video-recorded with separate devices. The researcher have interviewed 23 central office administrators and campus-level school leaders, 9 schoolteachers, 13 high school students, and 1 school counselor. All participants completed individual questionnaires for the purpose of collecting their demographic background information for later reference in the data analysis phase. Although there were no direct conversations regarding the issues of school-to-prison pipeline, strategies and conversations regarding student behavioral issues and the use of disciplinary practices, which are the major contributor to the exposure of the school-to-prison pipeline, were brought up from the participants. The researcher also collected presentation powerpoints and publicly available documents on the BISD website regarding the use of the ESSER fund. All collected data are imported into Nvivo qualitative data analysis software.

The researcher coded the interview data using a hybrid method (Miles et al., 2020), in which the researcher first developed deductive codes from the literature and the theoretical framework on disciplinary strategies and the use of the ESSER Fund. While coding, the researcher defined boundaries between subcategories through a constant comparative method (Glaser & Strauss, 1967). Through dialogue between the data and literature, the researcher modified and omitted deductive codes as necessary, replacing or expanding upon them. The researcher then created matrices and wrote and refined analytic memos on emerging findings to address the study's central questions about disciplinary strategies during the pandemic and how the ESSER Fund supports schools' efforts to address student behavioral issues.

FINDINGS

Sun (2022) found that, before the COVID-19 pandemic, school principals were willing to have open discussions regarding general issues of racial inequalities and systemic racism, including issues of gentrification. However, Principals avoided in-depth discussions and reflections on the issues related to racial disparities and racialized discretionary disciplinary decisions on their campuses. The participants centered the conversations on correcting behavioral issues and the rationale for punishing undesired behaviors. There was no mention of childhood trauma. As mentioned in the introduction section, more students experienced trauma in remote learning and the pandemic. Remote learning has made traditional disciplinary measures more challenging. The findings illuminated the justifications of behavioral issues from student perspectives, disciplinary priorities in BISD, and how the ESSER Fund supports the implementations of the district-wide disciplinary priorities.

Practicing Compassion

Before returning to in-person learning in August 2021, students expressed their frustration with online learning:

I have to help with house chores and watch my siblings at home when I am actually in class. My mom sometimes tells me to help with cooking. I told her, "I am in class." But she thinks I am just listening to my teacher so I should be able to multitask and help out with house chores, you know. She doesn't understand that my teacher asks us to do a lot of activities on the computer. And I have to be on the computer all the time to complete the tasks.

Students feel that they are being pushed to grow up faster and become more like adults in the house during remote learning and have to take more responsibilities at home while attending classes online. This is a more general experience for the student participants. Some students experienced the death of family members.

We tried to build compassion with our teachers and students. Working from home is hard. Learning from home is hard. The most challenging part of our work is to keep students attending online classes.

School principals acknowledge the challenge of disciplining students during the remote learning phase primarily concerns student attendance. The increasing emphasis on compassion for teachers and students did not seem to be a common practice before the pandemic.

We [including school administrators, teachers, and students] are all being impacted by COVID at some point. Suspension is our last resort before we try every disciplinary option we have in school.

The interview and focus group data revealed that experiencing the loss of family members occurs at all levels in school during the pandemic. District-level and school-level leadership frequently and heavily stressed addressing trauma instead of disciplinary actions to punish unwanted behaviors. This type of leadership practice echoes the CRSL framework, which promotes an inclusive school environment (Alston, 2005; Gooden, 2005; Gooden & O'Doherty, 2015; Shields, 2010). Instead of using exclusionary discipline practices, school leaders were actively practicing compassion regarding behavioral issues triggered by trauma. School leaders practiced compassion more after returning to an in-person learning environment in August 2021.

When we were in the virtual learning phase, we had school buses to deliver meals to our students, sent our school resource officers to knock door to door to check on students who had trouble attending online classes, and reminded our staff and teachers that we are all struggling at some point working and learning from home. There was so much going on at the same time. It is not easy to take care of all students' needs when they have trouble focusing on learning.

Culturally-Responsive Disciplinary Strategies

Although in-person learning does not require the same amount of effort to check on student needs, the same level of compassion continues at all levels in BISD. And the use of suspension remains at the minimum level after returning to in-person learning.

Prioritizing Mental Health

Behavioral issues started to surface in the beginning of the in-person learning phase. According to BISD school principals, students who experienced online learning during their transition year to elementary school (first grade), middle school (sixth grade), and high school (ninth grade) had more behavioral issues than other students.

Our first graders [were] having trouble learning to hold pencils properly. . . . Some of them didn't know how to speak to teachers properly and throw tantrums a lot more than we had ever experienced before. . . . I think part of it is because their parents were "serving" them during the remote learning. And kids carried the same behavior to treat teachers like how they treat their parents at home. We spent a lot of time [demonstrating] proper behaviors to our kids. Because if we don't address behavioral issues, teachers cannot continue the teaching part.

One elementary school principal expressed the challenge to address behavioral issues and prioritize addressing behavioral issues than instructional goals.

Kids in [sixth] grade and [ninth] grade are still acting like elementary school and middle school kids. They missed the first part of the academic year in school to have senior students modeling proper behaviors in middle and high schools. We also see an increase of anxiety and depression among students.

The associate superintendent of secondary schools pointed out the different behavioral challenges secondary school students have after returning to school. One high school principal expressed that one possible explanation for the increasing misbehaviors could be students miss interacting with their peers. Some students experienced not being able to see their family members or were forced to stay with their grandparents due to the closing of the border. Some high school students were forced to work or experience homelessness due to parent job loss. Some students experienced increased unsupervised time during the online learning phase, which led to increased access to vaping materials.

We see . . . unprecedented behavioral issues in the first month of returning to school. Students vandalized school properties, [threw] tantrums at teachers, were anxious being around . . . others, and had increased numbers of depression and suicidal thoughts.

School administrators expressed that the level of attention on student behavioral issues was a surprise after returning to school. Before the semester started, school administrators and teachers were focusing on preparing to address students' learning loss. However, student behavioral issues become the priority when students return to school.

Having an understanding of different trends of behavioral issues that occurred in the remote learning and in-person learning phases, it is apparent that the use of disciplinary strategies in BISD diverged from the traditional disciplinary strategies, including in-school and out-of-school suspensions.

Our kids have spent almost a year learning from home and being away from school; we try not to send kids home again before we exhaust all the possible ways to address behavioral issues. I think kids also don't want to be [sent] home again. So far, we haven't had any case [such] that we must send kids home.

Instead of using suspensions, BISD increased the use of school counselors, promoted senior teachers who had received social-emotional learning training to provide social-emotional support to students, implemented a social-emotional learning curriculum to help students identify their emotional needs, and had a social-emotional wellness check with students every morning. Central office administrators also recognized the need to address mental health and family trauma beyond the student population; the BISD leadership team also worked on expanding their care from students to family and community by collaborating with local counseling services.

I have one student whose family experienced a death of their father. Kids seem to handle the loss of their father better than their mom. Their mom still talks to us about her husband in present tense. Mom seems to have a harder time to process the loss.

The director of school counselors shared an example of the need to provide counseling services to family members other than the counseling services at school. BISD, like school districts in the borderland city in Texas, is a Title I school district with a majority Latina/o student population. The majority of the student population received free and reduced-cost lunches and lived in highly concentrated poverty areas. Many of the families in this district do not have health insurance to cover mental health services. BISD leadership team recognized the needs of the neighborhood community and serve as an advocate and social activist for the school and neighborhood community (Capper et al., 2002; Gooden, 2005; Johnson, 2006;

Khalifa, 2012) and sought to provide free mental health services to both students and family members. The heavy focus on student and family mental health is strong evidence of culturally responsive school leadership practices. Instead of using exclusionary disciplinary strategies, BISD implemented a series of services and professional development training to promote an inclusive environment and engage student and parent contexts (Khalifa et al., 2016).

The ESSER Fund Support

BISD is located in a city where all the school districts are Title I school districts. This indicated that the majority of the students live in a concentrated poverty area. Mainstream news media and policy reports regarding student learning experiences during the pandemic centered on the issues related to the increasing rates of domestic violence and learning loss; however, the BISD central office administrators expressed that homelessness and anxiety about going back to school are more prevalent among students in the district. Elementary school students have more emotional meltdown moments in class than secondary school students. Families were dealing with divorce and the loss of family members because of the pandemic and job loss. The director of counseling explained that parents have difficulty coping with the loss of a family member more so than their children. School leaders recognize that the social-emotional well-being of family members of their students can have an impact on students' social-emotional well-being as well. The district leaders distributed part of the ESSER Fund to collaborate with community mental health service facilities to provide mental health services to family members of their students.

BISD was able to receive fifteen million dollars from ESSER II and additional three million dollars from ESSER III. Echoing a national discourse related to students' increasing exposure to childhood trauma, the BISD leadership utilized the ESSER Fund to hire school counselors, provide professional development training regarding social-emotional learning to teachers, promote senior teachers to become social-emotional liaisons on campus, hire more school counselors, and create calming corners on campus. BISD also utilized the ESSER Fund to increase foster care services due to the increased numbers of foster care and homeless students. During the pandemic, students experienced parental job loss, deaths in families, and domestic abuse. Some families became homeless, and some students were removed from their families, in need of child protection services.

In addition to the increasing need for mental health services and foster care support, after the passing of SB 179 in the 2021 Texas legislature, which requires school counselors to spend at least 80% of their work time on duties related to school counseling programs instead of administrative work, school counselors can focus on building meaningful relationships with students, meeting with students one-on-one to address emotional issues and trauma. This means school counselors need more quality time with each student who needs mental health services. With the increased demand for counseling services in school, BISD used the ESSER Fund to hire more school counselors, provided professional development training to senior teachers about social and emotional learning, implemented a district-wide positive behavioral intervention system, and installed health and wellness programs.

We know these programs and initiatives are essential to our student's well-being for a long time. But with the limited state and federal funding, we were not able to implement anything that can bring systemic change to address students' mental health. Some students need more mental health support than others. Like, I have this one girl who were sexually abused before the pandemic. I was working with her on this issue. But it is very obvious that the pandemic aggregated the abuse. Now, returning to school, she is very easily trigger[ed] by little things because of the amount of trauma she experienced at home. I am meeting with her a lot more than before. But I also have served a lot more students before. I am glad that we are able to hire more counselors so more students can receive the mental health support they need.

The director of school counselors expressed her gratitude for being able to hire more school counselors with the ESSER Fund. BISD was able to promote one of their school counselors to be the director of school counselors and appointed her to oversee hiring more school counselors. As mentioned earlier, principals acknowledge the behavioral challenges students have after the school reopening in the 2021 fall semester, and school leaders have discussed behavioral issues with compassion since students are not the only population experiencing trauma such as loss and grieving during the pandemic. Having compassion and acknowledging the need for mental health services without financial capacity cannot provide sufficient services that students need. The ESSER Fund has become a critical resource for BISD to address the root causes of behavioral issues as civil rights organizations have advocated for increased access to mental health services at school for years (Mann et al., 2019). Although the systemic implementation of mental health services in BISD is worth celebrating, there is a genuine concern about the sustainability of these mental health services after the district runs out of ESSER Fund support.

Our superintendent told us that we will continue the mental health services after the ESSER Fund because we do see the benefit of these services. However, we are still in the process of brainstorming what we can move around in our budget to sustain the mental health system we implemented right now.

As for now, the ESSER Fund is one-time funding. The director of federal funding said that the district leadership is in the process of assessing the use of Title I, II, III, IV Part A funding from the Every Student Succeeds Act (ESSA) to develop a budget plan to sustain mental health services to students beyond the ESSER Fund. With the ESSER Fund, BISD is able to increase the resources to support students' mental health services and provide training to equip staff and teachers to identify student mental health needs.

To conclude, the in-depth understanding of disciplinary strategies used in BISD during the pandemic shows a promising and positive organizational change that can truly address the root cause of misbehaviors instead of punishing students or pushing students out of school. Although the COVID-19 pandemic has brought devastating impacts on students in various ways, the pandemic has also forced school leaders to re-examine educational priorities and illuminate the importance of caring for student mental health and childhood trauma. With the ESSER Fund, school districts can fulfill the pathway of transforming the school environment from exclusion to inclusion and strengthen a school's relationship with the community. As the associate superintendent of secondary schools said that "we, [the school district], are the only educational and social resource to our community in this rural area. We have the responsibility to provide resources to our students and to the community to ensure the wellness of the community."

CONCLUSION AND IMPLICATIONS

It is apparent that the COVID-19 pandemic has transformed the BISD ways of disciplining students at an organizational level. Echoing the literature on environmental crisis and education, the rising numbers of anxiety and depression amount students are unprecedented during the COVID-19 pandemic. The COVID-19 pandemic is not just a crisis that happened in a certain state or part of the world but on a global scale. The pandemic has brought school administrators, teachers, and students together and increased the practice of compassion when interpreting student misbehavior. The case of BISD leadership shows an exemplary leadership response to student behavioral issues in a predominately Latina/o population school district. Instead of viewing student misbehaviors from a deficit standpoint (Davis, 2001; Flessa, 2009), BISD school leaders have focused on reducing anxiety among students (Madhlangobe & Gordon, 2012) and advocating for the community (Capper et al., 2002; Gooden, 2005; Johnson, 2006; Khalifa, 2012).

Findings show that school leaders prioritized mental health services to replace the use of exclusionary disciplinary practices. This is a form of challenging exclusionary practice (Khalifa, 2011, Madhlangobe & Gordon, 2012). Choosing to address the root cause of student behavior issues rather than punishing student reactions to the struggles, trauma, and challenges students carry from home to school. After school closure and the experience of the COVID-19 pandemic, there has been a significant shift from the focus of implementing alternative disciplinary practices to addressing the root causes of misbehaviors, including childhood trauma. This is a critical and important finding since civil rights activists have been trying to break the linkage of the school-to-prison pipeline to address trauma by promoting the increase in hiring school counselors (Mann et al., 2019) and the implementation of culturally responsive restorative practices (Lustick, 2017). With the ESSER Fund, schools are taking more actions to implement programs, including a social-emotional learning curriculum and hiring more school counselors to address childhood trauma. More importantly, school leaders are more compassionate when discussing misbehaviors since the pandemic is an experience for all. With the paradigm shift in viewing student behavioral issues and financial support from the ESSER Fund, schools have more opportunities to challenge exclusionary policy practices (Khalifa, 2011; Madhlangobe & Gordon, 2012), promote a culturally responsive and inclusive school environment (Khalifa et al., 2016), develop meaningful, positive relationships with the community (Gardiner & Enomoto, 2006; Johnson, 2006; Walker, 2001), and serve as an advocate and social activist for the community (Capper et al., 2002; Gooden, 2005; Johnson, 2006; Khalifa, 2012).

Indeed, schooling disruptions were more frequent in districts with a greater proportion of students of color (Oster et al., 2021). National narratives of schooling experiences of students of color disproportionally focus on the struggle and the negative impact of the pandemic. The practice of focusing on the negative impact on students who are racially minoritized does not bring meaningful solutions to the already challenging learning experiences of racially minoritized students. The BISD leadership has broken the narrative of the suffering of Latina/o students during the pandemic and has focused on the opportunity to change and transform disciplinary practices. BISD is an example of implementing a culturally responsive school leadership framework to address childhood trauma and mitigate student exposure to the school-to-prison pipeline.

REFERENCES

Alston, J. A. (2005). Tempered radicals and servant leaders: Black females persevering in the superintendency. *Educational Administration Quarterly*, *41*(4), 675–688. doi:10.1177/0013161X04274275

Bell, D. (1987). *And we are not saved: The elusive quest for racial justice*. Basic Books.

Billups, F. D. (2020). *Qualitative data collection tools: Design, development, and applications*. SAGE Publications.

Capper, C. A., Hafner, M. M., & Keyes, M. W. (2002). The role of community in spiritual centered leadership for justice. In G. Furman (Ed.), *School as community: From promise to practice* (pp. 77–94). State University of New York Press.

Davis, J. (2001). American Indian boarding school experiences: Recent studies from Native perspectives. *Magazine of History*, *15*(2), 20–22. doi:10.1093/maghis/15.2.20

Delgado, R. (1989). Storytelling for oppositionists and others: A plea for narrative. *Michigan Law Review*, *87*(8), 2411–2441. doi:10.2307/1289308

Evans, M. L., Lindauer, M., & Farrell, M. E. (2020). A pandemic within a pandemic: Intimate partner violence during COVID-19. *The New England Journal of Medicine*, *383*(24), 2302–2304. doi:10.1056/NEJMp2024046 PMID:32937063

Fetterman, D., Kaftarian, S. J., & Wandersman, A. (2014). *Empowerment evaluation: Knowledge and tools for self-assessment, evaluation capacity building, and accountability* (2nd ed.). Sage.

Flessa, J. (2009). Urban school principals, deficit frameworks, and implications for leadership. *Journal of School Leadership*, *19*(3), 334–373. doi:10.1177/105268460901900304

Ford, T., Reber, S., & Reeves, R. V. (2020, June 16). *Race gaps in COVID-19 deaths are even bigger than they appear*. Brookings Institute. https://www.brookings.edu/blog/up-front/2020/06/16/race-gaps-in-covid-19-deaths-are-even-bigger-than-they-appear/

Gagnon, D. J., & Mattingly, M. J. (2016). *Most US school districts have low access to school counselors: Poor, diverse, and city school districts exhibit particularly high student-to-counselor ratios* (Report No. 108). Carsey School of Public Policy. doi:10.34051/p/2020.275

Gardiner, M. E., & Enomoto, E. (2006). Urban school principals and their role as multicultural leaders. *Urban Education*, *41*(6), 560–584. doi:10.1177/0042085906294504

Glaser, B. G., & Strauss, A. L. (1967). *The discovery of grounded theory*. Aldine.

Gooden, M. A. (2005). The role of an African American principal in an urban information technology high school. *Educational Administration Quarterly*, *41*(4), 630–650. doi:10.1177/0013161X04274273

Gooden, M. A., & O'Doherty, A. (2015). Do you see what I see? Fostering aspiring leaders' racial awareness. *Urban Education*, *50*(2), 225–255. doi:10.1177/0042085914534273

Gross, B., Tuchman, S., & Yatsko, S. (2016). *Grappling with discipline in autonomous schools: New approaches from DC and New Orleans*. Center on Reinventing Public Education.

Heitzeg, N. A. (2009). Education or incarceration: Zero tolerance policies and the school-to-prison pipeline. *Forum on Public Policy Online*. https://files.eric.ed.gov/fulltext/EJ870076.pdf

Johnson, L. S. (2006). "Making her community a better place to live": Culturally responsive urban school leadership in historical context. *Leadership and Policy in Schools*, *5*(1), 19–36. doi:10.1080/15700760500484019

Khalifa, M. A. (2011). Teacher expectations and principal behavior: Responding to teacher acquiescence. *The Urban Review*, *43*(5), 702–727. doi:10.100711256-011-0176-z

Khalifa, M. A. (2012). A re-new-ed paradigm in successful urban school leadership principal as community leader. *Educational Administration Quarterly*, *48*(3), 424–467. doi:10.1177/0013161X11432922

Khalifa, M. A., Gooden, M. A., & Davis, J. E. (2016). Culturally responsive school leadership: A synthesis of the literature. *Review of Educational Research*, *86*(4), 1272–1311. doi:10.3102/0034654316630383

Lustick, H. (2017). Making discipline relevant: Toward a theory of culturally responsive positive schoolwide discipline. *Race, Ethnicity and Education*, *20*(5), 681–695. doi:10.1080/13613324.2016.1150828

Madhlangobe, L., & Gordon, S. P. (2012). Culturally responsive leadership in a diverse school: A case study of a high school leader. *NASSP Bulletin*, *96*(3), 177–202. doi:10.1177/0192636512450909

Mann, A., Whitaker, A., Torres-Gullien, S., Morton, M., Jordan, H., Coyle, S., & Sun, W. (2019). *Cops and no counselors: How the lack of school mental health staff is harming students.* American Civil Liberties Union. https://www.aclu.org/issues/juvenile-justice/school-prison-pipeline/cops-and-no-counselors

Miles, M. B., Huberman, A. M., & Saldaña, J. (2020). *Qualitative data analysis: A methods sourcebook* (4th ed.). Sage.

Muñiz, J. O. (2021). Exclusionary discipline policies, School–police partnerships, surveillance technologies and disproportionality: A review of the school to prison pipeline literature. *The Urban Review*, *53*(5), 735–760. doi:10.100711256-021-00595-1

Novak, A. (2019). The school-to-prison pipeline: An examination of the association between suspension and justice system involvement. *Criminal Justice and Behavior*, *46*(8), 1165–1180. doi:10.1177/0093854819846917

Nyumba, T. O., Wilson, K., Derrick, C. J., & Mukherjee, N. (2018). The use of focus group discussion methodology: Insights from two decades of application in conversation. *Qualitative Methods for Eliciting Judgements for Decision Making*, *9*(1), 20–32. doi:10.1111/2041-210X.12860

Oster, E., Jack, R., Halloran, C., Schoof, J., McLeod, D., Yang, H., Roche, J., & Roche, D. (2021). Disparities in learning mode access among K–12 students during the COVID-19 pandemic, by race/ethnicity, geography, and grade level. *Morbidity, and Mortality Weekly Report*, *70*(26), 953–958. doi:10.15585/mmwr.mm7026e2 PMID:34197363

Rodríguez, L. F., & Greer, W. (2017). (Un)expected scholars: Counter-narratives from two (boys) men of color across the educational pipeline. *Equity & Excellence in Education*, *50*(1), 108–120. doi:10.1080/10665684.2016.1256004

Schwartz, R. M., Sison, C., Kerath, S. M., Murphy, L., Breil, T., Sikavi, D., & Taioli, E. (2015). The impact of Hurricane Sandy on the mental health of New York area residents. *American Journal of Disaster Medicine*, *10*(4), 339–346. doi:10.5055/ajdm.2015.0216 PMID:27149315

Shields, C. M. (2010). Transformative leadership: Working for equity in diverse contexts. *Educational Administration Quarterly*, *46*(4), 558–589. doi:10.1177/0013161X10375609

Skiba, R. J., Arredondo, M. I., & Williams, N. T. (2014). More than a metaphor: The contribution of exclusionary discipline to a school-to-prison pipeline. *Equity & Excellence in Education*, *47*(4), 546–564. doi:10.1080/10665684.2014.958965

Solórzano, D. G., & Delgado Bernal, D. (2001). Examining transformational resistance through a critical race and LatCrit theory framework—Chicana and Chicano students in an urban context. *Urban Education*, *36*(3), 308–324. doi:10.1177/0042085901363002

Solórzano, D. G., & Yosso, T. J. (2001). Maintaining social justice hopes within academic realities: A Freirean approach to critical race/LatCrit pedagogy. *Denver Law Review*, *78*(4), 595–612.

Sun, W. (2022). *Finding alternative pathways beyond the rhetoric of the racial disparities in disciplinary practices: Racialized politics of principals' reasonings of disciplinary practices* [Manuscript submitted for publication].

Swedo, E., Idaikkadar, N., Leemis, R., Dias, T., Radhakrishnan, L., Stein, Z., Chen, M., Agathis, N., & Holland, K. (2020). Trends in U.S. emergency department visits related to suspected or confirmed child abuse and neglect among children and adolescents age < 18 years before and during the COVID-19 pandemic: United States, January 2019 – September 2020. *MMWR. Morbidity and Mortality Weekly Report*, *69*(49), 1841–1847. doi:10.15585/mmwr.mm6949a1 PMID:33301436

Taub, A. (2020). A new COVID-19 crisis: Domestic abuse rises worldwide. *The New York Times*. https://www.nytimes.com/2020/04/06/world/coronavirus-domestic-violence.html

Usher, K., Bhullar, N., Durkin, J., Gyamfi, N., & Jackson, D. (2020). Family violence and COVID-19: Increased vulnerability and reduced options for support. *International Journal of Mental Health Nursing*, *29*(4), 549–552. doi:10.1111/inm.12735 PMID:32314526

Walker, V. S. (2001). African American teaching in the South: 1940–1960. *American Educational Research Journal*, *38*(4), 751–799. doi:10.3102/00028312038004751

Ward, M. E., Shelley, K., Kaase, K., & Pane, J. F. (2008). Hurricane Katrina: A longitudinal study of the achievement and behavior of displaced students. *Journal of Education for Students Placed at Risk*, *13*(2–3), 297–317. doi:10.1080/10824660802350391

Welsh, R. O., & Little, S. (2018). The school discipline dilemma: A comprehensive review of disparities and alternative approaches. *Review of Educational Research*, *88*(5), 752–794. doi:10.3102/0034654318791582

Yin, R. (2017). *Case study research and applications: Design and methods* (6th ed.). SAGE Publications.

ENDNOTES

[1] HB 4545 required students to pass standardized tests for schools to continue receive state funding. See https://tea.texas.gov/about-tea/news-and-multimedia/correspondence/taa-letters/house-bill-4545-implementation-overview

[2] I collected participants' background and demographic information via questionnaires via QuestionPro.

[3] School leaders feel more comfortable to have high school students to participate in this research than middle school and elementary school students since the school leaders believe middle and elementary schoolers are too young to speak up for their minds. From an IRB standpoint, it is easier to access to high schoolers than middle and elementary schoolers due to the longer IRB board reviewing timeline.

Chapter 4
Using Trauma-Informed Care and Horticulture Therapy With College Students:
A Counseling Approach Modeled After a Refugee Resettlement Community

Jon N. Trauth
https://orcid.org/0000-0001-9792-5584
Central State University, USA

Nikkita Jackson
https://orcid.org/0000-0001-6543-123X
Central State University, USA

Karleah Harris
University of Arkansas at Pine Bluff, USA

ABSTRACT

Trauma-informed care has been considered for high schools since 2010. Both teachers and support staff realize that it is important to make sure to meet students' basic needs for any learning to occur. This information rings true for all college students, especially since the pandemic. The trauma-informed care model has been presented to faculty and staff at Central State University to engage them and allow them to learn new strategies that will help them work with a traumatized student population. This chapter addresses how the model of trauma-informed care training on the website starr.org will help students to complete their college courses more effectively. The small mid-western college in the United States pulls from a few models that were used at the lighthouse community school and the St Leo Burundi refugee resettlement programs. School challenges can be from, according to previous research, being bored with school programs, missing too many days, and being unable to catch up. The chapter will consider how these issues can be combated using the TIC model.

DOI: 10.4018/978-1-6684-5713-9.ch004

Copyright © 2023, IGI Global. Copying or distributing in print or electronic forms without written permission of IGI Global is prohibited.

INTRODUCTION

In March 2020, Central State University (CSU) closed due to coronavirus known as COVID-19, which is an infectious disease caused by the SARS-CoV-2 virus (World Health Organization, n.d.). The closure was unexpected, and it happened fast. Although the prediction was that the university would only close for two weeks, CSU subsequently closed until the end of the Spring semester. Summer classes were offered online, while some of the fall classes were offered to students in both online and hybrid formats. As a result of the COVID-19 pandemic, students as well as school staff experienced anxiety, trauma, and feelings of being overwhelmed.

According to Najjar et al. (2018), horticulture therapy had been used to decrease psychological symptoms, increasing organizational function and the memory of males that were chronically depressed. Pinpointing a need for its returning students, CSU saw an opportunity to positively impact its incoming students. CSU Counseling Centers added aromatherapy that was posited by Lin & Chu (2020) to improve sleep, increase relaxation and comforts while diminishing pain. Combining horticulture therapy and counseling services for the CSU students appeared to offer many benefits including increased well-being, better health, social cohesion, improved sleep and more relaxation. This chapter discusses some of the academic and psychological challenges students experienced as a result of school closure, overviews CSU's response and recommendation for a trauma-sensitive learning approach to reduce trauma and exposure to the school-to-prison pipeline.

BACKROUND

Trauma is referred to "as situations that threaten death or serious injury, or threat to the physical integrity of self or others and overwhelm a person's coping resources" (Brooks et al., 2018. p. 370). According to Champagne and Stromberg (2004), trauma-informed care is referred to "as mental health care that addresses the significant effect that trauma may have on a person's neurobiology, psychology, and social relationships, and the high prevalence of traumatic experiences and disorders in people who receive mental health services" (p. 37). Following the onset of the pandemic, it became clear that many students at CSU had experienced traumatic events in their daily lives, and some of these may include substance abuse dependency, food insecurity, threats to their overall well-being, and health and safety (Steele, 2013). Many of these challenges existed prior to the pandemic and were exacerbated following the onset of the pandemic.

The source of traumatic events may be both from within and outside the family, resulting in a loss of a loved one, abuse, war experiences, and natural disasters

(National Child Traumatic Stress Network [NCTSN], n.d.). Additionally, trauma has been associated with earlier biological aging, early puberty, cellular aging and changes in the brain structure (Colich et al., 2020). Having a good social support system that provides space to express emotions where individuals may feel cared for reduces the impact of trauma (SAMHSA, 2022). Traditionally, counseling centers offer individual and group support services that may address many of the needs of college students.

According to the American Civil Liberties Union (ACLU, n.d.), the term school-to-prison pipeline refers to a disturbing trend wherein youth are funneled out of public schools and into juvenile and criminal legal systems. Many of these youth have learning disabilities or histories of poverty, abuse or neglect, and would benefit from additional educational and counseling services (ACLU, n.d.). The high correlation between trauma and contact with the criminal justice system experienced by impoverished and minority populations in the United States points to the fact perpetrators and victims often share the same physical environment (Sampson & Lauritsen, 1994). Because CSU recognized this opportunity to better serve its diverse student base and mitigate their exposure to the school-to-prison pipeline, their focus was on maximizing its existing counseling services and expanding to further address student needs. CSU reimagined its counseling environment to address their incoming student learners with nontraditional alternatives.

Counseling services at CSU had been a staple for many students over the past several decades. The enrollment at CSU for in-person classes at the Historically Black College is about 2000 students. CSU is the only public Historically Black College and University in the state of Ohio. Both teachers and staff were encouraged to inform their students about the services that are offered. This is especially important during a pandemic when students are experiencing even more trauma and anxiety. In order to ensure that students and teachers have the best experience in the classroom and their learning environment, a trauma-informed approach was used at CSU from the starr.org curriculum (Seigel, 2015). Trauma-sensitive training was used to prepare faculty for in-person students returning to campus following the pandemic (Briere & Scott, 2015).

Horticulture therapy offered many positive benefits. Research conducted by Haller and Capra (2016) resulted in rewarding and positive experiences when the participants and therapists interacted with gardens and the growing environment. Horticultural therapy has been used in recovery from mental and physical illnesses as well as assisting with the vocalization rehabilitation, a process that enables individuals with physical, mental or emotional disabilities to return to employment or other useful occupation (Capra et al., 2019). Because of the versatility of horticultural therapy, the programs may be conducted in different ways individually, in groups, cover areas, outside, and inside (Scott, 2015). Horticulture is used as a method of treatment for different ages groups in different environments to promote health, well-being and social cohesion (Harris & Trauth, 2020). The positive results with a variety of environments and ages groups made it an obvious choice for minimizing trauma with college students and reducing their exposure to the school-to-prison pipeline.

Coronavirus Pandemic Challenges

Because of the effects of the coronavirus pandemic and the challenges many students and their families faced both psychologically and financially, CSU offered their first trauma-informed care training in fall 2021 when most students returned to in-person classes. CSU also maintained an option to attend classes online. Subsequently, CSU engaged in a large push to have both in-person classes and faculty trained in some of the trauma-informed guidelines (Steele, 2013). This effort sought to decrease childhood trauma and mitigate its effects. Similar to students in the Lighthouse Community School, CSU mirrors their philosophy:

The students need challenging work to facilitate their learning and must see their education as a way to foster civility, good citizenship, responsible behavior, and self-reliance. The TIC model attempts to meet each student wherever he or she is in life

(Trauth & Harris, 2019 p. 26).

Several mediums for counseling may use a sensory-based approach. Some schools use only one or two, such as aromatherapy and music therapy. CSU opted to add several more sensory-based approaches such as horticulture, art, and music therapies, and theater. It is anticipated that the horticulture therapy will begin with the current resources at the university; however, it is anticipated that the program will grow and thrive if awarded the grant currently under review from the team at CSU.

The Counseling Centers

The counseling center at CSU used both safe and appropriate measures during the coronavirus pandemic and welcomed tactics such as using immediately noticeable aromatherapy as students and teachers enter (Lin & Chiu, 2020). The effects of aromatherapy have been studied and used in many counseling centers throughout the United States. Champagne and Stromberg (2004) posited that aromatherapy improves sleep, increases relaxation and comforts while diminishing pain. Lin & Chiu (2020) combined aromatherapy and horticulture therapy for use with their students. This approach may be beneficial in other counseling centers in the future to help students who experience childhood trauma.

The model used at CSU is similar to the trauma-informed care (TIC) paradigm that was used for public mental health and human services for many years. This rehabilitation model encourages students to set goals and participate in activities and programs that help accomplish these goals (Trauth, 2017). Some of the interventions that are used at the CSU Counseling Center include art, music, yoga practice, theatrical arts as an expressive tool for healing, and other sensory-based interventions. Many of these interventions are critical to understanding the detrimental effects of trauma on the body.

Sensory Based Approaches

Champagne and Stromberg (2004) explained that "sensory-based approaches and multisensory classrooms are valuable resources as cultures of care shift to become more responsive and collaborative" (p.35). The sensory-based approaches that are used at CSU Counseling Center begin with aromatherapy. Additionally, students are provided opportunities to use small rooms or learning spaces for art therapy (Kuban, 2015) and work in silence or discuss things they are going through while using both paint and colored pencils to create different things that are therapeutic for them. This encourages the sensory-based approach using the left brain as described in a trauma-informed care approach (Steele, 2013). Another sensory-based approach uses the music room where students can come and spend time playing the piano or guitar. The music room is being further developed to include drums.

The importance of using a sensory-based approach for trauma-informed care, especially in counseling centers, are critical and should be incorporated effectively to help faculty and students cope with trauma. Both faculty and staff should be trained to use trauma-informed care approaches when people experience trauma in their lives to promote health, well-being and social cohesion (Trauth, 2017). This model should be considered for many students, especially after the challenges that made academia extremely difficult following the 2020 pandemic. Moving forward, it will be imperative to use such approaches and also train both faculty and staff at the University level to be knowledgeable about the trauma informed care approach when dealing with students. By maintaining up to date training and being knowledgeable of updated research on trauma informed care, university staff may better prepare professors and student leaders to respond to the dynamic needs and challenges as they appear throughout the year.

Horticulture therapy offered a sensory based connection to the growing environment that creates an organic connection to nature. Haller and Capra (2017) posited that horticulture therapy encourages rewarding and positive experiences connecting individuals and the growing environment. Horticulture therapy "is one of the most effective treatments for people of all ages backgrounds and abilities"

(Pouya, 2019, p. 19). Horticulture is used as a method of treatment for a wide range of ages in a variety of environments to promote health, well-being and social cohesion (Harris & Trauth, 2020). CSU hopes to incorporate these benefits for their staff and students.

Counseling Approaches

Many students present with symptoms of depression and anxiety when exposed to trauma. CSU counseling services incorporate Cognitive Based Therapy (CBT) (Gutermann et al., 2016) techniques and activities to assist students in reaching their therapeutic goals and to help build their relational capacity. In addition to CBT interventions, CSU counseling services employ a strength-based approach (Lucio & Nelson, 2016), which promotes resiliency (McClery & Figlye, 2017).

Psychoeducation (Black et al., 2012) and expressive interventions (Relojo-Howell, 2020) are used to aid students in expressing feelings, reducing distressing symptoms, self-awareness, identifying strengths, and building effective coping skills. In addition to traditional dialogue, CSU counseling services include journaling, artistic creation, music, and physical movement (walking, dancing). CSU counseling services also included horticultural interventions and Healing Through Expression theater productions.

The power of partnership is vital to a thriving counseling program. CSU counseling services partnered with the National Alliance on Mental Illness (NAMI), Northeast Ohio Medical University (NEOMED), Mental Health Recovery Board of Clark, Green, and Madison Counties. In addition, they have developed partnerships with departments within the institution. These partnerships have been instrumental in assisting counseling services to have a broader impact and to assist in reducing the stigma of mental illness and the effects of trauma. All these efforts have been instrumental in helping to decrease a mental health crisis and increase the institutional retention rate. CSU counseling services has a 98% satisfaction rate and 83% retention rate.

Counseling Individuals with Trauma

When assessing a trauma-informed care approach, it is important to consider some of the models that have been used previously. Several other schools, both at the high school and college level have used some of the curricula that include yoga, cooking, art therapy, and horticulture to increase engagement. Students at CSU have access to a monthly food pantry that utilizes on-premises services and distributes refrigerated and frozen foods along with traditional foods through the food pantry at the counseling center.

Urban agriculture has offered access to land and seeds that have become increasingly popular at CSU. The decision to add horticulture therapy to other sensory-based approaches was considered after reviewing the research on several multi-century approaches. It has been proven effective at reducing childhood trauma by helping them regulate emotions that last into adulthood. It also teaches practical skills such as responsibility and having interactions with the community, along with the idea of working hard to prepare a harvest for the fall (Trauth & Harris, 2019).

.... the lighthouse community school represents an example of the impact of trauma informed care on the lives of at-risk students. Century based programs such as the urban agriculture program help with the experience for students and are proving to have successful impact on traumatized students by giving them alternative opportunities for self-care, self-expression, and the opportunity to develop coping skills. At risk students attend school with a myriad of problems that necessitate adoption of alternative strategies for teaching. Trauma informed care provides a multi-sensory and experimental learning approach for addressing emotional and social needs of students while providing academic education in a more sensory-based environment. Schools can use this to incorporate alternative experiences for trauma affected students that have strong components of horticulture and hands-on learning as well as arts yoga and many other alternative experiences (p. 28).

It is important to show that these different interventions have been effective in many environments to increase their options. The Lighthouse community school model highlights that these interventions are helpful and effective. It will be essential to carry on the widely-studied interventions with students at the college level to respond to their changing needs. In the past several months, there have been fear and challenges with school shootings. Because of this, CSU has formed a safety committee for students to feel safe at school when they are away from home. With many students coming from large cities with high murder rates, such as St. Louis and Chicago, feeling safe on campus is the number one priority. Without the feeling of safety, trauma can be exacerbated and made worse.

Services Available Through the St. Leo Holistic Program Important for TIC in Colleges

A similar program to treat people with Post Traumatic Stress Disorder (PTSD) was used at St. Leo the Great Catholic Parish in Cincinnati, just one hour south of CSU. Many ideas and programs were researched before final selection of the ecological model used today.

In 2008, as part of a doctoral program project, Dr. Ellen Cook, Professor of Counseling at the University of Cincinnati, introduced her students to this unique inner-city parish that begun to serve recently resettled African immigrants (Conyne & Cook, 2004). Her purpose was to enlighten and enlist others who could aid the already established urban Catholic parish in its mission. These doctoral students assessed the situation and suggested several interventions. With the help of an interpreter, many interviews were conducted. Based on the feedback obtained, some interventions were set in motion. These programs were instrumental in shaping programs at CSU.

Considering the research and the significant needs of post-civil war refugees upon their arrival to the United States, the administration and community of St. Leo organized several services and programs to address the short-term, long-term, and mental health needs of the Burundian refugees. These services address physical, cultural, psychological, and spiritual needs through a case management approach, i.e., the St. Leo Burundi Refugee Ministry Program.

The St. Leo Burundi Refugee Ministry Program is one of the programs working under the broader umbrella of St. Leo's. Other programs offered by the St. Leo staff and volunteers include a parish nursing program, the food pantry, a parish library, transportation assistance, school facilitators, and referral services to specialists. The Burundian refugees and other refugees within the parish utilize these services to a great extent. Additionally, programs offered from resources outside St. Leo benefit the entire refugee population, including the Burundians. Catholic Charities, the Cincinnati Metropolitan Housing Authority, and other professionals offer the following services: locating and subsidizing housing, legal advising, social work support for case management, and work and mental health counseling referrals. Their approach encompasses a community-based strategy to meet the needs of their clients.

Although St. Leo is limited to seven staff positions, including the Pastor, all employees assume responsibilities for contributing to the St. Leo Burundi Refugee Ministry Program. While some government funding is received, it remains very limited. Most financial support was provided through donations and benevolent services, that is, volunteer time. Occasionally grant opportunities were sought when appropriate. The vast array of services currently available to support the broader refugee population at St. Leo is designed to meet the growing needs at all levels and ages of the refugee families. The following sections elaborate on the scope and support provided by these individual services.

Tutoring is offered one night per week for ninety minutes each session to help elementary and high school students complete homework assignments and special school projects. This program is offered through the generosity of volunteers. Similarly, CSU offers tutors access to a safe space to do research papers and create presentations in the counseling center. Positive experiences and effective communication can help reduce the imprints of unpleasant happenings of the past often linked to childhood trauma (International Schooling, n.d.).

At St. Leo, there is a women's support group also initiated by the Pastoral Counselor that meets once a week. This group advises refugee women on daily responsibilities such as child-rearing, hygiene, cooking, shopping, employment and job search, economic issues including banking and money management, and completing governmental forms, among other topics. The services of a translator are also available for this group. Within the Women's Group is a gathering of women known as the "Women of Peace." This empowerment group offers refugee women an opportunity to earn some supplemental income by making and selling handcrafted bags of various shapes and sizes. For their crafts, staff at St. Leo collects recycled plastic bags that the refugee women use to crochet into new bags that they sell at the church, local markets, and the nonprofit fair-trade store, Ten Thousand Villages. CSU's college continues to offer mental health support groups and individual counseling in a beneficial partnership that mitigates the effects of trauma.

Various modifications have been implemented to support the spirituality of the Burundian population and accommodate the language barriers. The guiding belief addresses the spiritual side of their lives can beneficially impact the refugee's adjustment process as they settle into this new culture. Parts of Mass, such as the readings, hymns, and the gospel, have been translated to Kirundi, which not only facilitates the Burundians' opportunities to participate in Mass but also allows them to use their prayer books brought with them from their homeland. Other materials facilitate their spirituality, such as Bibles that have been made available through a donation from a Jesuit priest from Burundi but now studying at Georgetown University. The spiritual side of their lives has a significant impact in helping the adjustment phase of life in a new city and country. The St. Leo website also includes an online dictionary resource with translations between English and Kirundi to help the Burundians interact and function in their daily lives. In a similar vein, CSU encourages spirituality and a space that is safe for students to worship how they choose. In some instances, as mentioned before, students use the music therapy room for musical worship to help them feel safe and at home at CSU.

As a parish with a large refugee population comprised of many nationalities, including Burundians, Guatemalans, and Tanzanians, various other programs at St. Leo address the common issues faced by any refugee population. These services often overlap and support the goals of the Burundian Refugee Ministry as previously described. Similarly, CSU offers vehicles for food security, such as a daily food pantry with dry goods and monthly delivery of frozen and refrigerated goods. CSU teaches its students about community responsibility, volunteerism and being a good neighbor.

The Food Pantry housed in the basement of St. Leo is well stocked with fresh produce, canned goods, meat, and toiletry items acquired from generous donations from across the city of Cincinnati. It is open to the refugees and residents of the immediate neighborhood during regular hours and is staffed by the church. A Community Garden has been established and maintained, allowing participants to grow produce to meet their needs and share the surplus with the food pantry. Located on the terraced hillside directly behind St. Leo, this garden allows any St. Leo parishioner to garden and grow food.

Often questions arise from the refugee population about where they can seek help pertaining to a particular topic or issue, such as medical care, employment, banking, and the like. The pastoral staff and social workers from the University of Cincinnati provide referral services and case management to help refugees locate resources that can fulfill these additional needs.

The Parish Nursing Program is supported on a full-time basis through Tri health of Cincinnati. A full-time nurse, a part-time nurse, and a translator are employed and available for assistance at St. Leo. The nurses' jobs include supporting and assisting refugees navigating the healthcare system. Assessments provided by the Parish Nurses detail the refugees' specific needs, the current crisis they are experiencing, and cultural components needing to be addressed. CSU added these services to address the health needs of their students. During the pandemic, there was also a weekly coronavirus testing clinic for students and faculty to maintain a safe learning environment.

Transportation is provided to and from Mass and other church activities, the food pantry, the Parish Nurse for medical care, the gardens and other places as needed. Many volunteers have stepped forward to help meet these ongoing needs. As the refugee youth enter the American school systems, they may experience a level of discordance such as being coerced into unfamiliar institutional practices and expectations. St. Leo volunteers strive to serve as facilitators and intermediaries to help the youth. Cincinnati Metropolitan Housing Authority (CMHA) helps arriving refugees find immediate and suitable housing. St. Leo's staff and volunteers connect the refugees to CMHA, where they assist in arranging rent subsidies. Many legal needs, including completing the citizenship application, arise as the refugees establish their lives in a new and unfamiliar culture. A volunteer lawyer provides services at St. Leo as needed to assist in legal advising.

This holistic approach is essential to ensuring that all areas in a counseling environment are addressed. Although it may appear that some of the work done for counseling is under the area of case management, this highlights the importance of covering basic needs to ensure that the individual feels safe and secure before proceeding to higher level goals addressed at the counseling center. This chapter concludes with the many current activities CSU offers to address life goals and successfully completing college using a trauma-informed care model.

Continued Work with Trauma and Trauma Informed Care

Many schools are currently using the Trauma-Informed Care Model. Many schools, including Lighthouse Community School, are modeled after the documentary "Paper Tigers," which expresses the effectiveness of continued research about the trauma-informed care model. There are several activities included in a trauma-informed model at the high school and collegiate levels. For example, CSU students presented "Healing Through Expression Out of Darkness" at the Ohio NAMI Conference on May 13, 2022. The production was used as an expressive tool for emotional healing. They also used dance as a therapeutic tool to reduce stress and trauma (Serlin, 2020). The dance intervention was started during the pandemic. Dance Movement Therapy is an intervention that supports emotional and mood regulation. It has the potential to help by reducing stress and anxiety and is an effective response to trauma (Serlin, 2020).

In addition, CSU Counseling Services has a National Alliance on Mental Illness chapter on campus. This is a student organization that helps to support CSU's Remove the Stigma efforts. NAMI student members are mental health advocates trained in suicide prevention, trauma-informed care, and mental health first aid. The NAMI on Campus has weekly outreach to encourage other students to seek help when needed. This holistic approach, similar to the components of the Ecological Model, which incorporates individual, relational, community, and societal components, have been shown for decades to be effective and new information and programs such as Lighthouse Youth Services and the counseling center at Central State University. Future considerations may include both Horticulture therapy coupled with the Cooking Classes and other ways students may become completely self-supporting upon completion of their first year of college or even the first semester in many cases.

FUTHER RESEARCH

Trauma-informed care has been researched for more than a quarter of a century. However, more of the mind and body connection should be considered for future research. Sensory-based interventions like those used at CSU are paramount to healing and mitigating trauma using the mind and body connection. More work should be considered as a holistic approach to overall wellness for our students, which may even include an infusion of personal spirituality. Counselors should be open to discussing and training in multicultural approaches and exploring the students' thoughts on spirituality and wellness. Horticulture therapy offers a great venue to discuss things such as feeding and caring for others and self-care. Wellness begins with self-care and can be passed on using horticulture therapy to reduce the impact of trauma.

CONCLUSION

As a result of the coronavirus pandemic, CSU students and staff experienced anxiety, trauma and feelings of being overwhelmed. Research and data analysis allowed CSU to focus on the specific needs of its incoming students and staff. Research conducted by Haller and Capra (2016) resulted in rewarding and positive experiences when the participants and therapists interacted with gardens and the growing environment. Horticultural therapy had been used in the recovery from mental and physical illnesses as well as assisting with the vocalization rehabilitation, a process enables individuals with physical, mental or emotional disabilities return to employment or other useful occupation (Capra et al., 2019). Because of the versatility of horticultural therapy, the programs could be conducted in different ways individually, in groups, cover areas, outside, and inside (Scott, 2015). Horticulture is used as a method of treatment for different ages groups in different environments to promote health, well-being and social cohesion (Harris & Trauth, 2020). The positive results with a variety of environments and ages groups made it an obvious choice for minimizing trauma with college students.

Champagne and Stromberg (2004) posited that aromatherapy improved sleep, increased relaxation and comforted while diminishing pain. Lin & Chiu (2020) combined aromatherapy and horticulture therapy for use with their students. This approach may be beneficial in other counseling centers in the future to help students who experience childhood trauma. Counseling services had been a staple for many students over decades and offered an opportunity to expand services to further meet the needs of their students.

Trauma-informed colleges are essential to our future because of the global trauma experienced by many college students during and following the coronavirus pandemic to promote health, well-being and social cohesion. Schools with a history of treating students with trauma will be essential in leading and addressing the needs of students with trauma-informed care similar to the sensory-based approaches implemented at CSU. Horticulture therapy and artistic expression are recommended for all counseling centers considering a trauma-informed approach to promote health and well-being of its students. Seed starting and urban gardens may be initiated in many climates throughout the United States and globally. For colleges and universities concerned about inclement weather, indoor gardens and greenhouses may be considered.

Choosing a comprehensive evidence-based approach to address the needs of their students, CSU is leading with sensory-based approaches following the pandemic.

The counseling center serves as the central hub of resources and engagement for students. Aromatherapy greets students initially as they enter the counseling center to improve sleep, increase relaxation, and comfort while diminishing pain and the effects of trauma. Other interventions used at CSU include art, music, dance, yoga practice, and the use of theatrical arts as an expressive tool for healing and reducing trauma.

Based on the St. Leo Burundi Refugee Ministry Program, CSU mirrors services to its students to meet their needs holistically. For example, CSU provides access to a food pantry, library, transportation assistance, school facilitators, and referral services to specialists. Additionally, tutoring and safe space for studying are provided, a music therapy room, health care services, financial assistance, and strategies for reaching life goals. The CSU model extends beyond the boundaries of the college, partnering with the community agencies to meet the needs of each individual student and staff member.

For the above reasons, trauma-informed care coupled with sensory-based therapy including horticulture therapy are recommended to meet the changing needs of college students. Increased positive experiences coupled with effective communication (International Schooling, n.d.), and expressive interventions (Relojo-Howell, 2020) aid students in expressing feelings, reducing distressing symptoms, self-awareness, identifying strengths, and building coping skills to reduce the effects of trauma. CSU embraced these sensory-based strategies to reduce childhood trauma, stress and anxiety in their learning environments while mitigating exposure to the school-to-prison pipeline.

REFERENCES

American Civil Liberties Union. (n.d.). *School-to-prison pipeline.* ACLU. https://www.aclu.org/issues/juvenile-justice/juvenile-justice-school-prison-pipeline

Black, P. J., Woodworth, M., Tremblay, M., & Carpenter, T. (2012). A review of trauma-informed treatment for adolescents. *Canadian Psychology, 53*(3), 192–203. doi:10.1037/a0028441

Briere, J., & Scott, C. (2015). Complex trauma in adolescents and adults: Effects and treatment. *The Psychiatric Clinics of North America, 38*(3), 515–527. doi:10.1016/j.psc.2015.05.004 PMID:26300036

Brooks, M., Barclay, L., & Hooker, C. (2018). Trauma-informed care in general Practice: Findings from a women's health centre evaluation. *Australian Journal of General Practice, 47*(6), 370–375. doi:10.31128/AJGP-11-17-4406 PMID:29966183

Capra, C., Haller, R., & Kennedy, K. (2019). *Introduction to the profession of horticulture therapy*. CRC Press.

Champagne, T., & Stromberg, N. (2004). Sensory Approaches in inpatient Psychiatric settings: Innovative alternatives to seclusion & restraint. *Journal of Psychosocial Nursing and Mental Health Services, 42*(9), 34–44. doi:10.3928/02793695-20040901-06 PMID:15493494

Colich, N., Rosen, M., Williams, E., & McLaughlin, K. (2020). Biological aging in childhood and adolescence following experiences of threat and deprivation: A systematic review and meta-analysis. *Psychological Bulletin, 146*(9), 721–764. doi:10.1037/bul0000270 PMID:32744840

Conyne, R. K., & Cook, E. P. (2004). *Ecological Counseling: An innovative approach to conceptualizing person-environment interaction*. American Counseling Association.

Gutermann, J., Schreiber, F., Matulis, S., Schwartzkopff, L., Deppe, J., & Steil, R. (2016). Psychological treatments for symptoms of posttraumatic stress disorder in children, adolescents, and young adults: A meta-analysis. *Clinical Child and Family Psychology Review, 19*(2), 77–93. doi:10.100710567-016-0202-5 PMID:27059619

Haller, R. L., & Capra, C. L. (Eds.). (2016). *Horticultural therapy methods: Connecting people and plants in health care, human services, and therapeutic programs*. CRC Press. doi:10.1201/9781315369563

Harris, K., & Trauth, J. (2020). Horticulture therapy benefits: A report. *International Journal of Current Science and Multidisciplinary Research, 3*(4), 61–65.

International Schooling. (n.d.). Six ways to minimize the effects of childhood trauma. *International Schooling*. https://internationalschooling.org/blog/6-ways-to-minimize-the-effect-of-childhood-trauma/

Kuban, C. (2015). Healing trauma through art. *Reclaiming Children and Youth, 24*(2), 18.

Lin, Y. N., & Chiu, Y. H. C. (2020). Applying integrated Horticultural Therapy and aromatherapy to assist undergraduates in Taiwan. *College Student Journal, 54*(1), 8–12.

Lucio, R., & Nelson, T. L. (2016). Effective practices in the treatment of trauma in children and adolescents: From guidelines to organizational practices. *Journal of Evidence-Informed Social Work, 13*(5), 469–478. doi:10.1080/23761407.2016.11 66839 PMID:27104619

McCleary, J., & Figley, C. (2017). Resilience and trauma: Expanding definitions, uses, and contexts. *Traumatology, 23*(1), 1–3. doi:10.1037/trm0000103 PMID:29755296

Najjar, A., Foroozandeah, E., & Gharneh, A. (2018). Horticulture therapy effects on memory and psycho-logical symptoms of depressed male outpatients. *Iranian Rehabilitation Journal, 16*(2), 147–154. doi:10.32598/irj.16.2.147

National Child Traumatic Stress Network. (n.d.). *About child trauma.* NCTSN. https://www.nctsn.org/what-is-child-trauma/about-child-trauma

Pouya, S. (2019). The importance of horticulture therapy and gardening for older adults in nursing home. *Anadolu University, 8*(2), 146–166. doi:10.20488anattasarim.529734

Relojo-Howell, D. (2020). Book review of 'Wales High School: First Diagnosis'. Psychreg. *The Journal of Psychology, 4*(2), 140–142.

Sampson, R., & Lauritsen, J. (1994). Violent victimization and offending: Individual, situational, and community level risk factors. In A. J. Reiss Jr & J. A. Roth (Eds.), *Understanding and preventing violence* (Vol. 3, pp. 1–114). National Academy Press.

Scott, T. (2015). Horticultural therapy. In N. Pachana (Ed.), *Encyclopedia of Geropsychology* (pp. 1–5). Springer. doi:10.1007/978-981-287-080-3_268-1

Serlin, I. A. (2020). Dance/movement therapy: A whole person approach to working with trauma and building resilience. *American Journal of Dance Therapy, 42*(2), 176–193. doi:10.100710465-020-09335-6 PMID:33250545

Siegel, D. J. (2015). The developing mind: How relationships and the brain interact to shape who we are (2nd, rev. ed). The Guilford Press.

Steele, W., & Kuban, C. (2013). *Working with grieving and traumatized children and adolescents: Discovering what matters most through evidence-based, sensory interventions.* Wiley.

Substance Abuse and Mental Health Services Administration. (2022). *Trauma and Violence.* SAMHSA. https://www.samhsa.gov/trauma-violence

Trauth, J. (2017). Lighthouse community school: A case study of a school for behaviorally challenged youth. *Journal of Therapeutic Horticulture, 27*(1), 60–65.

Trauth, J., & Harris, K. (2019). Lighthouse community school: An in-depth look at successful strategies used with at-risk students. *Multicultural Education, 27*(1), 24–28.

World Health Organization. (n.d.). *Coronavirus disease (COVID-19)*. WHO. https://www.who.int/health-topics/coronavirus#tab=tab_1

ADDITIONAL READING

Bederian-Gardner, D., Hobbs, S. D., Ogle, C. M., Goodman, G. S., Cordón, I. M., Bakanosky, S., Narr, R., Chae, Y., & Chong, J. Y. (2018). Instability in the lives of foster and non-foster youth: Mental health impediments and attachment insecurities. *Children and Youth Services Review, 84*, 159–167. doi:10.1016/j.childyouth.2017.10.019

Briere, J., & Scott, C. (2013). *Principles of trauma therapy: A guide to symptoms, evaluation, and treatment*. SAGE Publications.

Brown, R. C., Witt, A., Fegert, J. M., Keller, F., Rassenhofer, M., & Plener, P. L. (2017, August). Psychosocial interventions for children and adolescents after man-made and natural disasters: A meta-analysis and systematic review. *Psychological Medicine, 47*(11), 1893–1905. doi:10.1017/S0033291717000496 PMID:28397633

Chen, R., Gillespie, A., Zhao, Y., Xi, Y., Ren, Y., & McLean, L. (2018). The efficacy of Eye movement desensitization and reprocessing in children and adults who have experienced complex childhood trauma: A systematic review of randomized controlled trials. *Frontiers in Psychology, 9*, 534. doi:10.3389/fpsyg.2018.00534 PMID:29695993

Cohen, J. A., Mannarino, A. P., & Murray, L. K. (2011). Trauma-focused CBT for youth who experience ongoing traumas. *Child Abuse & Neglect, 35*(8), 637–646. doi:10.1016/j.chiabu.2011.05.002 PMID:21855140

Edwards, C., & Karnilowicz, W. (2013). An ecological perspective: Therapist practices with children who experienced abuse and trauma. *Australian Psychologist, 48*(5), 321–328. doi:10.1111/j.1742-9544.2012.00073.x

Fraser, K., MacKenzie, D., & Versnel, J. (2017). Complex trauma in children and youth: A scoping review of sensory-based interventions. *Occupational Therapy in Mental Health, 33*(3), 199–216. doi:10.1080/0164212X.2016.1265475

Jee, S., Couderc, J., Swanson, D., Gallegos, A., Hilliard, C., Blumkin, A., Cunningham, S., & Heinert, S. (2015). A pilot randomized trial teaching mindfulness-based stress reduction to traumatized youth in foster care. *Complementary Therapies in Clinical Practice*, *21*(3), 201–209. doi:10.1016/j.ctcp.2015.06.007 PMID:26256140

Lanktree, C. B., & Briere, J. (2017). *Treating complex trauma in children and their families: An integrative approach*. SAGE Publications. doi:10.4135/9781071801291

National Academies of Sciences, Engineering, and Medicine. (2019). The promise of adolescence: Realizing opportunity for all youth. *National Academies Press*.

Steele, W., & Kuban, C. (2014). Healing trauma, building resilience: SITCAP in action. *Reclaiming Children and Youth*, *22*(4), 18–20.

KEY TERMS AND DEFINITIONS

Trauma: mental, physical, and/or emotional outcomes stemming from harmful or distressing situations or events which can have both immediate and long-term impacts on an individual's health, well-being, and ability to function.

Holistic Approach: techniques and/or philosophies that consider an entity or phenomenon in totality, rather than as an aggregate of constituent parts.

Young Adults: approximately 18-30 years of age.

Gardening: The laying out and care of a plot of ground devoted partially or wholly to the growing of plants such as flowers, herbs, or vegetables.

Chapter 5
Emotional Coaching:
A Technique to Regulate School Bullying

Sruthi Suresh
https://orcid.org/0000-0002-2505-9872
CHRIST University (Deemed), India

R. Vijaya
CHRIST University (Deemed), India

ABSTRACT

The present chapter aims to address school bullying as a source of childhood trauma and recommends the use of emotional coaching as a regulatory strategy. The chapter will begin with an introduction to the concept, types, occurrence, and impact of school bullying. Next, the authors will outline the role of school bullying in pushing students to enter the school-to-prison pipeline and the challenges involved in identifying and supporting these students. The chapter will then explore the process of emotional coaching, the steps involved, the role of teachers, and the challenges they could face during this process. Finally, the chapter will end by providing practical strategies to incorporate emotional coaching in traditional and virtual classrooms as well as provide a sample template script for the same. The summary and key points section will briefly review the content and highlight the key takeaways for the readers to keep in mind.

DOI: 10.4018/978-1-6684-5713-9.ch005

INTRODUCTION

According to the American Psychological Association (APA, 2019), trauma is "an emotional response to a terrible event like an accident, rape, or natural disaster". It includes events that occur once or multiple times and long-lasting repetitive incidents (Substance Abuse and Mental Health Services Administration [SAMHSA], 2014). Childhood trauma can be painful or distressing experiences that impact a child physically and psychologically. Otherwise known as adverse childhood experiences (ACEs), these events refer to a child's experiences before the age of 18 and have long-lasting impacts on children that can persist into adulthood (Wisner, 2022). These incidents may differ from child to child and include events like car accidents and chronic occurrences like abuse. It also includes events that a child witnesses, but may not be directly involved in. Additionally, traumatic events for a child can be both from within and outside the family, such as the loss of a loved one, abuse, war experiences, and natural disasters (The National Child Traumatic Stress Network [NCTSN], n.d.).

One such incident is school bullying, another common cause of childhood trauma prevalent among children worldwide. Trauma and bullying are intertwined with each other. Children who experience trauma are more likely to be involved in bullying, and experiencing bullying can lead to traumatic reactions such as Post Traumatic Stress Disorder (PTSD) (Plexousakis et al., 2019). These traumatic bullying experiences not only mar a child temporarily, hindering their academic and social development, but also lead to lasting changes in their behavior and biology (Dye, 2018). Additionally, research has indicated that children involved in bullying are more likely to have delinquent thoughts and engage in violent and criminal behavior, such as dating and domestic violence, thereby contributing to the school-to-prison pipeline (Bender & Lösel, 2011). Studies have shown that early experiences of trauma predict both mental and physical health outcomes such as depression, anxiety, cancer, and cardiovascular diseases. Trauma is also associated with earlier biological aging, including early puberty, cellular aging, and changes in the brain structure (Colich et al., 2020).

Immediate responses to traumatic incidents include shock, denial, sadness, and anxiety. Long-term responses to such incidents can manifest in the form of nightmares, sleep disorders, emotional dysregulation, and somatization (SAMHSA, 2014). However, having a good social support system that provides the child with a space to express their emotions and feel cared for can help reduce the impact of trauma on a child (SAMHSA, 2022). With the right help, children can heal from such trauma and become more resilient to face their day-to-day stressors effectively. Hence, the current chapter will focus on the role of school bullying as a childhood traumatic experience and explore emotional coaching as a strategy to break the school-to-prison pipeline by building resilience and regulating bullying among children.

Chapter Objectives

The chapter aims to give the readers:

1. An outline of bullying as childhood trauma, its occurrence, and its impact on children.
2. An understanding of the direct and indirect ways bullying contributes to the school-to-prison pipeline.
3. Suggestions to identify and support students experiencing bullying as trauma.
4. An insight into the concept of emotional coaching, the steps involved, the role of teachers, and the challenges they may face during this process.
5. Practical strategies to incorporate emotional coaching in the classroom to regulate school bullying.

BULLYING

The term "bullying" refers to aggressive behavior that is more often repeated, negative, intentional, and based on some imbalance of power between the individuals involved (United Nations Educational, Scientific, and Cultural Organization [UNESCO], 2019). It occurs in schools, families, neighborhoods, and workplaces. Even in these different contexts, the bullying behavior can be between individuals of different roles, such as parent versus child, teacher versus student or between peers, such as students or office colleagues. The present chapter will focus on bullying in the school environment between peers, that is, school children bullying each other.

Irrespective of the context where the behavior occurs, bullying entails discomfort or injury to the individual who is targeted. It can include short- and long-term consequences that affect the physical, psychological, social, and academic spheres of an individual's life. Some effects of school bullying include health complaints, stress, feeling rejected, poor self-esteem, weak relational skills, and low academic performance (NCTSN, n.d.). Further, school bullying can be considered a "part of life" that can make it difficult for individuals to identify and report such incidents (Blake & Louw, 2010).

Defining School Bullying

The first systematic examination of school bullying occurred in the 1970s by Dan Olweus in Scandinavia. Eventually, other parts of the world, such as the United States, Japan, Australia, and England, joined in the process and started examining bullying experiences in the 1980s and 1990s. From the 1970s until the most recent

International Conference in 2020, the definition of bullying has been debated and updated regularly. The initial definition provided by Olweus stated that "a person is being bullied or victimized when he or she is exposed, repeatedly and over time, to negative actions on the part of one or more other persons" (Olweus, 1994). After further examination, a theoretical redefinition of the concept highlighted that "bullying is aggressive goal-directed behavior that harms another individual within the context of a power imbalance" (Volk et al., 2014). Finally, the most recent recommendations suggested at the International Conference urge experts to rethink the requirement of behavior to be intentional and repeated for it to be recognized as bullying (UNESCO, 2020).

Types of School Bullying

Different types of behavior are classified under the umbrella term of school bullying. Based on the actions involved, it can be sub-classified as physical, verbal, social/relational, and cyberbullying. Additionally, bullying can also be psychological or sexual. In psychological bullying, the target is made to feel emotionally disturbed or uncomfortable through intimidating, manipulating, and stalking (Antiri, 2016). Sexual bullying is another type of bullying that involves making sexual jokes, comments, and gestures (UNESCO, 2019).

Bullying behavior can also be said to be direct or indirect. Direct bullying refers to acts that are obvious and easier to identify and acknowledge as bullying, such as physical bullying. On the other hand, indirect bullying is anonymous and difficult to identify, such as cyberbullying (National Bullying Prevention Center [NBPC], 2019). In this process of identifying bullying, it is essential to understand that mutual conflicts between students who are equal and have similar physical or social power do not come under the term bullying. Hence, it is imperative to assess a situation for the imbalance in power between the individuals involved to understand whether it is bullying (Kaufman et al., 2020).

Occurrence of School Bullying

According to students, incidents of bullying commonly occur in certain places of the school environment in classrooms, playgrounds, school buses, bathrooms, and hallways (Weinhold, 2000). These spots generally have limited adult supervision and are accessed during the break times in schools that can easily be used to corner and target children. Although a target of bullying does not necessarily cause their experience, certain factors make some individuals more vulnerable to bullying than others. It includes individual, familial, social, and cultural factors. Studies have shown that children experience bullying based on their facial features, physical appearance, sexual orientation, and academic performance (de Oliveira et al., 2015; Weinhold, 2000). It is to be noted that children who tend to have poor peer relationships and low parental education levels are more likely to become targets of bullying (Wang et al., 2021; Wong et al., 2013). Further, sociocultural factors such as socioeconomic status, religion, race, color, and place of origin also make children vulnerable to bullying (de Oliveira et al., 2015; UNESCO, 2019).

The UNESCO report titled "Behind the numbers: Ending school violence and bullying" (2019) states that every one in three children is experiencing bullying worldwide. This prevalence of bullying differs based on factors such as age, gender, and geographical location of the child. The type of bullying experienced also differs for each socio-demographic group. Studies have indicated that boys tend to be more involved as both bullies and victims; however, at the global level, no gender differences were reported in the prevalence of bullying. When boys are more likely to be involved in physical bullying, it is found that girls are more often engaging in psychological bullying. Further, as age increases, physical bullying, psychological bullying, and the overall prevalence of bullying are also seen to decrease. The overall prevalence of bullying among children again varies from place to place, with the highest levels of bullying being reported in sub-Saharan Africa (11.3%) and the lowest level in Central America (4.1%). Certain regions, such as sub-Saharan Africa and the Pacific, are seen to report high levels of physical bullying. Sexual bullying is most prevalent in Central America, the Middle East, and North Africa. In contrast, other places, such as Northern America and Europe, are known to have higher levels of psychological bullying.

Impact of School Bullying

When a child is involved in bullying, it can affect their physical, psychological, academic, and social life. A child may be involved in a bullying incident in various roles such as bully, target, or bystander. However, no matter the role played by the child, there is some impact on their life. Further, being part of a bullying experience in any role can impact a child in the short and long term.

Short-Term Impact

The short-term impact of bullying on students includes how the experience affects them immediately or gradually within a few years. Children who are targets of bullying may experience low self-esteem, internalization, substance abuse, low life satisfaction, reduced physical activity, and a lack of healthy peer relationships (Pulido et al., 2019; UNESCO, 2019). They begin to feel lonely, depressed, anxious, and sad and are no longer interested in or enjoying the activities they previously loved (Arseneault, 2017). These children also exhibit changes in their eating habits, shifts in sleeping patterns, symptoms of psychosomatic illnesses, and a drop in their academic performance levels (Kshirsagar et al., 2007; Oliveira et al., 2018). In addition, students who are victimized may indulge in self-harm and experience suicidal ideation (Ttofi et al., 2011). They feel like an outsider at school, tend to skip school, and even drop out of school (Wang et al., 2020). Studies have shown that being bullied can lead to addictive internet usage (Guo et al, 2020), use of non-prescription analgesics to alleviate pain (Chai et al., 2020), non-suicidal self-injury (Wu et al., 2021), and possible sleep bruxism (Fulgencio et al, 2016). In some cases, the students may become bullies themselves and are categorized as bully victims (Yang & Salmivalli, 2015) which can lead to a vicious circle of low self-esteem and consequent victimization of the bully victims (Choi & Park, 2021). Finally, children who witness the bullying incident as a bystander may feel confused, anxious, guilty about not taking action, experience helplessness, and feel a lack of safety and security (Hutchinson, 2012). They are also seen to report greater levels of substance abuse, interpersonal sensitivity, and suicidal ideation (National Academies of Sciences, Engineering, and Medicine, 2016). Further, they may experience mental health problems and are more likely to drop out of or miss school (StopBullying.gov, 2021).

Long-Term Impact

Bullying involvement is known to impact children long term by influencing their adult personalities, beliefs, attitudes, and worldviews. Children who experience bullying at school, both victims and bully-victims, are more likely to experience mental health issues such as anxiety, psychosis, and depression, be involved in domestic violence, and face issues in their interpersonal relationships. They are also more likely to experience poor health, including somatic and psychosomatic issues such as colds, headaches, and stomachaches (Wolke & Lereya, 2015). These children also grow up to become adults who earn less or remain unemployed (Anti-Bullying Alliance, n.d.). It has also been found that children who experience bullying are more likely to face depression, social withdrawal, and somatization (Ttofi et al., 2011). These children found it difficult to make and maintain friendships and relationships as well. In all aspects, children who were bully-victims were more severely affected than pure victims (Wolke & Lereya, 2015). On the other hand, children who bullied others were physically and psychologically healthier than their peers but went on to indulge in criminal activities. They were seen to engage in property and traffic offenses, exhibit delinquent behavior, vandalizing, antisocial behavior, substance abuse, sexual abuse, dating violence, and domestic violence into adulthood (StopBullying.gov, 2021). These children were more likely seen to face serious criminal charges in their young adulthood due to these issues. Children who bullied others were also seen to exhibit increased aggressiveness, psychopathy, and impulsivity in their young adulthood. Finally, all three groups - bullies, bully-victims, and victims - faced certain challenges in their physical, and social life. Findings indicate that all three groups had an increased risk for self-harm and suicidal ideation. They also showed poor academic performance and had trouble being employed. Research also indicated that these children faced challenges in making and keeping friends (Wolke & Lereya, 2015).

THEORETICAL FRAMEWORKS IN RELATION TO SCHOOL BULLYING

Numerous theoretical frameworks have been adapted from different fields to understand and explain school bullying behavior. However, these theories focus on explaining bullying perpetration more often than victimization. Some theories include the social information processing theory, social dominance theory, social cognition theory, social-cultural theory, and organizational culture theory (Subedi, 2020).

The recent research focuses on the socio-ecological framework, based on Bronfrenbrenners's socio-ecological theory, to understand bullying behavior. This approach incorporates the influence of multiple environments on a child's development and thereby examines the behavior in the context of these multiple overlapping environments. It states that a child's bullying behavior is not only because of the child but is a result of numerous influences from parents, teachers, peers, community, media, and much more (Espelage & Swearer, 2009). Hence, the current focus on understanding and regulating bullying involves both the child and the community around the child. Since teachers are most closely associated with and interacting with children during most of their day, it becomes imperative to provide them with the right skill set to help guide students away from engaging in bullying.

School Bullying and the School-to-Prison Pipeline

According to the American Civil Liberties Union (ACLU, n.d.), the term 'school-to-prison pipeline' refers to "a disturbing national trend wherein youth are funneled out of public schools and into the juvenile and criminal legal systems." This trend is also known by other names such as the 'school-to-prison link,' 'school-prison nexus,' or 'schoolhouse-to-jailhouse track.' It includes factors such as a zero-tolerance policy, stringent school rules to discipline children, high testing requirements, discouragement, and involvement of police in minor school issues (New York Civil Liberties Union [NYCLU], n.d.). Schools need to enforce rules to ensure discipline among students. However, it is also important to ensure that no innocent student should be punished. According to Benjamin Franklin (1706–90), "it is better 100 guilty persons should escape than that one innocent person should suffer."

As discussed in the previous section, children involved in bullying are more likely to commit minor and major infractions such as substance abuse, and missing or skipping school. When such behavior is attempted to be disciplined using stringent school policies and the involvement of the police, it further pushes these children into the rabbit hole of the school-to-prison pipeline. As rightly stated by Hence (2018), children end up "behind bars more than behind desks" as a result of such actions. Studies have noted that children who study in stricter schools with higher suspension rates are more likely to be involved in criminal activities, not just during their school life but well into adulthood (Bacher-Hicks et al., 2021). Additionally, students who belong to minority groups and have disabilities are more vulnerable to both being involved in bullying and entering the school-to-prison pipeline (Hence, 2018; National Criminal Justice Reference Service, 2014).

Students who are involved in bullying may directly or indirectly be pushed into this pipeline. Children who play different roles in the bullying scenario are equally impacted. Consequently, children who are bullies, victims, bully victims, and bystanders are more vulnerable to being pulled up for lack of discipline, issues with peers, involvement in alcohol and substance abuse, and missing out on school. With involvement in bullying already predisposing them to engage in criminal activities, being punished, expelled, or suspended for resultant behavior further increases this risk. This not only makes it more difficult for the child to continue their education but also hinders their healthy overall development. It is also essential to note that in cross-cultural learning environments, adults should be aware of and recognize the different patterns of communication and interpersonal interactions. It will avoid misinterpretation of casual, friendly behavior as bullying and misconduct (Berlowitz et al., 2014).

Once a child is punished severely, they carry around the label of being a bad person. Resultantly, they could experience ostracization from their peers and be pushed into the company of other wrongdoers. Teachers may also differentiate the student from the others by pulling them up for minor issues, ignoring them, or providing them less attention and opportunities than they would normally do. Bringing to mind the "self-fulfilling prophecy" (Rosenthal, 2012) at this moment, being involved in bullying creates a vicious chain of events that impacts every aspect of a child's life. The bullying experience leads to certain changes in the child and how they are treated; the experience may directly or indirectly make the child more vulnerable to entering the school-to-prison pipeline, which again limits their opportunities to get back on track in their life (ACLU; n.d.).

Identifying and Supporting Students Involved in School Bullying

In a school environment filled with children of different age groups, sexual orientations, sociocultural backgrounds, interests, and challenges, it can be overwhelming for an adult to identify and support students who are involved in bullying. In some cases, it is specifically so because bullying is not always obvious, and the child involved in it may hesitate to seek help. Many times, the child may even be unaware that they require help. The students may not report such incidents out of fear of being bullied further by peers or being punished by an adult (Hicks et al., 2018). Findings show that many students felt that teachers did not intervene and support the child appropriately when it came to bullying (O'Brien et al., 2018). Teachers state that they intervene in most bullying scenarios, however, they feel incompetent and unsure about how to deal with such incidents (Craig et al., 2011; Luca et al., 2019). Further, a child's response to traumatic incidents like bullying also differs with their age. Preschool and young school-age children may exhibit behavior such as clinginess whereas adolescents may withdraw from their family and friends (NCTSN, n.d.). This makes it challenging for teachers to observe, identify and provide support within the school environment and time limits.

In 2015, all the UN member nations adopted a set of goals through the 2030 Agenda for Sustainable Development. This agenda put forth a 15-year plan to fulfill 17 sustainable development goals (SDGs). SDG 4, and 16 focusing on 'Quality Education' and 'Peace, Justice and Strong Institutions' indirectly highlights the need to regulate bullying by 2030. Reviews and assessments have been conducted by UNESCO Mahatma Gandhi Institute of Education and Peace and Sustainable Development in 2018 and 2019 to measure and monitor the progress towards achieving the target SDG 4.7. These reviews highlight the importance of holistic development for students and implicate Social-Emotional Learning (SEL) in fulfilling SDG 4.7. In order to promote SEL skills among children, teachers need to be trained in these skills through emotional coaching.

In response to the experience of bullying, children may experience a range of emotions and as a result, exhibit changes in behavior as well. Even though they may be unable to recognize their need and ask for support, it is the responsibility of adults around them to do their best to help them. Hence, teachers who are with the children most of the time can make an effort to provide at least some generalized support to every student. One way of doing this is by using the framework of the engagement model used to support learners "who are working below the level of the national curriculum and not engaged in the subject-specific study" (p.6). The model is pupil-centered, focuses on the child's abilities, and values the knowledge of all stakeholders working with the child. Moreover, it is a method of observation that helps to improve a student's insight. Encouraging children who have experienced bullying and trauma to develop insight can help them identify their feelings and understand themselves better. It will not only enable them to feel more in control but also promote self-regulation in place of acting out in response to challenging events. The engagement model outlines five areas of engagement, which include (a) exploration, (b) realization, (c) anticipation, (d) persistence, and (e) initiation. Using this model, teachers can support children to connect with and engage with their emotions to better understand and regulate themselves. A process that is in line with this model is emotional coaching (Standards and Testing Agency, 2020).

EMOTIONAL COACHING

Emotional coaching is a "structured relationship that encourages young people to take action and to develop competence in social and emotional skills in a safe and supportive environment" (Hromek, 2007). The concept of emotional coaching was first observed and identified by John Gottman (1996) while studying parenting styles. Parents who used the emotional coaching style were seen to be more supportive of their child's emotional needs, provided them with guidance to regulate their emotions, and were emotionally intelligent themselves. This parenting style encouraged children to take ownership of their behavior and develop into emotionally healthy individuals. It also resulted in children being better able to self-soothe, delay gratification, and perform better both, academically and socially (Emotional Coaching UK [ECUK], 2020).

The process is based on the understanding that all behavior is a form of communication. With this approach, behavior is seen as a medium for expressing and understanding the emotions that lie behind it. All the same, children are supported in understanding that although all emotions are equally acceptable, not all behavior is acceptable. This enables the child to differentiate and separate their emotions, and behavior thereby promoting their abilities to regulate themselves. The research and later exploration into the concept of emotional coaching have identified that it has numerous benefits for the child. Children who are emotionally coached have better relationships with those adults, feel more self-confident, and perform better in social and academic contexts. When the child observes and is guided by emotionally intelligent role models such as parents and teachers, they eventually learn to manage their stress response and become well-regulated adults. It is also interesting to note that this process focuses on regulating the emotion that is a source of misbehavior and does not aim at behavior modification directly (Colosi, 2019).

Steps in Emotional Coaching

The process of emotional coaching comprises five steps through which a teacher can connect with and provide support for students to recognize and regulate their emotions (Colosi, 2019).

Step 1: Be aware of emotions
Step 2: Connect with the student
Step 3: Listen to the student
Step 4: Name the emotion
Step 5: Find good solutions

Step 1: Be Aware of Emotions

Social and cultural expectations ingrain children with ideas of good versus bad emotions, socially acceptable versus unacceptable emotions. Therefore, when students come to school, they may have preset ideas about which are socially acceptable emotions and have categories such as good and bad emotions. This may make them hesitant or resistant to identifying the emotion they are experiencing. To smooth over such challenges, teachers can use tools such as emotion vocabulary charts and emoji icons to help students expand their emotional vocabulary (Siregar & Suparno, 2018). Additionally, teachers can encourage students to identify emotions as comfortable or uncomfortable, in contrast to positive and negative. The importance of all emotions and the role they play in an individual's life can also be discussed; for instance, anger could indicate that the person is feeling vulnerable and threatened, whereas anxiety tells the individual that they need better coping strategies to deal with a threat. Teachers can also assist students in this process by examining their body language and facial expressions which provide a clue as to what they are feeling.

Step 2: Connect With the Student

A teacher can consider emotional expressions in a student as opportunities to connect with them at a deeper level. Students can be encouraged to look within themselves and explore what they feel. In such instances, teachers can open the floor to non-judgemental discussions about emotions which will then provide a safe environment for a child to feel what they feel. Statements such as, "You seem to be frowning, is something upsetting you?" could act as gateways to begin conversations about uncomfortable emotions. It is also important to note that teachers need to accept and acknowledge the emotion instead of being dismissive or disapproving (ECUK, 2020).

Step 3: Listen to the Student

Once a student has identified that they are experiencing some emotion, a teacher can be there for them by listening to and empathizing with their experience. It does not require the teacher to have undergone the same experience, but the understanding that the student is in a difficult situation and they require someone to listen to them. If and when required, the teacher can also share any relevant parallels from their own life experiences to share and bond with the student. However, the focus should remain on the student and their emotional experience. Many adults tend to minimize or dismiss the emotional experience of a child, indirectly telling them that their emotions are not valued. Hence, it is imperative that the teacher takes the student seriously and ensures the student is aware of it. Being an active listener, without being distracted, and being non-judgmental can go a long way in helping the student feel heard.

Step 4: Name the Emotion

Listening to the student's experience can shed light on the emotion they are experiencing. Here, the teachers can actively step in to help the student name the emotion. This can be done by paraphrasing their experience, acknowledging the changes in their body language, and suggesting a possible emotion. For example, a teacher who interacts with a student who has been bullied could say something like, "I hear that you were hit by someone bigger than you in front of your classmates. Your face is flushed and I see tears in your eyes. Is it possible that you may be feeling humiliated by the incident?" The use of props such as the feelings wheel can assist the student and teacher work together to name the emotion. The teacher can also act as a model by giving an example of their life experiences, such as, "When my boss yelled at me in front of my colleagues, I felt humiliated. Does that relate to what you are feeling now?" (Dewar, 2021).

Step 5: Find Good Solutions

In this final stage, teachers can assist students in choosing and practicing self-regulation strategies. This could range from simple breathing exercises to regular habits to be incorporated into their daily routines, such as adequate sleep and exercise. It is also at this step that teachers guide students to differentiate between acceptable and unacceptable behaviors to express their emotions. They can remind students that, 'It is acceptable for you to feel angry, however not to beat up another student to express your anger. What could be another way for you to express your anger?' This ensures that students become aware of healthy ways to express their emotions. Teachers need to merely encourage the student to come up with ways to express their emotions and help them pick a strategy that is a win-win for everyone involved. At this stage, teachers need to be patient, recognize and identify harmful behavior, and appreciate students when they come up with healthy ways to express their emotions (Dewar, 2021).

ROLE OF TEACHERS

With the existing workload and many roles a teacher is expected to perform, it is only natural that another question pops up - another additional role? What if this role just requires a few minutes a day, ensures a disciplined classroom environment, and promotes learner engagement? Although emotional coaching specifically focuses on enabling a child to get in touch with their emotions, the learner also experiences many positive side effects. Children engaged through emotional coaching are known to have better academic success, peer relationships, student-teacher relationships, and problem-solving abilities required to perform well at school (Gottman et al., as cited in Rose et al., 2015; Gus et al., 2017).

Basic qualifications that make a teacher capable of emotionally coaching a student include knowledge and experience in the fields of education and psychology. It is also essential that the teacher likes children, and is able to develop and maintain a good rapport with them. In addition, good communication skills, the ability to self-regulate, and sufficient interpersonal skills can prove to be helpful in the process of emotional coaching (Hromek, 2007). Furthermore, in order to support a student through emotional coaching, the teacher first needs to be emotionally intelligent. Before an aircraft takes off, people are instructed to put their own oxygen masks first, before helping another person; similarly, a person who is not self-regulated cannot support another person through emotional coaching.

Self-Check for Teachers

Before assisting a student through emotional coaching, a teacher has to look within to see how they feel in a situation and then respond to the student's emotional expression. Some questions they can ask themselves are given below.

- Am I feeling calm and composed?
- Am I well-regulated?
- Do I need some time to calm down before supporting my student?

- Do I have the physical and emotional energy to support my student now?
- Do I have adequate resources to support my students now?
- Will I be able to model the required behavior to emotionally coach my student?

When teachers ask themselves these questions, they will be better in tune with their own selves. They will also be able to check whether or not they are ready to take on the role of an emotional coach. Only if the teacher is well-regulated and ready to be an emotional coach can they support a student effectively throughout the process. If not, they can refer the student to another trained adult, or schedule another time for the emotional coaching process (ECUK, 2020).

Challenges in Emotional Coaching

While teachers and students work together in the process of emotional coaching, there are some challenges they may face. The four key aspects that could raise issues include (a) trust, (b) resources, (c) expectation, and (d) boundaries. Initially, it is essential that the students are comfortable with the said teacher. If the teacher has not built trust with the students and they do not have a good rapport, the students are not going to be able to relax and be vulnerable with their emotions. Further, the teacher should ensure that they have the required time and space to begin the process, lest they have to end it mid-way leaving the child raw with emotion, without resolving the issue. They should also have the space to express themselves in a safe and supportive environment without being rushed or interrupted (Hromek, 2007).

In a class with about 20 to 40 students, it is not expected that teachers delve deeply into each student's emotions. They can merely take on the role of a guide and encourage children to look within themselves to build their understanding of their emotions. Hence, at the beginning of the process, the teachers, as emotional coaches, should set expectations of what can be expected throughout the process. They can outline the timings, frequency, and space where the process would take place including any other details required for each specific group. Finally, it is important to know where to limit the emotional coaching process and support the child with their therapeutic needs. When required, for instance in cases when the child exhibits overwhelming emotions, the teacher needs to step back and refer them to the required professional. It is not on them to take on the role of a mental health professional and overextend themselves to meet the needs of the child (Hromek, 2007).

PRACTICAL STRATEGIES FOR CLASSROOMS

The process of emotional coaching has numerous benefits for the teaching-learning relationships shared in different learning environments. In this final section, strategies to practice emotional coaching step-by-step in both traditional and virtual classrooms as well as their specific role in regulating bullying will be discussed. In addition to this, a sample template (Template A) for teachers to use in their classrooms will also be provided at the end of this section.

Awareness

To build children's awareness of emotions, teachers can weave it into their lessons. For example, while discussing a story, the teacher can ask questions such as, 'What do you think the character is feeling now?', 'What would you feel if you were in this situation?', 'How have you responded to such a situation if you have experienced it previously?' However, it is understood that not all subjects will have such relatable strategies to weave emotions into lessons. In such scenarios, teachers can simply share their experiences within or outside of the classroom. For example, a teacher who is experiencing a bad day could say something like, 'I am feeling frustrated as I am having a bad day. It is an unpleasant experience for me so I would like to take a minute to calm down and then we can get back to the lesson.'

Teachers can discuss different emotions and encourage children to explore how these emotions are felt in their bodies. In certain cultures where emotional expression is restrained or discouraged, it can be difficult to talk about emotions, but children may feel more comfortable expressing physical sensations. Once children learn that there can be numerous emotions and they are all acceptable, it will help them be more accepting and kind to themselves. In a bullying situation, it can help all students recognize that they are feeling emotional and understand it as an acceptable experience. This will reduce their need to suppress emotions or override them by acting out (Waliski & Carlson, 2008).

Connecting

In some cases if a student is experiencing an emotion it can be difficult to connect with it, even if they are aware of and accept it. In cases of unpleasant and traumatic events, children may be afraid to get in touch with their emotions and process them. Doing so may also unleash overwhelming feelings that the child is unable to manage on their own (Pur, 2014). Teachers can demonstrate connecting with feelings by encouraging students to read each other's facial expressions and body language.

This could be done as a break time activity in between classes or practiced when any specific incident occurs in class. For instance, when one student calls another student by a nickname, the teacher can suggest that the student pause and guess what the other student is feeling. Questions like, 'What made you say that?', 'How did you feel after you did that?', 'How do you think the behavior made your classmate feel?', 'Has someone done this to you before? How did you feel then?' can provide students with the space to reflect on their behavior and understand themselves better.

Encouraging students to connect with their emotions will support them to look within themselves and understand what they feel. Many children find it difficult to deconstruct complex and difficult emotions. They may not have the skills to accept the situation (Goldsmith & Freyd, 2005). As a result, this will hinder the process of healing their emotional wounds which could be exhibited as bullying or victimization. Even those students who have witnessed incidents of bullying may experience unpleasant feelings of helplessness, guilt, and shame. The process of connecting with emotions allows children to try to explore these feelings in a non-judgemental way.

Listening

At times adults can seem dismissive and disapproving of a child's emotions. They may feel that children may grow out of it or learn to stop feeling those emotions. Unfortunately, a child feels that their emotions are being ignored. As a teacher, an effective strategy to incorporate listening is to talk to the students about their day. This can be done at the beginning of the session while waiting for the other students, or during classroom breaks. Simple questions can be used such as, 'How have you been?' 'Have you eaten?' 'I see that you are not sitting with your friends today, is everything all right?', 'What prevented you from completing this work?' or even asking, 'What is on your mind today?' These interactions can not only help build the child's standard, but can also have a huge impact on their classroom performance, assist to develop classroom rapport, and bring awareness to the child that the teacher cares for them.

Listening drastically helps the teacher engage with students during in-class activities. In the teaching session, this can be followed by asking students if they are ready to move to a new topic, by allowing them to choose the next topic, or by asking them to pick from the given choices. Such activities will provide them with some amount of autonomy in their classrooms and let them know that they have control of their lives and there is someone to listen to them (Deci & Ryan, 1987; Ruzek et al., 2016). It is important to note that while engaging in such interactions, teachers need to follow the suggestions or choices made by the students and not modify them to something that has been pre-planned.

More often, children involved in bullying, in all roles, may experience a loss of control - of themselves, of others, and even of the world. Giving students the opportunity to control some aspects of their life in the protection of their classroom will help them practice their freedom of choice and learn to use it in a way. Further, when students feel heard, they are more likely to come forward and discuss their issues or experiences of bullying; thereby increasing the opportunities for adults to step up and support them. Research has also shown that children who have better relationships with their teachers are less likely to be involved in bullying (Huang et al., 2018).

Naming

Once children are in tune with their feelings, they can be exposed to a wide vocabulary of emotions. Simple tools such as emojis, the wheel of emotions, the emotions color wheel, face cards, and much more can be easily used in classrooms or displayed on boards. As a one-minute exercise, children can be asked questions like, 'What color are you feeling like today?', and 'Which emoji best describes how you feel now?' Such exercises will encourage children to pay attention to the different types of emotions, how they are expressed, and what they could mean. They will also learn that recognizing and expressing emotions can be done in a variety of ways.

Students who are involved in bullying are known to have difficulties in self-regulation, demonstrating behavioral and emotional difficulties (Cross et al., 2015; Miller et al., 2005). When they have opportunities to learn about, recognize, and express their emotions, it can help them be more connected with themselves and others. This will improve their ability to empathize with others, and regulate their emotions and resultant behavior. Exposing them to a wide range of emotions also helps them narrow down their feelings without generally resorting to anger or sadness and thereby acting upon it. Students can assess the intensity of their emotions using tools such as the feelings thermometer (Wyman et al., 2010).

Resolving

In the final step of resolving, students are encouraged to look within themselves to find healthy, harmless ways to work with their emotions. In order to practice this, teachers can encourage perspective taking and group activities in the classroom. The key focus here is to urge students to become more open minded and explore strategies and solutions they would not have previously considered. Such tasks could improve their ability to think of alternative solutions when they are faced with difficult situations and choices. It can also provide them with an insight into how others think and get involved in seeking and helping each other out. Further, relaxation techniques such as breathing exercises, grounding, the 5-4-3-2-1 technique, and visualization can be practiced or recommended to the students as quick self-regulation techniques.

When a child is engaged in a bullying situation, they are sure to experience some emotion. Many a time, these emotions are either externalized or internalized leading to numerous physical, psychological, and social issues in their life. Being aware of and learning to use self-regulatory strategies can give these children a chance to resolve their feelings in a safe and healthy way. Following the process will help them feel better and healthier. It will allow them to skip the consequences of impulsive actions. Most often children resort to crime, substance abuse, and other harmful behavior due to a lack of self-regulation and an inability to pause before taking a decision. These strategies can give them that extra moment to think and make better and wiser decisions. Additionally, in situations where a child does not have the power to resolve the issue, techniques such as the invisible shield and imaginary umbrella can be used to feel safe and protected (Wyman et al., 2010).

Template A. Sample Script for Emotional Coaching in Traditional and Virtual Classrooms

The current template is based on the assumption that the students and the teachers have already oriented themselves to the process of emotional coaching and have practiced a few previous sessions. In the initial sessions, the teacher can share their feelings and thoughts at each stage to model how the process works. This will help children understand how to participate in the process and actively engage in each session. Here is a sample script that a teacher, who is an emotional coach, can use regularly before beginning their session.

[Once students enter and settle down in the classroom - TRADITIONAL CLASSROOM

OR

Once all or a majority of the students join the classroom - VIRTUAL CLASSROOM]

Good day students! Happy (morning/afternoon/evening)!

Welcome to our session on (subject). Today we will be working on (topic).

Before we start the topic, let us take five minutes to connect with and regulate ourselves. We will go through five steps together - becoming aware of our emotions,

Emotional Coaching

connecting with them, listening to ourselves, trying to name our emotions, and thinking of a possible way to exhibit them.

While going through these steps, it would help all of us to remain silent and look within ourselves. However, at any point in time, if you would like me to support you, kindly raise your hand and I shall come up to you. - TRADITIONAL CLASSROOM

OR

While going through these steps, it would help all of us to remain on mute, in a silent environment, and look within ourselves. However, at any point in time, if you would like me to support you, kindly use the raise hand button or message me personally and I shall respond to you. - VIRTUAL CLASSROOM

Do you have any questions or comments, or shall we start?

[Give them a minute to be prepared and sit comfortably or ask any questions]

[Awareness]

Let us all take this moment to listen to what our body is feeling.

We have discussed that emotions can be expressed by our body, so try to listen to what your body is feeling now. Are you experiencing any pleasant, neutral, or unpleasant sensations in your body?

Take a moment to scan your body and choose a sensation that you would like to explore further in today's session.

[Connecting]

Now let us connect with the sensation you have chosen for today. What emotion or feeling do you think your body is experiencing now? How long have you been feeling this way? Is this a feeling you are familiar with or does this feel new?

[Listening]

What do you think your sensation is trying to tell you? Have you expressed this feeling yet? Is there something you like to do while feeling this way?

[Naming]

What would you like to name this feeling? We have six basic emotions - happiness, surprise, anger, sadness, fear, and disgust. Would your emotion broadly fall under any of these categories?

[Resolving]

How would you like to exhibit this emotion? If you have already experienced this emotion, is there something you would like to do differently this time?

Is your behavior harmless and effective in exhibiting your emotion? If not, what could you do differently?

[Bringing back attention to the session]

Now, let us all take a deep breath in and breathe out. Are we able to feel the seat we are sitting on? Do we feel the floor beneath our feet? Can you spot something blue in the room?

Is there something anyone would like to share or shall we move on to our topic?

[Give them a minute to respond and go ahead accordingly]

KEY POINTS

The key points identified from the chapter are given below:

- Bullying refers to aggressive behavior that is more often repeated, negative, intentional, and based on some imbalance of power between the individuals involved (UNESCO, 2019). It can be sub-categorized as direct or indirect; and physical, verbal, social/relational, psychological, sexual, or cyberbullying.
- Numerous factors at the individual, familial and sociocultural levels influence a child's involvement in bullying, and it can have both short term and long term impacts on the child. Being involved in bullying can directly or indirectly push a child into the school-to-prison pipeline.
- It can be challenging to identify and support children who are involved in bullying. Hence, using the model of engagement, teachers can provide a base level of support for all students through emotional coaching.

Emotional Coaching

- Emotional coaching is a "structured relationship that encourages young people to take action and to develop competence in social and emotional skills in a safe and supportive environment" (Hromek, 2007). It encompasses the following five steps - (a) be aware of emotions, (b) connect with the student, (c) listen to the student, (d) name the emotion, (e) find good solutions.
- Teachers play a significant role in the process of emotional coaching in the classroom and may face certain challenges during the process. However, some practical strategies to use in the classroom include the emotions wheel to improve awareness of different emotions, breathing, and calming exercise to regulate emotions, and problem-solving techniques.

REFERENCES

American Civil Liberties Union. (n.d.). *School-to-prison pipeline*. ACLU. https://www.aclu.org/issues/juvenile-justice/juvenile-justice-school-prison-pipeline

American Psychological Association. (2019). *Trauma*. APA. https://www.apa.org/topics/trauma

Anti-Bullying Alliance. (n.d.). *The impact of bullying*. ABA. https://anti-bullyingalliance.org.uk/tools-information/all-about-bullying/prevalence-and-impact-bullying/impact-bullying

Antiri, K. O. (2016). Types of bullying in the senior high schools in Ghana. *Journal of Education and Practice*, *7*(36), 131–138.

Arseneault, L. (2017). The long-term impact of bullying victimization on mental health. *World Psychiatry; Official Journal of the World Psychiatric Association (WPA)*, *16*(1), 27–28. doi:10.1002/wps.20399 PMID:28127927

Bacher-Hicks, A., Billings, S., & Deming, D. (2021). Proving the school-to-prison pipeline: Stricter middle schools raise the risk of adult arrest. *Education Next*, *21*(4), 52–57.

Bender, D., & Lösel, F. (2011). Bullying at school as a predictor of delinquency, violence and other anti-social behaviour in adulthood. *Criminal Behaviour and Mental Health*, *21*(2), 99–106. doi:10.1002/cbm.799 PMID:21370295

Berlowitz, M., Frye, R., & Jette, K. (2014). Bullying and zero-tolerance policies: The school to prison pipeline. *Multicultural Learning and Teaching*, *12*(1), 7–25. doi:10.1515/mlt-2014-0004

Blake, P., & Louw, J. (2010). Exploring high school learners' perceptions of bullying. *Journal of Child and Adolescent Mental Health*, *22*(2), 111–118. doi:10.2989/17280583.2010.536657 PMID:25859768

Chai, L., Xue, J., & Han, Z. (2020). Excessive weight and academic performance among Chinese children and adolescents: Assessing the mediating effects of bullying victimization and self-rated health and life satisfaction. *Children and Youth Services Review*, *119*, 105586. doi:10.1016/j.childyouth.2020.105586

Choi, B., & Park, S. (2021). Bullying perpetration, victimization, and low self-esteem: Examining their relationship over time. *Journal of Youth and Adolescence*, *50*(4), 739–742. doi:10.100710964-020-01379-8 PMID:33428081

Colich, N., Rosen, M., Williams, E., & McLaughlin, K. (2020). Biological aging in childhood and adolescence following experiences of threat and deprivation: A systematic review and meta-analysis. *Psychological Bulletin*, *146*(9), 721–764. doi:10.1037/bul0000270 PMID:32744840

Colosi, A. (2019). Teaching emotion coaching to teachers of toddlers. [Capstone Projects and Master's Theses, California State University, USA]. https://digitalcommons.csumb.edu/caps_thes_all/706

Craig, K., Bell, D., & Leschied, A. (2011). Pre-service teachers' knowledge and attitudes regarding school-based bullying. *Canadian Journal of Education*, *34*(2), 21–33.

Cross, D., Lester, L., & Barnes, A. (2015). A longitudinal study of the social and emotional predictors and consequences of cyber and traditional bullying victimisation. *International Journal of Public Health*, *60*(2), 207–217. doi:10.100700038-015-0655-1 PMID:25645100

de Oliveira, W., Silva, M., de Mello, F., Porto, D., Yoshinaga, A., & Malta, D. (2015). The causes of bullying: Results from the National Survey of School Health (PeNSE). *Revista Latino-Americana de Enfermagem*, *23*(2), 275–282. doi:10.1590/0104-1169.0022.2552 PMID:26039298

Deci, E., & Ryan, R. (1987). The support of autonomy and the control of behavior. *Journal of Personality and Social Psychology*, *53*(6), 1024–1037. doi:10.1037/0022-3514.53.6.1024 PMID:3320334

Dewar, G. (2021). Emotion coaching: Helping kids cope with negative feelings. *Parenting Science*. https://parentingscience.com/emotion-coaching/

Dye, H. (2018). The impact and long-term effects of childhood trauma. *Journal of Human Behavior in the Social Environment*, *28*(3), 381–392. doi:10.1080/10911359.2018.1435328

Emotional Coaching, U. K. (2020). *Our emotions, brain, and stress: Emotion coaching to support health and wellbeing*. ECUK. https://www.emotioncoachinguk.com/_files/ugd/994674_d5e9463056a64632ac45298c5ab577a6.pdf

Espelage, D., & Swearer, S. (2009). Contributions of three social theories to understanding bullying perpetration and victimization among school-aged youth. In J. M. Harris (Ed.), *Bullying, rejection, and peer victimization: A social cognitive neuroscience perspective* (pp. 151–170). Springer Publishing Company.

Fulgencio, L., Corrêa-Faria, P., Lage, C., Paiva, S., Pordeus, I., & Serra-Negra, J. (2016). Diagnosis of sleep bruxism can assist in the detection of cases of verbal school bullying and measure the life satisfaction of adolescents. *International Journal of Paediatric Dentistry*, *27*(4), 293–301. doi:10.1111/ipd.12264 PMID:27598528

Goldsmith, R., & Freyd, J. (2005). Awareness for emotional abuse. *Journal of Emotional Abuse*, *5*(1), 95–123. doi:10.1300/J135v05n01_04

Guo, J., Zhu, Y., Fang, L., Zhang, B., Liu, D., Fu, M., & Wang, X. (2020). The relationship between being bullied and addictive internet use among Chinese rural adolescents: The mediating effect of adult attachment. *Journal of Interpersonal Violence*, *37*(9-10), NP6466–NP6486. doi:10.1177/0886260520966681 PMID:33084482

Gus, L., Rose, J., Gilbert, L., & Kilby, R. (2017). The introduction of emotion coaching as a whole school approach in a primary specialist social emotional and mental health setting: Positive outcomes for all. *The Open Family Studies Journal*, *9*(S1, M3), 95-110. doi:10.2174/1874922401709010095

Hence, A. (2018). Bullying in grade school children and its connection to the school-to-prison pipeline. [Senior Honors Theses and Projects, EMU, USA]. https://commons.emich.edu/honors/596

Hicks, J., Jennings, L., Jennings, S., Berry, S., & Green, D. (2018). Middle school bullying: Student reported perceptions and prevalence. *Journal of Child and Adolescent Counseling*, *4*(3), 195–208. doi:10.1080/23727810.2017.1422645

Hromek, R. (2007). Emotional coaching: A practical programme to support young people. *Psychology*.

Huang, F., Lewis, C., Cohen, D., Prewett, S., & Herman, K. (2018). Bullying involvement, teacher–student relationships, and psychosocial outcomes. *School Psychology Quarterly*, *33*(2), 223–234. doi:10.1037pq0000249 PMID:29878821

Hutchinson, M. (2012). Exploring the impact of bullying on young bystanders. *Educational Psychology in Practice*, *28*(4), 425–442. doi:10.1080/02667363.2012.727785

Kaufman, T., Huitsing, G., & Veenstra, R. (2020). Refining victims' self-reports on bullying: Assessing frequency, intensity, power imbalance, and goal-directedness. *Social Development*, *29*(2), 375–390. doi:10.1111ode.12441

Kshirsagar, V., Agarwal, R., & Bavdekar, S. (2007). Bullying in schools: Prevalence and short-term impact. *Indian Pediatrics*, *44*, 25–28. PMID:17277427

Luca, L., Nocentini, A., & Menesini, E. (2019). The teacher's role in preventing bullying. *Frontiers in Psychology*, *10*, 1830. doi:10.3389/fpsyg.2019.01830 PMID:31474902

Miller, A., Gouley, K., Seifer, R., Zakriski, A., Eguia, M., & Vergnani, M. (2005). Emotion knowledge skills in low-income elementary school children: Associations with social status and peer experiences. *Social Development*, *14*(4), 637–651. doi:10.1111/j.1467-9507.2005.00321.x

National Academies of Sciences, Engineering, and Medicine. (2016). *Preventing bullying through science, policy, and practice.* NASEM. doi:10.17226/23482

National Bullying Prevention Center. (2019). *How is "direct bullying" different from "indirect bullying"?* Pacer. https://www.pacer.org/bullying/info/questions-answered/direct-vs-indirect.asp

National Criminal Justice Reference Service. (2014). Beyond bullying: How hostile school climate perpetuates the school-to-prison pipeline for LGBT youth (NCJ Number 246129). Center for American Progress.

New York Civil Liberties Union. (n.d.). *School-to-prison pipeline.* NYCLU. https://www.nyclu.org/en/issues/racial-justice/school-prison-pipeline

O'Brien, N., Munn-Giddings, C., & Moules, T. (2018). The repercussions of reporting bullying: Some experiences of students at an independent secondary school. *Pastoral Care in Education*, *36*(1), 29–43. doi:10.1080/02643944.2017.1422004

Oliveira, F., de Menezes, T., Irffi, G., & Oliveira, G. (2018). Bullying effect on student's performance. *Economía*, *19*(1), 57–73. doi:10.1016/j.econ.2017.10.001

Olweus, D. (1994). Bullying at School. In L. R. Huesmann (Ed.), *Aggressive Behavior* (pp. 97–130). Springer., doi:10.1007/978-1-4757-9116-7_5

Plexousakis, S., Kourkoutas, E., Giovazolias, T., Chatira, K., & Nikolopoulos, D. (2019). School bullying and post-traumatic stress disorder symptoms: The role of parental bonding. *Frontiers in Public Health*, *7*, 75. doi:10.3389/fpubh.2019.00075 PMID:31024876

Pulido, R., Banks, C., Ragan, K., Pang, D., Blake, J., & McKyer, E. (2019). The impact of school bullying on physical activity in overweight youth: Exploring race and ethnic differences. *The Journal of School Health*, *89*(4), 319–327. doi:10.1111/josh.12740 PMID:30843227

Pur, I. (2014). Emotion regulation intervention for complex developmental trauma: Working with street children. *Procedia: Social and Behavioral Sciences*, *159*, 697–701. doi:10.1016/j.sbspro.2014.12.471

Rose, J., McGuire-Snieckus, R., & Gilbert, L. (2015). Emotion coaching - a strategy for promoting behavioural self-regulation in children/young people in schools: A pilot study. *The European Journal of Social and Behavioural Sciences*, *13*(2), 130–157. doi:10.15405/ejsbs.159

Rosenthal, R. (2012). Self-fulfilling prophecy. In *Encyclopedia of Human Behavior* (2nd ed., pp. 328–335). Elsevier. doi:10.1016/B978-0-12-375000-6.00314-1

Ruzek, E., Hafen, C., Allen, J., Gregory, A., Mikami, A., & Pianta, R. (2016). How teacher emotional support motivates students: The mediating roles of perceived peer relatedness, autonomy support, and competence. *Learning and Instruction*, *42*, 95–103. doi:10.1016/j.learninstruc.2016.01.004 PMID:28190936

Siregar, S., & Suparno, S. (2018). *Understanding child's emotions and responses to the food using words and emojis fat and thin child*. Proceedings of the International Conference on Special and Inclusive Education (ICSIE 2018), *296*, 315-319. 10.2991/icsie-18.2019.57

Standards & Testing Agency. (2020). The engagement model. *Assets*. https://assets.publishing.service.gov.uk/government/uploads/system/uploads/attachment_data/file/903458/Engagement_Model_Guidance_2020.pdf

StopBullying.gov. (2021, May 21). *Effects of bullying*. Stopbullying. https://www.stopbullying.gov/bullying/effects

Subedi, K. (2020). Theoretical perspective of bullying. *International Journal of Health Sciences and Research*, *10*(8), 83–89.

Substance Abuse and Mental Health Services Administration. (2014). Understanding the Impact of Trauma. In *Trauma-Informed Care in Behavioral Health Services* (pp. 59–89). HHS Publication.

Substance Abuse and Mental Health Services Administration. (2022). *Understanding child trauma*. SAMHSA. https://www.samhsa.gov/child-trauma/understanding-child-trauma

The National Child Traumatic Stress Network. (n.d.). *About child trauma*. NCTSN. https://www.nctsn.org/what-is-child-trauma/about-child-trauma

Ttofi, M., Farrington, D., & Losel, F. (2011). Health consequences of school bullying. *Journal of Aggression, Conflict and Peace Research, 3*(2). doi:10.1108/jacpr.2011.55003baa.002

United Nations Educational, Scientific, and Cultural Organization. (2019). *Behind the numbers: Ending school violence and bullying*. UNESCO. https://unesdoc.unesco.org/ark:/48223/pf0000366483

United Nations Educational, Scientific, and Cultural Organization. (2020). *International conference on school bullying: Recommendations by the scientific committee on preventing and addressing school bullying and cyberbullying.* UNESCO. https://unesdoc.unesco.org/ark:/48223/pf0000374794.locale=en

Volk, A., Dane, A., & Marini, Z. (2014). What is bullying? A theoretical redefinition. *Developmental Review, 34*(4), 327–343. doi:10.1016/j.dr.2014.09.001

Waliski, A., & Carlson, L. (2008). Group work with preschool children: Effect on emotional awareness and behavior. *Journal for Specialists in Group Work, 33*(1), 3–21. doi:10.1080/01933920701476714

Wang, G., Han, A., Zhang, G., Xu, N., Xie, G., Chen, L., Yuan, M., & Su, P. (2020). Sensitive periods for the effect of bullying victimization on suicidal behaviors among university students in China: The roles of timing and chronicity. *Journal of Affective Disorders, 268*, 12–19. doi:10.1016/j.jad.2020.02.049 PMID:32158002

Wang, H., Wang, Y., Wang, G., Wilson, A., Jin, T., Zhu, L., Yu, R., Wang, S., Yin, W., Song, H., Li, S., Jia, Q., Zhang, X., & Yang, Y. (2021). Structural family factors and bullying at school: A large scale investigation based on a Chinese adolescent sample. *BMC Public Health, 21*(1), 2249. doi:10.118612889-021-12367-3 PMID:34895204

Weinhold, B. (2000). Uncovering the hidden causes of bullying and school violence. *Counseling and Human Development, 32*(6), 1–18.

Wisner, W. (2022, February 24). What are adverse childhood experiences? *Very Well Mind*. https://www.verywellmind.com/what-are-aces-adverse-childhood-experiences-5219030

Wolke, D., & Lereya, S. (2015). Long-term effects of bullying. *Archives of Disease in Childhood*, *100*(9), 879–885. doi:10.1136/archdischild-2014-306667 PMID:25670406

Wong, C., Cheng, Y., & Chen, L. (2013). Multiple perspectives on the targets and causes of school bullying. *Educational Psychology in Practice*, *29*(3), 278–292. doi:10.1080/02667363.2013.837030

Wu, N., Hou, Y., Zeng, Q., Cai, H., & You, J. (2021). Bullying experiences and nonsuicidal self-injury among Chinese adolescents: A longitudinal moderated mediation model. *Journal of Youth and Adolescence*, *50*(4), 753–766. doi:10.100710964-020-01380-1 PMID:33428080

Wyman, P., Cross, W., Brown, C., Yu, Q., Tu, X., & Eberly, S. (2010). Intervention to strengthen emotional self-regulation in children with emerging mental health problems: Proximal impact on school behavior. *Journal of Abnormal Child Psychology*, *38*(5), 707–720. doi:10.100710802-010-9398-x PMID:20180009

Yang, A., & Salmivalli, C. (2015). Effectiveness of the KiVa antibullying programme on bully-victims, bullies and victims. *Educational Research*, *57*(1), 80–90. doi:10.1080/00131881.2014.983724

KEY TERMS AND DEFINITIONS

Adverse Childhood Experiences (ACEs): Events that are experienced before the age of 18 years which are potentially traumatic to the child experiencing it and the impact of which persists into adulthood.

Childhood Trauma: Any incident that poses psychological or physical, real or perceived harm to a child. It includes single and multiple occurrences as well as chronic repeated occurrences.

Direct Bullying: Any form of bullying that involves obvious, overt behavior wherein the target is aware of being bullied. It mostly occurs face-to-face and includes acts such as hitting, punching, and teasing, to name a few.

Emotional Coaching: The process through which one individual, mostly an adult, assists another individual, mostly a child, to recognize, understand, and regulate their emotions and their expression.

Indirect Bullying: Any form of bullying that involves not-so-obvious, covert behavior wherein the target may not be aware of being bullied until a later point in time. It includes behavior such as cyberbullying and spreading rumors.

School Bullying: A form of peer-to-peer interaction wherein one student is physically, psychologically, or socially harmed by one or more other students.

School-to-Prison Pipeline: The trend in which children are channeled into criminal justice and legal systems through suspensions and expulsions based on their misconduct at school. More often these minor infractions can be disciplined within the school system. Further, this trend is seen to disproportionately affect children from minority communities or with disabilities.

Chapter 6
Leveraging Literacy Instruction to Support Learners Who Have Experienced Compounded Trauma

Karyn A. Allee
https://orcid.org/0000-0003-0764-4792
Mercer University, USA

Annemarie Bazzo Kaczmarczyk
Mercer University, USA

ABSTRACT

Children can experience trauma in multiple ways and spaces which can have profound effects on their development and impact student engagement, approaches to learning, and student outcomes. In this chapter, the authors break down various types of trauma, adversity, and stress that can contribute to delays in children's development. Schools can impact children's pre-existing trauma (or cause new trauma), even unintentionally, and children's classroom behaviors can signal that trauma may be affecting them. Teachers can use instructional strategies that both buffer students to potentially mitigate the harmful effects of systemic and compounded trauma, and also meet academic learning goals. The authors provide some suggestions on how to use literacy learning strategies in elementary school to support learners, especially those who may be historically marginalized due to systemic conditions like racism. They conclude by providing their thoughts on how future research can continue to identify evidence-based ways to support vulnerable learners.

DOI: 10.4018/978-1-6684-5713-9.ch006

INTRODUCTION

Since the return to "business as usual" schooling amid the COVID-19 pandemic, educators have begun to notice an uptick in "negative" student behaviors in the classroom. Students seem to be struggling to self-regulate and cooperate and have been expressing more anger and defiance towards teachers and administrators, thus impacting some of the daily functions in the classroom. Children can experience trauma, both in and outside of the school setting, in multiple ways and spaces. The compounded trauma and stress experienced by children can powerfully impact student engagement, approaches to learning, learning outcomes, and behaviors in the classroom. It is imperative for educators to understand the ways trauma can affect children's development and how it may manifest itself in the classroom to be able to respond to children's needs appropriately. In this chapter, we will provide background on how stress and trauma are inter-related and impact young children's development, specifically illustrate how this may manifest in classroom learning behaviors, and suggest literacy-based instructional strategies that can help mitigate exposure to conditions and experiences frequently associated with the "school-to-prison pipeline."

BACKGROUND

Trauma is a word that seems more ubiquitous than ever as we emerge into a quasi-post-pandemic world. Words may lose their power when over-used or used differently by context or user. In this section, we will provide background information to explain how stress and trauma are related, how schools as systems can inadvertently inflict further trauma on children, and how to recognize potential behavioral markers of children's stress and trauma.

DEFINING STRESS AND TRAUMA

Let's begin by understanding what trauma is. Simply experiencing emotionally unpleasant events is not in itself traumatic, despite how the term is frequently used colloquially. *Trauma* is a term even psychologists tend to define differently, and a commonly accepted understanding remains elusive – as experts are themselves subjectively applying meaning – but it is generally accepted as "the experience of certain events and by universal or specific cognitive or emotional reactions to such events" (Dalenberg et al., 2017, p. 27). These events can include high magnitude stressors (HMSs; referring to the nature of the event), acute stress (a HMS that has an immediate significant impact), and traumatic stressors (those HMS events that cause long-term impact emotionally or cognitively). HMS events can be happenings like assault, disasters, combat, homicide of close friends or family members, etc. (van der Kolk et al., 2005). Dalenberg and her colleagues (2017) suggest we could develop a more nuanced understanding of trauma and its effects on individuals by distinguishing between the types of events "commonly associated" with HMSs that generate acute stress and the types "that have been followed by a constellation of trauma-related symptoms" or changes in behavior and perspective (p. 27). Each of these varying viewpoints on the causes and impacts of trauma and attempts to define trauma, however, are focused on individual experience, usually resulting from a singular event, but trauma can also affect groups of people.

There is a growing body of scholars and scientists studying more expansive understandings of trauma. For example, emerging research is beginning to suggest that individual trauma may be heritable. *Inherited trauma*, or genetic trauma, refers to how trauma can be transmitted to offspring, either through behaviors or *epigenetic mechanisms*, the nongenetic influences on gene expression that affect how our bodies interpret the genetic code in our DNA (Yehuda & Lehrner, 2018). For example, let us imagine someone who has experienced intimate partner domestic violence. They may unconsciously tense, flinch, or otherwise express fear bodily around people of the abuser's same gender and physical appearance. Their children may perceive the parent's behaviors, even subconsciously, and internalize a similar fear thus "inheriting" the fear behaviorally. Alternatively, assuming the victim of domestic violence was a pregnant female, the physiological stress response she may experience during instances of domestic violence can trigger the release of stress hormones that affect not only her, but also her fetus. If the fetus is also female, theoretically the mother's stress hormone can also affect the eggs already in the fetus' body, potentially impacting how the genetic code of the DNA is interpreted by three generations. These examples illustrate two different ways trauma may be generational and affect families.

"*Systemic* [emphasis added] trauma [however, refers to the] contextual features of environments and institutions that give rise to trauma, maintain it, and impact posttraumatic responses" (Goldsmith et al., 2014, Abstract). When we think of trauma in this systemic manner, we begin to recognize that the larger environments of institutions (e.g., schools, government, the criminal justice system), agencies and systems (e.g., foster care, public assistance, law enforcement, immigration), conflicts (e.g., refugees, war, geopolitics), and social dynamics (e.g., systemic prejudice and bias, political and cultural divide) can cause trauma writ large. Acknowledging the pervasiveness and insidiousness of the myriad sources perpetuating systemic trauma on children, families, and communities, researchers and practitioners in the social sciences, including education, are shifting their approaches and broadening their perspectives of trauma accordingly. These systems understandably can and do impact *social determinants of health*, the conditions of a person's environment that affect their wellness outcomes which are driven largely by "socioeconomic factors such as income, wealth, and education[al]" factors (Braveman & Gottlieb, 2014, p. 19). The Centers for Disease Control explains social determinants of health are "shaped by the distribution of money, power, and resources throughout local communities, nations, and the world. Differences in these conditions lead to health inequities or the unfair and avoidable differences in health status seen within and between countries" (Centers for Disease Control and Prevention, n.d., para. 1). They define these determinants as: education access and quality; health care and quality; neighborhood and built environment; social and community context; and economic stability.

Each of these social determinants of health, but especially education for the context of this chapter, have a direct connection to children's life outcomes, including their academic outcomes and likelihood of incarceration. First used in the early 21st century, the term *school-to-prison pipeline*, or the more current phrase *school-to-prison nexus*, refers to the impact of educational reform and legislative practices that effectively steer children out of school and toward prison. These harsh policies and practices disproportionately affect *historically marginalized students*, particularly high poverty or low-income students, students of Color, limited English proficiency students, and other disenfranchised groups (Wald & Losen, 2003). Reform efforts requiring evidence of student learning through high-stakes testing and zero-tolerance exclusionary discipline policies have created disparities that mirror, with shocking similarity, the demographic makeup of citizens most harshly sanctioned by our US legal system. The systemic failure of schools to proactively provide appropriate behavioral interventions, the use of severe exclusionary discipline practices, and the non-existence or ineffective application of interventions aimed to reduce risk and enhance protective factors that support "at-risk" children contributes to this pipeline or nexus (Wald & Losen, 2003). The policies of mass incarceration in the US influences the criminalization of children in schools (Heitzeg, 2009), and the population of incarcerated persons are 33% more likely to have experienced adverse childhood events than non-incarcerated persons (Hurley, 2021) thus illustrating a causality dilemma. Are the children who "struggle" most in school more likely to become incarcerated or is the system skewed in such a way as to generate inhospitable and unforgiving environs in schools that push children toward prisons, especially those who have experienced adversity and marginalization? We believe it is the latter.

ADVERSE CHILDHOOD EXPERIENCES

The concept of Adverse Childhood Experiences (ACEs; Felitti et al., 1998) is not new and influences how educators (and others in the social sciences) consider the impact of trauma on children. ACEs are events that occur in childhood that are potentially traumatic and are linked to potentially chronic physical, emotional, cognitive, and social problems throughout a person's lifespan. The effects of experiencing adverse childhood circumstances have been linked to adult substance abuse, chronic health issues, mental illness, the aforementioned incarceration, career success and earning potential, early morbidity, and family and relationship stability. It is important to note that the original list of ACEs from the Kaiser-Permanente study is not exhaustive, there are other traumatic experiences that can affect wellness, and ACEs can be prevented. Those original ACEs (Felitti et al., 1998) include a child experiencing:

- Physical abuse by a parent
- Emotional abuse by a parent
- Sexual abuse by anyone
- Growing up with an alcohol and/or drug abuser in the household
- Experiencing the incarceration of a household member
- Living with a family member experiencing mental illness
- Domestic violence
- Loss of a parent
- Emotional neglect
- Physical neglect

Subsequent studies (e.g., Cronholm et al., 2015; Merritt et al., 2013) have expanded the list of ACEs children may experience to include neighborhood safety levels, living in foster care, bullying, community violence, and racism (see Figure 1). Adding in these new ACE characteristics, the percentage of adult study participants experiencing at least one ACE rose from 69.9% (Felitti et al., 1998) to 83.2% (Merritt et al., 2013). The more ACEs a child experiences, the more at risk they are for poor academic achievement and negative outcomes throughout life (Dhaliwal, 2015; see Figure 2), but there are interventions that can buffer these traumas and support children so that they are less likely to experience these negative long-term outcomes including future incarceration. Children (or adults) who have experienced zero ACEs are at low risk for potential negative outcomes, those who have experienced one to three are at intermediate risk (high risk if the individual also has an associated health condition), and those who have experienced four or more ACEs (regardless of health status) are considered to be at high risk for negative outcomes (Iniguez & Stankowski, 2016). Like trauma, ACEs can follow intergenerational patterns

(Widom & Maxfield, 2001) and affect us physiologically which can impair children's development and affect positive outcomes across a variety of measures.

Figure 1. Types of ACEs (Created based on Cronholm et al., 2015 by the National Human Trafficking Training and Technical Assistance Center)
Source: National Human Trafficking Training and Technical Assistance Center, n.d.

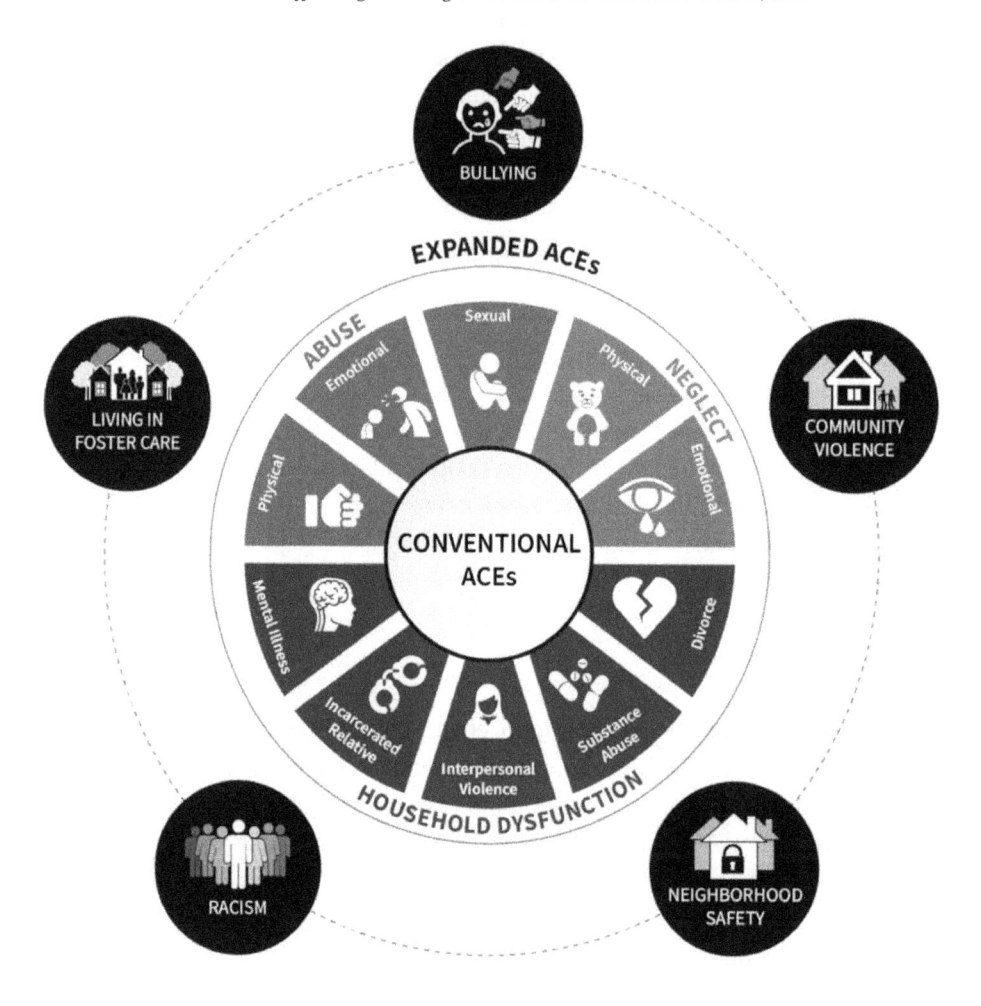

Figure 2. Initial Conceptualization of ACE Effects (Adapted from the CDC by The RYSE Center)
Source: Dhaliwal, 2015

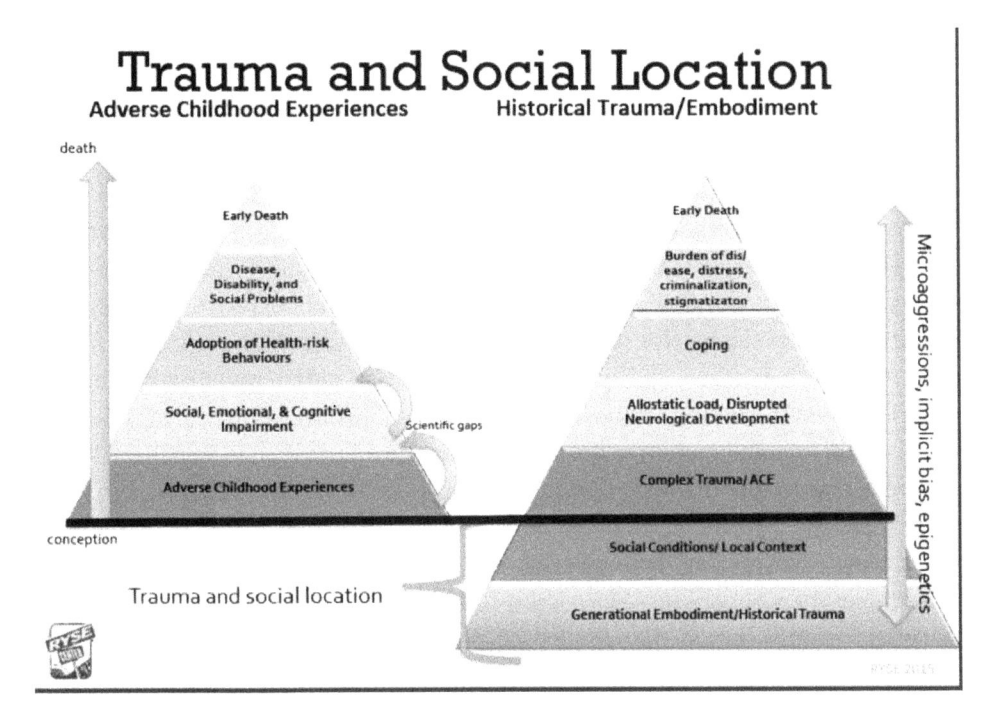

IMPACTS OF STRESS AND TRAUMA ON YOUNG LEARNERS

We all experience stress periodically, and sometimes a small amount of stress can actually make us focus more and perform better (e.g., stress before an exam or presentation). Think back to the example of the pregnant victim of intimate partner domestic violence shared earlier to explain how trauma may be heritable as you think about this stress hormone response. Our bodies have an endocrine response that triggers our fight/flight/freeze/fawn reactions by releasing stress hormones like cortisol and adrenaline designed to trigger responses in our bodies to enable us to survive in the face of a threat (Harvard Health, 2020). *Toxic stress*, however, is when a body experiences a long-term, ongoing physiological stress response such that a person stays in a chronic state of fight/flight/freeze/fawn thus creating wear and tear on our physical, emotional, and cognitive health. In times of normal stress, our bodies release hormones to deescalate our endocrine response and return to a resting state, but in cases of chronic, toxic stress, our bodies remain on high alert. Children experiencing (or adults who have experienced) ACEs and systemic trauma who do not have supportive adults buffering these stressors can experience stress that is chronic and toxic (Center on the Developing Child at Harvard University, 2020). It is this constant state of being at DEFCON 1 (the highest state of Defense Ready Condition) that eventually causes long term wear and tear on the body which leads to later health and wellness concerns (Center on the Developing Child at Harvard University, 2020; Franke, 2014). As with educational and incarceration disparities and ACEs, chronic toxic stress levels are influenced by systemic racism (Shonkoff et al., 2021).

We need not wait until adulthood to see the impacts of systemic trauma on children. The typical developmental trajectory for children from infancy on moves from survival → regulation → social-emotional → cognitive with the most amount of mental energy and bandwidth dedicated to social-emotional and cognitive development. Children who have experienced trauma impacting their development tend to follow the same pattern, but the majority of their mental energy and bandwidth are dedicated to survival and regulation (Agorastos et al., 2019). This necessarily means that the social-emotional and cognitive domains of their development are impaired. When children come to school, this type of trauma-influenced development presents itself in multiple ways including poor social-emotional behaviors, negative approaches to learning, a lack of foundational academic knowledge, and inabilities to meet the expectations of school (Allee-Herndon & Roberts, 2019, 2021). Without significant and effective intervention, the gaps that are already present among children who have experienced or are experiencing trauma and those who have not experienced as much adversity at kindergarten entry continues to widen throughout their K-12 experience (Allee-Herndon et al., 2022). Classroom culture and practices can serve to either mitigate or perpetuate the traumas many of our students have already experienced.

CLASSROOM IMPACTS ON TRAUMA

As discussed above, children can experience trauma of all sorts (i.e., high magnitude stressors, acute stress, traumatic stressors, systemic trauma, and potentially inherited trauma) which can stem from, and be compounded by, adverse childhood experiences and toxic stress. Almost half of American children (45%) have experienced at least one ACE, a statistic that has remained fairly consistent for over a decade, and 10% have experienced three or more ACEs (Bellazaire, 2018; Sacks, 2021). As schools grow increasingly diverse (de Brey et al., 2019; National Center for Education Statistics, 2022), with the understanding that trauma and ACEs disproportionately affect children of Color (National Conference on State Legislatures, 2021), educators and educational researchers must consider how schools can compound children's trauma.

Schools Further Inflict Stress and Trauma

While schools are spaces where students are meant to thrive and receive support from educators, they are often places that, intentionally or unwittingly, inflict further stress and trauma. Students who are already grappling with external-to-school causes of trauma, specifically ACEs, find themselves at odds in school and classroom settings that are misaligned with their needs. There are various disconnects between the culture of academia and the culture of the students it is meant to serve. The "culture of power" and its effects are part of nearly every institution in the United States, including the institution of schooling (Delpit, 1988). Issues of power are enacted in classrooms and there are codes or rules for participating in power. Scholars like David Stovall argue that our schools, in many ways, train children for incarceration using this culture of power (2018).

Classrooms and schools reflect the rules of the culture of those who have power. While some teachers never outwardly state their "power" and control in the classroom, this often manifests itself in the list of classroom rules themselves that some teachers present to their students during the first weeks of school. Sometimes rules are presented as finite and punitive and are often constructed without student input. While not overtly expressed, this presentation of preset rules often shows students that the teacher is meant to have overall power in the classroom. Thus, traditional classrooms are structured to give the teacher the most power and therefore creates several cultural disconnects between teacher and learner. Students often experience cross-racial, cross-cultural, and cross-lingual disconnects that become present in the classroom.

The teaching force is working to become more diverse, but it still remains predominantly White and female (Goodman, 2001; Kerssen-Griep & Eifler, 2008; Sleeter, 2001; US Department of Education, 1997). With increased and growing diversity among student populations, cross-racial, cross-cultural, and cross-lingual disconnects become more evident in schools and individual classrooms. With increased diversity in schools and classrooms, educators will also be more likely to have students who have experienced disproportionately more trauma, ACEs, and stress. It is also important to note that the diversity of our student population will continue to increase over the next decade (Figure 3). Educators who persist with the types of instructional and disciplinary practices that emphasize the culture of power, promote systemic trauma, and exacerbate students' stress and marginalization instead of mitigating it will create situations where more children struggle in schools as a result of these disconnects, and examples are provided below.

Figure 3. Percentage distribution of student enrollment in public elementary and secondary schools, by race/ethnicity: Fall 2009, fall 2020, and fall 2030
Source: National Center for Education Statistics, 2022

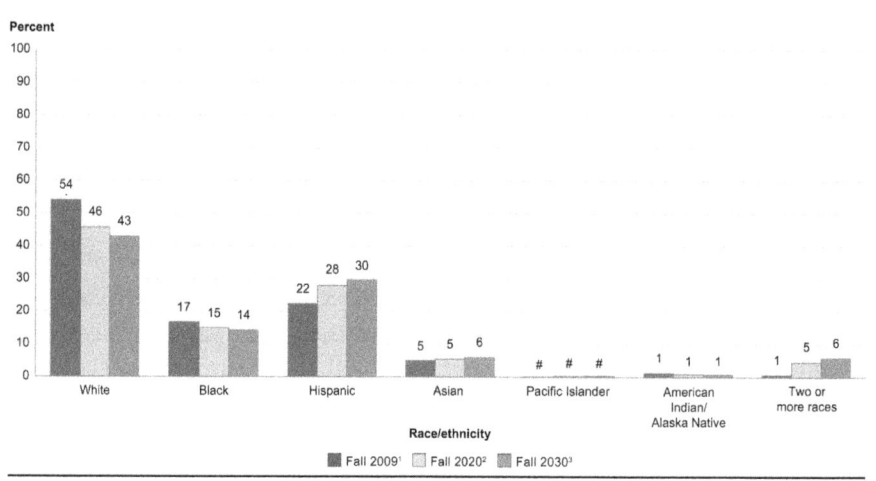

Rounds to zero.
[1] For fall 2009, data on students who were Pacific Islander and of Two or more races were reported by only a small number of states. Therefore, the data are not comparable to figures for later years.
[2] Includes imputations for nonreported enrollment for all grades in Illinois. Also includes imputations for nonreported prekindergarten enrollment in California and Oregon.
[3] Data for fall 2030 are projected.
NOTE: Data are for the 50 states and the District of Columbia. Race categories exclude persons of Hispanic ethnicity. Details may not sum to 100 percent because of rounding. Although rounded numbers are displayed, the figures are based on unrounded data.
SOURCE: U.S. Department of Education, National Center for Education Statistics, Common Core of Data (CCD), "State Nonfiscal Survey of Public Elementary and Secondary Education," 2009–10 and 2020–21; and National Elementary and Secondary Enrollment by Race/Ethnicity Projection Model, through 2030. See *Digest of Education Statistics 2021*, table 203.50.

Cross-Racial Disconnects

The continued increase in students' racial and ethnic diversity in public schools as predicted by the National Center for Educational Statistics (NCES) illustrates the importance of teachers understanding how cross-racial disconnects impact the relationships they build with their students, the interactions that occur in and out of the classroom, and ways they may inadvertently be inflicting more trauma and stress on their students through their "rules" and power structures in the classroom. A study by Downey and Pribesh (2004) explores the theory that White teachers often give harsher consequences to Black students because White teachers misinterpret aspects of their Black students' behavior. Through the implementation of punitive measures based on cultural behaviors, the wedge between teacher and student is driven deeper. Students begin to question their own known behavior and the place it has in the classroom, ultimately questioning their own place in the classroom.

Cross-Cultural (and -Lingual) Disconnects

Cross-cultural and cross-lingual disconnects occur when the culture of the teacher and classroom do not correspond with the culture of the students. In Jacqueline Jordan Irvine's text *In Search of Wholeness: African American Teachers and Their Culturally Specific Classroom Practices,* she states that

when teachers and students are out of sync, they clash and confront each other, both consciously and unconsciously, in matters concerning proxemics (use of interpersonal distance), paralanguage (behaviors accompanying speech, such as voice tone and pitch... rate and length), and coverbal behavior (gesture, facial expression, and eye gaze) (Irvine, 2002, p. xix).

These disconnects create many unintended barriers between the teacher and students. These barriers can be physical, perceptual, emotional, cultural, gendered, interpersonal, and even linguistic.

Cross-Lingual Disconnects

Cross-lingual disconnects can occur when the teacher and student speak a different native language. Continued correction of student language can inflict further trauma and stress on students, even when the teacher feels they are aiding students' linguistic development. Linguistic barriers can create silence-prompted trauma when there is no shared vocabulary for communication between teacher and student, outside of Standard English which is the language of power (Irvine, 2002). Students often then choose to be silent in the classroom as a result. Educators may mistake this silence for defiance or dissonance, when most likely the student has just come to the realization that they do not share the power in the classroom and do not feel the need (or ability) to participate. Additionally, some students may choose silence in the classroom as an emotional response when they experience trauma outside of the school setting. Teachers who send students messages to "leave what happened at the door" are showing students that their experiences and feelings are not validated in the classroom. Students may then not see the classroom as a space where they feel safe.

Microaggressions

Microaggressions can be another source of trauma for students in the classroom. "Microaggressions are the subtle, everyday verbal and nonverbal slights, snubs, or insults which communicate hostile, derogatory, or negative messages" to students (Hammond, 2015, p.47). Educators and other students may sometimes unconsciously send messages that invalidate another student's identity or even trivialize their experiences. These comments often create unsafe and threatening environments for students, thus adding to trauma experiences within the school environment. Examples of microaggressions that can occur (almost daily) in the classroom are

- Continued mispronunciation of a student's name
- Setting low expectations for students from particular racial or cultural backgrounds
- Providing narrow representation of ethnic and racial groups
- Using othering language

Often microaggressions are not intentionally harmful, and their use may go unnoticed or unaddressed by "well-intentioned" teachers. With more resources available focused on anti-bias/anti-racist teaching strategies, teachers – a majority of whom are White – believe they are being more inclusive with their classroom practices and instruction. Due to the culture of power still present in classrooms, these inclusive practices can still be shrouded in White privilege and be disenfranchising to students of color (Miller & Harris, 2018). Teachers still need to examine their implicit beliefs and attitudes when rigorously and persistently reflecting on the racial, cultural, and linguistic disconnects in their classrooms to better support students, especially those already "at-risk" because of prior trauma, ACEs, and the experience of toxic stress. If we truly believe all children are capable of succeeding at school, but the persistent and predictable achievement and behavioral gaps exist, we must interrogate the ways the systemic structure of schooling perpetuates these inequities and challenge our assumptions about children's abilities, effort, and behaviors.

TRAUMA'S IMPACT ON BEHAVIOR IN THE CLASSROOM

The stress and trauma that students experience outside of school does not vanish as they enter the classroom. Students often "bring" those experiences and memories of traumatic interactions with them as they interact with educators and classmates. Educators should understand the role that trauma plays on their students' learning and behavior by becoming familiar with some neuroscience basics. While nothing about neuroscience is basic per se, it does help to appreciate just how past experiences can shape interactions in and outside of the classroom, as well as to understand how students may react to these exchanges.

All brains come with a default setting that acts as its prime directive regardless of race, class, language, or culture: Avoid threats to safety at all costs and seek well-being at every opportunity (Hammond, 2015). Students from marginalized communities already have their safety-threat detection cued to be on alert for social and physiological threats based on past traumatic experiences, either individual, familial, systemic, and/or compounded, both in and out of the classroom. Educators can pay careful attention to the limbic region, or emotional portion of the brain, and its primary roles to help individuals learn from their experiences, manage their emotions, and remember events (Hammond, 2015). This portion of the brain also records memories of experiences and behaviors that produced positive and negative results in the past.

When working with school-aged children a large portion of these positive and negative experiences may be tied to occurrences in the classroom, with teachers, and with fellow classmates. The amygdala is a part of the limbic region. In Zaretta Hammond's book *Culturally Responsive Teaching and the Brain* (2015) she refers to the amygdala as the brain's "guard dog," and explains that students can experience an *amygdala hijack* when the brain senses a hint of distress. This distress could send students into a flight/fight/freeze/fawn response (McInerney & McKlindon, 2014). To most educators one of these responses may appear as disrespect or defiance, but in actuality it is the brain's natural response to the traumatic trigger. In other words, the child's brain automatically signals to their bodies that they need to prepare to defend themselves to survive. This reaction can be more successfully mediated when children have stronger self-regulation skills, adults who support them and teach them stress response strategies, and feel a sense of belonging. When children have experienced compounded trauma, however, they are less prepared to respond "appropriately." It becomes imperative, then, to understand how to build positive social relationships that signal to the brain a sense of physical, psychological, and social safety so that learning is possible.

The behaviors children may exhibit while in the stress response state discussed above are commonly misinterpreted as deliberate misbehavior or willful defiance requiring correction when displayed in the classroom. Well-intentioned, "nice" teachers who may just want to ensure proper classroom behavior should take a moment to reflect and reassess the situation. Is the behavior a flagrant disobedience of the classroom rules and structure? Or is there an underlying contributor to the student's response? As previously discussed, disconnects in the classroom, whether racial, cultural, and lingual, and microaggressions may create stress for a student, therefore leading that student to a stress response (Frothingham, 2021; Imad, 2022; Todd, 2021). Establishing social and emotional safety in the classroom, focusing on positive reinforcement when it comes to a behavior plan, and increasing one's own self-awareness and trauma competency can aid teacher's in re-evaluating their own understanding of outright defiance or displays of stress and trauma responses (Responding to trauma in your classroom, 2016). As an added bonus, becoming more understanding and supportive of students can help buffer and mitigate the negative effects of trauma.

Fight and flight are two of the possible behavioral responses to trauma and stress in the classroom can be more visual and easier to identify by classroom teachers. When a student goes into the *fight* response, they may yell, scream, appear defiant or oppositional, and they may seem aggressive. Students may also get physical and hit or kick in a fight response. Understanding an individual student's circumstances can aid teachers in understanding how a stress-based trauma response may be at the root of this behavior. Doing so can also affirm students' identity and cultivate empathy (Responding to trauma in your classroom, 2016). Conversely, a student may also exhibit a *flight* response. This may cause the student to physically leave the classroom, emotionally or mentally leave by becoming preoccupied with everything but the required task, move away from what they feel the threat is, or appear anxious or panicked (Frothingham, 2021; Todd, 2021).

The freeze and fawn, or appease, responses to trauma and stress may not be as easily recognizable as the first two, and sometimes go unnoticed by classroom teachers (Frothingham, 2021; Hammond, 2015). When a student exhibits the *freeze* response, they may isolate themselves or shut down. They may appear zoned out or have difficulty completing tasks. A teacher may view this as a student who is being apathetic or is disinterested, but this response is just as important to note as any physical response such as fight or flight. Lastly, a student could resort to a *fawn* response. This is typically used to avoid conflict and is seen as people-pleasing or appeasing. The student may be more concerned with just making the teacher or another student happy than about their own work or wellbeing (Frothingham, 2021). Just as with the freeze response, it is just as important to be aware of this less visually obvious response. Children exhibiting these responses can easily "fly under the radar" of a teacher's attention.

These trauma responses affect how students interact with peers and teachers in the classroom (McInerney & McKlindon, 2014) and impact their ability to focus and learn (Hammond, 2015). When a student has an "amygdala hijack" (Hammond, 2015, p. 40) their ability to take in added information is blocked. Students who go into fight or flight cannot actively engage in content instruction and may even negatively impact the instruction of their peers. Some school behavior plans would have a student removed from the classroom if they were being a distraction (which reaffirms the school power dynamic and contributes to the school/prison nexus dynamic). This removal additionally impacts a student's ability to learn by removing opportunities to learn and engage with academic content. While students who go into freeze or fawn may not always appear to be off task for distracted, they too could find it difficult to focus and comprehend parts of a lesson. "Learning isn't a passive event but a dynamic action" (Hammond, 2015, p. 48). Students need to be engaged in learning and not pulled from that learning by a trauma response, either emotionally and cognitively or physically through stringent exclusionary discipline policies. Creating relationships, communities of trust, and safe spaces in classrooms is imperative to the success and learning of students who have experienced trauma.

SOLUTIONS AND RECOMMENDATIONS

Teachers are often inundated with numerous professional development experiences and trainings during the course of an academic year as well as during summer break. Trainings and book talks focused on trauma-informed classroom practices (as well as similar topics like restorative justice, social-emotional learning, ACEs, and social justice in education) are becoming increasingly prominent. This professional learning focus has become even more of a priority for school districts and building leaders as teachers and students are experiencing collectively traumatic events. In the past three years, we have faced a global pandemic, more school shootings, legislative attacks on educators and public schools, racial justice and police violence issues, and additional topics that directly impact students' lived experiences. Being intentional in the way teachers show up for their students can provide students with the support they need.

One way teachers can help students feel heard and seen is through the use of books in the classroom. Books can act as vessels for students to connect and express their feelings. They can be spaces where students can heal through stories similar to their own without sharing personal details about their own lives. It is also important to recognize that books can also create a space where students may feel a form of erasure in the classroom. Diversity in children's books is increasing, but it does not accurately represent our diverse population of classroom students. According to 2020 statistics collected by the Cooperative Children's Book Center, diverse characters are still fairly scarce among children's books (Godfrey, 2021). In a survey of 3,600 titles, only about 12% of characters were Black, 9% Asian, 6% Latinx, and 2.1% Pacific Islander. Representation of White characters was about 41%, and animals overshadowed the remaining ethnicities at 29% (CCBC Diversity Statistics, 2021). Teachers must critically analyze their own classroom libraries and use of texts in the classroom. Literature can be a powerful classroom tool to support students who have experienced trauma, but classroom teachers must make sure students are, in fact, seeing themselves in the texts they are reading.

Using Literacy to Support Learners Exposed to Compounded Trauma

Literacy instruction occurs daily in classrooms across the country. Stories can be a strong tool to engage students in personal reflection and create spaces where they feel "seen" and therefore send their brains a sense of physical, psychological, and social safety. There are a handful of specific strategies educators can build upon and add to that are centered both on meeting academic learning goals and on addressing systemic perpetrators of childhood trauma like racism, bias, poverty, immigration, etc. These strategies are: 1) the use of picture books to promote conversation, 2) extending the conversation through literature circles, 3) journaling to personalize the conversation, and 4) taking the conversation to a broader audience through publishing.

Use of Picture Books

Utilizing books and storytelling taps into some of the cultural archetypes connected to our students' backgrounds. It is through storytelling that we learn about other's experiences and make personal connections. These connections are vital to understanding who our students are and their life experiences. Children's picture books can provide students with snapshots of current and historical social issues (Botelho & Rudman, 2010; Mathis, 2020). Reading also builds social understanding in readers, improving their ability to empathize and sympathize with other's thoughts, feelings, and actions (Kozak & Recchia, 2019; Taylor et al., 2017). Picture books allow safe spaces for students to see characters who may experience things similar to them and grasp how the character responds to those experiences. Furthermore, books that focus on or highlight social issues can benefit students by creating space for critical dialogue and exchanging ideas, enabling children to unpack the roles of power in society and their own lives (Gopalakrishnan, 2010).

Picture books can be used to promote reflection and conversation in the classroom. Stories such as Recorvits' (2003) *My Name is Yoon* or Thompkins-Bigelow's (2020) *Your Name is a Song* can be used within a writing center to personalize a student's experience with hearing their name mispronounced. For example, students could write advice for the character or how they would react if they were in that situation. This task does not require them to outwardly share their own experience, to try to moderate further stress, but rather lets children express how they would put themselves in the character's shoes. Integrating stories with characters that represent the classroom diversity can help facilitate opportunities for book talks that shift away from Colorblindness or Color preference to an awareness of the impact of Color in the classroom.

Book talks can also be used to focus on advocacy and activism using books like Nagara's (2021) *A is for Activist* or Clark-Robinson's (2018) *Let the Children March*. Such books can inspire personal action plan posters, writing about inequality in personal journals, or making a class book on ways student can be activists in their own school or home communities.

Literature Circles

A source of trauma and stress for students can stem from racial inequality that they may be experiencing within their communities, as well as in their own school and classrooms. Using literature circles (Daniels, 2002; Peterson & Eeds, 1987/2007) can engage students in authentic conversations around such inequality. Similar to experiences possible with picture books above, students can choose to share personal connections to characters, or use the voice of the character as a safe way to discuss their own lived experiences. Even without outwardly sharing, students can individually reflect on a character's experiences and how they handled adversity.

Understanding classroom power dynamics was previously mentioned as a possible source of stress and trauma for students (Delpit, 1988). Literature circles can be a way to return some of that power to the students by providing them both voice and choice (Daniels, 2002). Children are able to choose their own book (with adult guidance), hold one another accountable for literature circle meetings, and complete student-led projects that focus on the theme of the book. Books like Tonatiuh's (2014) *Separate is Never Equal* focus on inequality, discrimination, and privilege. Alexander's (2014) *The Crossover* and Booth's (2015) *Kinda Like Brothers* are coming-of-age stories that address issues of power and friendship among people of Color, dealing with death in the family, and navigating the foster care system. Both stories feature Black male main characters through compelling stories with positive, feel-good endings. The stories can be relatable for students and show strong, positive characters when similar characters are often written in a more negative, stereotypical light. As with the strategies for utilizing picture books above, students can engage in conversation around their literature circles books or write personal responses through journaling.

Journaling

Journaling has long been recognized as an effective, authentic literacy learning strategy that supports differentiated learning (e.g., Adams & Pierce, 2006; Gilbert & Graham, 2010; Hayes et al., 1998; Tompkins, 2022). Teachers can facilitate writing opportunities for different purposes and for different content areas. Students can use a variety of journaling strategies depending on the learning or affective goals. Reflective journaling, daily journaling, question journaling, concept journaling, private journaling, and dialogue journaling are some examples of the types of journal writing experiences students may engage in at school. Through journaling, students can voluntarily record their own experiences without the threat of having to share with others in private journals, engage in recursive dialogue with the teacher, and reflecting on thought-provoking writing prompts provides a space for students to grapple with potentially challenging themes of equity, advocacy, inequality, and sociopolitical issues. Even early elementary children are aware of these issues, affected by current events, and are capable of facing challenging issues (Kaczmarczyk et al., 2018), and journal prompts can be a logical extension of the reading strategies above.

Just as the available resources to identify diverse, inclusive, and thought-provoking children's literature, teachers have writing resources available to them, also. While teachers must be discerning about the quality and purpose of writing prompts, as well as the instructional and developmental appropriateness of the prompts, print and online resources can help teachers find or develop journal prompts that stretch children to think more deeply about a focus topic. Below are some sample prompts from *1200 Creative Writing Prompts* (Donovan, 2014) and *Over 1,000 Writing Prompts for Students* (Gonchar, 2021).

- Donovan, 2014
  - Use all of the following words in a poem: humanity, hunger, equality, power, greed, redemption, freedom.
  - If you could change one thing in the world, what would you change and why?
  - Think of a major worldwide problem: for example, hunger, climate change, or political corruption. Write an article outlining a solution (or steps toward a solution).
  - Write a poem about disenfranchised or marginalized people.
- Gonchar, 2021
  - What are you really learning at school?
  - What do you think of grouping students by ability in schools?
  - How do you define 'family'?
  - What's the story behind your name?
  - Have you ever changed your mind about a hot-button issue?

These particular prompts are more appropriate for middle grades or intermediate elementary students, but they can be easily adapted to be more appropriate for younger children or simply provide a basis for teachers to generate their own ideas. Students' own lived experiences will often generate authentic opportunities to not just journal, but also to write for a broader audience.

Broadening the Conversation

Mark Hansen describes scenarios where through his 3rd grade students' shared personal experiences, he was able to push them "in a more editorial direction" (Hansen, 2020). For example, when students were angered that many parents had been detained by US Immigration and Customs Enforcement (ICE), the students wrote letters to the mayor and ICE and created a petition. His students turned their reactions and feelings about current events like the redevelopment of public housing, environmental disasters, and solving inter-personal problems into writing assignments for authentic audiences beyond the classroom. Robert Bahruth engaged in similar types of meaningful writing for various forms of "publication" including creating class books that could be checked out of the school library, letters to the editor of the local newspaper, and public service announcements for other students and the community (Hayes et al., 1998).

Research supports the ways these practitioners engaged their students in these authentic writing experiences with varied audiences (e.g., Foulger & Jimenez-Silva, 2007; Schwieter, 2010; Spanke & Paul, 2015; Zawilinski, 2016). Whether using a technology-based writing tool or more analog paper and pencil techniques, effective writing practices include providing "time and opportunity to write, a reason for writing, a genuine audience, access to role models, a safe environment, useful feedback, and [building] a sense of community" (Foulger & Jimenez-Silva, 2007). As an added bonus, the more teachers can establish and use these effective writing practices, the stronger the classroom community can be to support engaging in critical and transformative learning experiences and buffering work to mitigate trauma, toxic stress, and ACEs (Allee-Herndon et al., 2021; Kaczmarczyk et al., 2018). Writing exercises can also give voice to students who may be reluctant to speak otherwise because their trauma has marginalized them in the educational space.

Breaking the Silence

Students who are experiencing trauma can be retraumatized in school through poorly chosen readings, activities, and assignments (Alexander, 2019; Gorski, 2013). Literacy can provide a powerful tool in helping students break their silence-prompted trauma. Allowing opportunities for students to engage with authentic stories, seeing their own experiences through the eyes of another person/character, and using literacy strategies to engage with these stories can be a valuable way to tap into student voice. In addition to the strategies discussed above, teachers must heavily rely on visuals when working with students who have chosen silence. Just as teachers would use visuals with language learners, it is just as important to incorporate visuals with those who feel as though there is a cross-lingual disconnect. Students who don't speak Standard English often feel that their home language is inferior based on teacher comments (and microaggressions), thus building onto their trauma and stress in the classroom (Hollie, 2018).

Teachers should refrain from correcting a student's language or dialect if it deviates from Standard English. Just as with regular classroom instruction, modeling language use can help students recognize and acquire the preferred language of the classroom. As students are thoughtfully exposed to academic language, teachers can validate students and build their available language reserves (Hollie, 2018). In addition to the silence, the trauma responses of freeze and fawn also create moments where students may seem disinterested or minimally focused (Frothingham, 2021; Todd, 2021). Creating opportunities for students to engage non-verbally can help scaffold students and allow them to engage and have a sense of voice. For example, teachers can create physical or digital "parking lot" spaces where students can place sticky notes with questions/concerns throughout the day. This can be a vehicle for students to demonstrate understanding, request clarification, or generate ideas. Lastly, teachers must take the time and effort to learn student names. Names are a part of one's identity, and the effort to pronounce and spell names correctly is an act of caring. Mispronouncing or assigning arbitrary nicknames can erode the rapport-building process (*Responding to trauma in your classroom*, 2016; Todd, 2021). Learning and using students' correct names further affirms who they are and models respect in the classroom.

FUTURE RESEARCH DIRECTIONS

The focus of trauma-informed literacy instruction is both on social justice in education and improving learning experiences and outcomes for historically marginalized students who have experienced systemic or compounded trauma. While ACEs, *trauma-informed education*, social justice work in schools, and anti-bias/anti-racist work is growing in focus and popularity in education spaces, more work needs to be done. A 2020 bibliometric analysis of multiple school psychology journals (Graves et al.) actually identified an uncommon *practice to research* gap. Typically, educational researchers struggle to close the *research to practice gap* by making our findings more accessible to practitioners, but in this case the authors found

that practice is tackling topics (e.g., White privilege and school-to-prison pipeline) that are not present in the social justice research literature. [Their] implications... encourage proponents of social justice to begin to expand their research beyond definition rhetoric to include outcomes associated with [application]. (Graves et al., 2020, p. 358).

The body of research on the school-to-prison nexus, trauma-informed education, ACEs, and other equity-focused topics is growing with some topics more longstanding (e.g., school-to-prison nexus and ACEs) than others (e.g., trauma-informed education). The more comprehensively we study these issues, the more starkly the impact of systemic trauma on historically marginalized students is evident. What is less parsed out, however, is the research on the effectiveness of the application of instructional strategies intended to mitigate negative effects on children. Differentiated approaches that support social-emotional learning, self-regulation, and executive function development are purported to help (e.g., Allee-Herndon & Roberts, 2019; Hulvershorn & Mulholland, 2018; Parker & Hodgson, 2020), but there are also studies warning against misapplying the research in ways that harm students (e.g., Bath, 2017; Winninghoff, 2020). Additionally, the current literacy instructional climate is hyper-assessment-focused at the expense of centering trauma-sensitive instructional strategies (e.g., Allee-Herndon, Roberts, et al., 2021). For our efforts to support students and dismantle systems of oppression, trauma, and marginalization in our schools, we must carefully guard against "programatizing" or "commercializing" strategies meant to mitigate or buffer but which simply maintain the systems.

CONCLUSION

Educators must learn how to recognize constraints constructed by privileges associated with power created by the culture of academia. They must create spaces where students have the safety to explore and take risks with their learning and share in the power of the classroom creating democratic spaces. Building meaningful relationships with students and creating classroom cultures that prioritize student voices shows students that they are in a welcoming environment, therefore easing the brain's safety-threat detection and avoiding an amygdala hijack. This work can begin through the work of literacy instruction and allowing students to see their stories told in text. As teachers, it is critical we allow introspection and reflection to create the spaces where students feel safe, even if just in the classroom. Lastly, educators must be willing to seek out additional learning and support from mentors in the field and within the work of trauma-informed teaching. It is impossible to do the rigorous, messy work of social justice teaching without the benefit of the experience of others.

ACKNOWLEDGEMENTS

We would like to thank Dr. Wynnetta Scott-Simmons, Professor Emerita at Mercer University, for her thought contributions that provided the foundation for much of our thinking for this chapter, particularly the Breaking the Silence section.

This research received no specific grant from any funding agency in the public, commercial, or not-for-profit sectors.

REFERENCES

Adams, C. M., & Pierce, R. L. (2006). *Differentiating instruction: A practical guide to tiered lessons in the elementary grades.* Prufrock Press.

Agorastos, A., Pervanidou, P., Chrousos, G. P., & Baker, D. G. (2019). Developmental trajectories of early life stress and trauma: A narrative review on neurobiological aspects beyond stress system dysregulation. *Frontiers in Psychiatry, 10*, 118. doi:10.3389/fpsyt.2019.00118 PMID:30914979

Alexander, J. (2019). *Building trauma-sensitive schools: Your guide to create, safe, supportive learning environments for all students.* Brookes Publishing.

Alexander, K. (2014). *The crossover* (D. Anyabwile, Illus.). Clarion Books.

Allee-Herndon, K. A., Kaczmarczyk, A. B., & Buchanan, R. (2021). Is it "just" planning? Exploring the integration of social justice education in an elementary language arts methods course thematic unit. *Journal for Multicultural Education, 15*(1), 103–116. doi:10.1108/JME-07-2020-0071

Allee-Herndon, K. A., & Roberts, S. K. (2019). Poverty, self-regulation and executive function, and learning in K-2 classrooms: A systematic literature review of current empirical research. *Journal of Research in Childhood Education, 33*(3), 345–362. doi:10.1080/02568543.2019.1613273

Allee-Herndon, K. A., & Roberts, S. K. (2021). The power of purposeful play in primary grades: Adjusting pedagogy for children's needs and academic gains. *Journal of Education, 201*(1), 54–63. doi:10.1177/0022057420903272

Allee-Herndon, K. A., Roberts, S. K., Hu, B. Y., Clark, M. H., & Stewart, M. L. (2022). Let's talk play! Exploring the possible benefits of play-based pedagogy on language and literacy learning in Title I kindergarten classrooms. *Early Childhood Education Journal, 50*(1), 119–132. doi:10.100710643-020-01141-6

Bath, H. (2017). The trouble with trauma. *Scottish Journal of Residential Child Care, 16*(1), 1–12. https://www.traumebevisst.no/program/etgodthjem/filer/Bath_H_The_Trouble_with_Trauma.pdf

Bellazaire, A. (2018, August). *Preventing and mitigating the effects of adverse childhood experiences.* National Conference of State Legislatures. https://www.ncsl.org/Portals/1/HTML_LargeReports/ACEs_2018_3 2691.pdf

Booth, C. (2015). *Kinda like brothers.* Scholastic.

Botelho, M., & Rudman, M. (2010). *Critical multicultural analysis of children's literature: Mirrors, windows, and doors*. Routledge.

Braveman, P., & Gottlieb, L. (2014). The social determinants of health: It's time to consider the causes of the causes. *Public Health Reports*, *129*(1, suppl2), 19–31. doi:10.1177/00333549141291S206 PMID:24385661

Center on the Developing Child at Harvard University. (2020, October 30). *What are ACEs? And how do they relate to toxic stress?* Harvard University Press.https://developingchild.harvard.edu/resources/aces-and-toxic-stress-frequently-asked-questions/

Centers for Disease Control and Prevention. (n.d.). *Social determinants of health*. Social Determinants of Health. https://www.cdc.gov/publichealthgateway/sdoh/index.html

Clark-Robinson, M. (2018). *Let the children march* (F. Morrison, Illus.). HMH Books for Young Readers.

Cooperative Children's Book Center. (2021). *CCBC Diversity Statistics*. Cooperative Children's Book Center. https://ccbc.education.wisc.edu/

Cronholm, P. F., Forke, C. M., Wade, R., Bair-Merritt, M. H., Davis, M., Harkins-Schwarz, M., Pachter, L. M., & Fein, J. A. (2015). Adverse childhood experiences: Expanding the concept of adversity. *American Journal of Preventive Medicine*, *49*(3), 354–361. doi:10.1016/j.amepre.2015.02.001 PMID:26296440

Dalenberg, C. J., Straus, E., & Carlson, E. B. (2017). Defining trauma. In S. N. Gold (Ed.), *APA handbook of trauma psychology: Foundations in knowledge* (pp. 15–33). American Psychological Association., doi:10.1037/0000019-002

Daniels, H. (2002). *Literature circles: Voice and choice in book clubs and reading groups*. Stenhouse.

de Brey, C., Musu, L., McFarland, J., Wilkinson-Flicker, S., Diliberti, M., Zhang, A., Branstetter, C., & Wang, X. (2019, February). *Status and trends in the education of racial and ethnic groups 2018* (NCES 2019–038). National Center for Education Statistics and American Institutes for Research. https://nces.ed.gov/pubs2019/2019038.pdf

Delpit, L. (1988). The silenced dialogue: Power and pedagogy in education other people's children. *Harvard Educational Review*, *53*(3), 280–298. doi:10.17763/haer.58.3.c43481778r528qw4

Dhaliwal, K. (2015). *Initial Conceptualization of ACE Effects*. RYSE Center Richmond. [Online image]. http://www.acesconnection.com/blog/adding-layers-to-the-aces-pyramid-what-do-you-think

Donovan, M. (2014). *1200 creative writing prompts (Adventures in writing)*. Swan Hatch Press.

Downey, D., & Pribesh, S. (2004). When race matters: Teachers' evaluations of students' classroom behavior. *Sociology of Education, 77*(4), 267–282. doi:10.1177/003804070407700401

Felitti, V. J., Anda, R. F., Nordenberg, D., Williamson, D. F., Spitz, A. M., Edwards, V., Koss, M. P., & Marks, J. S. (1998). Relationship of childhood abuse and household dysfunction to many of the leading causes of death in adults: The Adverse Childhood Experience (ACE) study. *American Journal of Preventive Medicine, 14*(4), 245–258. doi:10.1016/S0749-3797(98)00017-8 PMID:9635069

Foulger, T. S., & Jimenez-Silva, M. (2007). Enhancing the writing development of English language learners: Teacher perceptions of common technology in project-based learning. *Journal of Research in Childhood Education, 22*(2), 109–124. doi:10.1080/02568540709594616

Franke, H. (2014). Toxic stress: Effects, prevention and treatment. *Children (Basel, Switzerland), 1*(3), 390–402. doi:10.3390/children1030390 PMID:27417486

Frothingham, M. (2021). Fight, flight, freeze, or fawn: What this response means. *Simply Psychology*. www.simplypsychology.org/fight-flight-freeze-fawn.html

Gilbert, J., & Graham, S. (2010). Teaching writing to elementary students in grades 4–6: A national survey. *The Elementary School Journal, 110*(4), 494–518. doi:10.1086/651193

Godfrey, M. (2021). *Diversity in children's books from 2012 to 2020*. Jambo Books Blog. https://blog.jambobooks.com/diversity-in-childrens-books-from-2012-to-2020/

Goldsmith, R. E., Martin, C. G., & Smith, C. P. (2014). Systemic trauma. *Journal of Trauma & Dissociation, 15*(2), 117–132. doi:10.1080/15299732.2014.871666 PMID:24617751

Gonchar, M. (2021, October 14). Over 1,000 writing prompts for students. *The New York Times*. https://www.nytimes.com/2018/04/12/learning/over-1000-writing-prompts-for-students.html

Goodman, W. (2001). Living (and teaching) in an unjust world. In W. Goodman (Ed.), *Living and teaching in an unjust world: New perspectives on multicultural education* (pp. 1–25). Heinemann.

Gopalakrishnan, A. (2010). Multicultural children's literature: A critical issues approach. *Sage (Atlanta, Ga.)*.

Gorski, P. (2013). *Reaching and teaching students in poverty: Strategies for erasing the opportunity gap*. Teachers College Press.

Graves, S. L. Jr, Phillips, S., Johnson, K., Jones, M. A. Jr, & Thornton, D. (2020). Pseudoscience, an emerging field, or just a framework without outcomes? A bibliometric analysis and case study presentation of social justice research. *Contemporary School Psychology, 25*(3), 358–366. doi:10.100740688-020-00310-z

Hammond, Z. (2015). *Culturally responsive teaching and the brain: Promoting authentic engagement and rigor among culturally and linguistically diverse students*. Corwin.

Hansen, M. (2020, August 25). *Writing for justice*. Rethinking Schools. https://rethinkingschools.org/articles/writing-for-justice-persuasion-from-the-inside-out/

Harvard Health. (2020, July 6). *Understanding the stress response*. Harvard University Press. https://www.health.harvard.edu/staying-healthy/understanding-the-stress-response

Hayes, C., Bahruth, R., & Kessler, C. (1998). *Literacy con cariño: A story of migrant children's success* (9.8.1998 ed.). Heinemann.

Heitzeg, N. A. (2009). Education or incarceration: Zero tolerance policies and the school to prison pipeline. *Forum on Public Policy Online, 2009*(2), 1-21. https://eric.ed.gov/?id=EJ870076

Hollie, S. (2018). *Culturally and linguistically responsive teaching and learning* (2nd ed.). Shell Education.

Hulvershorn, K., & Mulholland, S. (2018). Restorative practices and the integration of social emotional learning as a path to positive school climates. *Journal of Research in Innovative Teaching &amp. Learning, 11*(1), 110–123. doi:10.1108/JRIT-08-2017-0015

Hurley, B. (2021, December 15). *Adverse childhood events more common among adults in prison.* Interrogating Justice. https://interrogatingjustice.org/ending-mass-incarceration/adverse-childhood-events-more-common-among-adults-in-prison/

Imad, M. (2022). Trauma-informed education for wholeness: Strategies for faculty & advisors. *New Directions for Student Services, 2022*(177), 39–47. doi:10.1002s.20413

Iniguez, K. C., & Stankowski, R. V. (2016). Adverse childhood experiences and health in adulthood in a rural population-based sample. *Clinical Medicine & Research, 14*(3-4), 126–137. doi:10.3121/cmr.2016.1306 PMID:27503793

Irvine, J. (2002). The common experience, In J. Irvine (Ed.), In search of wholeness: African American teachers and their culturally specific classroom practices (p.1-8). Palgrave Macmillan.

Kaczmarczyk, A., Allee-Herndon, K. A., & Roberts, S. K. (2018). Using literacy approaches to begin the conversation on racial illiteracy. *The Reading Teacher, 72*(4), 523–528. doi:10.1002/trtr.1757

Kerssen-Griep, J., & Eifler, K. (2008). When cross-racial contact transforms intercultural communication competence: White novice teachers learn alongside their African American high school mentees. *Journal of Transformative Education, 6*(4), 251–269. doi:10.1177/1541344608330125

Kozak, S., & Recchia, H. (2019). Reading and the development of social understanding: Implications for the literacy classroom. *The Reading Teacher, 72*(5), 569–577. doi:10.1002/trtr.1760

Learning for Justice. (2016). *Responding to trauma in your classroom.* Learning for Justice. https://www.learningforjustice.org/magazine/spring-2016/responding-to-trauma-in-your-classroom

Mathis, J. (2020). Global picture books to provide critical perspectives. *English Journal, 109*(5), 102–104.

McInerney, M., & McKlindon, A. (2014). Unlocking the door to learning: Trauma-informed classrooms & transformational schools. *Education law center*, 1-24.

Merritt, M. B., Cronholm, P., Davis, M., Dempsey, S., Fein, J., Kuykendall, S. A., & Wade, R. (2013). *Findings from the Philadelphia Urban ACE Survey.* Institute for Safe Families. https://www.rwjf.org/en/library/research/2013/09/findings-from-the-philadelphia-urban-ace-survey.html

Miller, L., & Harris, V. (2018). I can't be racist: I teach in an urban school, and I'm a nice white lady. *World Journal of Education, 8*(3). doi:10.5430/wje.v8n3p1

Nagara, I. (2016). *A is for activist*. Seven Stories Press.

National Center for Education Statistics. (2022). *Racial/ethnic enrollment in public schools*. NCES. https://nces.ed.gov/programs/coe/indicator/cge/racial-ethnic-enrollment

National Conference on State Legislatures. (2021, August 12). *Adverse childhood experiences*. NCSL. https://www.ncsl.org/research/health/adverse-childhood-experiences-aces.aspx

National Human Trafficking Training and Technical Assistance Center. (n.d.). *Adverse childhood experiences*. US Department of Health and Human Services. https://nhttac.acf.hhs.gov/soar/eguide/stop/adverse_childhood_experiences

National Human Trafficking Training and Technical Assistance Center. (n.d.). *Types of ACEs* [Online image]. US Department of Health and Human Services. https://nhttac.acf.hhs.gov/soar/eguide/stop/adverse_childhood_experiences

Parker, R., & Hodgson, D. (2020). "One size does not fit all": Engaging students who have experienced trauma. *Issues in Educational Research, 30*(1), 245–259. https://search.informit.org/doi/abs/10.3316/ielapa.086214776638143

Peterson, R., & Eeds, M. (1987/ 2007). *Grand conversations: Literature groups in action*. Scholastic.

Recorvits, H. (2003). My name is Yoon (G. Swiatkowska, Illus.). Macmillan.

RYSE. (2015). Trauma and social location [Online image]. RYSE. https://www.pacesconnection.com/fileSendAction/fcType/0/fcOid/416618476901050324/filePointer/425769210363174323/fodoid/425769210363174317/RYSEACEsDisorderDistressSocialLocation2015.pdf

Sacks, V. (2021, March 8). *The prevalence of adverse childhood experiences, nationally, by state, and by race or ethnicity*. Child Trends. https://www.childtrends.org/publications/prevalence-adverse-childhood-experiences-nationally-state-race-ethnicity

Schwieter, J. W. (2010). Developing second language writing through scaffolding in the ZPD: A magazine project for an authentic audience. *Journal of College Teaching and Learning, 7*(10), 31–46. doi:10.19030/tlc.v7i10.154

Shonkoff, J. P., Slopen, N., & Williams, D. R. (2021). Early childhood adversity, Toxic stress, and the impacts of racism on the foundations of health. *Annual Review of Public Health, 42*(1), 115–134. doi:10.1146/annurev-publhealth-090419-101940 PMID:33497247

Sleeter, C. E. (2001). Preparing teachers for culturally diverse schools: Research and the overwhelming presence of Whiteness. *Journal of Teacher Education, 52*(2), 94–106. doi:10.1177/0022487101052002002

Spanke, J., & Paul, K. A. (2015). From the pens of babes: Authentic audiences for talented, young writers. *Gifted Child Today, 38*(3), 177–186. doi:10.1177/1076217515583743

Stovall, D. (2018). Are we ready for 'school' abolition?: Thoughts and practices of radical imaginary in education. *Taboo: The Journal of Culture and Education, 17*(1), 6. doi:10.31390/taboo.17.1.06

Taylor, R., Oberle, E., Durlak, J., & Weissberg, R. (2017). Promoting positive youth development through schoolbased social and emotional learning interventions: A meta-analysis of follow-up effects. *Child Development, 88*(4), 1156–1171. doi:10.1111/cdev.12864 PMID:28685826

Thompkins-Bigelow, J. (2020). *Your name is a song* (L. Uribe, Illus.). The Innovation Press.

Todd, R. (2021). *Recognizing the signs of trauma*. Edutopia. https://www.edutopia.org/article/recognizing-signs-trauma#:~:text=Some%20classroom%20signs%20of%20trauma,%2C%20excessive%20crying%2C%20etc)

Tompkins, G. E. (2022). *Literacy for the 21st century: A balanced approach* (5th ed.). Pearson.

Tonatiuh, D. (2014). *Separate is never equal: Sylvia Mendez and her family's fight for desegregation*. Harry N. Abrams.

US Department of Education. (1997). *America's teachers: Profile of a profession, 1993-94*. National Center for Educational Statistics. https://nces.ed.gov/pubs97/97460.pdf

van der Kolk, B. A., Roth, S., Pelcovitz, D., Sunday, S., & Spinazzola, J. (2005). Disorders of extreme stress: The empirical foundation of a complex adaptation to trauma. *Journal of Traumatic Stress, 18*(5), 389–399. doi:10.1002/jts.20047 PMID:16281237

Wald, J., & Losen, D. J. (2003). Defining and redirecting a school-to-prison pipeline. *New Directions for Youth Development, 2003*(99), 9–15. doi:10.1002/yd.51 PMID:14635431

Widom, C. S., & Maxfield, M. G. (2001, February). *An update on the "Cycle of Violence"* (NCJ 184894). National Institute of Justice. https://www.ojp.gov/pdffiles1/nij/184894.pdf

Winninghoff, A. (2020). Trauma by numbers: Warnings against the use of ACE scores in trauma-informed schools. *Occasional Paper Series, 2020*(43), 4.

Yehuda, R., & Lehrner, A. (2018). Intergenerational transmission of trauma effects: Putative role of epigenetic mechanisms. *World Psychiatry; Official Journal of the World Psychiatric Association (WPA), 17*(3), 243–257. doi:10.1002/wps.20568 PMID:30192087

Zawilinski, L. M. (2016). Primary grade students create science eBooks on iPads: Authentic audiences, purposes and technologies for writing. *New England Reading Association Journal, 51*(2), 81.

KEY TERMS AND DEFINITIONS

Adverse Childhood Experiences: Events children experience that can act as high magnitude stressors, are cumulatively impactful, and have lifelong health and wellness outcome implications.

Children's Literature: For the purpose of this chapter, this is literature that includes picture books and some chapter books that can be effectively and appropriately used with elementary school-aged children to read for pleasure, to accomplish a specific learning goal, and/or to facilitate discourse on a particular subject.

Elementary Education: In the US, compulsory education begins at the elementary school level (although kindergarten is not required in many states), and elementary-aged students typically range from 4-11 years old depending on whether the school includes pre-kindergarten and/or 6th grade.

Epigenetics: The study of how traumatic events and the subsequently triggered behaviors in response to trauma can affect how bodies interpret genetic coding in DNA.

Historically Marginalized Students: Students, who by virtue of their race/ethnicity, gender, geographical location, language, learning status, sexual orientation, religion, physical/cognitive abilities, etc. have been pushed to the margins of the educational system and are therefore underserved or disadvantaged.

Inherited Trauma: Also frequently referred to as *transgenerational trauma* or *genetic trauma*, this is a growing theory that trauma can impact our behaviors and reactions and/or our DNA through epigenetics such that future generations are affected behaviorally, cognitively, or emotionally.

Instructional Strategies: Techniques teachers use to help students become more strategic, self-regulated learners where they can effectively select strategies to accomplish a particular learning goal or task.

School-to-Prison Nexus: The statistical tendency that children from "disadvantaged" backgrounds are more likely to become incarcerated as a result of increasingly harsh, punitive school and legal policies that disproportionately impact historically marginalized students.

Social Determinants: Environmental and social conditions in a person's living, learning, or working environment that affect health and wellness outcomes, either positively or negatively.

Social Justice (in Education): The equitable distribution of resources, interventions, and teaching/learning environments such that all children feel welcomed, safe, supported, and valued academically, socially, behaviorally, and physically. It also refers to instructional practices that specifically engage in critical and transformative work to disrupt social injustice.

Systemic Trauma: Trauma resulting from the systemic and maintained practices and procedures that cause direct or indirect harm to communities or specific groups of people in physical, psychological, emotional, economical, educational, and other ways.

Toxic Stress: The prolonged activation of the body's physiological stress response system, often stemming from chronic stress and the lack of a supportive caregiver buffering these experiences, that prohibits the body from recovering fully, which can cause long-term trauma responses.

Trauma: An emotional, cognitive, physiological, and/or behavioral response to a deeply distressing or disturbing event.

Trauma-Informed Education: An approach to education that attempts to understand, redress, and disrupt the academic, social, emotional, cognitive, and physical impacts of trauma and adversity on students.

Chapter 7
Practical Strategies for Higher Hope Learning Spaces:
Reducing Childhood Trauma in a Post-Pandemic Era

Belinda M. Alexander-Ashley
 https://orcid.org/0000-0002-9991-3971
Independent Researcher, USA

ABSTRACT

Childhood trauma was found to increase the risk of aggression and disruptive behavior in classrooms. The disruptive behavior risks exposure to the school-to-prison nexus, a result of inequities in zero tolerance and exclusionary policies. The coronavirus disease (COVID-19) pandemic disrupted the world's learning systems leaving in its wake feelings of anxiety, depression, fear, uncertainty, and hopelessness. This exacerbated the existing trauma experienced by students. Thousands of studies involving hope theory advanced to a science with predictable outcomes and progressively more benefits for dealing with childhood trauma. The eight recommended practical strategies for higher hope include acknowledging that hope takes work, understanding the tenets of hope theory, emphasizing a personal approach to student needs, protecting educators from vicarious trauma, listening more and talking less, developing ambassadors of hope, and creating partnerships of hope focused on positive experiences, effective communication, and resilience to reduce the effects of childhood trauma.

DOI: 10.4018/978-1-6684-5713-9.ch007

Copyright © 2023, IGI Global. Copying or distributing in print or electronic forms without written permission of IGI Global is prohibited.

INTRODUCTION

The coronavirus disease (COVID-19) pandemic created a massive disruption to the world's educational systems affecting nearly 1.6 billion learners and more than 190 countries (Chaturvedi et al., 2021). This highly infectious disease resulted in global contamination, elevated mortality rates, and widespread uncertainty about the future (Chaturvedi et al., 2021). In its aftermath, students, their families, and educators were left feeling anxious, depressed, scared, and overwhelmed. This exacerbated the existing trauma experienced by students and their teachers. While not caused by the pandemic, childhood trauma was found to increase the risk of violent and aggressive behavior in adulthood that often leads to criminality (Kalmuss, 1984; Straus et al., 1980; Widom, 1989). The rates of childhood and adult trauma are high among the incarcerated (Wolff & Shi, 2012), resulting in a need to reduce childhood trauma within the education system and disciplinary referrals that increase exposure to the school-to-prison pipeline or recently referred to as the school-to-prison nexus.

Racial disparities resulting from inequities in discipline and exclusionary policies in the education system have left poor and disadvantaged students, especially Black and Brown students, exposed to the school-to-prison nexus (Basford et al., 2020). Because similar patterns exist within both the educational and criminal justice systems, their linkages are difficult to ignore (Wald & Losen, 2003). Understanding the earlier points within the educational system where positive impact could be made, existing trauma with elementary students became the focus of the chapter. The author explored the question of how to create higher hope for a brighter future in the post-pandemic learning space using practical strategies. Hope offered more than a positive attitude, wishful thinking or optimism. The science of hope is an evidence-based life strategy or plan of action with predictable outcomes. This chapter outlines eight strategies for implementing higher hope in an elementary learning space based on the tenets of hope theory developed by Snyder (1996, 1998) and Snyder et.al. (2002), focusing on positive experiences, effective communication, and resilience to reduce the effects of childhood trauma.

CHILDHOOD TRAUMA AND THE SCHOOL-TO-PRISON NEXUS

A fair and just criminal justice system must provide due process, protect the rights of the innocent, and provide those protections equally to all people (Hayes, 2020). A well-functioning criminal justice system may be characterized by low or declining crime rates, low recidivism rates, and victims compensated for the wrongs committed against them (Hayes, 2020). This is a balanced system that responds to the needs of the population by protecting, restoring and holding responsible parties accountable, while not erroneously representing itself as perfection for everyone within the system. Ultimately, the criminal justice system is a work in progress that should engage in continuously striving for equity as well as equality for all. When the system is wholly out of balance, a portion of society including those within the criminal justice and educational systems may be disproportionately impacted resulting in negative outcomes for generations to come.

Research has shown that putting a high percentage of a nation's population in prison has a negative impact on society as a whole, perpetuating a cycle of crime and violence that may extend to future generations (Simpson, 2020). Because incarceration has not resulted in society feeling safer or declining crime, more is needed to respond to the needs of all youth while balancing inequities. Minorities are heavily overrepresented among those most harshly sanctioned in the education system (Wald & Losen, 2003) and many of those impacted have experienced trauma that follows them into adulthood. Their behavioral responses to trauma have exposed them to the criminal justice system. Additionally, educators who are ill equipped to deal with this trauma have inadvertently ushered trauma victims into the criminal justice system. This has become a cycle of trauma, negative responses to trauma, transition to juvenile justice programs, and at adulthood to the prison system. This cycle has resulted in increased mass incarceration and the existence of the original problem of unaddressed trauma.

While similar data patterns exist in the global incarcerated population, the United States has a significantly higher prison population that disproportionately impacts Black and Brown youth and adults. The United States has the highest incarceration rate with well over 2 million prisoners and China comes in second with 1.5 million. However, China's incarceration rate is only 118 per 100,000 people and the United States has 655 per 100,000 people (Simpson, 2020). In 2015, the United States had 5% of the world's population, but 22% of the incarcerated population (Simpson, 2020). The high correlation between trauma and contact with the criminal justice system experienced by impoverished and minority populations in the United States points to the fact that victims (especially victims of violent trauma) and perpetrators of crime often share the same physical environment (Sampson & Lauritsen, 1994). These commonalities are opportunities to prevent and reduce trauma, which subsequently reduces the number of perpetrators in the juvenile or criminal justice systems. This is not an easy fix, but each perpetrator that is eliminated reduces their sphere of victims and the associated cost of care or incarceration.

The racial disparities within the educational and judicial systems are so similar that it becomes impossible not to recognize the linkages between the two (Wald & Losen, 2003). Terms such as prison track and school-to-prison nexus have been used to describe the trends contributing to mass incarceration (Wald & Losen, 2003). Childhood trauma is associated with risk for emotional disorders (e.g., depression and anxiety) and co-morbid conditions such as substance abuse and antisocial behaviors in adulthood (Wolff & Shi, 2012). Subsequently, reducing trauma and the risk to the school-to-prison pipeline also reduces these health conditions. Intentionally equipping educators with strategies to reduce trauma and restrict the flow of students into the school-to-prison nexus enhances the health of young people within the educational system which positively impacts incarceration rates.

The school-to-prison nexus is a theoretical construct that results from inequities in discipline and exclusionary polices in the educational system that leaves poor and disadvantaged students, especially Black and Brown students, outside the confines of school ushering them into the criminal justice system (Basford et al., 2020). This is important because research demonstrates a correlation between the societal trend of mass incarceration and the school-to-prison nexus (Heitzeg, 2009; Nocella et al., 2014). Understanding the school-to-prison nexus broadens understanding of mass incarceration, its ties to childhood trauma, and the education system's role in increasing the overall well-being of society.

Those exposed to the school-to-prison nexus carry trauma into adulthood. For this reason, it is not surprising to find elevated rates of trauma among the incarcerated especially men (Wolff & Shi, 2012). Being in prison is difficult to live through (Simpson, 2020), but it also impacts the children and families left behind. In 2015, there were more than 10.3 million people imprisoned worldwide (Baranyi et al., 2017). Women constitute 6.8% of the total prison population, and their proportion is rising in most countries (Walmsley, 2016). However, the overwhelming majority of the prison population at 93.2% are men. Many studies have focused on men because of this disproportionality.

Learning conditions tend to be worst for the poor or disadvantaged, and the pattern continues for their learning outcomes (The World Bank, 2018). Without an equitable learning process, youth may become locked into systems of poverty and exclusion when the education system fails those most in need of a good education (The World Bank, 2018). While equality encourages everyone to be treated the same, equity specifically provides the resources the individual needs to be successful (Horner, 2019). Focused attention from educators and researchers may appropriately assess the needs of each student through the lens of both equity and equality for the success of all students.

For example, every student may be provided a computer for their homework. While this is good, it may be of no value for a child without access to the Internet. Equity takes into account individual needs (Horner, 2019), which are very different from treating everyone the same. This gives rise to the notion of privilege, which is when decisions are made to benefit enough people, but not all people (Horner, 2019). The issues of equity, equality, and privilege are complex issues that have caused disparities in the educational system requiring a shift in thinking to a more personalized approach and resolution. Because of the pandemic, this personalized approach intensified the need to reshape the educational system to include strategies to address trauma and inequities.

The Center for Disease Control and Kaiser Permanente (1995) conducted one of the largest studies of childhood abuse, neglect, and household challenges that negatively impacted their well-being. Collectively, the traumatic events that occur in childhood were referred to as adverse childhood experiences (ACEs) (Center for Disease Control and Prevention [CDC], 1995). ACEs have both personal and environmental factors. For example, personal ACEs may include violence, abuse, neglect, witnessed violence, or exposure to suicide. Environmental factors contribute to childhood trauma undermining feelings of safety, stability and bonding. While not an all-inclusive list of factors, these were accentuated by the disruption of educational system and social stability during the pandemic.

Mental disorders associated with childhood trauma include depression, anxiety disorders, post-traumatic stress disorder, dissociative disorders and psychosis (Chapman et al., 2004; Stein et al., 1988; Springer et al., 2007). In learning spaces, students who have experienced trauma may elicit a multitude of responses. For example, responses to trauma may include anger, aggression towards others, and self-destructive and suicidal behaviors (Brodsky et al., 2001; Dube et al, 2001; van der Kolk et al., 1996). Educators that understand these responses to trauma may be better equipped to respond to the behavior and alter the trajectory of their student's lives. Childhood abuse also has been found to significantly predict adult arrests for substance abuse related offenses (Ireland & Widom, 1989).

With the prevalence of ACEs in homes and the community, children experience increased levels of trauma and exposure to the school-to-prison nexus. If this increased level of trauma is not addressed, the economic and social costs to families, community, and society may translate into hundreds of billions of dollars each year (CDC, 1995). ACEs have long-term negative effects on health, well-being, educational and employment opportunities (CDC, 1995). For these reasons, it is imperative that solutions and alternatives be offered to reduce its financial, economic and social costs.

With more than 22 years working in the federal probation system, the author conducted hundreds of interviews gaining an understanding of the depth of traumatic experiences, their impact and the importance of hope. Many releasees interviewed during that time self-reported the presence of childhood trauma or posttraumatic stress disorder. Consistent with the interviewees, the research indicated that over half the male releasees (56%) reported experiencing childhood physical trauma (Wolff & Shi, 2012). This connection to the releasing population made the author keenly aware of the plight of formerly incarcerated people, who were often from poor, disadvantaged, underrepresented, and especially vulnerable to trauma during the pandemic. For these reasons, the author focused on preventive measures that circumvented the flow of students into the school-to-prison nexus and reduced or prevented trauma.

Elementary students were primary targets for higher hope spaces in this chapter because the development of hope becomes more refined as youth mature (Snyder et al., 2002). This natural progression of expanding vocabulary, memorization skills, development of writing, and collaborative team building makes hope a productive starting place for building skills for more complex future strategies. By developing and becoming more familiar with the tenets of hope earlier, students may apply the principles to life applications, as they build on their sense of identity and peer relationships when difficulties occur (Snyder et al., 2002). The constructivist learning theory offered support for the underpinnings of hopeful thinking.

CONSTRUCTIVIST LEARNING THEORY

The constructivist learning theory is an approach where learners use prior knowledge and experiences in pursuing learning objectives and problem solving (Brown & King, 2000). Learners work together sharing their ideas, processing new information and previous knowledge to achieve their learning objectives while assessing alternatives. Similarly, the theory of hope is a goal-directed thinking strategy that creates pathways to objectives and uses motivation (agency) to maintain momentum on that path (Snyder, 1996). Because learners share in the goal-directed team building, they share lessons learned and gain a deeper understanding of one another while building transferable skills for the future.

The constructivist learning theory is especially important because practices and strategies used in the tenets of hope to reduce trauma and mitigate exposure to the school-to-prison nexus. Learners are required to methodically process information, prove or disprove misconceptions and construct solutions from current and previous knowledge to build a better future. This process is unique to each learner based on a continuum of processing current and past information while constructing new ideas and solutions. As students mature and broaden their understanding of themselves and their environment, the tools learned can be used to problem solve with others and may be transferred to more complex circumstances. The constructivist learning theory provides the structure needed in learning and applying the tenets of hope.

THE SCIENCE OF HOPE

Hope is commonly understood to mean "desire accompanied by expectation" or "to want something to happen or be true" (Merriam-Webster, n.d., para. 1). If the desire

Practical Strategies for Higher Hope Learning Spaces

of that anticipation or expectation has not yet manifested, the outcome is slated for some point in the future. If there is no expectation or envisioning for the desire in the future, there may be a sense of hopelessness or despair. Generally, hopelessness occurs when the outcome has already been determined and nothing can be done to alter the results (Gwinn & Hellman, 2019). Not everyone believes that hopelessness is an option. Hopper (2020b) asserts "there's always hope, no matter how difficult or dire a situation may seem" (p. 5). In any case, as more focus is placed on the individual's inability to alter the outcome, negativity, anger, and frustration manifest reducing the level of hope. Intentionality, choices, and forward looking are required to achieve higher hope. Hope filled adolescents are mentally healthier than those filled with hopelessness (Afzal et al., 2014).

Supported by more than 2,000 studies that produced predictive outcomes, hope has transitioned from a simple theory to a science of hope (Gwinn & Hellman, 2019). The science of hope is defined as goal-directed thinking based on two tenets including developing workable alternatives to achieving goals and the sustained momentum to achieve it (Snyder, 1996). In short, an individual must have the capacity to set clear goals for the future, map alternative route(s) to those goals, and be sufficiently motivated to follow them through to achievement. However, there are instances when an anticipated goal is not achieved or there is an inevitable loss.

Snyder (1996) identifies two types of losses, those anticipated and those that are the result of an unattainable goal. In the first type, it is accepted that hopeful thinking characteristically reflects the 50% probability that success will be attained (Snyder, 1996). This may mean preparing several possibilities in anticipation that one or more may not result in the desired results. For example, a 100-meter competitive race will only result in one winner although two or more athletes may compete. The second type of loss or failure is unanticipated and may be painful to process (Snyder, 1996). For example, children may experience the death of a beloved pet which may cause an emotional deflation or mental draining of energy. One of the characteristics of higher hope people when confronted with loss is that they are hopeful during the loss and bounce back to a more hopeful state following the natural grieving process (Snyder, 1996). The idea is not to replace or make light of the loss, but allow the child to experience the process and flow to other goal pursuits.

Learning to process loss is similar to managing through trauma. Some degree of trauma is inevitable to everyone at one time or another. At its core, hope is the innate introspective cognitive ability that each individual possesses to achieve a future outcome. This is within each person's purview to journey to a state of higher hope with guidance and an expectation that better future outcomes are available even when confronted with loss and trauma. In short, the science of hope is accessible to everyone with the capacity for goal-directed thinking. While striving for hope may accompany feelings of stress or being overwhelmed, building hope may start with small manageable steps to building a hopeful state (Hopper, 2020b). Research indicates that hope is positively correlated with life satisfaction (Telef, 2020). The constructivist learning theory is helpful in creating the structure for processing past information to set new goals or alternative ones with pathways to achieve the unique goals of the learner.

The science of hope is a holistic approach to initiating a higher hope learning space that involves multiple active roles and pathways to achievable outcomes. A methodical approach is critical to students exposed to ACEs in creating positive experiences and effective communication that reduce childhood trauma (International Schooling, n.d.). This is an ongoing process where teachers recognize the value and benefits of a higher hope learning space while serving as curriculum drivers. Teachers who establish a safe environment where expectations are outlined clearly psychologically support children who have experienced trauma (Pickens & Tschopp, 2017). To prepare educators, they must be supported with resources and training including trauma-informed practices that not only protect students, but protect educators from vicarious trauma. Compassion fatigue also known as vicarious trauma can lead to emotional exhaustion and disengagement or burnout which is especially hazardous to teachers (Gwinn & Hellman, 2019). Since the pandemic began, teachers leaving the profession have accelerated to a rate of 44% (Jagannathan, 2021). If we are to address this exodus, more has to be done to address the inequities within the educational system.

Because children live and learn in multiple environments, family and support systems are important to maintain the positive progress reflected in a higher hope learning space. Although a personalized journey for the student, many supports have to be in place for higher hope to exist and thrive. When children and educators are protected, nurtured, and given a platform to voice their concerns, celebrate achievements, and pursue their goals, everyone benefits. Having sufficient goal-oriented energy enables people to have life satisfaction (Wong & Lim, 2009). The eight strategies outlined provide a practical starting place for a higher hope learning space consistent with the introspective, strategic, intentional, and predictive nature of higher hope focused on positive experiences, effective communication and resilience to reduce the effects of childhood trauma and exposure to the school-to-prison nexus.

Strategy 1: Acknowledge That Hope Takes Work

While the hope concepts are straight forward, the routes to the goals may require detours and alternative paths as life changes to achieve desired outcomes. Using hope strategies in a higher hope learning space requires planning, motivation, and work (Gwinn & Hellman, 2019). The science of hope may be a used as a tool to achieve healthier relationships, higher daily attendance, higher grades, better test scores, health, mental health, recovery from trauma, and reduced behavioral issues (Gwinn & Hellman, 2019). Learning about the value of hope's long-term benefits may be leveraged into transferrable skills applicable to more complex achievements in the future.

Recentering is not meant to disregard feelings of frustration and despair that inevitably occur as a part of human nature. Being hope-centered means making a decision to remain focused on hopeful thinking and recentering when necessary to receive the benefits of goal-directed thoughts (Gwinn & Hellman, 2019). Although important to acknowledge that hope takes work, there is also an equally important ever hopeful strategy that may be pursued. Hopper (2020b) asserts that "perhaps the first step is to acknowledge that there is always hope, no matter how difficult or dire a situation may seem" (p. 5). This simple assertion helps to reframe any negative situation and refocus on the fact that there is a future and it comes with hope. Again, each person is unique and may require their own time and space to process through pain, grief and difficulties to position themselves to move toward a more hopeful state.

For example, a child may find it hard to concentrate and recenter on a cause-and-effect relationship, when their family environment is chaotic (Snyder et al., 2002). As a result, the child may relinquish a goal of achieving a perfect score in each class and choose an alternative path or invest their energies elsewhere. Alternative routing and motivation to recenter on a hope-centered life offers benefits and life lessons such as overcoming and reimaging what success looks like. However, success may sometimes come after time and space to grieve and recenter on more hopeful goals. The important thing is to have a process available when the person is ready to move on to other goal pursuits. Hopeful thinking is not an excuse to not engage in life and/or with others. Success is more than achieving a goal, but applying practices and principles to life circumstances that enhance outcomes. In addition, being hopeful and managing emotions reduces the effects of traumatic events by decreasing outbursts or disruptive behaviors that may result in fewer disciplinary actions and increasing life satisfaction (Valle et al., 2006).

Incorporating the language of hope into school projects and assignments increases familiarity and normalizes hope theory as a tool. For example, a school assignment may include a written report on the impact of COVID-19 on their personal lives. Teachers may provide guidance designing the assignment with the final outcome of a personal presentation in mind. Guidance may be given on how students should develop steps or pathways to their envisioned report or presentation and how they plan to maintain their motivation toward this goal. Predictable routines and expectations help children who have experienced trauma heal (Bartlett & Smith, 2019). For some, motivation may be in the form of favorable grades, rewards or satisfaction with achieving the outcome. Each student is different and may be motivated by different incentives prompting a personalized approach to incentives.

Teaching the language of hope helps students recognize and model the language and affiliated behavior encourages a shift in thinking (Gwinn & Hellman, 2019). Routine in the classroom and clear expectations reduce the risk of additional trauma (Bartlett & Smith, 2019). Normalizing the language of hope in the classroom reduces negative emotions and experiences such as fear and hostility with the added benefit of mitigating the risk of trauma and exposure to the school-to-prison nexus. After completing the assignment, students may share their approaches with their classmates while engaging in authentic discussions. Shared learning from other classmates is important to gain insight and perspective. When children are encouraged to pursue the broader goal of life satisfaction by discovering and exploring their world and life around them, they strive for personal development and are more equipped to face difficulties (Park, 2004).

Best elementary classroom practices include creating a safe, secure space where students' physical and emotional needs are met (Education Staffing Space [ESS], n.d.). To achieve this goal, educators may establish a caring and supportive classroom experience by promoting open honest sharing without judgement. No judgement is not the same as accepting misinformation, bullying or teasing. Educators may provide guided learning and correction when needed in a healthy exchange as a model for class behavior based on respect. Helping children heal from trauma by ensuring that they have predictable routines, safe learning spaces, and setting expectations appropriate for their level of functioning is paramount (Bartlett & Smith, 2019). In this context, working to foster feelings of hope in uncertainty increases feelings of well-being and empowerment toward a better future (Hopper, 2020b).

Strategy 2: Understand the Tenets of Hope Theory and Its Benefits

The pandemic created not only educational challenges, but opportunities as well. Because of the inequities exacerbated by the pandemic, favorable circumstances exist to change the educational process to include higher hope strategies. The benefits include encouraging healthier relationships, optimistic thinking, reduced trauma, empowerment of students, fewer mental health issues (Gwinn & Hellman, 2019), and teachers and students united as curriculum drivers. The strategies recommended are foundational steps that are transferrable to other aspects of life that benefit the whole person. Assisting students to think critically and generate solutions offers opportunities to develop additional skills (ESS, n.d.).

Psychologist Rick Snyder, known as the original "hope scientist," and his colleagues developed a hope theory based on two concepts: pathways and agentic thinking (Snyder, 1996, 1998). In achieving desired goals, pathways or routes were developed to reach each goal and willpower served as the fuel for motivation to complete it. Currently, there are more than 2,000 published studies of hope theory demonstrating its power in the areas of education, employment, health, mental health, social relationships, family, and trauma resulting in an evidentiary base incuding predictive positive outcomes (Gwinn & Hellman, 2019). These positive outcomes reduce the imprint of unpleasant experiences related to childhood trauma (International Schooling, n.d.).

Hope can predict academic achievement for school-aged children to graduate level students (Gwinn & Hellman, 2019). Because of its applicability to a wide range of youth and adults, the author focused on younger elementary students to serve as a foundation of transferrable skills in building student confidence as they matured and progressed in school. The higher the hope of a child, the higher the daily attendance, the lower the tardiness rate, the higher the grades, and better the test scores (Gwinn & Hellman, 2019). However, additional research is required to expand the field of study to include specific grade levels, ages, classroom subjects, and genders among others.

The science of hope encourages powerful goal-directed thinking (Snyder, 1996) to offset the effects of childhood trauma by strategically providing tools needed to manage behavioral responses to trauma. Students experiencing negative emotions have fewer streams of thought and actions and, thus, may have restricted pathways to goal achievement (Franke et al., 2017). Understanding how students who have experienced trauma respond helps equip teachers with tools that reduce exposure to disproportionate disciplinary actions. Educators are encouraged to use project-based and/or problem-based activities that engage the student in active learning as a part of best practices (ESS, n.d.). For these reasons, the science is hope is recommended to navigate the negative results of trauma along with its disruptive behaviors by managing emotional responses and reducing the risk of exposure to the school-to-prison nexus.

In a study published by Katelyn Long of Harvard University, researchers found that more hopeful participants reported higher levels of positive emotions, lower levels of depression, a stronger sense of purpose and meaning, and less loneliness (Hopper, 2020b). Psychologists have found that people who score higher on measures of hope also tend to have a higher level of well-being (Hopper, 2020b). This hopeful mindset makes setting clearly defined goals possible, even when facing significant trauma and adversity (Hopper, 2020b). The decision to focus on a higher hope learning spaces provides scaffolding from an impossible future to one with possibilities. Positive lifestyle reduces the effects of childhood trauma (International Schooling, n.d.).

A higher hope learning space offers an opportunity to reshape the educational system. By weaving opportunities for students to problem solving, they learn to think critically and generate unique solutions that follow them into adulthood. It is also important to develop assignments and projects that encourage students to regularly set goals, develop pathways to reaching their goals, and provide motivation to continue their pursuit to its desired conclusion. The focus in a higher hope learning space is on the process and not necessarily about the destination and/or detours in the beginning. Table 1 summarizes the benefits of a higher hope learning space and uses the acronym "Hopeful" to serve as a reminder of the benefits.

Table 1. Benefits of a higher hope learning space

Designation	Benefits
H	Healthier relationships.
O	Optimistic thinking.
P	Power of hope.
E	Empowerment.
F	Fewer mental health problems.
U	Unites students, teachers, and school staff as curriculum drivers.
L	Less exposure to the school-to-prison pipeline.

Strategy 3: Emphasize a Personalized Approach to Student Needs

In a higher hope learning space, the psychological strengths of hope are nurtured by encouraging strategic thinking when adversity comes. Undoubtedly, no life is without adversity at one time or another. The focus should be on resilience, overcoming pain, and recentering when necessary (Gwinn & Hellman, 2019). By nurturing the unique characteristics of each child, they are celebrated and valued as individuals with the ability to choose the direction for their future. Sustaining motivation to achieve goals is essential to gaining higher hope. Consideration may be required in meeting the student's basic needs before they can be sufficiently motivated to complete higher level thinking.

Maslow's hierarchy of needs provides a basis for motivating students to maximize their potential (McLeod, 2022). Physiological needs required for human survival such as food and water, safety and stability ensure personal and financial security, social belonging such as being a part of a family or group of friends, and self-esteem needs (McLeod, 2022). If these basic needs are met, students may be motivated by higher level thinking such as cognitive (curiosity), self-esteem (respect), and self-actualization, a need to realize one's own potential (Basford et al., 2020). These motivations may occur simultaneously, based on the underlying needs. A personalized approach is required to identify the needs of each student and define a plan of how best to address them.

Understanding these basic motivations outlined in Maslow's hierarchy of needs assists in understanding what may be motivating the student's behavior. For example, when a student misbehaves or acts out of character, a caring trauma-informed adult may ask narrative questions requiring more than single word answers. As students learn to navigate problems and create solutions, they simulate real world applications that better prepare them for the future (ESS, n.d.). Learning in a variety of ways and being encouraged to develop their own unique positive solutions may make the difference whether students feel supported or are referred to the judicial system risking exposure to the school-to-prison nexus. Positive experiences reduce childhood trauma (International Schooling, n.d.).

If a student becomes combative because of a subject discussed in class, a more trauma-informed follow up question may be appropriate. The teacher may ask "What has happened that caused this behavior?" instead of "How do I deal with the misbehavior?" Many children display disruptive behavior as a result of trauma (e.g., sexualized or aggressive acts, and withdrawal) and are at risk of being stigmatized and isolated (Pynoos et al., 1996). Oftentimes, student misbehavior leads to a student being labeled as a "bad student" or "incorrigible." These labels travel with the student and can taint their relationship with other teachers or adults in the future. Effective communication strategies reduce the effects of childhood trauma (International Schooling, n.d.).

Because teaching and learning are dynamic endeavors, teachers must remain open-minded and willing to learn themselves (ESS, n.d.). Teachers cannot be expected to know how to respond to trauma without proper training. The child's fears, frustrations, and trauma should be priority even when the schedule is hectic. Misbehavior and outbursts never seem to occur at the most convenient time, but placing a priority on the health and well-being of each student reenforces to the child that they are valued and their frustrations taken seriously. Because of these caring adults, teachers become experts on their students while helping the child manage their emotional responses which reduce exposure to the student-to-prison nexus. Creating an environment with clear expectations, positive experiences and effective communications reduces childhood trauma (International Schooling, n.d.).

Strategy 4: Protect Teachers and School Staff from Vicarious Trauma

Bartlett and Smith (2019) report that early childhood trauma is a major public health problem with severe consequences for children, families, and society as a whole.

Trauma can be defined broadly as "an event or series of events or set of circumstances experienced that are physically or emotionally harmful or life-threatening" (Substance Abuse and Mental Health Services Administration, 2014, p. 7). When exposed to traumatic experiences of their students, teachers and school staff may become victims of vicarious trauma by simply doing the critical work of caring adults. Therefore, teachers and school staff must be protected from vicarious trauma. A safe learning environment includes all those within the educational system and preparation is key.

An estimated 17% of public-school teachers reported leaving the teaching profession before their fifth year, often as a result of low salary and insufficient school resources as major reasons for their departure (Gray & Taie, 2015). Since the pandemic began, teachers leaving the educational field increased to 44% (Jagannathan, 2021). For many of these teachers, the pandemic added to the stress and despair of the teaching profession. Serving as caring adults in the lives of their students, teachers were exposed to trauma oftentimes without the support to adequately serve their students' needs. This must be considered in reshaping the teaching profession and halting the exodus.

Educators are not able to give what they do not have or do not know (Gwinn & Hellman, 2019). By establishing comforting and predictable routines, teachers set the stage for cognitive development (ESS, n.d.). These supportive caring adults deserve the investment of resources to obtain care for themselves, so that they do not become victims of vicarious trauma. A psychologically supportive learning space celebrates each child, respects and listens to their concerns, and encourages them to share their vulnerabilities and fears (Pickens & Tschopp, 2017). It is critical that the voice of the student, teacher, and other educational professionals are not overlooked.

When educators are afforded an opportunity for trauma-informed training that highlights best practices, they are less likely to become distracted by disruptive behavior focusing instead on the underlying trauma (Gwinn & Hellman, 2019). Professional development for educators and parents provides a symbiotic relationship with the student while surrounding each with the skilled, caring people necessary to support a higher hope learning space. Educating the school district, community leaders, and government officials ensures that the resources required to provide trauma-informed care is accessible to all those who engage with students. This partnership is important to the community's long-term success. Focusing on the goal of arming students and teachers with the tools necessary to prevent or minimize childhood trauma provides the potential for successful futures using the science of hope.

Strategy 5: Surround Students with Caring Adults

Teachers, parents, family members, and school staff influence student behavior and expose them to an array of factors. For example, caring adults that recognize needs such as food, clothing or other essentials are critical to satisfying their student's basic needs. Maslow's hierarchy of needs assists with identifying multiple levels of needs (Hopper, 2020a). Additionally, empowering teachers that have their higher order needs met may be more equipped to engage students and their families on a personal level. The messages communicated by teachers, verbally and nonverbally, about expectations contribute to a psychologically safe environment, providing a foundation for a trauma-informed learning environment (Pickens & Tschopp, 2017). Given that today's student are tomorrow's global citizens, leaders, and workforce, a good education is an investment with enduring benefits (The World Bank, 2018).

The educational system involves many contributors including students, parents, guardians, teachers, administrative staff, cafeteria works, assistants, technical staff, and bus drivers, among others. For the system to work properly, all facets of the system must be valued for the contributions made in fulfilling the needs of the student. Oftentimes, cafeteria works are overlooked because they do not teach. However, cafeteria staff are responsible for fulfilling the basic nutritional needs of the students. Without their services or contributions, many students may be unfocused and distracted because they are hungry. Bus drivers, too, are often overlooked for their contributions of transporting students to and from school and/or other activities. If students are unable to attend class, the system breaks down. Therefore, it is imperative to celebrate all the everyday heroes.

Best practices for teachers necessitate that they create a safe, secure environment where students' physical and emotional needs are met (ESS, n.d.). In reshaping the educational system, it must be acknowledged that teachers, too, have needs that must be met. Communications must include the voices of those directly and indirectly impacting the student. They must not be forgotten in the process and provided a voice and platform to shape the educational system of the future. Otherwise, the exodus from the teaching profession that began before the pandemic will continue on its accelerated course following the pandemic. Communication and compassion will be important in modeling the priority that should be placed on the teaching and educational community.

Strategy 6: More Listening, Less Talking

Trauma-informed adults provide the caring voices that encourage a young person's sharing and further safe development. Creating a higher hope learning space requires that teachers and school staff listen to the student, ask narrative questions that prompt explanation (Gwinn & Hellman, 2019), process this information before responding, and listen more. In short, caring adults should be listening more than they are talking and asking questions that require a narrative answer. For example, a teacher might ask a student "What did you most like about today?" In response, children need to be able to tell their story without interruptions or anyone trying to fix them. They want to be validated, heard, and not judged (Gwinn & Hellman, 2019).

A student's closest social circle of peers, partners, and family members influences their behavior, contributing to their magnitude of experiences (Centers for Disease Control and Prevention, 2022). Negative people and their behavior can influence others. Helping students to be critical thinkers in controlling who and what influences their behavior increases their self-confidence and self-actualization. Prevention strategies may include parenting or family focused prevention programs, and mentoring and peer programs designed to reduce conflict, foster problem-solving skills, and promote healthy relationships (Centers for Disease Control and Prevention, 2022). Building these aspects into the school strategies drives curriculum building to a higher-level reinforcing well-being and constructive thinking.

It is important that students feel comfortable sharing among their peers, learning the tenets of hope, and continuing to look to taking an active role in preparing for a brighter future. Effective discipline begins with setting expectations and providing consistent reinforcement of expected behaviors (Pickens & Tschopp, 2017). The ultimate goal for discipline is to ensure young people choose a better set of actions to reach their desired goals in the future or self-regulate to delay achieving that goal (Pickens & Tschopp, 2017). Surrounding learners with other excited hope-filled learners equipped with strategies to building a better future builds excitement. This helps learners to manage the controllable parts of their future, while accepting that there are always unexpected variables. In addition, learning to manage emotions, communicate effectively and build rapport reduces childhood trauma (International Schooling, n.d.). As a result, young people learn to detour, take alternative routes to meeting goals, and reset when the process becomes derailed. Learning in authentic contexts anchor students learning to familiar people, places and things (ESS, n.d.).

Strategy 7: Develop Students and Educators as Ambassadors of Hope

By creating a hopeful learning space and arming students with these strategies, they become empowered ambassadors of hope. Maintaining meaningful connections involves creating routines that promote healthy coping strategies and improved self-regulation skills, while integrating them into learning expectations, rules, and lessons (Pickens & Tschopp, 2017). Improved self-regulation and coping skills reduces the risk of trauma and mitigates the need for referral to the school-to-prison pipeline.

Practical Strategies for Higher Hope Learning Spaces

Once students and teachers understand and can benefit from the higher hope learning space, it breeds interest from others. This fueled interest expands to others seeking the benefits of a higher hope environment. Those successfully using hopeful thinking provide the sparks that generate hope in the community encouraging partnerships.

Ambassadors of hope are important to creating enthusiasm, interest, excitement, and funding opportunities that support educational professionals. Members of the community and local leaders are more supportive when they see measurable outcomes and positive results. Hope scales, worksheets, surveys, and research are available to assist in providing funders with output for justification of financial supports. For example, Rick Snyder developed the hope scale to measure both agency and pathways thinking toward goals (Snyder, 1996, 1998). The hope scale reflects four measures for willpower for past, present, and future goals and four items reflecting mental roadmaps toward goal attainment (Snyder, 1996, 1998). Active roles and strategic planning are crucial to establishing, maintaining and funding a higher hope learning space. Raising awareness of the needs for trauma-informed training increases positives responses to childhood trauma reducing the risk of additional trauma and further restricting flow into the school-to-prison pipeline.

Newsletters, podcasts or social media events highlighting the long-term benefits and measurable outcomes may serve to generate excitement about the progressive work done in the hopeful learning space. When student families and community supporters see the benefit in individual students, they are more likely to talk about it with others and inspire additional support. Allowing educators and young people to create platforms surrounding the higher hope learning environment creates a voice for the teaching profession to share their concerns and contribute to their field of expertise.

While each school district is different, it is important to focus on the strengths of the school and collaborate with local leaders to support the higher hope learning space. Giving students, teachers, and school staff the opportunity to add their voices may contribute to the overall support needed to bring a higher hope learning space to fruition. The ability of students to learn in a variety of ways and experience content through multiple modalities strengthens communication and neutral connections in multiple centers of the brain (ESS, n.d.). These positive experiences, rapport building and effectively learning to manage communication reduces childhood trauma (International Schooling, n.d.).

Strategy 8: Create Partnerships of Hope

Implementing trauma-informed care curricula and establishing partnerships with early childhood education programs, mental health programs, and trauma-informed services create a holistic higher hope support system (Bartlett & Smith, 2019). The resources and training made available to educators reduces and prevents future trauma and places educators in a better position to execute their important jobs. Education is not restricted to the classroom or school district boundaries. Global education and social platforms link academic subjects with students around the globe by emphasizing how their lives are inextricably connected to one another (Mokuria et al., 2020). Sharing knowledge and problem-solving skills creates invaluable partnerships by eliminating duplication of resources, research, and funding sources. For example, the research involved in the developing children's vaccines for COVID-19 saved countless lives globally. Creating partnerships as a regular practice before emergencies occur is a preventative strategy for maintaining global health in a learning environment.

Allotting time in the class schedule for creative team building activities focused on topics related to the pandemic and stressful situations offers many benefits. For example, students may be asked to paint a picture related to COVID-19 pandemic. During guided instruction, students may be taught to look to the future picture that they desire, develop steps to painting the picture, and verbalize how they will motivate themselves to complete it. The steps are the process which helps each student to visualize the outcome from their perspective and build steps while remaining motivated through to its completion. Afterward, students present their picture to their classmates and describe the steps that led to its completion. Teachers and classmates listen and encourage during the discussion of why and how the student came to their conclusions. If there are inaccuracies about COVID-19, the teacher provides support and facts to reassure and comfort. This is an opportunity for the student to voice concerns and share thoughts that exist in their reality. Additionally, movement in an around the learning space between different modalities helps students reduce stress and bring oxygen to the brain, priming them to create and innovate (ESS, n.d.). Building hopeful partnerships are valuable for empowerment for students and those that support them.

CONCLUSION

It would be disingenuous to pretend that building higher hope learning spaces that reduce trauma, build confidence, encourage empathy, and mitigate the school-to-prison pipeline is without challenges. No amount of money alone can resolve this issue. There is no panacea or quick fix for managing trauma and existing inequities in school discipline and exclusionary policies that impact Black and Brown students disproportionately. However, there is hope for a more inclusive school system that benefits all students, including those with special challenges. Interjecting a diverse representation of students, teachers, parents, educational staff, and supporters allows for new perspectives to be heard and exchanged. It is important to understand that the systemic nature of the educational system has existed for many, many years and will require a commitment from caring adults and informed partnerships to begin healing. The science of hope provides goal-directed thinking that focuses on students and families, and advocates pathways and motivations for a more personalized approach to a better future that benefits the entire educational system one student at a time.

The complexities and interconnectedness of the higher hope learning spaces are unquestionably worth the investment to future students. Each person that engages with a child has a role in contributing to a higher hope learning space. The student and educator must be open and moved toward developing and building a new future while acknowledging the challenges presented by the pandemic or other stressful events. Educators and parents or guardians must be equipped with the appropriate training to become trauma-informed care givers. Additionally, community leaders educated in trauma-informed care may introduce beneficial legislation in reshaping the educational community. It will take the combined efforts at all levels to reshape the existing educational system that responds to student and teacher needs while reducing trauma and flow into the school-to-prison nexus.

Phillip Zimbardo and Rosemary Sword suggest that one way to become more hopeful is to help others and lobby for social change (Hopper, 2020b). Focusing on the future, the benefits for both individuals and society become clearer. Education promotes employment, earnings, and health (The World Bank, 2018). The probability for a healthy future with the potential and capacity to provide sustainable earnings is life changing for most. A quality education encourages confidence, self-trust, and self-actualization in reaching the highest potential.

Additionally, more research with the science of hope is needed in diverse environments involving multiple age groups and cultures to further expand the body of research. When faced with pressing social issues, embracing hope can be beneficial to bring about change in a broader community (Hopper, 2020b). The science of hope process is complex requiring work, but is achievable if caring adults commit to responding to what children and adults have gone through (Gwinn & Hellman, 2019).

As teachers continue to leave the teaching profession, much must be done to hear their concerns and challenges if the exodus is to halted. This will require reshaping the educational system to be more inclusive of their ideas and their voice in shaping the future. Other large societal factors include the health, economic, educational, and social policies that help to reduce economic or social inequalities between groups in society (Centers for Disease Control and Prevention, 2022). While recognizing the monumental task of reshaping the education system, it is achievable if all contribute at their level of influence. Every voice is important at every level of influence. Everyone counts.

There are eight practical strategies recommended to encourage a higher hope learning space. They are not meant to be all-inclusive because each learning space and school district are different. They are simply a starting place to increase equity and establish a thoughtful, intentional, and hope-centered environment consistent with best practices for elementary schools. First, acknowledge that an authentic higher hope learning space takes work, but is worth the investment. Second, understanding the tenets of hope including goals, pathways, and agency provide an evidence-based strategic foundation from which to measure progress. Third, emphasize a personalized approach to student needs. Fourth, protect teachers and school staff from vicarious trauma. Fifth, surround students with caring adults to encourage and build confidence. Sixth, listen to everyone, ask narrative questions, process information before responding, and, after responding, be willing to listen more. This requires keeping an open mind. In short, more listening and less talking. Seventh, develop students and teachers as ambassadors of hope. Finally, create partnerships of hope with local communities as part of a larger society supporting the educational system. Table 2 summarizes these practical strategies for higher hope learning spaces.

Table 2. Strategies for higher hope learning spaces

Strategies for Higher Hope Learning Spaces
1. Acknowledge that hope takes work.
2. Understand the tenets of hope theory and its benefits.
3. Emphasize a personalized approach to student needs.
4. Protect teachers and school staff from vicarious trauma.
5. Surround students with caring adults.
6. More listening, less talking.
7. Develop student and teachers as ambassadors of hope.
8. Create partnerships of hope.

ACKNOWLEDGMENT

This research received no specific grant from any funding agency in the public, commercial or not-for-profit sectors.

REFERENCES

Afzal, A., Malik, N. I., & Atta, M. (2014). The moderating role of positive and negative emotions in relationship between positive psychological capital and subjective well-being among adolescents. *International Journal of Research Studies in Psychology*, *3*(3), 29–42. doi:10.5861/ijrsp.2014.687

Baranyi, G., Cassidy, M., Fazel, S., Priebe, S., & Mundt, A. (2017). Prevalence of posttraumatic stress disorder in prisoners. *Epidemiologic Reviews*, *40*(1), 134–145. doi:10.1093/epirev/mxx015 PMID:29596582

Bartlett, J. D., & Smith, S. (2019). The role of early care and education in addressing early childhood trauma. *American Journal of Community Psychology*, *64*(1), 1–14. doi:10.1002/ajcp.12380 PMID:31449682

Basford, L., Lewis, J., & Trout, M. (2020). It can be done: How one charter school combats the school-to-prison pipeline. *The Urban Review*, *53*(3), 540–562. doi:10.100711256-020-00583-x

Brodsky, B. S., Oquendo, M., Ellis, S. P., Haas, G. L., Malone, K. M., & Mann, J. J. (2001). The relationship of childhood abuse is impulsivity and suicidal behavior in adults with major depression. *The American Journal of Psychiatry*, *158*(11), 1871–1877. doi:10.1176/appi.ajp.158.11.1871 PMID:11691694

Brown, S. W., & King, F. B. (2000). Constructivist pedagogy and how we learn: Educational psychology meets international studies. *Oxford University Press, 1*(3), 245-254. https://www.jstor.org/stable/44218131

Center for Disease Control and Prevention. (1995). *Fast Facts: Preventing adverse childhood experiences*. Retrieved on July 21, 2022, from https://www.cdc.gov/violenceprevention/aces/fastfact.html

Centers for Disease Control and Prevention. (2022, January 18). *The social-ecological model: A framework for prevention*. https://www.cdc.gov/violenceprevention/about/social-ecologicalmodel.html

Chapman, D., Whitfield, C., Felitti, V., Dube, S., Edwards, V., & Anda, R. (2004). Adverse childhood experiences and the risk of depressive disorders in adulthood. *Journal of Affective Disorders*, *82*(2), 217–225. doi:10.1016/j.jad.2003.12.013 PMID:15488250

Chaturvedi, S., Purohit, S., & Verma, M. (2021). Effective teaching practices for success during Covid-19 pandemic: Toward phygital learning. *Frontiers in Education*, 6, 1–10. doi:10.3389/feduc.2021.646557

Dube, S. R., Anda, R. F., Felitti, V. J., Chapman, D. P., Williamson, D. F., & Giles, W. H. (2001). Childhood abuse, household dysfunction, and the risk of attempted suicide throughout the life span: Findings from the adverse childhood experiences study. *Journal of the American Medical Association*, 286(24), 3089–3096. doi:10.1001/jama.286.24.3089 PMID:11754674

Education Staffing Space. (n.d.). *Best practices in teaching and learning elementary education*. https://ess.com/blog/articles-best-practices-in-teaching-and-learning-in-elementary-school/

Franke, K. B., Huebner, E. S., & Hills, K. J. (2017). Cross-sectional and prospective associations between positive emotions and general life satisfaction in adolescents. *Journal of Happiness Studies: An Interdisciplinary Forum on Subjective Well-Being*, 18(4), 1075–1093. doi:10.100710902-016-9763-8

Gray, L., & Taie, S. (2015). *Public school teacher attrition and mobility in the first five years: Results from the first through fifth waves of the 2007-08 beginning teacher longitudinal study*. U.S. Department of Education. https://nces.ed.gov/pubs2015/2015337.pdf

Gwinn, C., & Hellman, C. (2019). *Hope rising: How the science of hope can change your life*. Morgan James Publishing.

Hayes, T. O. (2020). *The economic costs of the U.S. Criminal Justice System*. American Action Forum. https://www.americanactionforum.org/research/the-economic-costs-of-the-u-s-criminal-justice-system/

Heitzeg, N. A. (2009). *Education or incarceration: Zero tolerance policies and the school to prison pipeline*. Forum for Public Policy. https://files.eric.ed.gov/fulltext/EJ870076.pdf

Hopper, E. (2020a). *Maslow's hierarchy of needs explained*. https://www.christianworldmedia.com/client/docs/603_15850795 40_17.pdf

Hopper, E. (2020b, July 6). *The psychology of hope: How to build hope and a better future*. https://healthypsych.com/psychology-of-hope

Horner, J. (2019, May 1). *Let's think about equity, equality and justice.* https://psychology.wisheights.org/2019/05/01/lets-think-abou t-equity-equality-justice/

International Schooling. (n.d.). *Six ways to minimize the effect of childhood trauma.* Retrieved August 15, 2022, from https://internationalschooling.org/blog/6-ways-to-minimize-t he-effect-of-childhood-trauma/

Ireland, T., & Widom, C. S. (1994). Childhood victimization and risk for alcohol and drug arrests. *The International Journal of the Addictions, 27*(2), 251–271. doi:10.3109/10826089409047380 PMID:8144278

Jagannathan, M. (2021, February 22). *Teachers were already leaving the profession due to stress then covid-19 hit.* https://www.marketwatch.com/story/teachers-were-already-leav ing-the-profession-due-to-stress-then-covid-19-hit-116140252 13

Kalmuss, D. S. (1984). The intergenerational transmission of marital aggression. *Journal of Marriage and Family, 46*(1), 11–19. doi:10.2307/351858

McLeod, S. (2022, April 4). *Maslow's hierarchy of needs.* https://www.simplypsychology.org/maslow.html

Merriam-Webster. (n.d.). *Hope.* Retrieved May 31, 2022, from https://www.merriam-webster.com/dictionary/hope

Mokuria, V., Williams, A., & Page, W. (2020). There has been no remorse over it: A narrative inquiry exploring enslaved ancestral roots through a critical family history project. *Genealogy, 4*(26), 1–13. doi:10.3390/genealogy4010026

Nocella, A., Parmar, P., & Stovall, W. (2014). *From education to incarceration: Dismantling the school-to-prison pipeline* (2nd ed.). Peter Lang.

Park, N. (2004). The role of subjective well-being in positive youth development. *The Annals of the American Academy of Political and Social Science, 591*(1), 25–29. doi:10.1177/0002716203260078

Pickens, I. B., & Tschopp, N. (2017, October 24). *Trauma-informed classrooms.* Council of Juvenile and Family Court Judges. https://www.ncjfcj.org/publications/trauma-informed-classroo ms/

Pynoos, R. S., Steinberg, A. M., & Goenjian, A. (1996). Traumatic stress in childhood and adolescence: Recent developments and current controversies. In B. A. van der Kolk, A. McFarlane, & L. Weisaeth (Eds.), *Traumatic stress: The effects of overwhelming experience on mind, body and society* (pp. 133–141). Guilford Press.

Sampson, R. J., & Lauritsen, J. L. (1994). Violent victimization and offending: Individual, situational, and community level risk factors. In A. J. Reiss Jr & J. A. Roth (Eds.), *Understanding and preventing violence* (Vol. 3, pp. 1–114). National Academy Press.

Simpson, V. (2020 September 14). *Incarceration rates by country*. World Atlas. https://www.worldatlas.com/articles/largest-prison-population-rates-in-the-world.html

Snyder, C. R. (1996). To hope, to lose, and to hope again. *Journal of Personal and Interpersonal Loss*, *1*(1), 1–16. doi:10.1080/15325029608415455

Snyder, C. R. (1998). To hope, to lose, and hope again. In J. H. Harvey, J. Omarzu, & E. Miller (Eds.), *Perspectives on loss: A sourcebook* (pp. 63–79). Taylor and Francis.

Snyder, C. R., Feldman, B. D., Shorey, H. S., & Rand, K. L. (2002). Hopeful choices: A school counselor's guide to hope theory. *Professional School Counseling*, *5*(5), 298–307. https://eric.ed.gov/?q=l&pg=808&id=EJ655195

Springer, K., Sheridan, J., Kuo, D., & Carnes, M. (2007). Long-term physical and mental health consequences of childhood physical abuse: Results from a large population-based sample of men and women. *Child Abuse & Neglect*, *31*(5), 517–530. doi:10.1016/j.chiabu.2007.01.003 PMID:17532465

Stein, J. A., Golding, J. M., Siegel, J. M., Burnam, M. A., & Sorenson, S. B. (1988). Long-term psychological sequelae of child sexual abuse: The Los Angeles epidemiologic catchment area study. In F. Sage, G. E. Wyatt, & Y. G. J. Powell (Eds.), *Lasting effects of child sexual abuse* (Vol. 100, pp. 135–154). Sage Publications.

Straus, M. A., Gelles, R. J., & Steinmetz, S. (1980). Behind closed doors: Violence in the American family. Anchor Press.

Substance Abuse and Mental Health Services Administration. (2014). *SAMHSA's concept of trauma and guidance for a trauma-informed approach*. Substance Abuse and Mental Health Services Administration. https://store.samhsa.gov/sites/default/files/d7/priv/sma14-4884.pdf

Telef, B. B. (2020). Hope and life satisfaction in elementary students: Mediation role of affective experiences. *Journal of Positive School Psychology*, *4*(2), 176–186. doi:10.47602/jpsp.v4i2.232

The World Bank. (2018). *World development report 2018: Learning to realize education's promise*. https://www.worldbank.org/en/publication/wdr2018

United Nations. (2020, August). *Policy Brief: Education during COVID-19 and beyond*. Retrieved from United Nations: https://unsdg.un.org/resources/policy-brief-education-during-covid-19-and-beyond

Valle, M. F., Huebner, E. S., & Suldo, S. M. (2006). An analysis of hope as a psychological strength. *Journal of School Psychology*, *44*(5), 393–406. doi:10.1016/j.jsp.2006.03.005

Van der Kolk, B. A., Pelcovitz, D., Roth, S., Mandel, F. S., McFarlane, A., & Herman, J. L. (1996). Dissociation, somatization, and affect dysregulation: The complexity of adaptation of trauma. *The American Journal of Psychiatry*, *153*(7), 83–93. doi:10.1176/ajp.153.7.83 PMID:8659645

Wald, J., & Losen, D. (2003, November 5). Defining and redirecting a school-to-prison pipeline. *New Directions for Youth Development*, *99*(99), 9–15. doi:10.1002/yd.51 PMID:14635431

Walmsley, R. (2016). *World prison population list* (11th ed.). Institute for Criminal Policy Research. https://www.prisonstudies.org/sites/default/files/resources/downloads/world_prison_population_list_11th_edition_0.pdf

Widom, C. S. (1989). Child abuse, neglect, and violent criminal behavior. *Criminology*, *27*(2), 251–271. doi:10.1111/j.1745-9125.1989.tb01032.x

Wolff, N., & Shi, J. (2012). Childhood and adult trauma experiences of incarcerated persons and their relationship to adult behavioral health problems and treatment. *International Journal of Environmental Research and Public Health*, *9*(5), 1908–1926. doi:10.3390/ijerph9051908 PMID:22754481

Wong, S. S., & Lim, T. (2009). Hope versus optimism in Singaporean adolescents: Contributions to depression and life satisfactions. *Personality and Individual Differences*, *45*(5-6), 648–652. doi:10.1016/j.paid.2009.01.009

Xiao, J. (2021). From equality to equity to justice: Should online education be the new normal in education? In A. Bozkurt (Ed.), *Emerging pedagogies for the future of education: Trauma-Informed, Care, and Pandemic Pedagogy* (pp. 1–15). IGI Global. doi:10.4018/978-1-7998-7275-7.ch001

ADDITIONAL READING

Gwinn, C. (2015). *Cheering for the children: Creating pathways to hope for children exposed to trauma*. Wheatmark Press.

Gwinn, J. D., & Hellman, C. (2019). *Hope rising: How the science of hope can change your life*. Morgan James Publishing.

Hellman, C. M., & Gwinn, C. (2017). Camp Hope as an intervention for children exposed to domestic violence: A program evaluation of hope and strength of character. *Child & Adolescent Social Work Journal*, *34*(3), 269–276. doi:10.100710560-016-0460-6

Lopez, S. J. (2014). *Making hope happen: Creating the future you want for yourself and others*. Atria Books.

Peale, N. V. (2003). *The power of positive thinking*. Simon and Schuster.

Pedrotti, J. T., & Edwards, L. (2008). Promoting hope: Suggestions for school counselors. *Professional School Counseling*, *12*(2), 100–107. doi:10.5330/PSC.n.2010-12.100

Snyder, C. R. (2000). *Handbook of hope: Theory, measures, and applications*. Academic Press.

Snyder, C. R. (2002). Hope theory: Rainbows in the mind. *Psychological Inquiry*, *13*(4), 249–275. doi:10.1207/S15327965PLI1304_01

KEY TERMS AND DEFINITIONS

Constructivist Learning Theory: It is an approach to learning based on building from knowledge and previous experiences.
Equality: It means being equal or treated the same.
Equity: It means a quality of fairness and taking into account individual needs.
Higher Hope: It is the capacity to envision a better future or outcome.

Hope: It means to desire or want something to be true.

Hopelessness: It means that there is no hope and/or the outcome has already been determined.

School-to-Prison Pipeline: It is the result of educational system inequities in discipline and exclusionary policies that place some students at a disadvantage ushering them into the criminal justice system.

Science of Hope: It is goal-directed thinking focusing on developing clear goals and sustainable momentum to achieve them.

Trauma: It is broadly defined as any event or series of events that are physically, emotionally, or spiritually harmful or life threatening.

Chapter 8
Integrating Family History Into the Post-Pandemic Elementary Learning Space:
Reducing Childhood Trauma

Belinda M. Alexander-Ashley
Independent Researcher, USA

ABSTRACT

The COVID-19 pandemic highlighted existing inequities as a result of zero tolerance and exclusionary policies that disproportionately impacted the world's learners living in poverty, people of color, and those experiencing special challenges. Under the existing educational system, marginalized students often feel devalued and without a voice. Integrating family history and genealogy into the elementary school learning space provides a methodology and framework that focuses on the historical conditions that promote healthy dialogues and sustain discourses connecting to other historical events. The process of creating positive experiences with family history, improving the classroom environment, effectively communicating, rapport and trust building, and strengthened socio-emotional skills reduce childhood trauma. The six recommended strategies include introspection and reflection, navigating parallel time periods, valuing genealogical tools, encouraging an environment of hope, normalizing authenticity, and transforming the learning environment.

DOI: 10.4018/978-1-6684-5713-9.ch008

INTRODUCTION

Although hugely disruptive, the COVID-19 pandemic impacted more than 1.6 billion learners worldwide in more than 190 countries (Chaturvedi et al., 2021). While the disparities predated the pandemic, COVID-19 further exposed and amplified existing inequities in the global education system (Sahlberg, 2020). The inequities including zero tolerance and exclusionary policies were especially disastrous for segments of the world's learners living in poverty, minority populations, and those experiencing special challenges. These inequities in the educational system further marginalize disadvantaged minority youth who are often overrepresented among those most harshly disciplined (Wald & Losen, 2003), exposing them to childhood trauma and the school-to-prison pipeline (STPP). The school-to-prison pipeline has more recently been referred to the school-to-prison nexus (Nunez-Eddy, 2022). Under the existing educational system, marginalized students often feel devalued and without a voice. Integrating family history into the curriculum along with the recommended strategies create a more inclusive learning space that encourages sharing personal histories that reduce childhood trauma by introducing positive experiences, increasing authentic communication, promoting resilience, and building a sense of personal identity and belonging (International Schooling, n.d.).

By integrating family history and storytelling into the elementary school curriculum, it serves as a transformational tool that encourages a deeper understanding of experiences, connectedness, and empathy. While some studies have sought to make students uncomfortable intentionally to undertake authentic discourses with older students (Case & Ngo, 2017), the focus with elementary students is sharing common histories and normalizing family experiences. Additionally, the strategies encourage the development of trauma-informed responses from elementary educators by creating safe, secure learning spaces, promoting self-awareness, and trusting relationships that reduce trauma and mitigate exposure to the school-to-prison nexus.

CHILDHOOD TRAUMA AND THE SCHOOL-TO-PRISON NEXUS

The Center for Disease Control and Kaiser Permanente (1995) conducted one of the largest studies involving childhood abuse, neglect, and household challenges that negatively impacted the well-being of children with generational consequences. Plaguing the educational system is its response to adverse childhood experiences (ACEs) which are traumatic events that occur prior to age seventeen (Center for Disease Control and Prevention [CDC], 1995). Childhood trauma, whether physical, sexual or emotional, has consequences that may create lifelong challenges (Stavrianos et al., 2011; Maniglio, 2009). The effects of trauma increase the risk for violent and aggressive behavior and criminality in adulthood creating a nexus between childhood trauma and the criminal justice system (Kalmuss, 1984; Straus et al., 1980; Widom, 1989). ACEs have both personal and environmental factors. Personal ACEs may include violence, abuse, neglect, witnessed violence, or exposure to suicide. Environmental factors that may contribute to childhood trauma by undermining feelings of safety, stability and bonding. While none originated with the pandemic, ACEs were accentuated with the disruption of educational system and social stability.

The racial disparities within the educational and judicial systems are so similar that it becomes impossible not to recognize the linkage between the two (Wald & Losen, 2003). Among those incarcerated, rates of childhood and adult trauma are high (Wolff & Shi, 2012), creating a portal between the STPP and mass incarceration. Terms such as prison track, school-to-prison nexus have been used to describe the trend toward mass incarceration (Wald & Losen, 2003). In addition, childhood trauma is associated with the risk for emotional disorders (e.g., depression and anxiety) and co-morbid conditions such as substance abuse and antisocial behaviors in adulthood (Wolff & Shi, 2012). Subsequently, reducing trauma enhances the health of young people within the educational system by lowering the risk to associated conditions.

The school-to-prison nexus is the result of disproportionate discipline and exclusionary policies that ultimately circumvent students, especially Black and Brown students, out of school systems and ushers them into the criminal justice system (Basford et al., 2020). Generations of exposure to these disciplinary and exclusionary policies may result in students being relegated to a permanent underclass without the ability to access the necessary tools to break free of its constraints (Alexander, 2010). The difference between being able to overcome and succumb to childhood trauma is simply having a trusting relationship with someone who believes in, values and respects the child (CDC, 1995). The system must be reshaped to encourage development of individuals with trusting relationships inclusive of all students – even those who seem to struggle the most with behavioral difficulties as a result of traumatic events. By reducing the negative effects of disruptive behavior, reducing delinquency, and managing emotions, the exposure to the student-to-prison nexus is mitigated (Wald & Losen, 2003).

Mitigating childhood trauma begins with building a school culture that values the realities of racially diverse youth, promotes transparent practices, and integrates families and community members into the governance and decision making (Henderson et al, 2019). By encouraging youth to value their own uniqueness by sharing their family history, they become aware of their families' place and contribution to history. When schools integrate the lived experiences and cultural realities of youth and promote a high degree of educational excellence, young people are likely to demonstrate academic performance and sense of belonging (Borreno et al., 2016; Dobbie & Fryer, 2011).

In learning spaces, students who have experienced trauma may elicit a multitude of responses. For example, responses to trauma may include anger, aggression towards others, and self-destructive and suicidal behaviors (Brodsky et al., 2001; Dube et al, 2001; van der Kolk et al., 1996). Educators that understand these responses and are equipped to respond to the behavior may alter the trajectory of their student's outcomes. Mental disorders associated with childhood trauma include depression, anxiety disorders, post-traumatic stress disorder, dissociative disorders and psychosis (Chapman et al., 2004; Stein et al., 1988; Springer et al., 2007). Childhood abuse also has been found to significantly predict adult arrests for alcohol and/or drug related offenses (Ireland & Widom, 1994). Those exposed to the school to prison nexus carry trauma into adulthood.

For many people, family history and genealogy are the same thing. However, Durie (2017) offers a useful distinction that critical family history builds on. According to Durie, "Genealogy is the retrieval of vital and familial data from records of various types, and its ordering into meaningful relationship patterns" (p. 2). Family history "takes the basic data of genealogical investigations, and includes the surrounding historical, economic, social, political, and other contexts to build a connected narrative" (p. 2). For the purpose of this chapter, genealogy may be thought of as a subset or part of family history.

After 22 years of working with underrepresented populations in the federal probation system, the author became concerned with the plight of the educational system and its connection to mass incarceration especially following the pandemic. This led to research involving the question of how family history could be used as a pedagogical tool to increase student engagement, encourage empathy, reduce trauma and mitigate exposure to the school-to-prison nexus. Introduction at the elementary grade level was pursued to normalize authenticity of shared narratives and common histories, not an attempt to make students intentionally uncomfortable.

INTEGRATED FAMILY HISTORY

Genealogy and family history provide critical methodology which focuses on the historical conditions that produce dialogue, how individuals have been shaped in a given time and space, as well as the mechanisms of power that produce and sustain such dialogues (Arribas-Ayllon & Walkerdine, 2008, p. 91). Researchers with diverse global perspectives recognize the power and influence of critical family history as a pedagogical tool of transformation that includes deeper introspection gleaned from one's family history (Mokuria et al., 2020). Transformational power lies in the ability to understand each person's unique experiences and integrate them into the curriculum to connect and engage on a deeper level. With greater understanding and knowledge of responses related to trauma, educators may be more impactful in recognizing and circumventing student behavior away from the school-to-prison nexus. Through deeper introspection, learning becomes more meaningful and engaging (Gay, 2000, 2002). These opportunities for positive experiences, rapport building and effective communication reduce the effects of childhood trauma (International Schooling, n.d.).

Mitigating race-related trauma begins by building a school culture that values the cultural reality and authenticity of racially diverse youth, advocates transparent practices, and integrates family and community members into shaping the learning experience and decision making (Henderson et al., 2019). Teachers learn motivate their students to reach for success using best classroom practices for elementary school students based on child development and how their brain learns (Education Staffing Space [ESS], n.d.). Family history in the elementary learning spaces is a starting place to begin integrating a personal family connection and providing positive sharing in the broader learning process. Research suggests schools that increase opportunities for teachers and students to communicate with each other in restorative circles and learn from these shared experiences report a reduction in discipline referrals (Fronius et al., 2017; Anfara et al., 2015), which restricts exposure to the STPP.

There is no one size fits all approach to integrating family history into a learning space to gain its benefits. An important point is to start with the teacher, educators, and school staff in valuing family history because they cannot pass on to their students what they do not understand or value. This is why it is so important teachers remain open-minded and willing to learn from the lives of their students (ESS, n.d.). For Sleeter (2015), a central idea of critical family histories for researchers is to locate their own families within the class structure, asking how family members came to be located where they were, analyzing their place in the larger world economy and examining their interest in it. Recognizing that all have a history creates a deeper connection to the greater historical tapestry.

A focus on training school personnel to identify responses to trauma may promote healthier learning spaces among racially diverse populations where educators may be positioned to serve as advocates in changing the school's culture (Henderson, 2019). Healthier learning spaces promote more engaged students. For example, coordinating best practices in elementary learning spaces such as multisensory learning through multiple modalities including visual, auditory, reading, writing or and kinesthetic activities increases learning effectiveness (ESS, n.d.). Trauma-informed practices that seek to eliminate inequities by promoting discipline and exclusionary policies that lessen immediate harm from disciplinary referrals and connect youth to resources and caring adults (CDC, 2021).

The path of family history exploration revealed common traumatic threads with connections to significant historical events that provided a deeper understanding and connectedness, leading to greater empathy and resilience. Resilience and skills were strengthened by seeking to understand family history and the trauma experienced. The knowledge and skills gained were transferable to other aspects of life, reducing anxiety, increasing self-awareness, and producing a greater sense of well-being. The three narratives referenced serve as exemplars that were found to contain common historical threads that guide the six strategies developed for integrating family history into the elementary curriculum.

Personal Tragedy Narrative

Research using newspaper inquiries unearthed a little-known tragedy that had not been passed down from the author's previous generations. A *Muskogee Times-Democrat* (1913) newspaper article indicated that ten-year-old William "Billy" Markham, the author's great uncle, was shot and killed on October 24, 1912, by an intoxicated neighbor. Like many other families, previous generations may have sought to protect later generations by not sharing the traumatic experiences of the past (Mokuria et al., 2020). The directly impacted generation carried the burden and trauma of the child's death while shielding future family members.

This tragic event occurred five years after Indian Territory became the state of Oklahoma in 1907. During that time, the newly established state struggled to maintain law and order. Studying parallel time periods lends context to the time period examined and assisted with gaining a deeper understanding of events through a personalized connection with family ties. Teachers should have knowledge about cultures that are represented in their classrooms to be able to adjust their teaching accordingly (Rychly & Graves, 2012). Transcripts from the *Alberty v. State* (1914) case indicated that the Markham family, including the child's mother and four siblings, testified during the trial. This was fairly unusual because, during that time, African Americans were not always allowed to testify in a court of law. Former enslaved people were often relegated to a position of property or less than full citizens. Students gain confidence through collaboration and a deeper connection with their peers (ESS, n.d.). Studies find that many people seek a sense of belonging to place and community, reporting that knowledge of the family's history deepens their sense of personal identity (Bottero, 2015; Kramer, 2011).

Although not atypical, the story of William "Billy" Markham had been hidden or lost to succeeding generations. Many families believed they were protecting their children by hiding secrets from them, and oftentimes those secrets remained hidden (Mokuria et al., 2020). In this case, a child's tragic death may have contributed to the author's family's response to sheltering their children by failing to talk about events that create great sadness and grief. Direct and indirect family members were exposed to the emotional and physical effects of this violent event. The author gained insight into who, where, and how the family beliefs came about and their responses to them. This journey reduced the trauma experienced with more recent events because of the resilience exhibited by the previous generation's response to trauma.

Historical trauma may cause parents without the skills to effectively guide their children to rise and overcome the situation as a survival mechanism (Moore, 2022). However, trauma experienced by earlier generations can influence the structure of genes in later generations, making them more likely to "switch on" negative responses to stress and trauma (Pember, 2016). Much research is being done on epigenetics and its impact on later generations, but much more is needed. By understanding where and how trauma presents in later generations, it clarified and reduced the risk of additional trauma in the author's family. Teachers equipped to respond with trauma-informed practices to disruptive behavior in response to traumatic events reduces disciplinary actions and their students' exposure to the school-to-prison nexus.

The science of epigenetics proposes that more is passed along with DNA in our genes, suggesting that genes carry memories of trauma experienced by our ancestors and can influence how individuals react to trauma and stress (Pember, 2016). For the Markham family, the trauma experienced with this critical incident may have predisposed later generations to negative responses to stress and trauma. Similar to the Markham family, the COVID-19 pandemic left students, parents, and educators ill-equipped to respond in its aftermath. Understanding previous generations has helped the author become more self-aware of responses to tragedy and grief. This phenomenon is not a new concept to some cultures. Folks in Indian Country wonder what took science so long to catch up with the traditional Native knowledge of intergenerational trauma being passed to later generations (Pember, 2016).

Tulsa Race Riot Narrative

The Tulsa Race Riot, which occurred in 1921 (Tulsa City-County Library, 2022), engages and resonates differently when known ancestors were directly involved and impacted. The race riot reportedly began with an incident involving a White elevator operator named Sarah Page and an African American man named Dick Roland (Tulsa City-County Library, 2022). There are differences of opinions about what actually happened between the two, but in the end, many lives were lost, businesses burned, and the Tulsa community was changed forever.

Prior to embarking on genealogy research, the author's family had never discussed this tragic event in relation to their family connections. Little had been written about this tragedy in Oklahoma history books available in school. However, family research revealed connections to the event that were previously unknown. Genealogy sites were used, including *ancestry*, *my heritage*, *family search*, *national archives*, and *Library of Congress*, among others. Historical databases proved invaluable to the research process. Research indicated that several of the author's family members were living in and around Tulsa in 1921 and survived the tragedy by sheltering with other families in the surrounding community. While the history was not shared with later generations, historical trauma can give rise to insecure parenting in later generations (Moore, 2022). This may have impacted an ancestor's propensity to parent in fear of repercussions when speaking out about injustices. This knowledge of the event brought about deeper understanding because family members were directly impacted as the result of the tragedy and personal accounts of their stories and their survival now persist and provide examples of resilience.

With the pandemic's negative impact on the educational system, new opportunities were presented to explore whether family genealogy could benefit the post-pandemic learning environment. Research indicated that teachers may build their knowledge base by learning about various elements of students' culture ranging from tangible culture or family experiences, artefacts, and events to intangible culture such as values, traditions, language, and identity through their own research and meaningful relationships with their students (Morrison et al., 2008). Integrating family history into the elementary curriculum is not an attempt to circumvent the teacher's own research on their students' culture, but an opportunity to learn first-hand about history from the students' perspective. There are also a multitude of ways that students' may share their history including reports, presentations, paintings, sculpture and other multisensory activities.

In order to circumvent the school-to-prison nexus, greater opportunities are needed to reengage students with activities that generate discussion supplemented by strategies and practices that reduce trauma. For example, allowing students to present their families' history encourages confidence, authenticity and healthier relationships with peers and teachers. With a wealth of information available on the newest technology, children may possess different skills than their parents did while preparing them for their future (ESS, n.d.). By appealing to their curiosity and giving them the proper tools and support, teachers are empowering their students to be engaged and self-directed learners (ESS, n.d.).

Integrated family events have been linked, blending the past and present and transforming the future with a personal historical connection. This more personalized approach to integrating historical events has multiple benefits, including shared understanding, integration of personal history into larger historical events, increased engagement, and a more global connection to a broader community (Mokuria et al., 2020). Students accompanied by their parents or guardians sharing their family stories may be critical in changing how students view history, critical thinking, and narratives in their learning spaces. As a result, students and teachers become curriculum drivers for the changing needs of their students.

Slavery Narrative

History books often minimize the contributions made by enslaved people to the United States and romanticize historical figures (Sandler, 2017). By introducing family history in elementary school, the conversations about unique family histories and their contributions are normalized preparing them for deeper future dialogues as they mature. Time and again, dialogues involving genealogy returned to some fascinating new piece of family history uncovered and how the knowledge of that information served to shift an understanding of the past – particularly around the "peculiar institution" of enslaving people of African descent that has never been fully addressed, acknowledged, dealt with, or squarely faced by most contemporary Americans (Mokuria et al, 2020, p. 3).

The author descends from Cherokee slaves that traveled to Oklahoma as part of the Trail of Tears, the forced relocation of Native Americans from 1830 to 1850 (Pauls, 2021). Little was spoken about the day-to-day living conditions within the institution of slavery among Native Americans. History books made brief mentions of this trek involving the Native American people and less about their slaves. Having a personal connection to the event created greater interest, introspection, and authentic sharing related to this two-level tragedy. First, the Native Americans were forced to relocate, leaving behind most of their belongings. Although slaves were considered property, they were forced to relocate while still in bondage. Second, the injustice experienced by Native Americans was even more oppressive for their slaves, human beings without the capacity to protect themselves or their families. Many Native Americans and their slaves died during the journey (Pauls, 2021).

Transformational learning was gained through the resilience of several surviving ancestors, giving rise to later generations. Parker-Drabble (2022) stressed the therapeutic value gleaned from hearing and discovering ancestral stories. The author found similar results. William Markham, Sr., an emancipated slave of the Cherokee Nation, operated a water ferry across Fort Gibson Lake near Wagoner, Oklahoma. His entrepreneurial endeavor in the wake of such personal tragedies was a testament to perseverance and resilience. He is remembered as one of the heroes among his ancestors. Recognizing the value of understanding an event from multiple perspectives enhances understanding, empathy, and the capacity to explore each person's humanity. Although not always easy to discuss, authentic sharing that improves effective communication helps with healing trauma (International Schooling, n.d.). Promoting social-norms that protect against violence and adversity through public education raises awareness and offers practical strategies to reduce trauma (CDC, 2021).

Family history, technology, and the capacity to learn from previous generations provided a foundation that may be used to further engage students in the educational system promoting a deeper understanding of their families' contributions to our global history. The knowledge gained strengthened the author's connection following emancipation from the manacles of slavery. Scientific developments such as epigenetics offer exciting new insights not only into how our bodies react but also into how we manage to survive it (Pember, 2016). Gene expression and regulation are also important influences on the behaviors of organisms (Dias et al., 2015). Future research may change the way many perceive generational trauma.

STRATEGIES FOR IMPLEMENTING INTEGRATED FAMILY HISTORY

The worldwide community must work together if we are to resolve the issues left in the aftermath of the global pandemic. The challenge is to innovate and implement an enhanced educational system and assessment strategies (Pokhrel & Chhetri, 2021) that connect and engage students. Genealogy and family history have recently gained popularity and offers opportunities to increase self-identify, gain a broadened historical perspective, and increase effective communication that reduces childhood trauma and provide tools to mitigate exposure to the school-to-prison nexus. Family history provides a vehicle for students to both learn about their personal families' histories, while simultaneously connecting histories with the broader political, historical, criminal justice landscape (Mokuria et al., 2020, p. 5).

Educators that understand themselves, their values and beliefs may assist their students similarly by remaining open-minded to learning more about other's culture and beliefs. Teachers who can take the perspectives of their students are able to better understand their students' different needs and adapt their instruction and curricula to match those needs (Darling-Hammond, 2000: McAllister & Irvine, 2002). If students are to be successful, they will need the joint support of educators, parents, guardians, family and the community to prepare them adequately. It is a joint venture to reshape the existing educational system. Drawing on relationships with professionals, colleagues, and students' families for continued guidance and support further enhance the learning environment (Institute of Education Sciences [IES], 2008). The six recommended strategies combine the efforts and relationships of students, teachers, parents and community advocates in an effort to reduce trauma and mitigate exposure to the school-to-prison nexus.

Strategy 1: Introspection and Reflection

For Sleeter (2015), a central idea for those researching focused on locating their own families within the class structure, identifying how their ancestors came to be located where they were, and assess how they engaged in the nation's economy and their vested interests in it (p. 3). This provided a means to connect from a historical perspective during the time period in which the family member existed and engaged. Integrated family history allows for a personalized connection, reflection, and empathy by listening and connecting with others. These skills are especially important in the post-pandemic learning space where students and educators may feel separated and disconnected. It becomes important to promote opportunities to connect and learn from one another. Diversifying school culture by increasing the number of professionals in the school environment who represent the cultural backgrounds of the students is also important to improving how schools reduce bias (Dobbie & Fryer, 2011).

Research indicates young people who possess a positive racial identity are more likely to perform better in school and possess a high level of assuredness and confidence in their social relationships (Sellers et al., 2006). Each person has a unique history, culture, and story to tell. Introspection and reflection on their personal values and historical background reflect a deeper dive into the past, gleaning greater self-awareness, perspective, and a deeper appreciation for ancestral roots. Comparatively, interactions with institutional and symbolic racism negatively influence how young people see themselves and how society characterizes them (Henderson, 2019). Educators may start the process of introspection and reflection to model these concepts to their students to create a positive experience which reduces childhood trauma (International Schooling, n.d.).

Working with school professionals in addressing their biases to respond to culturally and racially diverse youth is invaluable to potentially improve student-teacher relationships and increase school connectedness (Osher et al., 2012; Anafara et al., 2015). If educators do not value the process, they may be unable to transfer its importance to their students, parents, guardians, or administrators. Integrating family history into the curriculum assists teachers in actively collaborating with one another at a local level to improve teaching methods (Pokhrel & Chhetri, 2021). Teachers and school staff introduce students to the processes using specifically designed school assignments that integrate the processes into the curriculum. Not only do students learn about how they fit into the broader history, but they gain perspective and self-confidence and value their uniqueness (Mokuria et al., 2020).

For example, student research into their family's history may culminate in a book, video, or slideshow, which is presented to their classmates (Mokuria et al., 2020). The potential challenge is that the students become vulnerable to the responses of their classmates. A learning space where the strengths of each child are celebrated, respected, and heard helps them feel safe in a psychologically supportive environment (Pickens & Tschopp, 2017). A personalized response to education allows each student's needs to be addressed because they have a voice, feel empowered with authentic sharing, and know that they will be supported. Family history allows the student to tell their own story crafted with their unique family and presents their history to classmates. Awareness of ACEs and potential areas of trauma including emotional or emotional abuse helps to create an atmosphere of emotional and physical safety may reduce trauma and positively impact both their personal and academic lives (CDC, 1995).

Strategy 2: Navigate and Integrate Family History Using Parallel Time Periods

Developing knowledge and understanding from parallel times periods allows students to learn about family history, assess decisions made during applicable time frames, review the consequences of actions and gain historical perspective. Approaches aimed at improving school and classroom environments, including reducing the negative effects of disruptive or distracting behaviors, can enhance the chances that effective teaching and learning can occur, both for the student exhibiting disruptive behaviors and their classmates (IES, 2008). The effects of childhood trauma on psychological functionality can be reduced with effective communication that transmits a sense of empathy to the child making them feel more loved and heard (International Schooling, n.d.).

For example, if the targeted time period is between 1907 through 1915 in the United States, historical events involving family members from this period may be coordinated with a broader historical event of interest, such as Tulsa's race riot. Because every student's history and backgrounds are different, some may not be able to access family information in every case. In that situation, students may research newspaper articles and other information from the time period of interest to gain perspective of the time frame from people that lived during the targeted time period. The goal is for students to form personalized ties based on the information and circumstances that they research and relate to their family. They learn to analyze information critically, assess the sources of information, and conduct comparative studies of other information gleaned from the time period. The collective sharing and learning expand perspectives and exposure to different cultures, who may not have the same experiences during the same time period.

Educational professionals play a critical role in helping children heal from trauma by ensuring that they have predictable routines and safe places to learn limiting settings to those that are appropriate for their current level of functioning (Bartlett

& Smith, 2019). Educators who understand how their student functions and values family history may be able to develop guiding principles in the learning space based on respect, authentic learning, and a bully-free zone. Learning to listen without judgment may assist with receiving new information, broadening understanding of others and empathizing with their experiences. Family history is the bridge between the past and the present that may be interwoven into a fuller historical tapestry.

Strategy 3: Teach the Value of Genealogical Sites

Shaw (2020) observes that "Family history research, identified as one of the top three leisure pursuits in the world, is a multibillion-dollar industry with literally millions of participants around the globe" (p. 109). Learning about technology and genealogical tools expands and enhances the learning process. Educators that have learned to use these tools in their own personal journey are more likely to share them with the students because of their familiarity. By integrating family history into the school curriculum, teachers and students work collaboratively to become curriculum makers. Family history also brings about clarity and an understanding of self, classmates, family, and others using the tools and websites familiar to family historians. If students know, understand, and value their personal histories, their confidence is heightened while broadening the historical perspective and available tools. Making online teaching creative, innovative, and interactive through user-friendly tools is critical to research and development (Pokhrel & Chhetri, 2021).

Genealogy and family history have become more popular instilling a sense of identity and pride in diverse cultures. Learning to use new technology increases available skillset and helps students connect to the subject matter. Afterall, learning should be fun reducing anxiety and increasing confidence in using new technology. Research indicates that there is a need to increase the use of culturally responsive practices and representativeness in schools (Borreno et al., 2016). By allowing students and teachers the opportunity to become curriculum drivers, they become more engaged and responsive to the needs of the student and their learning processes.

Using creative, innovative, interactive, and user-friendly tools enhances research and development in family history (Pokhrel & Chhetri, 2021). Software provided by companies such as Ancestry, Genealogy, and Family Search, among others, may offer a platform to interpret historical records. No one knows what will happen in the future; however, incorporating new tools prepare the educational system to respond to uncertainties and resources in the future (Pokhrel & Chhetri, 2021). Transformation in the educational system occurs when teachers are allowed to integrate assignments that change the landscape of their learning space. Incorporating family stories, heroes, heroines, beliefs, and cultures unique to their families broadens the historical foundation. For example, teachers as curriculum drivers should intentionally incorporate family history or storytelling to integrate a personalized approach to assignments to promote critical thinking, authentic sharing, and collaborative learning.

Enhancing skills and technologies that are familiar and relevant assists students with assimilating new information, promoting friendship formation, prosocial interactions, and support for others learning. Strengthening student social-emotional skills reduces or prevents trauma (CDC, 1995) and increases alternative responses to potentially upsetting circumstances. Several recent studies suggest that schools that engage and keep students engaged can serve as powerful deterrents to delinquency (Wald & Losen, 2003). By reducing delinquency and engaging trauma-informed practices, exposure to the school-to-prison nexus is reduced.

Strategy 4: Encourage an Environment of Hope

Students and teachers have an active role in creating an environment of hope, a belief that the future can be brighter and better than the past (Gwinn & Hellman, 2019). Integrated family history weaves past and present together to strengthen skills and tools available to navigate the future educational system. Educators too have a role to play in creating a positive environment of hope. Working with school professionals in addressing their biases to respond to culturally and racially diverse youth in valuable ways potentially improve student-teacher relationships and increase school connectedness (Osher et al., 2012; Anafara et al., 2015). Research suggests schools that increase opportunities for teachers and students to communicate with each other in restorative circles and learn from these shared experiences report a reduction in discipline referrals (Fronius et al., 2016; Anafara et al., 2015).

A positive learning climate supports students' academic accomplishments (Sherblom et al., 2006) and helps to improve social-emotional well-being (Way et al., 2008). Teachers and school staff should find ways every day to encourage and praise their students, make an effort to reinforce their efforts to build character, celebrate efforts to complete tasks and assignments, and cheer efforts to help others (Gwinn & Hellman, 2019). Positive experiences can help reduce the traumatic events of the past and increase a sense of belonging and being emotionally supported (International Schooling, n.d.).

Instilling positive energy inspired by hope into the classroom environment whether in-person or virtual requires intentionally contributing resources to accompany their changing needs physically and psychologically. Teaching and increasing familiarity with the language of hope can assist students in recognizing and using the language, which encourages a shift in thinking (Gwinn & Hellman, 2019). Students share their unique family history results with their classmates while engaging in authentic discussions to promote dialogue and empathy toward others. Differences should be acknowledged, celebrated, and valued for their collaborative learning opportunity.

Race, ethnicity, heritage, cultures, and other characteristics should be given the same opportunities to succeed despite their differences (Horner, 2019). Creating a student-centered environment where students share the stories that make them unique and valued helps to develop balanced human beings.

To prepare for collaborative sharing, teachers and students together may co-create rules for etiquette in the classroom. Allowing students to voice concerns and assist with creating classroom rules empowers and develops their self-confidence in the creative process. Sharing information in the form of videos, slideshow presentations, art, or alternative means allows creativity for the student to express their family history. This is also a building block component that can be incorporated into higher-level learning as the assignments become more complex and comprehensive.

Strategy 5: Normalize Authenticity for Genuine Sharing

Creating a powerful inclusive social-emotional climate helps students to feel more at ease when they express personal opinions and experiences (Cuseo, 2000). Genuine sharing of history promotes authenticity and reflects on the realities experienced by the student. Students are encouraged to "keep it real" even if they fear negative responses from their classmates. Family history provides the conduit for students to normalize authentic sharing, present information that makes them unique, and collaborate with classmates on an area of expertise. Learners know themselves and their families better than any other instilling self-confidence and value to their ancestral roots. This collaborative sharing of knowledge and past experiences in pursuit of learning objectives and problem-solving is empowering. Improving authentic, effective communication and rapport building reduces the psychological effects of childhood trauma (International Schooling, n.d.).

Collaboration with parents or other family members offers an opportunity to filter information that they do not want publicly discussed in their child's classroom. For example, learning that a family member was committed to a debtors' prison or mental health institution should be accepted as historical facts instead of points of judgment against the family. Disclosure of this or any other sensitive information should be approved or filtered through the parent or guardian. Having a relationship with a student's family encourages an open exchange of information. Being able to facilitate authentic discourses with cultural elements assists with gaining skills to respond to behavior related to traumatic events in their learning spaces.

Strategy 6: Transform the Learning Space

Regardless of whether the learning space is in person or virtual, research indicates that schools that integrate the lived experiences and cultural realities of youth and promote a high degree of educational excellence, demonstrate increased academic performance and a sense of belonging (Borreno et al., 2016; Dobbie & Fryer, 2011). The education of each child is too important for any to be neglected or ignored. Developing a healthy culture in learning spaces depends on integrating overlapping systems that include the family and advocates from the community in reshaping the educational system (Henderson et al., 2019).

Students in high-poverty, high-minority schools are routinely provided fewer resources, fewer qualitied teachers, and fewer advanced-level courses that their more affluent peers (Brennan, 2002). As a result, they experience lower rates of high school graduation, lower levels of academic achievement, and higher rates of college attrition (Wald & Losen, 2003). Understanding that this may be happening does not negate the fact that it creates a disadvantage for the students within its educational sphere. This creates the urgent need to develop educators that understand child development and exemplify a growth mindset (ESS, n.d.). When educators take an active role responding to the needs of their students, they change the trajectory of their student's lives.

Because trauma, whether physical, mental, or sexual, may present itself in an array of behavioral responses, it is imperative that educators recognize and respond with trauma-informed skillsets. Each child deserves to reach their potential within the educational system which requires reshaping the current system to intentionally reduce trauma and mitigate exposure to the school-to-prison nexus. It will require that all levels of the educational system respond at the level at which they exist to contribute to the holistic success of each student in their learning space. Expanding understanding, providing supportive trauma-informed training and adjusting policies to meet the needs of each student will require that value be placed at all levels and that everyone contributes to making the system better.

CONCLUSION

By focusing on integrated family history, genealogy and storytelling at the elementary school level, their exposure to their family's contribution to the historical landscape becomes more prominent, familiar, and impactful. However, there is no one size fits all approach to integrating family history into the learning space (Carey, 2020). Different subjects and age groups require different approaches to learning based on the functionality of the student (Doucet et al., 2020). The important point is to start with teachers, school staff, and educational leadership in valuing family history because they cannot pass on to their students what they do not understand or value (Gwinn & Hellman, 2019). A holistic approach to assessing and integrating personal history with broader historical events unifies the historical tapestry, making it more inclusive. The benefits of sharing family stories include increased introspection, expanded capacity to empathize, and a more impactful pedagogy (Mokuria et al., 2020). When youth have access to cultural models and messages that reinforce positive racial socialization, they begin to develop a positive racial regard (Hughes et al., 2006).

Exposure to the school-to-prison pipeline is mitigated by teachers and educators establishing trusting relationships in the classroom with clear expectations and instructions, increasing parental contact on positive student accomplishments, and providing alternative trauma-informed responses to disruptive behavior. For example, parent or guardian support may be increased by calling the parent when the child does something awesome in the classroom or asking the question "why is this happening?" in response to outbursts instead of suspensions or referrals. Implications for school health include working with school districts and personnel to evaluate school policies and practices that lead to racial inequity, strengthen collaborations across multi-systems, and build culturally responsive and representative schools (Henderson et al., 2019).

The need of the hour is to innovate and implement an alternative educational system and assessment strategies (Pokhrel & Chhetri, 2021). Genealogy provides a critical methodology which focuses on historical conditions that produce meaning discussions, how each person has been shaped in a given time and space, and the mechanisms of empowerment that sustain the discussions (Arribas-Ayllon & Walkerdine, 2008). The United Nations (2015, p. 19) suggested that we "ensure inclusive and equitable quality education and promote lifelong learning opportunities for all." Justice can be achieved only all learners are given an opportunity to be the best version of themselves. Inequality, inequity, and injustice are deeply rooted in human society (Xiao, 2021). It is unrealistic to imagine that they can be eliminated; the best we can do and hope for is to enhance equality, equity, and justice (Xiao, 2021). We must look to today's students to reach their potential as tomorrow's leaders. However, to reach their potential, they must be given opportunities to learn, grow and thrive. Lifestyle changes that include interacting with friends and family while releasing thoughts that rob the mind of peace help reduce the effects of childhood trauma (International Schooling, n.d.).

In a post-pandemic educational environment, integrated family history reshapes the schema of the learning space, allowing students to work collaboratively in building relationships. Family histories have become an important contributor to public and social histories exploring and publicizing the micro-narratives of the past (Shaw & Donnelly, 2021). Integrating family history becomes the bridge to connect personally with macro historical narratives. A focus on training school personnel to respond to diverse student populations may place educators in a position to serve as advocates in changing the school's culture. A dynamic list of six strategies for integrating family history into the elementary school curriculum is recommended as a starting place because they introduce positive experiences, increase authentic communication and rapport building, promote resilience, and build a sense of personal identity.

The six recommended strategies are as follows. First, introspection and reflection help students to become self-aware in gaining valuable insights into an integrated family history. Second, navigation and integration of history using parallel periods creates a personalized approach to a more inclusive curriculum. Creating a positive experiences and effective communication reduce or prevent childhood trauma (International Schooling, n.d.). Third, teaching the values of pedagogical tools and genealogy increases familiarity and transportability of the concepts. Fourth, encouraging an environment of hope enhances a student's potential. Fifth, normalizing authenticity in genuine sharing within the learning space promotes empowerment. Building rapport, strengthened socio-emotional skills, and resilience reduce trauma and provide tools to managing behavior that mitigates exposure to the school-to-prison nexus. Finally, transform the educational system by intentionally integrating assignments that incorporate family stories, heroes, heroines, beliefs, and culture to encourage authentic sharing and collaborative learning. Table 1 summarizes the strategies for integrating family history into the elementary learning space; the acronym *INTENT* can assist in memorizing the information.

Table 1. Strategies for integrating family history into the learning space

Designation	Strategies for Implementing Family History
I	Introspection and reflection
N	Navigate and integrate family history using parallel time periods
T	Teach the value of genealogical sites
E	Encourage an environment of hope
N	Normalize authenticity for genuine sharing
T	Transform the learning environment

FUTURE RESEARCH

With increased interest in DNA testing and family history, there is an opportunity for empirical studies to assess the role that the knowledge of ancestors and previously unknown relatives plays in mental health and well-being (Moore, 2022). Junhong Xiao (2021) argues that the new normal for all should be a package of solutions able to cater to learners of various types, minimizing inequality and inequity to allow as many people as possible to access quality education. Family history presented as a pedagogical tool enhances equity and inclusiveness by valuing personal history and student narratives facilitating the need for evidence-based research. In all cases, research is needed at varying ages, grade levels, genders, and motivations to increase equity in educational alternatives, especially for younger students.

ACKNOWLEDGMENT

This research received no specific grant from any funding agency in the public, commercial, or not-for-profit sectors.

REFERENCES

Alberty v. State, 1914 OK CR 48 (1914). https://law.justia.com/cases/oklahoma/court-of-appeals-criminal/1914/21571.html

Alexander, M. (2010). The war on drugs and the new Jim Crow. *Race, Poverty, & Environment*. https://www.reimaginerpe.org/files/Alexander.20th.17-1.pdf

Anfara, V. A. Jr, Evans, K. R., & Lester, J. N. (2015). Restorative justice in education: What we know so far. *Middle School Journal*, *44*(5), 57–63. doi:10.1080/00940771.2013.11461873

Arribas-Ayllon, M., & Walkerdine, V. (2008). Foucauldian discourse analysis. In The Sage Handbook of Qualitative Research in Psychology (pp. 91-108). Sage Publications. doi:10.4135/9781848607927.n6

Bartlett, J. D., & Smith, S. (2019). The role of early care and education in addressing early childhood trauma. *American Journal of Community Psychology*, *64*(3–4), 359–372. doi:10.1002/ajcp.12380 PMID:31449682

Basford, L., Lewis, J., & Trout, M. (2020, May 22). It can be done: How one charter school combats the school-to-prison pipeline. *The Urban Review*. Advance online publication. doi:10.100711256-020-00583-x

Borreno, N. E., Flores, E., & de la Cruz, G. (2016). Developing and enacting culturally relevant pedagogy: Voices of new teachers of color. *Equity & Excellence*, *49*(1), 27-40. https://eric.ed.gov/?id=EJ1095807

Bottero, W. (2015). Practicing family history: "Identity" as a category of social justice. *The British Journal of Sociology*, *66*(3), 534–556. doi:10.1111/1468-4446.12133 PMID:26173995

Brennan, J. (Ed.). (2002). *The funding gap*. Education Trust.

Brodsky, B. S., Oquendo, M., Ellis, S. P., Haas, G. L., Malone, K. M., & Mann, J. J. (2001). The relationship of childhood abuse is impulsivity and suicidal behavior in adults with major depression. *The American Journal of Psychiatry*, *158*(11), 1871–1877. doi:10.1176/appi.ajp.158.11.1871 PMID:11691694

Carey, K. (2020, March 13). Everybody ready for the big migration to online college? Actually, no. *New York Times*. https://www.nytimes.com/2020/03/13/upshot/coronavirus-online-college-classes-unprepared.html

Case, A., & Ngo, B. (2017). Do we hae to call it that? The response to neoliberal multiculturalism to college antiracism efforts. *Multicultural Perspectives*, *19*(4), 215–222. doi:10.1080/15210960.2017.1366861

Center for Disease Control and Prevention. (1995). *Fast Facts: Preventing adverse childhood experiences*. Retrieved on July 21, 2022, from https://www.cdc.gov/violenceprevention/aces/fastfact.html

Chapman, D., Whitfield, C., Felitti, V., Dube, S., Edwards, V., & Anda, R. (2004). Adverse childhood experiences and the risk of depressive disorders in adulthood. *Journal of Affective Disorders*, *82*(2), 217–225. doi:10.1016/j.jad.2003.12.013 PMID:15488250

Chaturvedi, S., Purohit, S., & Verma, M. (2021). Effective teaching practices for success during COVID-19 pandemic: Towards phygital learning. *Frontiers in Education*, *6*, 1–10. doi:10.3389/feduc.2021.646557

Cuseo, J. (2000). Cooperative/collaborative structures explicitly designed to promote positive interdependence among group members. Illinois State University, Office of Academic Technologies, Center for Teaching, Learning, and Technology.

Darling-Hammond, L. (2000). How teacher education matters. *Journal of Teacher Education*, *51*(3), 166–173. doi:10.1177/0022487100051003002

Dias, B. G., Maddox, S., Klengel, T., & Ressler, K. J. (2015). Epigenetic mechanisms underlying learning and the inheritance of learned behaviors. *National Institute of Health*, *38*(2), 96–107. doi:10.1016/j.tins.2014.12.003

Dobbie, W., & Fryer, R. G. Jr. (2011). Are high-quality schools enough to increase achievement among the poor? Evidence from the Harlem children's zone. *American Economic Journal. Applied Economics, 3*(3), 158–187. https://www.jstor.org/stable/41288642. doi:10.1257/app.3.3.158

Doucet, A., Netolicky, D., Timmers, K., & Tuscano, F. J. (2020, March 29). *Thinking about pedagogy in an unfolding pandemic: An independent report on approaches to distance learning during COVID-19 school closures.* https://issuu.com/educationinternational/docs/2020_research_covid-19_eng

Dube, S. R., Anda, R. F., Felitti, V. J., Chapman, D. P., Williamson, D. F., & Giles, W. H. (2001). Childhood abuse, household dysfunction, and the risk of attempted suicide throughout the life span: Findings from the adverse childhood experiences study. *Journal of the American Medical Association, 286*(24), 3089–3096. doi:10.1001/jama.286.24.3089 PMID:11754674

Durie, B. (2017). What is genealogy? Philosophy, education motivations, and future prospects. *Genealogy, 1*(1), 1–4. doi:10.3390/genealogy1010004

Education Staffing Space. (n.d.). *Best practices in teaching and learning elementary education.* https://ess.com/blog/articles-best-practices-in-teaching-and-learning-in-elementary-school/

Fronius, T., Persson, H., Guckenburg, S., Hurley, N., & Petrosino, A. (2016). *Restorative justice in US schools: A research review.* WestEd. https://files.eric.ed.gov/fulltext/ED596786.pdf

Gay, G. (2000). *Culturally responsive teaching: Theory, research, and practice.* Teachers College Press.

Gay, G. (2002). Preparing for culturally responsive teaching. *Journal of Teacher Education, 53*(2), 106–116. doi:10.1177/0022487102053002003

Gwinn, C., & Hellman, C. (2019). *Hope rising: How the science of hope can change your life.* Morgan James Publishing.

Henderson, D. X., Walker, L., Barnes, R. R., Lundsford, A., Edwards, C., & Clark, C. (2019). A framework for race-related trauma in the public education system and implications on health for black youth. *The Journal of School Health, 89*(11), 926–933. doi:10.1111/josh.12832 PMID:31578726

Horner, J. (2019, May 01). *Let's think about equity, equality, and justice.* Wisconsin Heights School Psychology. https://psychology.wisheights.org/2019/05/01/lets-think-about-equity-equality-justice/

Hughes, D., Rodriguez, J., Smith, E. P., Johnson, D. J., Stevenson, H. J., & Spicer, P. (2006). Parents' ethnic-racial socialization practices: A review of research and direction for future study. *Developmental Psychology*, *42*(5), 747–770. doi:10.1037/0012-1649.42.5.747 PMID:16953684

Institute of Education Sciences. (2008). *IES practical guide: Reducing behavior problems in the elementary classroom.* U.S. Department of Education. https://ies.ed.gov/ncee/wwc/Docs/PracticeGuide/behavior_pg_092308.pdf

International Schooling. (n.d.). *Six ways to minimize the effect of childhood trauma.* Retrieved August 15, 2022, from https://internationalschooling.org/blog/6-ways-to-minimize-the-effect-of-childhood-trauma/

Ireland, T., & Widom, C. S. (1994). Childhood victimization and risk for alcohol and drug arrests. *The International Journal of the Addictions*, *27*(2), 251–271. doi:10.3109/10826089409047380 PMID:8144278

Kalmuss, D. S. (1984). The intergenerational transmission of marital aggression. *Journal of Marriage and Family*, *46*(1), 11–19. doi:10.2307/351858

Kramer, A. M. (2011). Kinship, affinity, and connectedness: Exploring the role of genealogy in personal lives. *Sociology*, *54*(3), 379–395. doi:10.1177/0038038511399622

Maniglio, R. (2009). The impact of child sexual abuse on health: A systematic review of reviews. *Clinical Psychology Review*, *29*(7), 647–657. doi:10.1016/j.cpr.2009.08.003 PMID:19733950

McAllister, G., & Irvine, J. J. (2002). The role of empathy in teaching culturally diverse students: A qualitative study of teachers' beliefs. *Journal of Teacher Education*, *53*(5), 433–443. doi:10.1177/002248702237397

Merriam-Webster. (n.d.). *Hope.* Retrieved on August 18, 2022, from https://www.merriam-webster.com/dictionary/hope

Mokuria, V., Williams, A., & Page, W. (2020). There has been no remorse over it: A narrative inquiry exploring enslaved ancestral roots through a critical family history project. *Genealogy*, *4*(26), 1–13. doi:10.3390/genealogy4010026

Moore, S. M. (2022). How ancestor research affects self-understanding ad well-being: Introduction to the special issue. *Genealogy, 6*(20), 1–6. doi:10.3390/genealogy6010020

Morrison, K. A., Robbins, H. H., & Rose, D. G. (2008). Operationalizing culturally relevant pedagogy: A synthesis of classroom-based research. *Equity & Excellence in Education, 41*(4), 433–452. doi:10.1080/10665680802400006

Muskogee Times-Democrat. (1913, February 15). *Death penalty for Negro.* https://www.newspapers.com/clip/50460331/february-15-1913-muskogee-times

Nunez-Eddy, E. (2020). *The coalescence of education and criminal justice in the United States: The school-to-prison nexus and the prison-industrial complex in a capitalist society.* Arizona State University. https://keep.lib.asu.edu/_flysystem/fedora/c7/224798/NunezEddy_asu_0010N_20092.pdf

Osher, D., Coggshall, J., Colombi, G., Woodruff, D., Francios, S., & Osher, T. (2012). Building school and teacher capacity to eliminate the school-to-prison pipeline. *Teacher Education and Special Education, 35*(4), 284–295. doi:10.1177/0888406412453930

Parker-Drabble, H. (2022). How key psychological theories can enrich our understanding of our ancestors and help improve mental health for present and future generations: A family history perspective. *Genealogy, 6*(1), 1–21. doi:10.3390/genealogy6010004

Pauls, E. P. (2021). Trail of tears. In *Encyclopædia Britannica.* Retrieved May 25, 2022, from https://www.britannica.com/event/Trail-of-Tears

Pember, M. A. (2016). *Intergenerational trauma: Understanding Natives' inherited pain.* Indian Country Today Media Network. https://amber-ic.org/wp-content/uploads/2017/01/ICMN-All-About-Generations-Trauma.pdf

Pickens, I. B., & Tschopp, N. (2017). *Trauma-informed classrooms.* National Council of Juvenile and Family Court Judges. https://www.ncjfcj.org/wp-content/uploads/2017/10/NCJFCJ_SJP_Trauma_Informed_Classrooms_Final.pdf

Pokhrel, S., & Chhetri, R. (2021). A literature review on impact of COVID-19 pandemic on teaching and learning. *Higher Education for the Future, 8*(1), 133–141. doi:10.1177/2347631120983481

Rychly, L., & Graves, E. (2012). Teacher characteristics for culturally responsive pedagogy. *Multicultural Perspectives*, *14*(1), 44–49. doi:10.1080/15210960.2012.646853

Sahlberg, P. (2020). Does the pandemic help us make education more equitable? *Educational Research for Policy and Practice*, *20*(1), 11–18. doi:10.100710671-020-09284-4

Sandler, J. D. (2017). African American language and American linguistic cultures: An analysis of language policies in education. *Working Papers in Educational Linguistics*, *22*(1), 105-134. Retrieved August 9, 2022, from https://repository.upenn.edu/wpel/vol22/iss1/6

Sellers, R. M., Copeland-Linder, N., Martin, P. P., & Lewis, R. H. (2006). Racial identity matters: The relationship between racial discrimination and psychological functioning in African American adolescents. *Journal of Research on Adolescence*, *16*(2), 187–216. doi:10.1111/j.1532-7795.2006.00128.x

Shaw, E. (2020). "Who we are and why we do it": A demographic overview and the cited motivations of Australian family historians. *Journal of Family History*, *45*(1), 109–124. doi:10.1177/0363199019880238

Shaw, E. L., & Donnelly, D. J. (2021). Rediscovering the familial past and its impact on historical consciousness. *Genealogy*, *5*(102), 102. Advance online publication. doi:10.3390/genealogy5040102

Sherblom, S. A., Marshall, J. C., & Sherblom, J. C. (2006). The relationship between school climate and math and reading achievement. *Journal of Research in Character Education*, *4*(1–2), 19–31.

Sleeter, C. (2015). *White Bread: Weaving cultural past into the present*. Sense Publishers. doi:10.1007/978-94-6300-067-3

Springer, K., Sheridan, J., Kuo, D., & Carnes, M. (2007). Long-term physical and mental health consequences of childhood physical abuse: Results from a large population-based sample of men and women. *Child Abuse & Neglect*, *31*(5), 517–530. doi:10.1016/j.chiabu.2007.01.003 PMID:17532465

Stavrianos, C., Stavrianou, P., Vasiliadis, L., Karamouzi, A., Mihailidou, D., & Mihail, G. (2011). Emotional maltreatment of children. *Social Sciences*, *6*(6), 441–446.

Stein, J. A., Golding, J. M., Siegel, J. M., Burnam, M. A., & Sorenson, S. B. (1988). Long-term psychological sequelae of child sexual abuse: The Los Angeles epidemiologic catchment area study. In F. Sage, G. E. Wyatt, & Y. G. J. Powell (Eds.), *Lasting effects of child sexual abuse* (Vol. 100, pp. 135–154). Sage Publications.

Straus, M. A., Gelles, R. J., & Steinmetz, S. (1980). Behind closed doors: Violence in the American family. Anchor Press.

Tulsa City-County Library. (2022, May 17). *Tulsa Race Massacre.* https://www.tulsalibrary.org/tulsa-race-riot-1921

United Nations. (2015). *Transforming our world: The 2030 agenda for sustainable development.* https://sdgs.un.org/2030agenda

van der Kolk, B. A., Pelcovitz, D., Roth, S., Mandel, F. S., McFarlane, A., & Herman, J. L. (1996). Dissociation, somatization, and affect dysregulation: The complexity of adaptation of trauma. *The American Journal of Psychiatry, 153*(7), 83–93. doi:10.1176/ajp.153.7.83 PMID:8659645

Wald, J., & Losen, D. (2003, November 5). Defining and redirecting a school-to-prison pipeline. *New Directions for Youth Development, 99*(99), 9–15. doi:10.1002/yd.51 PMID:14635431

Way, N., Reddy, R., & Rhodes, J. (2008). Students' perceptions of school climate during the middle school years: Associations with trajectories of psychological and behavioral adjustment. *American Journal of Community Psychology, 40*(3-4), 194–213. doi:10.100710464-007-9143-y PMID:17968655

Widom, C. S. (1989). Child abuse, neglect, and violent criminal behavior. *Criminology, 27*(2), 251–271. doi:10.1111/j.1745-9125.1989.tb01032.x

Wolff, N., & Shi, J. (2012). Childhood and adult trauma experiences of incarcerated persons and their relationship to adult behavioral health problems and treatment. *International Journal of Environmental Research and Public Health, 9*(5), 1908–1926. doi:10.3390/ijerph9051908 PMID:22754481

Xiao, J. (2021). From equality to equity to justice: Should online education be the new normal in education? In A. Bozkurt (Ed.), Emerging pedagogies for the future of education: Trauma-informed, care, and pandemic pedagogy (pp. 1–15). IGI Global. doi:10.4018/978-1-7998-7275-7.ch001

KEY TERMS AND DEFINITIONS

Constructivist Learning Theory: An approach to learning that is based on people building their own knowledge from the learner's experiences.

Epigenetics: The study of changes in organisms as a result of modification of gene expression as opposed to the alteration of the genetic code.

Family History: A study exploring the identities and backgrounds of ancestors.

Fixed Mindset: A belief that the ability to acquire knowledge and skills are immovable.

Genealogy: A line of decent traced continuously from a forebear.

Growth Mindset: A belief that a person's ability, skills, and talents have the capacity to improve.

Maslow's Hierarchy of Needs: A theory that proposes that human needs may be organized into a hierarchy ranging from basic survival needs such as food and water to abstract concepts such as self-actualization.

School-to-Prison Pipeline: A theoretical construct resulting from disproportionate disciplinary and exclusionary educational policies that are especially harmful to disadvantaged students who may be circumvented into the criminal justice system.

Story-Telling: An expression of oral or written stories.

Trauma: An emotional response to an upsetting experience, situation, or natural disaster.

Chapter 9
Teachers as Disruptors of the School-to-Prison Pipeline:
Creating Trauma-Sensitive Spaces in Classrooms

Michele McMahon Nobel
https://orcid.org/0000-0002-6032-714X
Ohio Wesleyan University, USA

ABSTRACT

This chapter seeks to provide context for teachers' overreliance on punitive discipline practices and how these practices contribute to the school-to-prison pipeline. If preservice teachers course content can be enhanced, it may help teachers learn about their own bias, more proactive responses to challenging behavior, trauma and its manifestations, and trauma-informed alternatives to challenging behavior. These changes may lead to classrooms that are more trauma-sensitive and culturally relevant, which will allow teachers to disrupt punitive discipline systems that are contributing to the school-to-prison pipeline. This chapter provides an overview of relevant literature and suggestions for ways that teacher training programs can prepare teachers to be more trauma-sensitive. Topics include positive behavioral interventions and supports, social-emotional learning, and trauma-informed approaches. Specific classroom practices will be described.

DOI: 10.4018/978-1-6684-5713-9.ch009

Copyright © 2023, IGI Global. Copying or distributing in print or electronic forms without written permission of IGI Global is prohibited.

Teachers as Disruptors of the School-to-Prison Pipeline

INTRODUCTION

Everyone remembers an influential teacher. These teachers connect with students, build relationships, and find ways to support students' holistic development. In many cases when students are asked how they overcome adversity in the classroom, they attribute a portion of their success to a teacher who believed in them.

Meet Corey–a 6th-grade student who loves art and playing basketball. Corey is biracial with parents who are Hispanic and Black. Corey's family lives below the poverty line and he utilizes school breakfast and lunch programs. He also gets weekend food through the school's program to combat food insecurity. He has a dual diagnosis of Emotional and Behavioral Disorder and Attention Deficit Hyperactivity Disorder. Corey spends a portion of his day in a special education classroom for English/language arts and math. He is with his grade mates for science and social studies. He participates in choir and enjoys his elective art course. Corey has strengths in the areas of visualization and creative arts. He is a gifted athlete and enjoys anything with physical activity. He has interests in drawing, basketball, video games, and professional wrestling. Corey is challenged by his low tolerance for failure which results in disruptive behavior in classrooms. Corey struggles when adults or peers give him constructive criticism or feedback on his performance or behavior. He is unsure how to express himself when he has big emotions or reactions to situations, which results in yelling, inappropriate language, and physical aggression like swiping materials off surfaces or assuming a fighting stance. Corey's family life has some challenges as well. His parents are divorced and his dad is living a couple of states away. Both parents have abused drugs. His mother is currently incarcerated and Corey is living with his maternal grandmother.

Corey's short biography, while fictional, is based on the realities many school children face every day. Now, suppose Corey's teacher is an early career social studies teacher, working in an urban area of the city unlike where she grew up. She is white, a first-generation college graduate, who is teaching students who are predominantly Black or brown. She has strengths in content knowledge but is challenged by managing the learning environment. In the past, she has relied heavily on the school's discipline ladder, which outlines increasingly punitive measures to control disruptive classroom behavior. If Corey misbehaves in her class, she will likely utilize these punitive options. Corey's teacher is lacking the training she needs to be proactive and supportive. For Corey, moving through the discipline ladder of detentions, suspensions, and expulsion could place him on an unintended trajectory from minor school misbehavior into the juvenile justice system, contributing to what is known as the school-to-prison pipeline.

This chapter seeks to provide context for punitive discipline and the school-to-prison pipeline, an overview of the literature regarding these topics, and identify ways that teacher training programs can enhance preparedness in the areas of classroom and behavior management to disrupt the pipeline. Positive behavioral interventions and supports, social-emotional learning, and trauma-informed approaches will be described, but the main focus of the chapter will center around the importance of teachers understanding trauma and how to create trauma-sensitive learning spaces using evidence-based strategies from the literature. Knowing more about trauma and trauma sensitivity can help early career teachers respond to challenging behavior in a supportive manner, rather than using punitive discipline measures that feed the school-to-prison pipeline. The chapter will conclude with guiding questions about Corey to help readers reflect on their practice.

DISCIPLINE AND THE SCHOOL-TO-PRISON PIPELINE

While teachers themselves can be strong advocates for children and young adults, they work in systems that can be draconian. Teachers who lack knowledge of Positive Behavioral Interventions and Supports (PBIS) or trauma-informed practices may follow the school's suggested disciplinary procedures without seeking other options. Researchers note another contributing factor to the use of punitive discipline is implicit bias. Skiba et al. (2011) found that teachers' racial bias leads to subjective interpretations of student behavior defined as 'disrespect' or 'excessive noise' and that students of color are given office referrals for such behavior, thus engaging the punitive discipline ladder. Often, early career teachers are in situations where they have limited support and may rely on school discipline ladders as their only method to change difficult classroom behavior. One way to help support teachers is through enhancing content taught in teacher training programs. If preservice course content can help teachers learn about proactive responses to challenging behavior through PBIS, trauma and its manifestations in youth, and trauma-informed approaches, it is possible that teacher behavior can be more trauma-sensitive and culturally relevant, which will allow teachers to disrupt punitive discipline systems that are contributing to the school-to-prison pipeline (Bryan, 2017).

Use of Punitive Disciplinary Measures

Schools have struggled with finding the balance of order, authority, and power. In the 1980s, schools attempted to maintain their learning environments in similar ways to the "get tough" era of the times (Brown et al, 2020; Mallett, 2016). More punitive measures and zero-tolerance policies (Akbar, 2017) infiltrated schools and forced teachers and administrators to follow strict discipline ladders. Oftentimes these proved to be inflexible measures that did not allow for individualized circumstances to be considered or for "common sense" to prevail. It is not difficult to find examples of young children drawing pictures of weapons and being expelled from schools because of zero-tolerance policies (Martinez, 2009).

Research has found connections between trauma and negative educational outcomes, such as lower grades, lower standardized test scores, and increased truancy (Brown et al., 2022; Leiter, 2007; Metzler et al., 2017; Raby et al., 2019). Negative impacts of trauma can have longer-term effects as well, such as an increased risk of dropping out of school or being less likely to pursue college or vocational training (Covey et al., 2013; Currie & Widom, 2010; Mills et al., 2019). For youth of color, the outcomes can be exacerbated by the combined effects of trauma (Brown et al., 2022), systemic inequities in the education system (NCTSN, 2017), teacher bias (Bryan, 2017), and over-reliance on punitive discipline policies by teachers (Akbar, 2017). To combat these factors, teachers must know more about trauma and its effects on students' health, well-being, and achievement. As Pemberton et al. (2021) note, change requires shifts in teacher agency within the school and classroom learning environments.

School-to-Prison Pipeline

As defined by Meek and Gilliam (2016), the school-to-prison pipeline refers to the trend of setting youth on a "trajectory toward the criminal justice system through practices such as early expulsion and suspension" (p. 1). There is increased recognition of the inequity and racist nature of these exclusionary policies, but many schools are still engaged in the use of punitive measures (Brown et al., 2022). Youth who have engaged in school misconduct continue to be at higher risk of being arrested and transferred into the juvenile justice system, which perpetuates the school-to-prison pipeline (Hirschfield, 2008; Meek & Gilliam, 2016).

How can teachers become more aware of these issues and disrupt the school-to-prison pipeline? It starts with the way preservice teachers are trained. Knowing more about PBIS, social-emotional learning, and trauma can help teachers gain relevant knowledge that is required to support all students in trauma-sensitive learning spaces. The next section will focus on key concepts that can be embedded into teacher training programs, followed by the types of strategies and activities teachers can use in their classrooms to create trauma-sensitive environments vital to the disruption of the school-to-prison pipeline (Souers & Hall, 2016).

KEY CONCEPTS FOR DISRUPTING THE SCHOOL-TO-PRISON PIPELINE

To disrupt the school-to-prison pipeline teachers must have an awareness of the pipeline and the factors that contribute. Teachers will need to reject punitive disciplinary tactics in favor of proactive approaches, like those associated with PBIS. Likewise, teachers will need an understanding of social-emotional learning and trauma and its effects on students' holistic development and subsequent performance in schools. Trauma is not limited to students. Teachers can experience secondary trauma associated with their interactions with students who have experienced trauma. Thus, teachers will need to be aware of their emotional well-being and how their bias and frustrations can lead to the utilization of punitive discipline. Teachers are in a unique position to model their coping skills while helping students focus on developing their social-emotional skills.

Figure 1. Components that lead to the rejection of punitive discipline and seek to create trauma-sensitive classrooms toward the goal of disrupting the school-to-prison pipeline

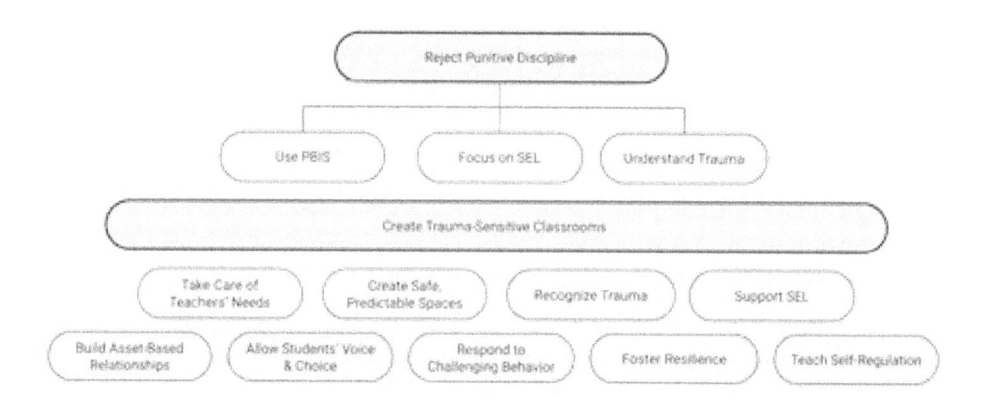

Positive Behavioral Interventions and Supports (PBIS)

According to the Center on Positive Intervention Behavioral Interventions and Supports (PBIS), "PBIS is an evidence-based, tiered framework for supporting students' behavioral, academic, social, emotional, and mental health. When implemented with fidelity, PBIS improves social and emotional competence, academic success, and school climate. It also improves teachers' health and well-being. It is a way to create positive, predictable, equitable, and safe learning environments where everyone thrives" (Positive Behavioral Interventions and Supports [PBIS], 2022).

When school districts and/or teachers commit to using proactive strategies with increasing levels of support, systems can change. According to the Center for PBIS, fully implementing PBIS into classrooms allows students to experience "improved behavioral, social, emotional, and academic outcomes" (PBIS, 2022) and improves the overall climate of their classrooms and learning spaces. In short, teachers who incorporate these practices should reduce their reliance on punitive or exclusionary measures of discipline, disrupting the school-to-prison pipeline.

Social-Emotional Learning (SEL)

The Collaborative for Academic, Social, and Emotional Learning (CASEL) defines SEL as "the process through which all young people and adults acquire and apply the knowledge, skills, and attitudes to develop healthy identities, manage emotions and achieve personal and collective goals, feel and show empathy for others, establish and maintain supportive relationships, and make responsible and caring decisions" (CASEL, 2022). CASEL suggests that partnerships between schools, families, and communities can advance educational equity and empower youth to create more just learning environments.

According to the CASEL SEL Framework, there are five core competencies: relationship skills, self-management, self-awareness, social awareness, and responsible decision-making (CASEL, 2022). Being aware of and including these competencies when teachers seek to create positive classroom environments should help reduce the need for punitive discipline. Teachable moments and SEL skill-building opportunities become available. Directly teaching students to develop self-awareness and self-management can lead to better decision-making–an important skill when faced with adversity. Working with students to achieve competency in these skill areas can help students find ways to manage when difficult situations arise and can give teachers ways to redirect and prompt prosocial behavior.

Trauma-Sensitive and Trauma-Informed

There are a variety of terms that are used somewhat interchangeably in the educational system–trauma-informed, trauma-sensitive, and trauma-responsive. However, there is a distinction according to the Massachusetts-based Trauma and Learning Policy Initiative (TLPI). Trauma-sensitive schools or learning spaces are places where "all students feel safe, welcomed, and supported" and the effect trauma has on learning would be addressed at a systems level, rather than in individual classrooms (Massachusetts Advocates for Children & Harvard Law School, 2022). Further, using the term trauma-sensitive makes it clear that teachers are not expected to take on the role of therapists, but they can contribute to the school and classroom culture of understanding trauma through the use of trauma-informed practices.

The term trauma-informed can be attributed to the behavioral health field (SAMHSA, 2014). However, the education field has used trauma-informed broadly to include any number of practices or approaches that take trauma and its effects into consideration. As Brown et al. (2022) note,

"there is a national movement towards creating and implementing trauma-informed schools that holistically recognize and respond to the needs of students who experience trauma (Overstreet & Chafouleas, 2016). Support for this movement is seen in local, state, and federal education policy and legislation, such as the federal Every Student Succeeds Act (2015) that includes grant funding provisions for trauma-informed services and in-service training" (p. 665).

The trauma-informed systems framework SAMHSA outlined includes four key features which can also be applied to teachers: (1) realize the prevalence and impact of trauma, (2) recognize trauma signs, (3) systematically respond using best practices and principles for recovery and resilience, and (4) resist re-traumatization of individuals (SAMHSA, 2014). In addition, Brown et al. (2022) suggest teachers also add "culturally responsive approaches that (1) recognize and validate the cultural and racial identity of the student, (2) understand the student's cultural group historical context and experiences in society, (3) affirm the student's learning style by having a flexible pedagogy, and (4) provide a positive representation of the students' culture in the learning environment and curriculum" (Blitz et al., 2016 as cited in Brown et al., 2022, p. 665).

Teachers, or other school-based personnel, have a unique ability to observe students' behaviors and emotions regularly as they may be the most consistent adults in a student's daily routine. This perspective may give teachers the ability to distinguish trauma-related changes from a student's typical disposition (Bell et al., 2013; Cohen & Mannarino, 2011; Gelkopf & Berger, 2009; Openshaw, 2011; Wiest-Stevenson & Lee, 2016).

There are a few cautions surrounding the use of trauma-informed practices found in the literature. Some practices may claim to be trauma-informed, but upon closer inspection, are not. Trauma-informed practices to avoid would be those that focus primarily on students' deficits (Nobel, 2022b), are not culturally responsive and therefore neglect historically excluded groups (Legette et al., 2020), ignore systemic inequities found in school systems and curricula, or fail to include school-wide efforts to affect change (Brown et al., 2022; Gaffney, 2019; Thomas et al., 2019).

Combining SEL & Trauma-Informed Approaches

There is research that suggests there is a correlation between students' SEL and academic success (Gregory & Fergus, 2017). Informed by this research, Pemberton and colleagues (2021) have identified a two-pronged approach that utilizes both SEL and trauma-informed practices. Specifically, "providing a two-prong approach that includes (a) SEL curricular interventions that are not color-blind embedded within (b) a trauma-informed framework supports racially minoritized students' well-being while simultaneously addressing the equity gap within the classroom" (p. 181). Pemberton et al. (2021) also include SAMSHA's six principles of trauma-informed environments in their approach. These principles are (1) safety; (2) trustworthiness and transparency; (3) peer support; (4) collaboration and mutuality; (5) empowerment, voice, and choice; and (6) cultural, historical, and gender issues (SAMSHA, 2018). The combination of the SEL, trauma-informed, and SAMSHA's principles may be the best way for classroom teachers to create supportive and proactive learning spaces where students' well-being can be prioritized.

HOW TEACHER PREPARATION PROGRAMS CAN HELP DISRUPT THE SCHOOL-TO-PRISON PIPELINE

Teacher preparation programs can do a great deal to help future teachers disrupt the school-to-prison pipeline. Preparation programs can introduce preservice teachers to PBIS, SEL, and trauma-sensitive approaches. When used together, these practices can create positive, proactive learning spaces for their students. Preparation programs can ensure that the trauma-sensitive content is embedded within at least one required course, perhaps classroom or behavior management, which also includes a field component to help bridge the theory-to-practice gap. If possible, content should be built across multiple courses and field experiences to help scaffold knowledge for future teachers and ensure they have multiple opportunities to engage with concepts (Brown et al., 2022; Bryan, 2017; Nobel, 2022a).

What content should be included in preservice teachers' coursework? Teacher preparation programs can build future teachers' awareness of their own implicit bias, address the effects trauma can have on students' holistic development, and help teachers understand the importance of using trauma-sensitive approaches to help disrupt punitive discipline measures. Overall, teachers are key to making positive classroom changes (Ellis, 2020).

Help Teachers Understand Implicit Bias

Ensuring that teachers understand who they are and how their experiences, personal identities, and implicit bias impact their teaching is vital to breaking the cycle of punitive discipline. Ukpokodu (2007) notes,

since most teacher educators are White and have been shaped by ideologies of color/culture blindness, it is critical that they learn to deconstruct who they are as socio-cultural/racial beings and how their socio-cultural/racial worldview and positionalities might influence their thinking, perception, knowledge base, relationship, and practice (p. 11).

Teacher preparation programs can help teachers become aware of their own biases and learn to use culturally responsive pedagogy (Bryan, 2017). One method described in the literature for expanding and exploring awareness of other cultures is through reading a variety of texts and articles that provide opportunities for critical reflection, journaling, and discussion about topics such as race, class, and gender (Ukpokodu, 2007). Carefully choosing texts and creating robust, diverse reading lists for multiple courses provides opportunities for teachers to explore issues of racism, intentionally interrogate their own bias, and reflect on how they can use this knowledge to empower themselves and their students in their future classrooms (Nobel, 2022b).

Build Awareness of the Effects of Trauma on Students

There is recognition that more teachers need to be aware of the effects of trauma on students. Trauma-informed instructional practices were being utilized before the COVID-19 pandemic; however, the inequities and difficulties spotlighted by the pandemic pushed trauma-informed practices to the forefront of teacher training and professional development (Jackson, 2021). Likewise, there is recognition that trauma can be debilitating and can change the trajectory of students' academic and behavioral journeys (Spence et al., 2020). Many teachers conceded that they needed to give more grace, to ask students how they were doing and what they needed to be successful in response to the global pandemic. These practices should not disappear as schools return to a sense of normalcy. On the contrary, these important aspects of SEL and trauma awareness need to stay in teachers' repertoires as they are crucial components to addressing inequities for students of color.

When teachers are unaware of the effects trauma can have on the development of children and young adults, they miss important opportunities to disrupt the cycle of trauma. Teachers who are trained to recognize the effects of trauma in their students can create safe spaces in their classrooms to foster social-emotional learning and are better equipped to send students on trajectories of success (Venet, 2021), and assist in disrupting the school-to-prison pipeline.

Adverse experiences and students' responses to trauma can make instruction more difficult for both teachers and students. When considering challenges students bring to the classroom, teachers can be coached to consider protective factors and focus on the assets students bring to the classroom. One key protective factor that has been identified is a caring adult who displays genuine care and understanding for students and their cultural backgrounds (Cooper, 2013; Portnoi & Kwong, 2015; Rodriguez, 2001; Swindler, et al., 2014). When students have a confidante they can go to when challenges arise, adults can guide and support them to increase their agency and self-advocacy skills.

Explain to Teachers Why Trauma-Informed Approaches are Important

Trauma-informed approaches are important because trauma can have profound effects on all areas of students' development, which is vital for teachers to consider when crafting lessons and establishing classroom expectations. According to the National Child Traumatic Stress Network (NCTSN) Complex Trauma Taskforce, trauma experienced by youth in their critical developmental years can affect multiple domains of functioning, including attachment, emotional and behavioral regulation, cognition, and learning (NCTSN, 2003). Adding to this evidence, neurobiological research has explored the effects of exposure to repeated and chronic trauma. Findings indicate that trauma can rewire the brain, making it more difficult for individuals to access higher-order cognitive processes that are critical to learning and executive functioning (Brown et al., 2022; Perry & Szalavitz, 2006; van der Kolk, 2005; van der Kolk et al., 2009). Teachers may notice that the effects of trauma are not limited to learning challenges, but may also appear in school settings in the form of emotional and behavioral dysregulation. Teachers may interpret this deregulation as misbehavior or 'acting out' without considering there may be systemic and/or environmental factors playing a role in shaping these behaviors (Akbar, 2017; Brown et al., 2022). Traditional classroom consequences used by teachers for misbehavior (e.g., detentions; suspensions), may not be well matched to the needs of youth who are experiencing dysregulation as a result of trauma.

How widespread is childhood trauma? According to Brown et al. (2022), data from the 2016 National Survey of Children's Health indicate almost half of children surveyed reported at least one Adverse Childhood Experience (ACE), with around 10% of children surveyed reporting three or more ACEs. Further, children reporting higher numbers of ACEs were from historically excluded racial and ethnic groups and households living at or below poverty levels (see Bethell et al., 2017; Sacks & Murphey, 2018).

Because of the prevalence of trauma and the likelihood that youth affected by trauma may be increasing, teachers need to be aware of trauma and what its effects might mean for students in their classes. Traditionally, trauma has been linked to those experiences measured by scales like ACEs; however, there is another form of trauma, "urban trauma", which relates to multigenerational, historical, and race-specific trauma (Akbar, 2017). Brown et al. (2022) note that urban trauma when combined with systematic disadvantages, results in continued oppression for students of color and those in poverty. This realization is particularly important for teachers working with youth of color and in urban settings.

To be most effective and supportive, teachers need to have an understanding of trauma and its effects on students' holistic well-being. One approach that can be utilized is culturally responsive trauma-informed education. In this approach, teachers can understand the contextual environments in which students exist, the potential effects of trauma on the physical, social, and emotional development of youth, and focus on practices that will allow students to thrive. In culturally responsive trauma-informed classrooms, teachers acknowledge students' emotions and experiences, teach students how to regulate themselves when something triggers their stress responses, and leverage the relationships that they are cultivating with their students (Brown et al., 2022; Wiest-Stevenson & Lee, 2016). Additionally, research has identified relationships with trusted adults as a protective factor for youth overcoming adversity (Bellis et al., 2018; Mortensen & Barnett, 2016; Robertson et al., 2021).

Maynard et al. (2017) caution that trauma-specific interventions that occur in isolation are not enough to support students' development across all domains. To be most beneficial, trauma-specific interventions need to be placed within a fully implemented trauma-informed system, like those programs that are being implemented by entire schools or districts. Brown et al. (2022) acknowledge that teachers engaging in culturally responsive trauma-informed practices who understand the intersection of systemic oppression and trauma are best positioned to effect change.

Given how important it is for teachers to understand trauma, its effects, and what that means for students in their classrooms, it is apparent that teachers need specific training to prepare them for the realities of the classroom, especially when teaching in urban environments or with students of color. The next section will provide specific emphasis on how to prepare teachers to create trauma-sensitive classrooms.

PREPARE TEACHERS TO CREATE TRAUMA-SENSITIVE CLASSROOMS

A major focus for disrupting the school-to-prison pipeline is to help teachers better understand why challenging behavior might be present in their classrooms and to provide an instructional response to this behavior rather than an exclusionary one. PBIS provides a structure for teachers to use with universal proactive support and opportunities to teach social-emotional skills. Teachers also need to develop an understanding of the role trauma plays in challenging behavior. The focus of this section is specific to initiatives around trauma sensitivity in classrooms and schools that have been shared in the educational literature (Atallah et al., 2019; Spence et al., 2020).

Support Students' SEL

Teachers are often looked upon by students as models for what to do in the face of challenges or adversity in the classroom. Research has shown that teachers who know how to recognize and regulate their social-emotional well-being are better equipped to guide students through similar situations (Schonert-Reichl, 2017). Doll et al. (2014) found that fostering qualities such as resilience contributed to more successful learning environments for students and teachers. Similarly, Souers and Hall (2016) highlight the importance of creating trauma-sensitive environments where students can thrive and work to build their resilience in conjunction with teachers. Finally, Boyd (2019) and Garcia (n.d.) indicate there is a need to ensure new teachers are aware of and can adequately use SEL strategies.

Recognize Trauma and Its Effects on Youth

Teachers need to be able to recognize misbehavior that is a manifestation of trauma and understand what the effects of trauma mean for students in their classrooms, especially if they are expected to create trauma-sensitive learning spaces in their future classrooms. Traumatized youth have the potential to exhibit effects long-term, which means academics and SEL could suffer (Bell et al., 2013).

Jaycox (2006) states that trauma occurs when a child perceives themselves or others around them to be threatened by serious injury, death, or psychological harm. This perceived threat can elicit responses of severe stress, fear, and/or feelings of helplessness. Further, Jaycox states, "that childhood trauma may cause several realms of the child's school life to be affected, including interpersonal communication skills, peer relationships, and academic achievement" (p. 140, as cited in Bell, et al., 2013). Teachers must account for these student needs and prepare to support and teach skills accordingly.

Types of Trauma

Teachers need to have a basic understanding of the types of trauma that may be affecting their students (Bell et al., 2013) but do not need to understand trauma in the same way as a counselor or mental health expert would. Having a basic understanding of how traumas are classified may help bridge communication between teachers, family members, and other specialized personnel. Traumas are generally divided into two categories: acute and chronic. The NCTSN (2006) defines acute trauma as singular, short-lived events occurring at a particular time and place. Chronic trauma occurs when related traumatic experiences continue over long periods. Examples of chronic traumas include child abuse, neglect, domestic violence, and chronic illness (Bell et al., 2013).

Effects of Trauma

As previously stated, the effects of a traumatic event or series of events can have lasting impacts on students' development. Traumatic experiences can impact functioning in neurobiological development, social-emotional development, cognition, and behavioral areas. Pemberton et al (2021) provides an overview of these effects as noted in the research literature. Cozolino (2017) and van der Kolk (2003) have documented the impact of trauma on neurochemistry and brain structures, including increased cortisol, norepinephrine, dopamine, endogenous endorphins, overactive amygdala, as well as decreased serotonin, and reductions in the hippocampus, corpus callosum, prefrontal cortex, and overall reduced brain activity. These neurochemical and brain activity changes can result in youth with

heightened startle responses, hypervigilance, emotional dysregulation, irritability, depression, dissociation, problems with executive functioning, learning, attention and concentration issues, memory impairment, problems with integration of information, difficulty modulating the fight or- flight reaction in response to anxiety, and other cognitive impairments (Pemberton & Edeburn, 2021, p. 185).

Perfect et al. (2016) adds youth exposed to trauma can also experience academic underachievement, anti-social behavior, and disruptive classroom behavior that may lead to increased school suspension and grade retention.

Hoppey et al. (2021) suggest that the prevalence of trauma diagnoses will likely increase due to contributing factors associated with the COVID-19 global pandemic.

Kanzler and Ogbeide (2020) predict increased diagnoses of post-traumatic stress disorder (PTSD) and post-traumatic stress syndrome (PTSS) will also occur, creating additional burdens on systems like education, that were already struggling to meet the needs of all students pre-pandemic. If these predictions come to fruition, it is even more important that teachers can recognize trauma and its manifestations in their students. Without this information, classroom misbehavior is likely to be misunderstood (Bell et al., 2013).

Implications for Teachers

Role of Teachers

When asked, teachers agree that they have an important role to support students who have experienced trauma (Berger et al., 2021). When trauma is missed by teachers or has not been identified, students' behavior in class may be falsely attributed to "laziness, lack of motivation, intentional oppositionality, or the student may be considered an overall bad student" (Pemberton & Edeburn, 2021, p. 189). Leading to the difficulties of providing adequate student support, teachers also state they are uncertain about how to respond to youth who have experienced trauma, largely due to their limited training and experience (Alisic, 2012; Berger et al., 2016). As such, teachers may revert to punitive behavioral control measures, rather than using trauma-informed approaches.

Teacher Retention

It is well documented that there is a shortage of teachers entering and remaining in the field (Carver-Thomas & Darling-Hammond, 2017; Sutcher, et al., 2016; Zhang & Zeller, 2016) and those in teacher education understand the challenges of the profession well—public scrutiny, issues around classroom management, high burnout rates, low salaries—to name a few. Faculty in teacher preparation programs also understand the need to ensure that teachers entering the field are ready to meet these challenges and stay in the profession (Ingersoll, et al., 2016; Sutcher, et al., 2016). This includes ensuring that future teachers have the knowledge and skills necessary to manage challenging student behavior and foster positive learning environments using trauma-informed practices.

Research on how teachers are trained in trauma-informed approaches is still limited. In 2021, Berger and colleagues conducted a study that sought to identify how teachers in the field responded to student trauma, the availability of resources and training for trauma response when necessary, and the wellbeing and professional practice issues of teachers regarding student trauma. The results of Berger et al.

(2021) contribute unique insight toward the development of targeted resources and school programs to reduce the negative impacts of trauma on children and the teachers who support them. Findings indicate most teachers expressed that more needs to be done to assist teachers in responding to trauma. Teachers suggested that "education and training about trauma would help deal with trauma-exposed students in the classroom" (p. 1052). Some teachers even suggested that learning about trauma and its effects on students in the classroom should be a part of their teacher training program.

Stress is often noted as a reason teachers leave the profession (Diliberti et al., 2021). There is research on secondary traumatic stress (STS), which would apply to teachers and should be discussed as an important aspect for future teachers to consider as they enter the field. Borntrager et al. (2012) found that teachers experience STS at very high rates; however, training in traumatic stress and STS awareness are not as readily available. Surveys conducted by Alisic (2012) and Bannister (2019) indicate teachers have the desire and need for training in traumatic stress to assist with managing students' traumatic stress, as well as their STS. Research regarding the implementation of trauma-informed education and the effectiveness of educator training remains limited (Brown et al, 2022; Lawson et al., 2019).

When teachers were asked about the type of content that would be appropriate to include for future or in-service teachers, responses from teachers included: understanding the different types of trauma, the impacts trauma can have on the brain, what students' responses to trauma may look like, how teachers can best respond to trauma, and how to respond to the parents of trauma-exposed children (Berger et al., 2021).

With the right training and awareness, teachers will be able to contextualize trauma responses as neurobiological responses that students need help navigating, rather than deliberate acts of misbehavior or challenges of power and authority in the classroom (Brown et al., 2022). This shift in thinking may allow teachers to respond with more intentionality to challenging behaviors, rather than punitively. Brown and colleagues (2022) suggest that rather than punishing misbehavior, teachers with training in trauma-informed approaches may be more apt to use evidence-based trauma-informed practices instead. They suggest these approaches "prioritize student needs, build community and connection, and allow students to learn prosocial behaviors" (p. 666) Examples of such programs include: Trauma-Informed Positive Education (TIPE); Cognitive Behavioral Intervention for Trauma in Schools (CBITS); and Restorative Practices (Baweja et al., 2016; Brunzell et al., 2015).

Barriers to Implementation

While the research is clear that trauma-informed approaches are beneficial and necessary for students who experience trauma, several barriers must be addressed. These barriers include lack of teacher training; lack of time during the school day to implement strategies; and varying levels of teachers' and administrators' buy-in of a trauma-informed mindset and approach (Baweja et al., 2016). Without buy-in, trauma-informed practices cannot be successful or sustainable in schools (Brown et al., 2022), which has dire consequences for student success and may contribute to an increase in punitive disciplinary actions.

PREPARE TEACHERS TO USE TRAUMA-INFORMED STRATEGIES

As established, there are many things that teachers need to know about trauma and its effects on student performance and behavior in the classroom (Robertson et al., 2021). Building awareness of what trauma is and how trauma responses can manifest in students' holistic development is an important first step in creating trauma-sensitive classroom spaces. From here, teachers need to have specific tools and teaching strategies available in their repertoire to assist when challenging student behavior does arise. The following collection of strategies could be included in coursework or field experiences for preservice teachers. The most logical place for these strategies to be included would be in classroom or behavior management courses or instructional methods, and some strategies could be modeled by university professors. In the field, guided observations in mentor teachers' classrooms and required reflection or journaling activities would further enhance the opportunities for future teachers to interrogate bias and gain exposure or experience with trauma-informed strategies. 16 states require some level of professional development for trauma-informed practices, but few states are addressing secondary traumatic stress (NASBE, 2022). Only five states require trauma-informed approaches during teacher preparation (Reddig & VanLone, 2022), however, more states require training in a single component of trauma-informed practice, such as culturally responsive pedagogy. The following compilation of evidence-based strategies may provide an accessible resource to add to existing coursework for preservice teachers or professional development of in-service teachers (See Appendix 1 for a list of these strategies with references).

Take Care of Teachers' Needs First

Teachers who recognize and regulate their stress and well-being can model strategies and support stronger social-emotional learning outcomes in their students (Schonert-Reichl, 2017). There is consensus in the literature that teachers need to prioritize their self-care to ensure they are not 'pouring from an empty cup' (Kaka & Tygret, 2020; Pawlo et al, 2019; Pemberton & Edeburn, 2021). For teachers to model self-regulation and SEL for their students, teachers need to stay as emotionally regulated as possible, no matter how difficult the situation. One way for teachers to ensure they can self-regulate in the classroom will be to know their triggers and how to adapt when something does become triggering. Souers and Hall (2020) suggest teachers should self-reflect to look for events, actions, circumstances, and interactions that can derail emotional equilibrium and create dysregulation. To help teachers identify triggers, they have identified the following common triggers for teachers: low energy, personal history, belief sets, implicit biases, expectations, and fear. Teacher education faculty can use this list as a starting point for discussion with preservice teachers.

Build Asset-Based Relationships

Previous studies have determined that teachers who build strong relationships with students can be motivating and are linked to improved student academic performance (Brown et al, 2022; Liebenberg et al. 2016; Masten et al. 2008; Masten et al., 2011; Skinner and Pitzer 2012). For some students, their teacher may be the only positive or consistent role model available, which means teachers' actions can have a lasting impact on a student (Brooks & Goldstein 2008; Masten et al. 2008). Asset or strengths-based relationships leverage the assets students bring to the classroom rather than focusing on the things that challenge them (Gardner & Stephens-Pisecco, 2019).

Building relationships with students is a good start, but preservice teachers also need to be culturally competent. Cultural competence is more than just recognizing diversity in the classroom. Lindsey et al. (2020) argue that teachers need continuous coaching and training to understand their own implicit biases and to become more culturally responsive to students of color. Jackson (2021) states cultural competence means having a system of discipline that is built on healthy relationships, trust, respect, empathy, and accountability, not on punitive measures of control. This shift in disciplinary tactics allows for more positive school environments and leads to higher achievement (Pemberton & Edeburn, 2021).

Zacarian et al. (2020) add that teachers should be building asset-based relationships with students because using an asset-based approach allows teachers to support students from their areas of strength while developing skills, competencies, and confidence in the classroom. Building culturally responsive relationships requires teachers to communicate to students that they are valued, belong, and are emotionally and physically safe in their classrooms.

Create Safe, Predictable Spaces

Teachers can create safe and predictable spaces in their classrooms by implementing routines and procedures that facilitate self-regulation and emotional awareness (Brown et al., 2022; Brunzell et al., 2019; Gardner & Stephens-Pisecco, 2019; Pawlo et al., 2019; Zacarian et al., 2020). Visual schedules and the use of predictable positive attention (i.e., "I will check back with you in five minutes") can assist students with self-regulation and can build trust when the teacher sets a timer and returns after five minutes to check on the student (Minahan, 2019).

Souers & Hall (2020) outline three required elements to create a "culture of safety" in classrooms. These elements are safety, predictability, and consistency. Safety means teachers have created a classroom space free from bullying, violence, or other physical threats to students' safety. Students feel safe to be who they are and trust those in the space with them. Predictability means that students know what to expect in the classroom space and what is expected of them. There is a sense of trust with clear communication between teachers and students. Finally, consistency means there is agreement on procedures, policies, and practices for success. Ideally, consistency would be school-wide and not just in classroom spaces.

According to Blaustein (2013), using the same routines in classrooms and during transitions allows students living with trauma to have stability in a calmer, more predictable, and positive space. Kris (2018) encourages teachers to establish a time for class or one-to-one meetings. These times can be used to set goals and co-construct norms (Pemberton & Edeburn, 2021), encourage students, check in with students, or practice strategies for self-regulation.

Encourage and Allow Student Choice and Voice

Pemberton et al. (2021) and Zacarian et al. (2020) suggest that teachers encourage student voice and choice in their classrooms to build students' sense of agency, shift the balance of power and authority (Bingham & Sidokin, 2004; Smyth, 2006), and recognize students' sense of identity as co-learners in the space (Morgan et al., 2015). Teachers who look for ways to incorporate students' voices and choices into their classrooms are utilizing relational pedagogy (Bingham & Sidokin, 2004; Smyth, 2006), which helps students recognize they are valued and trusted to make choices. Students who experience trauma may need to rebuild their confidence and capacity to speak up, address issues, take risks, and make decisions about things that matter to them. Teachers who can find safe ways for students to engage in such decisions will likely see growth in their students' ability to self-regulate.

Recognize Trauma Responses in Challenging Behavior

For students who have experienced trauma, developmentally appropriate emotional and social skills often are superseded by trauma-responsive survival skills (Cook et al., 2005). In the classroom, these behaviors can look like truancy, defiance, shutting down, struggling with boundaries, becoming overly self-reliant, or becoming too dependent on others (Pawlo et al., 2019). If students are experiencing overwhelming emotions in the classroom in response to triggers or stress, those emotions will limit the student's ability to process information and their social-emotional functioning. Pawlo and colleagues (2019) caution teachers need to recognize that the school setting itself may be stressful and teachers should be trained to recognize these stress responses in students (Berger et al, 2021). Depending on the level of student's needs, teachers may require additional support from mental health experts or counselors to best support students (Bell et al., 2013; Minahan, 2019). Venet (2019) cautions that teachers should seek clarity about their roles concerning students' mental health needs and establish boundaries when providing trauma-informed education. Teachers' sense of compassion seems to increase as they develop their trauma-informed practices (Morgan et al, 2015), which should lead to teachers choosing less punitive consequences for misbehavior.

Respond Appropriately to Challenging Behavior

Teachers help students feel safe, connected, and supported, even when they are exhibiting challenging behavior in the classroom. The role teachers play in students' mental health cannot be overstated, as they may be the first adults to recognize that a student needs additional support (Cohen & Mannarino, 2011). Students with trauma histories can react and behave in seemingly unexpected ways, which means teachers should expect the unexpected (Minahan, 2019).

When challenging behavior occurs in the classroom, teachers should attempt to determine what a student may be communicating through challenging behavior–whether there is an unmet need or a trigger or pattern that may help explain the student's response. Trauma responses can be "fight or flight" responses. One way to redirect trauma responses is by teaching students non-violent conflict resolution (Blaustein & Kinniburgh, 2018; Cook et al., 2005). Additionally, teaching decision-making skills can help replace the trauma responses over time. Like any new skill, initially, students will need explicit instruction and continuous prompting to acquire the skill, then opportunities for repeated practice (Pawlo et al, 2019).

Pemberton et al. (2021) add that creating safe spaces within and outside the classroom may also provide a sense of safety when students are trying to self-regulate. Students who are having difficulty with sensory regulation may need additional support to become more aware of their sensory needs and determine whether they require a reduction or increase in sensory stimulation. With a greater understanding of trauma response and students' needs, teachers can preemptively decrease problematic behaviors in the classroom (Opiola et al., 2020).

Foster Resilience

Resilience is the ability to positively function amid adversity (Noltemeyer & Robertson, 2015). Students who have experienced trauma bring a variety of adverse experiences into school, which can make instruction difficult. These students may need additional support to build their resilience (Souers & Hall, 2016). Building students' capacity for resilience may have short- and long-term benefits, resulting in fewer supports and less restrictive settings.

Teachers can build students' resilience by calling attention to resilience behavior when it is observed. Often in classrooms, teachable moments arise where teachers can model and guide students through a challenge. Similarly, teachers can model their problem solving by stating their thoughts aloud, making an internal process accessible for students. Teachers can encourage positive self-talk as students are working through a difficult situation. When students struggle to express themselves using words, teachers can encourage students to express themselves through play, art, or music. Finally, teachers can use lived experiences of others (e.g., podcasts; documentaries; books) to demonstrate that students are not alone in their challenges and that others have overcome similar circumstances.

Support SEL

Pemberton et al. (2021) suggest that teachers can help students practice SEL using skills from the CASEL framework. These include self-awareness, self-management, social awareness, relationship skills, and responsible decision-making. Skills can be embedded in curricular activities or teachers can use teachable moments to take advantage of situations occurring in real-time. Areas of emphasis include teaching students how to connect with others, helping students identify their needs and the needs of classmates, and recognizing and labeling emotions. Teachers can normalize making mistakes and model coping strategies in the classroom by pointing out their errors. Finally, teachers can use proactive management strategies such as redirection and choice to help build students' autonomy.

Teach Self-Regulation and Mindfulness

Teaching mindfulness in schools has proved to be beneficial for students of all ages (Maynard et al., 2017; Meiklejohn et al., 2012; Pemberton & Edeburn, 2021; Siegel, 2009). Mindfulness activities, like breathing, guided meditation, or yoga, can be easily embedded in classrooms as a quick start or ending of class or transition and is helpful to ground and emotionally regulate students and teachers (Pemberton & Edeburn, 2021). Other creative forms of expression, such as music, art, and writing, have been noted as having therapeutic benefits (Green, 2011) and can assist in the learning process (Pemberton & Edeburn, 2021). To enhance cultural competence and community building, teachers can incorporate music, poetry, and art from various cultures, ethnicities, and languages, which can be meaningful and relevant for students of color (Pemberton & Edeburn, 2021). Minahan (2019) notes that for some students, self-regulation may require a requested break from activities, but often students who are in a calming space with limited stimuli revert to the rumination of negative thoughts. Minahan advises that teachers should design calming spaces that utilize low stimuli activities that provide a cognitive distraction (e.g., listening center, find Waldo activity) to prevent rumination of negative thoughts while in the space. Building self-regulatory skills in students can help prevent the behavior from escalating, which means teachers will not consider punitive measures necessary.

AREAS FOR FUTURE RESEARCH

Three areas require additional research attention when reviewing the literature on trauma training, teacher preparation, and the effects of teacher training on the disruption of the school-to-prison pipeline. The first is investigating how widespread the inclusion of information on trauma, its effects on students' performance, and how teachers can support these students might be in teacher preparation programs. Second, for programs that do include such information, there is limited research on the effectiveness of trauma training. Additionally, there is a need to support in-service teachers through professional development, although information regarding this training is equally limited. Finally, there is limited research on the impact of teacher training on the reduction of punitive disciplinary approaches, which could disrupt the school-to-prison pipeline.

Inclusion of Trauma Training in Teacher Preparation Programs

There is a gap in the literature on the inclusion of trauma training in teacher preparation programs (Brown et al., 2022). In 2014, Freeman and colleagues reviewed standards and accreditation documentation and reported that only 28 states required training in evidence-based classroom management practices. It is unclear whether or not these classroom management practices include trauma-informed approaches or any trauma training. Since 2014, there have been initiatives to include more PBIS in public schools, but whether or not teachers are trained in these practices before employment remains largely unknown. Brown et al. (2022) point to several free and available resources that teacher preparation programs can utilize to close this training gap. They suggest free webinars hosted by the NCTSN and various resources covering the impact of trauma on learning and strategies for educators offered by the TLPI.

Research on the Effectiveness of Trauma Training for Preservice and In-Service Teachers

Brown et al (2022) report their study investigating the effects of trauma training for preservice teachers may be the first of its kind. Their findings suggest that positive changes occurred "in teacher candidates' attitudes, knowledge, and skills following trauma training" (p. 676). Their training consisted of 3.5 hours of trauma training and was structured as a mini-conference with a keynote speaker, several trauma-specific breakout sessions, and a presenter panel. Brown et al.'s findings are promising and their training could be easily replicated by other teacher preparation programs.

There is limited research on the availability or the effectiveness of professional development for teachers regarding trauma-informed approaches. Because of the prevalence of trauma among students, training cannot be limited to preservice teachers only but needs to be available for in-service teachers through professional development. There are specific training programs such as Compassionate Schools Training (Parker et al., 2020), but often these programs require whole district commitments, which may leave individual teachers with gaps in their knowledge and practice, and students with unmet needs in their classrooms. Teachers need supportive networks (Brown et al, 2022) to ensure they have healthy ways to handle the STS of working in schools, as well as the tools necessary to support all students.

Limited Research on the Effects of Teacher Training on the Disruption of the School-to-Prison Pipeline

Research is limited on the effects that improved teacher training could have on the reduction of punitive discipline measures and whether those reductions could have a profound effect on the disruption of the school-to-prison pipeline. It stands to reason that with additional awareness, empathy, and support for prosocial behaviors, there should be reductions in exclusionary discipline used by teachers. However, there is limited research to support this assertion.

CONCLUSION

Disrupting the school-to-prison pipeline may start with disrupting teachers' overreliance on punitive disciplinary measures and schools that allow such practices to continue. Teacher preparation programs have an important role to play when training future teachers to understand trauma and its effects on students' academic and behavioral performance. Teachers can be better equipped to meet the needs of all students, without punitive discipline. Removing harsh disciplinary tactics seeks to reduce the number of students who become disenfranchised by school systems and find themselves on pathways into the juvenile justice system. For students like Corey, having trauma-informed teachers who want to get to know him, leverage his strengths, and help him develop his self-regulatory skills will make all the difference.

REFLECTION

Returning to the case study student Corey, after reading this chapter and learning more about trauma, use the following reflective prompts to guide your thinking about Corey and students with similar traumatic experiences.

Reflective Prompts

- What strengths do you see in Corey? How could these strengths be leveraged in the classroom?
- What things seem to challenge Corey? Are there specific triggers to his behavior? What role could trauma play in the reactions Corey has in certain situations?
- What questions do you have about Corey and his situation? Who could help you seek additional information?
- How can you gain rapport and begin to develop a relationship with Corey?
- What strategies might be useful for Corey? List at least three challenging behaviors and strategies. Provide a rationale for why you matched these strategies to specific challenging behavior exhibited by Corey.
- What ideas do you have for fostering resilience for Corey or with other students?
- What things can you bring into your classroom tomorrow that could make a difference for Corey and others?

Now reflect on your knowledge regarding trauma-informed practices and how you can disrupt the school-to-prison pipeline:

- What did you learn in this chapter that was affirming?
- What do you feel is still challenging for you?
- What stereotypes or biases did you uncover as you read the chapter?
- How can you improve your resilience and your students?
- Where can you go for support if you need additional resources?
- How does being aware of trauma and its effects change the way you engage with students?
- What have you learned about the school-to-prison pipeline and how trauma-informed practices might lead to better outcomes for students?

ACKNOWLEDGMENT

This research received no specific grant from any funding agency in the public, commercial, or not-for-profit sectors.

REFERENCES

Akbar, M. (2017). *Urban trauma: A legacy of racism*. Publish Your Purpose Press.

Alisic, E. (2012). Teachers' perspectives on providing support to children after trauma: A qualitative study. *School Psychology Quarterly, 27*(1), 51–59. doi:10.1037/a0028590 PMID:22582936

Atallah, D., Koslouski, J., Perkins, K., Marsico, C., & Porche, M. (2019). *An Evaluation of Trauma and Learning Policy Initiative's (TLPI) Inquiry-Based Process: Year Three*. Boston University, Wheelock College of Education and Human Development. https://traumasensitiveschools.org/wp-content/uploads/2020/07/Evaluation-Trauma-Learning-Policy-Initiative-Inquiry-Based-Process-Year-3-BU.pdf

Bannister, T. (2019). *Teaching is a work of heart: A narrative inquiry on the impact of trauma-informed practice on teacher self-efficacy* [Master's thesis]. University of Victoria.

Baweja, S., Santiago, C., Vona, P., Pears, G., Langley, A., & Kataoka, S. (2016). Improving implementation of a school-based program for traumatized students: Identifying factors that promote teacher support and collaboration. *School Mental Health, 8*(1), 120–131. doi:10.100712310-015-9170-z

Bell, H., Limberg, D., & Robinson, M. III. (2013). Recognizing trauma in the classroom: A practical guide for educators. *Childhood Education, 89*(3), 139–145. doi:10.1080/00094056.2013.792629

Bellis, M. A., Hughes, K., Ford, K., Hardcastle, K., Sharp, C., Wood, S., Homolova, L., & Davies, A. (2018). Adverse childhood experiences and sources of childhood resilience: A retrospective study of their combined relationships with child health and educational attendance. *BMC Public Health, 18*(1), 1–12. doi:10.118612889-018-5699-8 PMID:29940920

Berger, E., Bearsley, A., & Lever, M. (2021). Qualitative evaluation of teacher trauma knowledge and response in schools. *Journal of Aggression, Maltreatment & Trauma, 30*(8), 1041–1057. doi:10.1080/10926771.2020.1806976

Berger, R., Abu-Raiya, H., & Benatov, J. (2016). Reducing primary and secondary traumatic stress symptoms among educators by training them to deliver a resiliency program (ERASE-stress) following the Christchurch earthquake in New Zealand. *The American Journal of Orthopsychiatry, 86*(2), 236–251. doi:10.1037/ort0000153 PMID:26963188

Bethell, C. D., Davis, M. B., Gombojav, N., Stumbo, S., & Powers, K. (2017). *Issue Brief: A national and across state profile on adverse childhood experiences among children and possibilities to heal and thrive*. Johns Hopkins Bloomberg School of Public Health.

Bingham, C., & Sidorkin, A. M. (2004). *No Education Without Relation*. Peter Lang.

Blaustein, M., & Kinniburgh, K. (2018). Treating traumatic stress in children and adolescents: How to foster resilience through attachment, self-regulation, and competency (2nd ed.). Guilford.

Blaustein, M. E. (2013). Childhood trauma and a framework for intervention. In E. Rossen & R. Hull (Eds.), Supporting and educating traumatized students: A guide for school-based professionals (pp. 3–21). Oxford University Press.

Blitz, L. V., Anderson, E. M., & Saastamoinen, M. (2016). Assessing perceptions of culture and trauma in an elementary school: Informing a model for culturally responsive trauma-informed schools. *The Urban Review, 48*(4), 520–542. doi:10.100711256-016-0366-9

Borntrager, C., Caringi, J. C., van den Pol, R., Crosby, L., O'Connell, K., Trautman, A., & McDonald, M. (2012). Secondary traumatic stress in school personnel. *Advances in School Mental Health Promotion, 5*(1), 38–50. doi:10.1080/1754730X.2012.664862

Boyd, M. (2019). *Incorporating SEL as a new teacher*. Edutopia. https://www.edutopia.org/article/incorporating-sel-new-teacher

Brooks, R. B., & Goldstein, S. (2008). The mindset of teachers capable of fostering resilience in students. *Canadian Journal of School Psychology, 23*(1), 114–126. doi:10.1177/0829573508316597

Brown, E. C., Freedle, A., Hurless, N. L., Miller, R. D., Martin, C., & Paul, Z. A. (2022). Preparing teacher candidates for trauma-informed practices. *Urban Education, 57*(4), 662–685. doi:10.1177/0042085920974084

Brown, S. J., Mears, D. P., Collier, N. L., Montes, A. N., Pesta, G. B., & Siennick, S. E. (2020). Education versus punishment? Silo effects and the school-to-prison pipeline. *Journal of Research in Crime and Delinquency, 57*(4), 403–443. doi:10.1177/0022427819897932

Brunzell, T., Stokes, H., & Waters, L. (2019). Shifting teacher practice in trauma-affected classrooms: Practice pedagogy strategies within a trauma-informed positive education model. *School Mental Health, 11*(3), 600–614. doi:10.100712310-018-09308-8

Brunzell, T., Waters, L., & Stokes, H. (2015). Teaching with strengths in trauma-affected students: A new approach to healing and growth in the classroom. *The American Journal of Orthopsychiatry, 85*(1), 3–9. doi:10.1037/ort0000048 PMID:25642652

Bryan, N. (2017). White teachers' role in sustaining the school-to-prison pipeline: Recommendations for teacher education. *The Urban Review, 49*(2), 326–345. doi:10.100711256-017-0403-3

Carver-Thomas, D., & Darling-Hammond, L. (2017). *Teacher turnover: Why it matters and what we can do about it*. Learning Policy Institute., doi:10.54300/454.278

Cohen, J. A., & Mannarino, A. P. (2011). Supporting children with traumatic grief: What educators need to know. *School Psychology International, 32*(2), 117–131. doi:10.1177/0143034311400827

Collaborative for Academic, Social, and Emotional Learning. (2022). *Fundamentals of SEL*. https://casel.org/fundamentals-of-sel/

Cook, A., Spinazzola, J., Ford, J., Lanktree, C., Blaustein, M., Cloitre, M., DeRosa, R., Hubbard, R., Kagan, R., Liautaud, J., Mallah, K., Olafson, E., & van der Kolk, B. (2005). Complex trauma in children and adolescents. *Psychiatric Annals*, *35*(5), 390–398. doi:10.3928/00485713-20050501-05

Cooper, K. (2013). Safe, affirming, and productive spaces: Classroom engagement among Latina high school students. *Urban Education*, *48*(4), 490–528. doi:10.1177/0042085912457164

Covey, H. C., Menard, S., & Franzese, R. J. (2013). Effects of adolescent physical abuse, exposure to neighborhood violence, and witnessing parental violence on adult socioeconomic status. *Child Maltreatment*, *18*(2), 85–97. doi:10.1177/1077559513477914 PMID:23420296

Cozolino, L. (2017). *The neuroscience of psychotherapy: Healing the social brain* (3rd ed.). Norton & Company.

Currie, J., & Widom, C. S. (2010). Long-term consequences of child abuse and neglect on adult economic well-being. *Child Maltreatment*, *15*(2), 111–120. doi:10.1177/1077559509355316 PMID:20425881

Diliberti, M. K., Schwartz, H. L., & Grant, D. (2021). *Stress topped the reasons why public school teachers quit, even before COVID-19*. RAND Corporation. doi:10.7249/RRA1121-2

Doll, B., Brehm, K., & Zucker, S. (2014). *Resilient classrooms: Creating healthy environments for learning*. The Guilford Press.

Doney, P. A. (2013). Fostering Resilience: A Necessary Skill for Teacher Retention. *Journal of Science Teacher Education*, *24*(4), 645–664. doi:10.100710972-012-9324-x

Ellis, W. R. (2020 October). *Healing communities to heal schools*. Educational Leadership, ACSD. https://www.ascd.org/el/articles/healing-communities-to-heal-schools

Freeman, J., Simonsen, B., Briere, D. E., & MacSuga-Gage, A. S. (2014). Pre-service teacher training in classroom management: A review of state accreditation policy and teacher preparation programs. *Teacher Education and Special Education*, *37*(2), 106–120. doi:10.1177/0888406413507002

Gaffney, C. (2019). When schools cause trauma. *Learning for Justice*, *62*. https://www.learningforjustice.org/magazine/summer-2019/when-schools-cause-trauma

Garcia, S. N. (n.d.). *How SEL helps you as a teacher*. Understood. https://www.understood.org/en/articles/how-sel-helps-you-as-a-teacher

Gardner, R., & Stephens-Pisecco, T. L. (2019). Empowering educators to foster student resilience. *The Clearing House: A Journal of Educational Strategies, Issues and Ideas*, *92*(4-5), 125–134. doi:10.1080/00098655.2019.1621258

Gelkopf, M., & Berger, R. (2009). A school-based, teacher-mediated prevention program (ERASE-Stress) for reducing terror-related traumatic reactions in Israeli youth: A quasi-randomized controlled trial. *Journal of Child Psychology and Psychiatry, and Allied Disciplines*, *50*(8), 962–971. doi:10.1111/j.1469-7610.2008.02021.x PMID:19207621

Gregory, A., & Fergus, E. (2017). Social and emotional learning and equity in school discipline. *The Future of Children*, *27*(1), 117–136. doi:10.1353/foc.2017.0006

Hirschfield, P. J. (2008). Preparing for prison? The criminalization of school discipline in the USA. *Theoretical Criminology*, *12*(1), 79–101. doi:10.1177/1362480607085795

Hoppey, D., Mills, K., Reed, D., & Collinsworth, C. (2021). Teacher candidates' perspectives of infusing innovative pedagogical methods and trauma-informed practices into a teacher education program during the COVID-19 pandemic. *School-University Partnerships*, *14*(3), 43–69.

Ingersoll, R., Merrill, L., & May, H. (2016). Do accountability policies push teachers out? *Educational Leadership*, *73*(8), 44–49. https://www.ascd.org/el/articles/do-accountability-policies-push-teachers-out

Jackson, R. (2021, October). After a year of trauma for all, how can we discipline more fairly? *Educational Leadership*, *79*(2), 45–49.

Jaycox, L. H. (2006). *How schools can help students recover from traumatic experiences: A tool-kit for supporting long-term recovery (Technical Report)*. RAND.

Kaka, S. J., & Tygret, J. A. (2020). 'You Can't Pour from an Empty Cup': 6 Things New Teachers Can Do to Promote Their Own Wellness. *Education Faculty Work*, 15. https://digitalcommons.owu.edu/educ_pubs/15

Kanzler, K. E., & Ogbeide, S. (2020). Addressing trauma and stress in the COVID-19 pandemic: Challenges and the promise of integrated primary care. *Psychological Trauma: Theory, Research, Practice, and Policy*, *12*(S1), S177–S179. doi:10.1037/tra0000761 PMID:32584101

Kris, D. F. (2018). *How to build a trauma-sensitive classroom where all learners feel safe.* https://www.kqed.org/mindshift/52566/how-to-build-a-trauma-Sensitiveclassroom-where-all-learners-feel-safe

Lawson, H. A., Caringi, J. C., Gottfried, R., Bride, B. E., & Hydon, S. P. (2019). Educators' secondary traumatic stress, children's trauma, and the need for trauma literacy. *Harvard Educational Review, 89*(3), 421–447. doi:10.17763/1943-5045-89.3.421

Legette, K. B., Rogers, L. O., & Warren, C. A. (2020). Humanizing student–teacher relationships for Black children: Implications for teachers' social–emotional training. *Urban Education, 57*(2), 278–288. doi:10.1177/0042085920933319

Leiter, J. (2007). School performance trajectories after the advent of reported maltreatment. *Children and Youth Services Review, 29*(3), 363–382. doi:10.1016/j.childyouth.2006.09.002

Liebenberg, L., Theron, L., Sanders, J., Munford, R., van Rensburg, A., Rothmann, S., & Ungar, M. (2016). Bolstering resilience through teacher-student interaction: Lessons from school psychologists. *School Psychology International, 37*(2), 140–154. doi:10.1177/0143034315614689

Lindsey, D. B., Martinez, R. S., Lindsey, R. B., & Myatt, K. (2020). *Culturally proficient coaching: Supporting educators to create equitable schools.* Corwin Press.

Mallett, C. A. (2016). The school-to-prison pipeline: From school punishment to rehabilitative inclusion. *Preventing School Failure, 60*(4), 296–304. doi:10.1080/1045988X.2016.1144554

Martinez, S. (2009). A system gone berserk: How are zero-tolerance policies really affecting schools? *Preventing School Failure, 53*(3), 153–158. doi:10.3200/PSFL.53.3.153-158

Massachusetts Advocates for Children & Harvard Law School. (2022). *Frequently asked questions about trauma-sensitive schools.* Trauma and Learning Policy Initiative. https://traumasensitiveschools.org/frequently-asked-questions/

Masten, A. S., Herbers, J. E., Cutuli, J. J., & Lafavor, T. L. (2008). Promoting competence and resilience in the school context. *Professional School Counseling, 12*(2), 76–84. doi:10.5330/PSC.n.2010-12.76

Masten, A. S., Monn, A. R., & Supkoff, L. M. (2011). Resilience in children and adolescents. In S. M. Southwick, B. T. Litz, D. Charney, & M. J. Friedman (Eds.), *Resilience and mental health: Challenges across the lifespan*. Cambridge University Press. doi:10.1017/CBO9780511994791.009

Maynard, B. R., Farina, A., & Dell, N. A. (2017). Protocol: Effects of trauma-informed approaches in schools. *Campbell Systematic Reviews, 13*(1), 1–32. doi:10.1002/CL2.177

Meek, S. E., & Gilliam, W. S. (2016). *Expulsion and suspension in early education as matters of social justice and health equity: NAM Perspectives*. Discussion Paper, National Academy of Medicine. doi:10.31478/201610e

Meiklejohn, J., Phillips, C., Freedman, M. L., Griffin, M. L., Biegel, G., Roach, A., Frank, J., Burke, C., Pinger, L., Soloway, G., Isberg, R., Sibinga, E., Grossman, L., & Saltzman, A. (2012). Integrating mindfulness training into K-12 education: Fostering the resilience of teachers and students. *Mindfulness, 3*(4), 291–307. doi:10.100712671-012-0094-5

Metzler, M., Merrick, M. T., Klevens, J., Ports, K. A., & Ford, D. C. (2017). Adverse childhood experiences and life opportunities: Shifting the narrative. *Children and Youth Services Review, 72*, 141–149. doi:10.1016/j.childyouth.2016.10.021

Mills, R., Kisely, S., Alati, R., Strahearn, L., & Naiman, J. M. (2019). Cognitive and educational outcomes of maltreated and non-maltreated youth: A birth cohort study. *The Australian and New Zealand Journal of Psychiatry, 53*(3), 248–255. doi:10.1177/0004867418768432 PMID:29696988

Minahan, J. (2019, October). Trauma-informed teaching strategies. *Educational Leadership*, 30–35. https://www.ascd.org/el/articles/trauma-informed-teaching-strategies

Morgan, A., Pendergast, D., Brown, R., & Heck, D. (2015). Relational ways of being an educator: Trauma-informed practice supporting disenfranchised young people. *International Journal of Inclusive Education, 19*(10), 1037–1051. doi:10.1080/13603116.2015.1035344

Mortensen, J. A., & Barnett, M. A. (2016). The role of child care in supporting the emotional regulatory needs of maltreated infants and toddlers. *Children and Youth Services Review, 64*, 73–81. doi:10.1016/j.childyouth.2016.03.004

National Association of Schools Boards of Education. (2022, June 14). *States adopt trauma-informed teacher training, few consider secondary traumatic stress*. NASBE. https://www.nasbe.org/states-adopt-trauma-informed-teacher-training-few-consider-secondary-traumatic-stress/

National Child Traumatic Stress Network. (2006). *Defining trauma and child traumatic stress*. https://www.nctsn.org/what-is-child-trauma/about-child-trauma

National Child Traumatic Stress Network. (2017). *Addressing race and trauma in the classroom: A resource for educators.*

National Child Traumatic Stress Network Complex Trauma Taskforce. (2003). *Complex trauma in children and adolescents*. https://www.nctsn.org/resources/complex-trauma-children-and-adolescents

Nobel, M. M. (2022a). Challenging deficit thinking in our schools: It starts during educator preparation. In R. D. Williams (Ed.), *Handbook of research on challenging deficit thinking for exceptional education improvement* (pp. 27–64). IGI Global. doi:10.4018/978-1-7998-8860-4.ch002

Nobel, M. M. (2022b). How a small, liberal arts university seeks to create socially conscious, resilient teachers. In O. S. Schepers, M. Brennan, & P. E. Bernhardt (Eds.), *Developing trauma-informed teachers: Creating classrooms that foster equity, resiliency, and asset-based approaches*. Information Age Publishing.

Noltemeyer, A., & Robertson, J. (2015). *Project AWARE Ohio Brief No. 2*. Ohio Department of Education. https://education.ohio.gov/getattachment/Topics/Other-Resources/School-Safety/Building-Better-Learning-Environments/PBIS-Resources/Project-AWARE-Ohio/Project-AWARE-Ohio-Statewide-Resources/Fostering-Resilience-in-a-Tiered-System.pdf.aspx

Openshaw, L. (2011). School-based support groups for traumatized students. *School Psychology International, 32*(2), 163–178. doi:10.1177/0143034311400830

Opiola, K. K., Alston, D. M., & Copeland-Kamp, B. L. (2020). The effectiveness of training and supervising urban elementary school teachers in child–teacher relationship training: A trauma-informed approach. *Professional School Counseling, 23*(1 part 2), 1–11. doi:10.1177/2156759X19899181

Overstreet, S., & Chafouleas, S. M. (2016). Trauma-informed schools: Introduction to the special issue. *School Mental Health, 8*(1), 1–6. doi:10.100712310-016-9184-1

Parker, J., Olson, S., & Bunde, J. (2020). The impact of trauma-based training on educators. *Journal of Child & Adolescent Trauma, 13*(2), 217–227. doi:10.100740653-019-00261-5 PMID:32549933

Pawlo, E., Lorenzo, A., Eichert, B., & Elias, M. J. (2019). All SEL should be trauma-informed. *Kappan, 101*(3), 37–41. doi:10.1177/0031721719885919

Pemberton, J. V., & Edeburn, E. K. (2021). Becoming a trauma-informed educational community with underserved students of color: What educators need to know. *Curriculum and Teaching Dialogue, 23*(1-2), 181–196.

Perfect, M. M., Turley, M. R., Carlson, J. S., Yohanna, J., & Saint Gilles, M. P. (2016). School-related outcomes of traumatic event exposure and traumatic stress symptoms in students: A systematic review of research from 1990 to 2015. *School Mental Health, 8*(1), 7–43. doi:10.100712310-016-9175-2

Perry, B., & Szalavitz, M. (2006). *The boy who was raised as a dog.* Basic Books.

Portnoi, L. M., & Kwong, T. M. (2015). Employing resistance and resilience in pursuing K-12 schooling and higher education lived experiences of successful female first-generation students of color. *Urban Education, 54*(3), 1–29. doi:10.1177/0042085915623333

Positive Behavioral Interventions and Supports. (2022). *What is PBIS?* https://pbis.org/pbis/what-is-pbis

Raby, K. L., Roisman, G. I., Labella, M. H., Martin, J., Fraley, R. C., & Simpson, J. A. (2019). The legacy of early abuse and neglect for social and academic competence from childhood to adulthood. *Child Development, 90*(5), 1684–1701. doi:10.1111/cdev.13033 PMID:29336018

Reddig, N., & VanLone, J. (2022). Pre-service teacher preparation in trauma-informed pedagogy: A review of state competencies. *Leadership and Policy in Schools*, 1–12. Advance online publication. doi:10.1080/15700763.2022.2066547

Robertson, H., Goodall, K., & Kay, D. (2021). Teachers' attitudes toward trauma-informed practice: Associations with attachment and adverse childhood experiences (ACEs). *The Psychology of Education Review, 45*(2), 62-74. https://www.research.ed.ac.uk/en/publications/teachers-attitudes-towards-trauma-informed-practice-associations-

Rodriguez, S. (2001). *Giants among us: First generation college graduates who lead activist lives.* Vanderbilt University Press. doi:10.2307/j.ctv16h2nct

Sacks, V., & Murphey, D. (2018). *The prevalence of adverse childhood experiences, nationally, by state, and by race/ethnicity* (Research Brief #2018-03). Child Trends. https://www.childtrends.org/wp-content/uploads/2018/02/ACESBrief_ChildTrends_February2018.pdf

Schonert-Reichl, K. (2017). Social and Emotional Learning and Teachers. *The Future of Children, 27*(1), 137–155. https://www.jstor.org/stable/44219025. doi:10.1353/foc.2017.0007

Siegel, D. (2009). Mindful awareness, mindsight, and neural integration. *The Humanistic Psychologist, 37*(2), 137–158. doi:10.1080/08873260902892220

Skiba, R., Horner, R., Chung, C., Rausch, M., May, S., & Tobin, T. (2011). Race is not neutral: A national investigation of African American and Latino disproportionality in school discipline. *School Psychology Review, 40*(1), 85–107. Advance online publication. doi:10.1080/02796015.2011.12087730

Skinner, E. A., & Pitzer, J. R. (2012). Developmental dynamics of student engagement, coping, and everyday resilience. In S. L. Christenson, A. L. Reschly, & C. Wylie (Eds.), *Handbook of research on student engagement*. Springer. doi:10.1007/978-1-4614-2018-7_2

Smyth, J. (2006). *When students have 'relational' power: The school as a site for identity formation around engagement and school retention*. Paper presented at the Australian Association for Research in Education, Adelaide, Australia.

Souers, K., & Hall, P. (2016). *Fostering resilient learners: Strategies for creating a trauma-sensitive classroom*. ASCD.

Souers, K., & Hall, P. (2020, October). Trauma is a word–not a sentence. *Educational Leadership, 78*(2), 34–39.

Spence, R., Kagan, L., Kljakovic, M., & Bifulco, A. (2021). Understanding trauma in children and young people in the school setting. *Educational and Child Psychology, 38*(1), 87–98.

Substance Abuse and Mental Health Services Administration. (2014). *SAMHSA's concept of trauma and guidance for a trauma-informed approach*. https://ncsacw.acf.hhs.gov/userfiles/files/SAMHSA_Trauma.pdf

Sutcher, L., Darling-Hammond, L., & Carver-Thomas, D. (2016). *A coming crisis in teaching? Teacher supply, demand, and shortages in the U.S.* Learning Policy Institute. https://learningpolicyinstitute.org/product/coming-crisis-teaching

Swindler Boutte, G., & Johnson, G. L. (2014). Community and family involvement in urban schools. In R. H. Milner & K. Lomotey (Eds.), *Handbook of urban education* (1st ed., pp. 167–187). Routledge.

Thomas, M. S., Crosby, S., & Vanderhaar, J. (2019). Trauma-informed practices in schools across two decades: An interdisciplinary review of research. *Review of Research in Education, 43*(1), 422–452. doi:10.3102/0091732X18821123

Trauma and Learning Policy Initiative. (2022). *Frequently asked questions about trauma-sensitive schools.* https://traumasensitiveschools.org/frequently-asked-questions/

Ukpokodu, O. N. (2007). Preparing socially conscious teachers: A social-justice oriented teacher education. *Multicultural Education, 15*(1), 8–15.

van der Kolk, B. A. (2003). The neurobiology of childhood trauma and abuse. *Child and Adolescent Psychiatric Clinics of North America, 12*(2), 293–317. doi:10.1016/S1056-4993(03)00003-8 PMID:12725013

van der Kolk, B. A. (2005). Developmental trauma disorder: Toward a rational diagnosis for children with complex trauma histories. *Psychiatric Annals, 35*(5), 401–408. doi:10.3928/00485713-20050501-06

van der Kolk, B. A., Pynoos, R. S., Cicchetti, D., Cloitre, M., D'Andrea, W., Ford, J. D., Lieberman, A. F., Putnam, F. W., Saxe, G., Spinazzola, J., Stolbach, B. C., & Teicher, M. (2009). *Proposal to include Developmental Trauma Disorder diagnosis for children and adolescents in DSM-V.* https://www.cttntraumatraining.org/uploads/4/6/2/3/46231093/dsm-v_proposal-dtd_taskforce.pdf

Venet, A. S. (2019). Role-clarity and boundaries for trauma-informed teachers. *Educational Considerations, 44*(2), 1–9. doi:10.4148/0146-9282.2175

Venet, A. S. (2021). *Equity-Centered Trauma-Informed Education.* W. W. Norton & Company.

Wiest-Stevenson, C., & Lee, C. (2016). Trauma-informed schools. *Journal of Evidence-Informed Social Work, 13*(5), 498–503. doi:10.1080/23761407.2016.1166855 PMID:27210273

Zacarian, D., Alvarez-Ortiz, L., & Haynes, J. (2020, October). Meeting trauma with an asset-based approach. *Educational Leadership,* 69–73.

Zhang, G., & Zeller, N. (2016, Spring). A longitudinal investigation of the relationship between teacher preparation and teacher. *Teacher Education Quarterly,* 73–92.

APPENDIX 1

Table 1. Evidence-based strategies and references for additional exploration

Evidence-Based Strategies	References
Take Care of Teachers' Needs First	Kaka & Tygret (2020) Pawlo et al. (2019) Pemberton & Edeburn (2021) Schonert-Reichl (2017) Souers & Hall (2020)
Build Asset-Based Relationships	Brooks & Goldstein (2008) Brown et al. (2022) Gardner & Stephens-Pisecco (2019) Jackson (2021) Liebenberg et al. (2016) Lindsey et al. (2020) Masten et al. (2008) Masten et al. (2011) Pemberton & Edeburn (2021) Skinner & Pitzer (2012) Zacarian et al. (2020)
Create Safe, Predictable Spaces	Blaustein (2013) Brown et al. (2022) Brunzell et al. (2019) Gardner & Stephens-Pisecco (2019) Minahan (2019) Pawlo et al. (2019) Pemberton & Edeburn (2021) Souers & Hall (2020) Zacarian et al. (2020)
Encourage Student Choice and Voice	Bingham & Sidokin (2004) Morgan et al. (2015) Pemberton et al. (2021) Smyth (2006) Zacarian et al. (2020)
Recognize Trauma Responses in Challenging Behavior	Bell et al. (2013) Berger et al, (2021) Cook et al. (2005) Minahan (2019) Morgan et al. (2015) Pawlo et al. (2019) Venet (2019)
Respond Appropriately to Challenging Behavior	Cohen & Mannarino (2011) Minahan (2019) Blaustein & Kinniburgh (2018) Cook et al. (2005) Pawlo et al. (2019) Pemberton & Edeburn (2021) Opiola et al. (2020)
Foster Resilience	Noltemeyer & Robertson (2015) Souers & Hall (2016)
Support SEL	Pemberton et al. (2021)
Teach Self-Regulation and Mindfulness	Green (2011) Maynard et al. (2017) Meiklejohn et al. (2012) Minahan (2019) Pemberton & Edeburn (2021) Siegel (2009)

Chapter 10
Increasing Readiness for Cultural Responsiveness and Trauma-Informed Practice:
Collective and Individual Readiness

Jerica Knox
National Center for School Mental Health, USA

Adam Alvarez
Rowan University, USA

Alexandrea Golden
University of Memphis, USA

Elan C. Hope
Policy Research Associates, USA

ABSTRACT

For years, the most prominent approaches to addressing youth trauma have been heavily influenced by whiteness and hegemonic systems of dominance. Rather than universal designs meant to address the needs of "all" children, it is imperative that trauma-informed practices be more culturally responsive. A major challenge, however, is that educators may be at various starting places when it comes to understanding and enacting culturally responsive practices that are also trauma-informed. In short, educators need learning opportunities that can increase their level of readiness—their attitudes and self-reported beliefs about their capacity—to implement culturally responsive, trauma-informed practices. The chapter has two overarching goals: (1) to contextualize trauma-informed practices within a culturally responsive framework and (2) to provide practical strategies and insights for promoting educators' readiness to engage in culturally responsive, trauma-informed professional learning.

DOI: 10.4018/978-1-6684-5713-9.ch010

INTRODUCTION

Increasing Readiness for Cultural Responsiveness and Trauma-Informed Practice

On May 14, 2022, an 18-year-old white man walked into a supermarket in a predominantly Black area of Buffalo, New York and opened fire. This hate crime–resulting in the death of 10 people–was the result of a gunman intentionally seeking out an area with a high concentration of Black people. Unfortunately, this story is not an anomaly, and racially-ethnically marginalized students across the US bear witness to racial trauma in their everyday lives (Saleem et al., 2020). Racially-ethnically marginalized students also face racial trauma in school as they seek an education within the context of biased-based bullying (Mulvey et al., 2016), racial microaggressions (Allen et al., 2013), and policies and practices that undermine the importance of race and culture in students' lives (Ladson-Billings & Tate, 1995). This is particularly detrimental as students of color are often punished for behaviors stemming from trauma and their own cultural context that do not meet the expectations of the white dominant culture of schools, further contributing to the school-to-prison pipeline (Tate et al., 2013). These experiences can create a cycle of traumatization for racially-ethnically marginalized students and prevent them from learning, warranting the need for educators to use trauma-informed practice alongside culturally responsive pedagogical approaches (Blitz et al., 2016).

Trauma-informed practice considers the impact of childhood trauma on student learning and behavior (Fondren et al., 2020). The most prominent approaches to trauma-informed practice are heavily influenced by whiteness and hegemonic systems of dominance (Alvarez, 2020). Trauma-informed practice does not, inherently, address the needs of those students whose manifested symptoms are a result of oppression and racial injustice (Curry, 2010). For example, researchers find that white educators often have a narrow view of how students should express their emotions, and this expectation of emotional expression is often in conflict with how Black students are actually feeling (e.g., incorrectly perceiving Black students as angry more often than white students; Halberstadt et al., 2022). Symptoms of sadness and depression in Black students who have experienced racial trauma may present as irritability or anger due to the vulnerabilities and risks associated with traditional expression of sadness. White educators' lack of awareness of these varying expressions of depression and sadness may result in misinterpretation of Black youth's sadness for aggression. Such mis-interpretation and misalignment in emotional expressions can result in punitive disciplinary actions (e.g., expulsion) that feed the school-to-prison pipeline (Halberstadt et al., 2018). These, and other, white-dominant approaches to trauma-informed practice devalue racially-ethnically marginalized students, creating a damaging cycle of re-traumatization. Thus, those looking to enact trauma-informed practice in schools should pair it with cultural responsiveness.

Cultural responsiveness centers students' individual and collective backgrounds, and is empowering and comprehensive of students' true selves (Gay, 2018). It acknowledges the accumulation of historical trauma and cross-cultural differences that result in punitive action for marginalized students. For this reason, prior research has suggested that there is a need to practice trauma-informed care within a culturally responsive framework in order to maximize its effectiveness (Blitz et al., 2016). Implementing cultural responsiveness effectively requires an understanding of systemic and racial oppression that serves to undermine ethnically marginalized students' cultural selves (Ladson-Billings, 1995). It is through this understanding that trauma-informed practice can be effective for racially-ethnically marginalized students. Similarly, trauma-informed professional development is not just about educators creating nurturing learning environments for students through simplistic measures like *only* replacing library books with representatives of different cultures. It addresses the power of racist systems and practices within schools that often traumatize students and feed the school-to-prison pipeline. Without the appropriate groundwork to create a safe and open environment, however, attempts to engage educators with these topics can backfire and result in feelings of shame and defensiveness (Blitz et al., 2016). Thus, more conversations and practical tools are needed to enhance educators' sense of readiness to integrate a culturally responsive approach with their pedagogy, inclusive of trauma informed practices.

In this chapter, we describe a readiness framework to better prepare educators and schools to implement cultural responsiveness and trauma-informed practice effectively and cohesively. We begin by providing insight into our positionalities as educators and researchers. We then introduce a novel framework for collective- and individual-level readiness to engage in culturally responsive, trauma-informed professional development. By collective readiness, we are referring to aspects at the school-level that can prepare the school community to engage in conversations related to trauma, racism, and cultural responsiveness. We consider four domains for collective readiness: Leadership, Awareness, Commitment, and Climate. Individual readiness includes factors that contribute to individual educators' preparedness to engage in a journey to becoming a culturally responsive and trauma-informed practitioner within their school. There are also four domains of individual readiness: Social, Cultural, Emotional, and Behavioral. We conclude with practical strategies for promoting collective and individual readiness in schools. We contend that educators who are prepared for culturally responsive and trauma-informed professional development will be better equipped to implement pedagogy and practice in their classrooms, which provides safe environments for racially-ethnically marginalized students to learn.

THE COLLECTIVE AND INDIVIDUAL READINESS FRAMEWORK

Author Positionalities

The Collective and Individual Readiness Framework was born out of conversations among the co-authors where we recognized the need to examine school and educator prerequisites for cultural responsiveness and trauma-informed practice that can enhance or hinder their effectiveness. We asked the question, "Is it enough to bring in diversity training and expect teachers and administrators to change in ways that support the academic, social, and emotional growth of all students?" We found that in our own research and practice, the answer was a resounding no. We concluded that both individual educators and the collective school community need to be prepared for on-going professional development and incremental long-term changes to practice and pedagogy to support a truly culturally responsive trauma-informed approach to schooling.

The first author identifies as a young, Black female school psychologist who takes an interest in disrupting the white-dominant discourse in US K-12 schools that contribute to educational inequities for students of color. As a first-generation college student, her previous educational experiences have highlighted the negative impact that systems have on individual students. Thus, her research is informed by a commitment to ensure that students of color are allotted safe, equitable school through systems-level advocacy. The second author, a Mexican-American man, comes to this work as a former elementary teacher for 6 years in a racially and culturally diverse school at a psychiatric treatment facility in Central Texas. His research and teaching interests focus on the intersection of race, violence, and trauma. These interests stem from his own experiences as a witness to domestic violence, a student of color, and a parent of children in US public schools. The third author is a Black woman scholar who was educated in predominantly Black urban schools in Detroit, Michigan which influenced her understanding and interests in race-based school inequities. Accordingly, her research focuses on the racially inequitable conditions within, but not limited to, the school environments that ethnically-racially minoritized youth must endure and navigate and the protective cultural mechanisms that aid them in successfully navigating those environments. The fourth author is a Black woman scientist and researcher with expertise in education and psychology, with a focus on the experiences of Black students in schools. She is also the parent of Black school-aged children, and serves in leadership in several education organizations that serve Black and Brown children and families in economically under-resourced communities. Grounded in these experiences and perspectives, the authors introduce the Collective and Individual Readiness Framework.

INTRODUCTION TO THE COLLECTIVE AND INDIVIDUAL READINESS FRAMEWORK

Researchers have noted the importance of individual characteristics and organizational contexts on the effectiveness of diversity-related professional development. For instance, Chung (2013) described how individual characteristics–like demographic attributes–and organizational characteristics–like diversity climate–influence one's readiness for diversity training. However, minimal research exists to center these characteristics within the school context. While some school research has evidenced the need for examining such individual characteristics (Blitz et al., 2016), no research to date has provided a framework for considering collective and individual readiness for diversity, racial equity, or culturally responsive professional development designed for the school context. The Collective and Individual Readiness Framework (see Figure 1) centers readiness of both the individual and the collective as a critical element for culturally responsive and trauma-informed professional development in school to translate into successful and well-implemented equitable practices within the school. Whole-school culturally responsive and trauma-informed professional development initiatives are often implemented with the assumption that educators who participate will be ready, able, or willing to engage with the content of the professional development and use their new knowledge in their own classrooms. However, researchers have found that educators often have deep resistance to engaging with topics related to the racial history of the US, culturally responsive pedagogy, and racial justice that hinder participation in and application of culturally responsive and trauma-informed professional development (Blitz et al., 2016). In this way, unlearning the white dominant cultural norms of education within a day- or week-long professional development can be challenging, uncomfortable, and arguably unrealistic. Through the Collective and Individual Readiness Framework, we highlight the prerequisites needed of both educators and schools in order for professional development that targets cultural responsiveness and racial justice to be effective. We contend that readiness is both individual, imbued to the individual educator, and collective, reflected in the school environment and culture. Within both the individual and the collective, we propose four domains that should be thought of as a multidimensional continuum. We do not consider readiness to be a dichotomous construct (i.e., one is ready or one is not ready), but, rather an ongoing journey where an educator or school can always be "more ready" to make culturally responsive and trauma-informed professional development effective. We also acknowledge that the school context is situated within districts, states, and regions with differing policies and resources that must be considered when engaging in culturally responsive and trauma-informed training and practice. Thus, following a culturally responsive and trauma-informed approach, we recommend using this framework in ways that align with the current needs of the school and the broader sociopolitical context of local education.

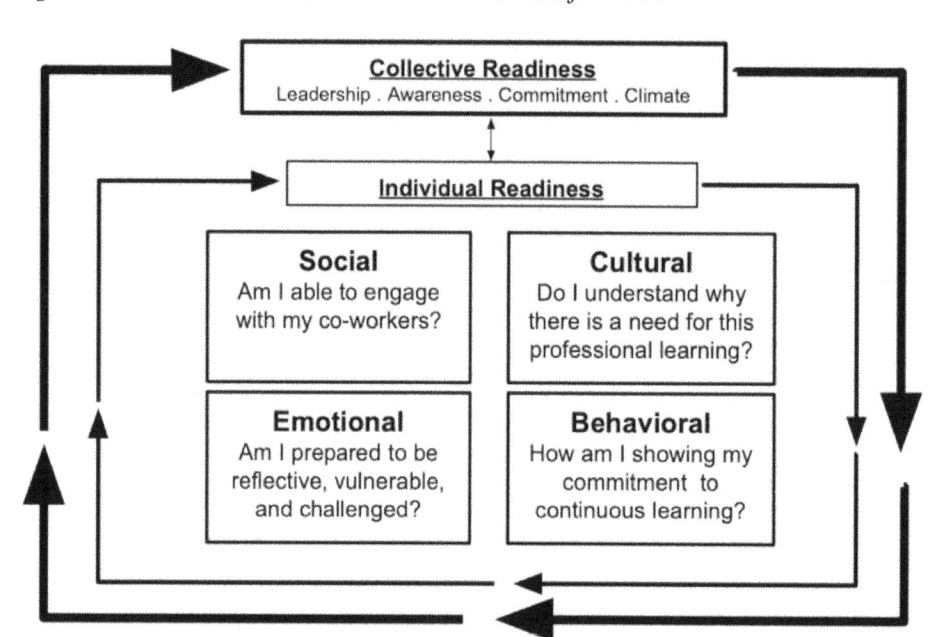

Figure 1. The collective and individual readiness framework

```
                    Collective Readiness
         Leadership . Awareness . Commitment . Climate
                              ↕
                    Individual Readiness

     ┌──────────────────────┐  ┌──────────────────────┐
     │        Social        │  │       Cultural       │
     │  Am I able to engage │  │  Do I understand why │
     │   with my co-workers?│  │  there is a need for │
     │                      │  │ this professional    │
     │                      │  │     learning?        │
     └──────────────────────┘  └──────────────────────┘

     ┌──────────────────────┐  ┌──────────────────────┐
     │      Emotional       │  │      Behavioral      │
     │  Am I prepared to be │  │  How am I showing my │
     │  reflective,         │  │    commitment to     │
     │  vulnerable, and     │  │  continuous learning?│
     │     challenged?      │  │                      │
     └──────────────────────┘  └──────────────────────┘
```

The Collective and Individual Readiness Framework applies previous research from school transformation, business, and economics literature, which acknowledge that both individual-level and organization-level prerequisites play a role in the effectiveness of professional development and school change (Chung et al., 2013; Wang et al., 2020). We build on this work to introduce a readiness framework that considers the reciprocal nature of both individual school staff and the school as a collective. Within the Collective and Individual Readiness Framework we assume that not *all* school staff within a school will be willing (and ready) to engage meaningfully in culturally responsive and trauma-informed professional development. We specifically use the word *collective* rather than *whole-school* to acknowledge this notion and assert that a large body of school staff can shift the culture of a school, while some members of the school community are not yet committed.

COLLECTIVE READINESS

Collective readiness refers to the preparedness of the school at the organizational level to engage in discourse related to cultural responsiveness and trauma-informed practice. This readiness acknowledges that individual school staff are limited in their ability to create widespread change with regards to culturally responsive and trauma-informed practice and that systems-level support is needed to make change across the school. Additionally, culturally responsive and trauma-informed school programs are often implemented at the school-level (Blitz et al., 2016; Dorado et al., 2016), putting further emphasis on readiness at the organizational level. Teachers and school staff who are not interested or ready for implementation are still required to engage, which can negatively impact overall effectiveness. Overall, there is a strong need for examining readiness at the system-level prior to and during implementation in order to engage in practices and increase support that can create effective culturally responsive and trauma-informed school environments. We present four distinct, yet overlapping, domains related to collective readiness: leadership, awareness, commitment, and climate. These four domains address group-based features, attributes, and characteristics that should be considered in working toward collective readiness. Here, we do not quantify how many school-based actors constitute a group because school size and number of faculty and staff can vary. Instead, we distinguish collective readiness from individual readiness by noting that collective readiness refers to a group of actors in the same school context and the structural features of schools. Here, we provide a conceptualization of each domain and then practical examples of engagement to increase overall collective readiness.

Domain 1: Leadership

Leadership is pivotal in making organizations run and is especially important for carrying out initiatives related to inclusion and equity (Young et al., 2010). Leadership within the context of collective readiness refers to the extent to which the school has motivated and vulnerable change makers in positions of power. This conceptualization emphasizes the leaders' motivation to learn and reflect on professional development, which is often associated with improved skills and confidence (Combs, 2002) that they can then bring back to the job and their team. School leaders may not initially have the knowledge and skills to regulate and direct deeper changes within the system to reflect cultural responsiveness and trauma-informed practice; however, readiness may help with that by providing motivation for learning and the transfer of that knowledge (Chung, 2013). Our conceptualization of leadership also emphasizes vulnerability as educational racial disparities and other critical issues of educational equity are often received with great trepidation

(Palmer & Louis, 2017). This fear, combined with the reality that leaders must engage in these challenging conversations, requires that school leaders must have the capacity to be vulnerable in order to facilitate discussions that can involve multiple and divergent perspectives, emotions, and beliefs while remaining committed to attending to and increasing equity.

Researchers of school leadership posits that strong, culturally responsive and social justice-oriented leadership is an area of need in schools (Bertrand & Rodela, 2018; Grooms et al., 2021; Khalifa et al., 2016). For example, Young and colleagues (2010) found that principals included in their study, although aware of diversity in their schools, were ill prepared to address needs related to that diversity. The principals also had trouble articulating key terms such as "diversity" and what that means for implementation of practices that could create inclusivity (2010). This is especially disappointing given that school leadership is responsible for establishing and maintaining shared understandings of terms like *equity* and *social justice* for the school (Riehl, 2009). Altogether, leadership can establish the priorities for the school and work to facilitate the other domains of collective readiness.

Engage in Critical Inquiry

Meaningful change starts with asking questions that provide awareness and insight into how school policies, procedures, and overall climate impact racially-ethnically marginalized students. These questions are especially important as racial inequity is deeply rooted in systems that produce educational disparities, even when school staff try to create equity-focused policies (Woodard, 2011). Developing collective readiness consists of asking questions related to mainstream, white-dominant ideologies and how they perpetuate educational disparities for students of color. It should be noted that the process of gaining awareness can produce discomfort or even be painful for many teachers and other school staff (Singleton, 2015) who learn how they have subscribed to oppressive ideologies and participated in oppressive acts as a part of the cultural norm and expectation of educators. Singleton (2015) suggests that this feeling of discomfort is necessary for personal growth and in this case–collective growth as a school. This discomfort should be attended to through vulnerable leadership and a positive school climate (discussed in further detail below). In Tables 1-4 throughout the Collective Readiness section, we offer examples of questions that provide a foundation for cultivating collective readiness wherein the terms *we* and *our* refer to the collective school. It will be important to continuously reflect on these questions as well as build off of them to create questions that are context-specific.

Table 1. Engaging in critical inquiry: leadership

Example Questions	Explanation
To what extent are we aware of general problems that racially-ethnically marginalized students face within the school context in the United States and locally?	Having an understanding of national disparities and issues within the U.S. educational system for racially-ethnically marginalized students can provide schools with a general understanding of what potential issues they should be examining.
To what extent are we aware of the current needs of our students and school staff and how we have or have not contributed to those needs?	A lack of clarity on current needs produces low readiness because schools are not prepared to embrace and implement opportunities and tools that can target those specific needs (Noguera, 2013).
How are school staff's cultural backgrounds different from our students and how does this distinction play a role in practices, policies, and procedures that do not work for our students?	Schools are never culturally neutral. That is, school staff practice through their own cultural lens, and this lens may not align with that of their students, causing disruption to learning. It will be important for the school staff to become aware of how their cultural backgrounds influence their practices, policies, and procedures and how they align or misalign with students' own cultural backgrounds.
How do we conceptualize culture? Cultural responsiveness? Trauma-informed practice?	Gathering a collective conceptualization of culture can provide clarity in conversations regarding addressing the needs of different students. Additionally, a collective conceptualization of cultural responsiveness and trauma-informed practice can provide clarity on what and where schools expect to see changes following ongoing professional development.

Domain 2: Awareness

Awareness within the context of collective readiness refers to a school's knowledge of needs related to cultural responsiveness and trauma-informed practice among their student body, their families, their staff, and community. *Knowledge* includes an understanding of systemic and racial oppression that often undermines racially-ethnically marginalized students' experiences in schools as well as the specific challenges experienced by racially-ethnically marginalized youth within the schools of focus. Awareness should not be limited to superficial realizations of cultural responsiveness, such as a lack of cultural celebration within the school (Sleeter et al., 2011). Simplistic awareness of cultural responsiveness or trauma-informed practice, alone or accompanied by superficial acts, ignores conditions of racism and other unjust practices within the system that continue to further educational disparities (Sleeter et al., 2011). For example, *only* engaging in cultural responsiveness through cultural celebration acknowledges cultural diversity, but does not inherently challenge unjust racialized practices within schools that impede the academic and social growth of students of color (Gray et al., 2018). Similarly, *only* considering that a student may have adverse conditions at home fails to be truly trauma-informed because there is a lack of realization that unjust practices can happen within the school as well (Venet, 2021).

Alternatively, *meaningful* awareness should begin with an understanding of the historical, social, and political degradation of racially marginalized students and their families and how that degradation has impacted their educational experiences (Ladson-Billings & Tate, 1995). Awareness should also include an understanding of school- and district-level policies and practices that serve to perpetuate racial inequities and normative whiteness within schools (Dixson & Anderson, 2018). Such policies include those that are vague, like students being subjected to consequences for insubordination or policies that blatantly target educators who take a culturally responsive approach to teaching (Johnson, et al., 2022). System change makers who practice meaningful awareness can point out that such a policy could run the risk of being inequitably enforced as biases against students of color could affect teachers' perceptions of what counts as insubordination (Venet, 2021). Schools should be aware that racially marginalized youth exist within white-dominant ideological schools and school systems that can further demean and traumatize them in the absence of awareness of (and related action to change) the structural and systematic ways that racism is embedded in schooling. This includes, but is not limited to, actively collecting disaggregated data to understand raced and gendered patterns in discipline referrals, placement into special education classes, and placement into gifted or advanced classes. Another example of awareness at the school-level could be a policy analysis to understand racialized effects of policies, even when policies were created with neutral intent. For example, dress code policies written from a lens of whiteness may disproportionately effect students of color because of racialized norms of whiteness for hairstyles that do not apply cross culturally. Additionally, schools can assess students' perceptions and experiences of the general and race-specific climates of the school to better understand the challenges faced by racially-ethnically marginalized students within their schools and appropriately remove barriers.

Awareness is a critical component of collective readiness as it serves as a foundation for cultural responsiveness and trauma-informed practice. Without awareness and understanding of the needs of students and how racial inequities are perpetuated by school systems, future practices and initiatives may be performative and not result in significant change. Additionally, awareness can provide motivation for professional development related to cultural responsiveness and trauma-informed practice. Awareness can help schools understand the strengths they have to build on and also identify strategic places for growth.

ENGAGE IN CRITICAL INQUIRY

Table 2. Engaging in critical inquiry: awareness

Example Questions	Explanation
How much time are we devoting to conversations related to cultural responsivity and trauma-informed practice in our instructional and leadership meetings?	Generally, showing a commitment to cultural responsivity and trauma-informed practice includes devoting ample time during the school day to discuss the ways in which the instruction and environment are meeting the needs of all students. This question also extends to reflection of practices throughout the school context. Integrating reflection can look like a number of routines, such as reviewing educational disparities during professional learning communities.
How many initiatives are we promoting designed to establish home-school-community collaboration?	Bridging gaps between home and school and home and community help to establish school environments that are culturally familiar to students.
To what extent are our school's mission and values representative of our students and school staff? To what extent are we pursuing our mission and values?	While schools can have the best of intentions through their missions and values, it will be important to ensure that they are aligned with current students' cultural backgrounds. What are your values saying or not saying? It will also be important to act on such values to ensure students' success.

Domain 3: Commitment

El-Amin (2022) conceptualized organizational commitment as taking a firm position on diversity, equity, and inclusion and providing resources to ensure their placement within the system. Collective *commitment* within the context of education refers to the extent to which schools are willing to acknowledge and respond to cultural responsivity and trauma-informed needs of students, their families, and the broader community. This domain should be thought of as action-oriented. Specifically, the more active and meaningful efforts schools take in their approach to cultural responsiveness and trauma-informed practice, the higher their collective commitment is. It is important to note that the term *meaningful* is significant as many simplistic actions, such as adopting a new diversity statement without attempting to actualize it, may not result in higher readiness. Commitment in this respect is actualized through the actions of the school to pursue racial justice and trauma-informed practice.

Collective commitment is essential for readiness as it provides individual educators with permission to engage in culturally responsive trauma-informed practices and pedagogy within their classrooms. School leaders can explicitly convey a message in which educators can enter into professional development settings with the understanding that they will receive support in deconstructing harmful beliefs and practices and in executing knowledge and skills from their professional development experiences. Commitment is also important for buy-in for educators who are not currently interested in equity work or who may have interest but have not made the first step toward practice. As these educators are exposed to tangible representations of commitment reflected in the school culture, school policy, and among colleagues they can explore and confront their own resistance and take steps towards building their own capacity for change. A demonstration of commitment to diversity, equity, and inclusion within the broad organizational context can include the creation of affinity groups (i.e., discussion groups for individuals with shared identities) and ally action groups, engagement in conversations related to efforts, and providing information and action-oriented equity-based training (Adejumo, 2020)—which is especially common and helpful within school organizations for cultural responsiveness and trauma-informed practice (Bottiani et al., 2018; Forber-Pratt et al., 2021; McIntyre et al., 2019; Mellom et al., 2018). This may also include professional development plans for staff and coaching support specific to trauma-informed cultural responsiveness within the building.

ENGAGE IN CRITICAL INQUIRY

Table 3. Engaging in critical inquiry: commitment

Example Questions	Explanation
To what extent is school leadership motivated to move toward cultural responsiveness and trauma-informed practice? How are they showing or not showing that motivation?	Motivation should be considered a top-down process. The more school leaders are motivated, the more motivated school staff will be.
To what extent is school leadership willing to be vulnerable to reflect on school practices, policies, and procedures that may be harming students? How are they showing or not showing that vulnerability?	Vulnerability in school leadership is essential to readiness as it provides modeling for other school staff.
To what extent is school leadership empowering individual school staff to integrate their various perspectives and cultural ways of knowing in the school policy and environment?	Taking perspectives from others, generally, is good practice; however, this will also help to increase readiness as school leaders will work towards changing policies and the environment for students.
To what extent is school leadership able to articulate what cultural responsiveness and trauma-informed practice means?	Having a common definition for cultural responsiveness and trauma-informed practice is important because it helps to formulate specific goals and solutions for professional development.
To what extent does school leadership understand the connection between cultural responsiveness and student achievement and trauma-informed practice and student achievement?	Student achievement should be at the core of both cultural responsiveness and trauma-informed practice. Implementing initiatives that do not center achievement and learning negate the purpose of both. Readiness for professional development increases when leaders can articulate how these practices can promote student achievement.
To what extent are school leaders prepared to guide teachers through uncomfortable conversations regarding their beliefs about race and culture?	Just as leaders must be vulnerable with their school staff, they must be prepared to help staff navigate their own vulnerability in uncomfortable conversations.

Domain 4: Climate

Climate refers to the elements of a school's environment to foster conversations and actions related to cultural responsivity and trauma-informed practice. It includes a number of factors, including academic press and community engagement (Uline & Tschannen-Moran, 2008), that work together to either serve or hinder cultural responsiveness and trauma-informed practice. According to Uline and colleagues (2008), academic press refers to the degree to which high standards for learning are implemented throughout the school. This is especially important as cultural responsiveness is rooted in academic achievement for racially-ethnically marginalized students (Ladson-Billings, 1995). Moreover, those who implement trauma-informed practice do so to create safe environments for students to learn and achieve (Cole et al., 2013). Community engagement pertains to the capacity of a school to engage with the broader community (Uline & Tschannen-Moran, 2008). Doing so can contribute to collective readiness by eliciting support and resources for implementation that are context-centered.

In addition to community engagement and academic press, climate includes *relational trust*–trust that is built through shared activity and goal setting between all involved parties (Bryk & Schneider, 2002). Relational trust within the context of readiness is particularly important because, when it is high, school staff feel comfortable learning from their own and others' challenges and are able to be vulnerable in sharing their own bias or ignorance to understand challenges (Bryk & Schneider, 2002). Academic press, community engagement, and relational trust can work together to create a supportive, yet challenging, climate for students. Moreover, these three elements can create the right conditions for school staff to be ready to engage in discourse regarding race and racism. For example, teachers can use professional learning communities to increase cultural awareness and engage in critical reflection regarding practices (Moore, 2018); however, having low relational trust can cause educators to be hesitant in sharing their practices in fear of criticism. Essentially, building climate is helpful for increasing collective readiness because it provides the space and culture for continual learning, reflecting, and growing amongst school staff.

ENGAGING IN CRITICAL INQUIRY

Table 4. Engaging in critical inquiry: climate

Example Questions	Explanation
To what extent is the climate conducive to talking about race and racism as it relates to our school and students?	The ability to talk about race and racism as it relates to specific schools and students is essential for readiness as it provides school staff with the foundational tool for identifying issues and proposing solutions.
To what extent do school staff believe talking about race and racism as it relates to our school and students is relevant?	Even if the climate is conducive to talking about race and racism, school staff may have varying opinions on whether talking about it is relevant. It will be important to understand these varying opinions and dispel any misconceptions that may result in order to increase readiness for further conversations.
To what extent does the climate empower organic relationships and support among school staff?	Students thrive in learning environments that are safe and comforting and the same should extend to school staff in order to increase the chances of school staff entering into collective conversations. For example, professional learning communities have the power to be effective when educators can share their innovative practices and ideas with others; however, when there is low trust in peers, educators are hesitant to share those practices in fear of criticism. Thus, it will be important to create a climate that is safe and supportive for educators to feel comfortable in sharing.

Practical Application and Strategies for Increasing Collective Readiness

We have provided several strategies below to begin thinking about and increase collective readiness within schools. It is important to note that these strategies should not be used as exact steps to follow; rather, these strategies serve as suggestions for schools if they have the capacity to implement them.

Seek Outside Resources

Seeking outside resources can help schools facilitate readiness for cultural responsivity and trauma-informed care by providing extra support and modeling. Such outside resources include instructional coaches from the school district or beyond, who use their knowledge to increase educators' teaching capacity (Hopkins et al., 2017) or outside consulting firms that can conduct equity audits to review policies and practices and work to create a strategic plan specific to the school's needs. As catalysts for change, instructional coaches and other outside consultants motivate teachers to engage in collective learning and, thus, get educators used to working with each other to facilitate better instruction and an environment conducive to learning. Challenges may arise when seeking outside support. Such challenges include a feeling of defensiveness among teachers who may believe they do not need instructional support. In these cases, it will be important for school leaders, instructional coaches, and/or outside consultants to attempt to shift mindsets from "needing to fix what is broken" to "improving upon the great work that is already happening."

Increase Color-Conscious Perspective

Color-evasiveness refers to comments made by individuals that dismiss the perception that racial/ethnic differences cause racially-ethnically marginalized people to be oppressed (Annamma et al., 2017). For example, a teacher might contend that they treat all of their students exactly the same and do not see race or color. Color-evasive beliefs can undermine awareness of systems-level issues within the school that feed educational disparities for racially-marginalized students. Blitz and colleagues (2016) found that many educators made color-evasive comments in response to a culturally responsive, trauma-informed school intervention. A later paper noted that the educators did not understand the role of racial oppression on students' experiences of trauma and adversity (Blitz et al., 2020). Through a *color-conscious perspective*, educators can better understand how racism exists and negatively affects racially-ethnically marginalized students and their families (Blitz et al., 2020; Ullucci & Battey, 2011). Moreover, it will be important for school leadership to reflect on and correct issues of color-evasiveness within their schools in order to push forward with collective readiness for trauma-informed and culturally responsive approaches.

Increase Collective Thought

School leaders must also include racially-ethnically marginalized school staff's perspectives in key decision-making. As critical race theory posits, the experiences and narratives of people of color have inherent value that their white counterparts are unlikely to know (Delgado & Stefanic, 2000). As such, amplifying diverse perspectives is essential to expand knowledge of underlying causes of challenging problems that impact racially-ethnically marginalized students. Increasing collective thought also provides a chance for increasing shared commitment to the solutions that emerge from such conversations (Supovits et al., 2019). Horsford (2010) acknowledged that exposure to counternarratives, coupled with confronting white privilege, can produce effective school leadership that is motivated to confront racial disparities in education.

Several challenges may arise as leadership looks to facilitate collective conversations regarding race, culture, and trauma. Of course, open discussion of uncomfortable topics, such as confronting and critiquing one's practice, can produce fear for many. However, avoidance of such topics can perpetuate negative practices. Additionally, increased exposure may reduce such anxiety of addressing these topics (Abramowitz, 2013; Kaczkurkin & Fao, 2022). Providing a specific time for reflection of practice during team meetings may help create a growth-oriented culture and decrease anxiety regarding critiques. Additionally, leadership should model the process of engaging in reflection and critiques of practices to decrease anxiety of less practiced staff regarding critiques. It may be helpful for staff to connect with other educators via online learning communities that can help to support educators in processing these potentially challenging topics. Leadership will have to navigate power differentials between themselves and their staff as well as among staff members as they may have an impact on the conversations that take place within team meetings. There must also be consideration of the fact that novice teachers and school staff may be afraid to challenge more senior school staff and leadership on their thoughts due to concerns of backlash for missteps. Leadership should make note of this and reflect on reactions to critiques to ensure that all feel safe in expressing their opinions.

INDIVIDUAL READINESS

Whereas collective readiness considers the school community, individual readiness is concerned with how people connect to the local environment when engaging in conversations about cultural responsiveness and trauma-informed practice. We think of these individual level domains in two groups: external and internal. First, the social and cultural domains are external insofar as they reflect how individuals move beyond themselves to connect to others in their shared environment. Second, the emotional and behavioral domains are internal because they represent the sensemaking individuals experience with regards to cultural responsiveness and trauma-informed work.

Domain 1: Social

The social aspect of individual readiness refers to the skills one has to engage with co-workers in discourse involving cultural responsiveness and trauma-informed practices. A central part of the social domain of individual readiness refers to having the knowledge of cultural responsiveness and trauma-informed practices, which we described in a previous section. Yet, to really grasp what it means to be culturally responsive and trauma-informed, people must engage in what Sealey-Ruiz (2022) refers to as the archaeology of the self. Through excavating their personal histories and exploring their own racial identities, for example, individuals enhance their knowledge uptake of cultural responsiveness and trauma-informed practice concepts. Indeed, such a deep exploration into one's various identities can shape how educators understand and view themselves and their students. Scholars who view cultural responsiveness and trauma-informed practice as a tool for enhancing equity and justice have stressed the importance of taking an anti-oppressive approach, meaning educators should be cognizant of their own privilege and how they demonstrate power through their interactions with others (Alvarez & Farinde-Wu, 2022; Duane et al, 2021; Venet, 2021). Essentially, to avoid misinterpretation, misinformation, and misrepresentation of other people and the systems that impact people's lives, it is critical for educators to recognize who they are, what motivated them to want to do culturally responsive and trauma-informed work, and why it matters. (Milner, 2007).

Although an educator may have the necessary cultural responsiveness and trauma-informed knowledge, the belief in one's ability, or efficacy, to engage in conversations about the subject matter is also necessary. Self-efficacy plays an important role in the social domain of individual readiness. Delale-O-Connor et al. (2017) argue that educators need a strong sense of self-efficacy when it comes to discussing issues related to race, culture and social problems. A strong sense of confidence, knowledge, and skill to navigate conversations about race and racism can play a role in contentious circumstances where colleagues may be opposed to integrating cultural responsiveness with trauma-informed practice. Bandura (1977) argued that efficacy beliefs refer to the capacity one has to perform certain tasks successfully. As Bandura noted, the context in which an individual was performing a given task could be a critical factor in their belief in themselves. In a previous study, Graham et al. (2019) found that the racial demographics of the school context was strongly related to teachers' feelings of preparedness, or readiness, to discuss race with students in class. Moreover, teachers in racially diverse schools often credited their sense of readiness for race talk to school support, strong collegiality with other teachers who cared about addressing race issues, and the needs of their students. This means that there could be a bidirectional relationship where collective readiness helps individual actors develop their own readiness and where individuals' readiness contributes to collective readiness.

Engage in Critical Inquiry

Similar to collective readiness, it will be important for educators to ask questions that provide awareness and insight into their capacity to engage with culturally responsive and trauma-informed work. We pull from our own research and practice as well as other scholars (Hammond, 2014) to provide initial questions to engage educators in reflection on individual readiness.

Table 5. Engaging in critical inquiry: social

Example Questions	Explanation
To what extent am I able to engage with my co-workers in conversations regarding race and racism?	Social dynamics within a room can influence the productivity of conversations. It will be important to reflect on one's ability to engage with co-workers regarding topics related to race and racism.
What do I think will happen if I were to speak about race and racism? How would others respond and how does that affect my ability to engage in conversation?	Fear of race talk is prevalent within the education field. One must reflect on their worries regarding having these conversations in order to dispel any misconceptions and feel more efficacious in doing so.

Domain 2: Cultural

The cultural domain of individual readiness refers to a deeper understanding of why cultural responsiveness and trauma-informed practices are necessary. In other words, how an individual thinks about broader systems of oppression, such as racism, can inform their understanding about how culture is influenced by historical, political, and economic interests. We view the cultural domain as an external part of individual readiness because it requires school-based actors to examine structural forces that shape people's lived experiences. Too often, people fail to recognize what drives culture–beliefs, values and assumptions. What is viewed in U.S. society as "normal" tends to be heavily influenced by white, middle-class, cisgendered, straight male-dominant ways of being and knowing, which is heavily influential of historical laws, beliefs, and practices. Moreover, people also view culture as something other people have, especially in cases where it deviates from what is "mainstream" or what they might consider normal. Consequently, researchers have learned that these singular ways of operating societal institutions contribute to disparities for marginalized groups, such as people of color, women, or people living in high-poverty areas (Hooks, 2014; Gay, 2018; Ladson-Billings, 2009).

Culture can be understood as a set of values, beliefs, and assumptions that groups and individuals construct. However, as some have argued, it is important to reimagine culture in non-essentializing and deficit-oriented ways (Gutierrez & Arzubiaga, 2012). A critical skill in developing the cultural domain of individual readiness, for educators, is to recognize the assets, uniqueness, and complexities within various communities. Seeing these community cultures as assets can be helpful for engaging in productive conversations about cultural responsiveness and trauma-informed practice. The Community Cultural Wealth framework offers six forms of cultural capital the individuals and communities can embody (Yosso, 2005):

- **Aspirational Capital:** An individual's ability to "dream of possibilities beyond their present circumstances"
- **Linguistic Capital:** The intellectual and social skills attained (e.g., speaking, storytelling skills, communicating via visual art, music, or poetry) when an individual speaks multiple languages and/or language styles
- **Familial Capital:** The knowledge nurtured by kin that "carry a sentence of community history, memory, and cultural intuition". The concept of "family" also refers to extended and chosen family, including living or deceased relatives, friends, and anyone else considered kin.
- **Social Capital:** One's ability to connect and tap into networks of people and community resources including social contacts and peers
- **Resistant Capital:** The knowledge and skills an individual can foster through oppositional behaviors that challenge inequality
- **Navigational Capital:** One's ability to maneuver through institutions (e.g., schools, health care spaces, housing). This can involve leveraging academic, social, personal, and institutional relationships.

The capacity to challenge one's own assumptions about people, their experiences and their value in a shared environment is a critical part of individual readiness. For educators, culture matters because any miscommunication or misunderstanding of cultural values and norms could lead to negative perceptions of students' abilities, families' level of care, or communities' assets and resources (Howard, 2020). One important insight for educators to grasp is that there is no one right or wrong culture, and whiteness is not the default "right" culture. Second, culture is not a static characteristic of an individual or group of people. Culture, for example, is often context-dependent, and it changes over time. That is to say, an individual's ways of being in school, at home, in a place of worship, or outside may look differently. Indeed, under varying conditions, people may adapt what they do, in the moment, to respond to their immediate needs or environment. Third, culture must be understood alongside historical and contemporary structures and systems that shape the rights and lives of people within that culture. A culturally responsive, trauma-informed approach cannot consider culture absent the systems and structures that cultures function in and around.

Engage in Critical Inquiry

Table 6. Engaging in critical inquiry: cultural

Example Questions	Explanation
What is the story of your family in America? Has your family been here for generations, a few decades, or just a few years?	If educators want to be ready for work regarding cultural responsiveness and trauma-informed practice, they must first accept and understand themselves as cultural beings. This self-knowledge serves as a reference point that shapes our mental models about teaching and learning. It will be important for individuals to take some time to identify their cultural frame of reference through the following questions. As individuals develop a great sense of their cultural frame of reference through these reflective questions and others, they should begin to have a clearer picture of their cultural self and, subsequently, increase their readiness to talk through how their culture may or may not align with that of their students. For example, individuals may have preconceived notions of students' discourse patterns, volume of interactions, how often they work together versus individually, and when these notions do not align with what a student is used to, educators must be ready to act.
What are some of your family traditions– holidays, foods, or rituals?	
What family stories are regularly told or referenced? What messages do they communicate about core values?	
What physical, social, or cultural attributes were praised in your community? Which ones were you taught to avoid?	
What got you shunned or shamed by your family?	
Were you allowed to question, or talk back to, adults?	
Were you taught to accomplish goals and tasks by yourself or as a team?	

Domain 3: Emotional

The emotional domain of individual readiness addresses the capacity of an individual to engage in reflection, vulnerability, and challenges that result from culturally responsive and trauma-informed conversations. The emotional domain is not static and may fluctuate daily as routine situational factors (e.g., interpersonal conflict with fellow staff) can influence one's emotional capacity. However, by its very nature, talking through inequities, racism, and trauma as it is experienced by racially-ethnically marginalized students and their families within schools is difficult. While researchers assert the importance of individuals within schools to confront their biases to be able to challenge the white-dominant culture that permeates US schools (Grineski et al., 2013; Singleton, 2015;), this has been easier said than done (Palmer & Louis, 2017). White educators, in particular, often experience fear of being called racist as well as having very negative reactions to conversations on race and racism in equity-based professional development despite seeing its value (Palmer & Louis, 2017).

Emotional readiness also pertains to Black and other racially-ethnically marginalized educators as they also must be willing to be reflective of their own racial experiences and perspectives, vulnerable in sharing those racial experiences and perspectives with others, and challenged regarding their beliefs of other marginalized groups. However, their readiness to show these characteristics are influenced by the fact that they may be part of the marginalized population that is being discussed. Racially-ethnically marginalized teachers have the added burden of reflecting on the racial inequity and microaggressions that experienced as students, and that they also encounter working in schools (Kohli, 2016; Mosely, 2018). Additionally, teachers of color also encounter "invisible taxes" that can weigh heavily on them, such as serving as liaisons between schools and families of color and serving as disciplinarians for students of color (King, 2016; McCready & Moseley, 2013). Certainly, we can posit that white teachers and teachers of color may, individually, come into collective spaces for professional development regarding race and racism with differing capacities to be reflective, vulnerable, and challenged. While one teacher may be coming into a culturally responsive training slightly nervous, but feeling supported, another may be coming in exhausted at, yet again, having to embark on a stressful journey where they are not part of the *ingroup*. These experiences can make professional development and conversations around cultural responsiveness and trauma-informed practice daunting, warranting the need for individual school staff to gain emotional readiness.

Engage in Critical Inquiry

Table 7. Engaging in critical inquiry: emotional

Example Questions	Explanation
To what extent am I prepared to be reflective and vulnerable *today*?	Minimal capacity to be reflective and vulnerable can result in minimal readiness to engage in conversations and professional development related to cultural responsiveness and trauma-informed practice.
To what extent am I willing to be challenged *today*?	Minimal capacity to be challenged may result in minimal readiness to buy-in to disagreed upon practices. For example, opting into an instructional coach for cultural responsiveness may prove hard if one does not believe they need one because they will have trouble being challenged.
How might my general disposition affect my social readiness?	One's disposition can affect how they engage with other school staff members during tough conversations. This can make for productive conversations or hinder what would have otherwise been productive.
To what extent do I know my emotional limits?	It will be important to know one's limits in order to engage in self-protective behaviors if needed.
Are there any school staff that I trust to divulge my emotional capacity to?	It will be important to lean on others within the school system during tough conversations. Doing so can increase readiness by having another person to talk through content with.

Domain 4: Behavioral

The fourth domain for individual readiness focuses on participation in actions that can promote preparation for engaging in collective conversations related to cultural responsiveness and trauma-informed practice. Similar to collective commitment, the behavioral readiness component is action-oriented (e.g., reading books, engaging in intentional conversations, watching documentaries); however, individual behavioral readiness focuses on individual school staff's personal, and perhaps solitary, behaviors that are meant to enact change outside of collective efforts. In this manner, educators can engage in behaviors that educate them on issues of racial-ethnic diversity and inequities that impact individuals beyond the school environment. Accordingly, individuals can grow their emotional, social, and cultural readiness, which may increase their interest in voluntarily attending more formal training (Chung, 2013).

Engage in Critical Inquiry

Table 8. Engaging in critical inquiry: behavioral

Example Questions	Explanation
How intentional am I with seeking information related to issues of racial-ethnic inequities and diversity?	Due to the social and racial climate in the United States, information on issues of racial-ethnic inequities is more frequently highlighted in the media. It is important that individuals are not passive consumers of information, but intentionally seek information to educate themselves on current and historical issues that contribute to racial-ethnic inequities.
To what extent am I engaging in continuous learning outside of school-led initiatives?	It will be important to get into a habit of continuous learning outside of initiatives that are led by the school. Does your curiosity stop once you leave the school or are you continuously attempting to learn and grow?
To what extent am I establishing rapport with my students and their families?	Establishing rapport and learning partnerships with students and families helps to understand their needs, background, and ways of knowing, which can help prepare school staff to engage deeply with professional learning related to cultural responsiveness and trauma-informed practice.

PRACTICAL APPLICATION AND STRATEGIES FOR INCREASING INDIVIDUAL READINESS

We have provided several strategies below to begin thinking about and increase individual readiness within schools. It is important to note that these strategies should not be used as exact steps to follow; rather, these strategies serve as suggestions for schools if they have the capacity to implement them.

Identity Development

Identity development can encompass activities such as drawing out and discussing family trees. Through family tree discussions, individuals can reflect on how their families came to be where they are. Furthermore, individuals should identify characteristics of people on the tree and what stories they have about those people. It is also helpful to think about how people on the family tree contributed to the individual's own identity. Another exercise to explore identity is discussing one's circle of influence. During this activity, individuals learn who, from a racial, cultural, and gendered perspective, the person is most closely connected with and how those relationships influence their understanding of themselves, others, and the world around them. For example, some questions, such as, "Who is your best friend?", "Who is your favorite teacher?", "Who is your spiritual leader/advisor?", "Who cuts your hair?", and "Who are you in a relationship with?", help people realize that they may rarely be in community with people from diverse backgrounds or the depth, or lack thereof, of their relationships with people from diverse backgrounds. It is also pertinent to consider guided sessions through the archaeology of the self to engage in meaningful reflections.

Engage in Restricted Protective Behaviors

We suggest that individual school staff develop emotion identification and regulation skills in order to engage in restricted protective behaviors. *Restricted protective behaviors* refer to emotion regulation strategies that can protect oneself from intensive discomfort. We propose this suggestion as we know that cultural responsiveness and trauma-informed practice professional development can be discomforting; however, it is important to note that we also recognize that some discomfort is conducive to growth. Thus, we propose enlisting protective behaviors with restrictions. That is, one should employ protective behaviors, such as dismissing oneself for the day, only when they are experiencing discomfort to the point where their presence is no longer productive. It is suggested that school staff engage in these restricted protective behaviors in all settings in order to the emotion identification and regulation skills necessary for emotional readiness.

CONCLUSION

Readiness to engage in professional learning regarding cultural responsiveness and trauma-informed practice is an essential, yet underutilized construct within the education system. We provided a framework from which schools can use to promote readiness, so that schools and educators can maximize professional development and training efforts to support students through culturally responsive and trauma-informed practices. In the Collective and Individual Readiness Framework we propose eight domains of readiness within two school contexts in order to promote productive conversations related to cultural responsiveness and trauma-informed practice. The collective domains–awareness, commitment, leadership, and climate–provide areas of focus at the systems-level in order to promote top-down processes for readiness. Such practical strategies for increasing collective readiness include engaging in critical reflection, using organizational screeners, and increasing color-conscious perspectives. The individual domains–social, cultural, emotional, and behavioral–focus on factors within individual school staff that can facilitate or hinder cultural responsiveness and trauma-informed practice professional learning. Practical strategies for increasing individual readiness include engaging in critical reflection, restricted protective behaviors, identity development, and efficacy building. We contend that these practical strategies can help to promote readiness at the individual and collective levels and, thus, promote productive professional learning related to cultural responsiveness and trauma-informed practice.

REFERENCES

Abramowitz, J. S. (2013). The practice of exposure therapy: Relevance of cognitive-behavioral theory and extinction theory. *Behavior Therapy*, *44*(4), 548–558. doi:10.1016/j.beth.2013.03.003 PMID:24094780

Adejumo, V. (2020). Beyond diversity, inclusion, and belonging. *Leadership*, *17*(1), 62–73. doi:10.1177/1742715020976202

Allen, A., Scott, L. M., & Lewis, C. W. (2013). Racial microaggressions and African American and Hispanic students in urban schools: A call for culturally affirming education. *Interdisciplinary Journal of Teaching and Learning*, *3*(2), 117–129.

Alvarez, A. (2020). Seeing race in the research on youth trauma and education: A critical review. *Review of Educational Research*, *90*(5), 583–626. doi:10.3102/0034654320938131

Alvarez, A., & Farinde-Wu, A. (2022). *Advancing a holistic trauma framework for collective healing from colonial abuses*. Sage Publications. doi:10.1177/23328584221083973

Alvarez, A., & Farinde-Wu, A. (2022). Advancing a Holistic Trauma Framework for Collective Healing from Colonial Abuses. *AERA Open*, *8*. Advance online publication. doi:10.1177/23328584221083973

Annamma, S. A., Jackson, D. D., & Morrison, D. (2017). Conceptualizing color-evasiveness: Using dis/ability critical race theory to expand a color-blind racial ideology in education and society. *Race, Ethnicity and Education*, *20*(2), 147–162. doi:10.1080/13613324.2016.1248837

Bandura, A. (1977). Self-efficacy: Toward a unifying theory of behavioral change. *Psychological Review*, *84*(2), 191–215. doi:10.1037/0033-295X.84.2.191 PMID:847061

Bertrand, M., & Rodela, K. C. (2018). A framework for rethinking educational leadership in the margins: Implications for social justice leadership preparation. *Journal of Research on Leadership Education*, *13*(1), 10–37. doi:10.1177/1942775117739414

Blitz, L. V., Anderson, E. M., & Saastamoinen, M. (2016). Assessing perceptions of culture and trauma in an elementary school: Informing a model for culturally responsive trauma-informed schools. *The Urban Review*, *48*(4), 520–542. doi:10.100711256-016-0366-9

Blitz, L. V., Yull, D., & Clauhs, M. (2020). Bringing sanctuary to school: Assessing school climate as a foundation for culturally responsive trauma-informed approaches for urban schools. *Urban Education*, *55*(1), 95–124. doi:10.1177/0042085916651323

Bottiani, J. H., Larson, K. E., Debnam, K. J., Bischoff, C. M., & Bradshaw, C. P. (2018). Promoting educators' use of culturally responsive practices: A systematic review of inservice interventions. *Journal of Teacher Education*, *69*(4), 367–385. doi:10.1177/0022487117722553

Bryk, A., & Schneider, B. (2002). *Trust in schools: A core resource for improvement*. Russell Sage Foundation.

Chung, Y. (2013). Trainee readiness for diversity training. *Journal of Diversity Management*, *8*(2), 77–84. doi:10.19030/jdm.v8i2.8234

Cole, S. F., Eisner, A., Gregory, M., & Ristuccia, J. (2013). *Creating and advocating for trauma-sensitive schools*. Trauma and Learning Policy Initiative, partnership of Massachusetts Advocates for Children and Harvard Law School. https://www.traumasensitiveschools.org

Combs, G. (2002). Meeting the leadership challenges of a diverse and pluralistic workplace: Implications of self-efficacy for diversity training. *Journal of Leadership & Organizational Studies*, *8*(4), 1–16. doi:10.1177/107179190200800401

Curry, J. R. (2010). Addressing the spiritual needs of African American students: Implications for school counselors. *The Journal of Negro Education*, *79*(3), 405–415.

Delale-O'Connor, L. A., Alvarez, A. J., Murray, I. E., & Milner, H. R. IV. (2017). Self-efficacy beliefs, classroom management, and the cradle-to-prison pipeline. *Theory into Practice*, *56*(3), 178–186. doi:10.1080/00405841.2017.1336038

Delgado, R., & Stefanic, J. (2000). *Critical Race Theory: The Cutting Edge* (2nd ed.). Temple University Press.

Dixson, A. D., & Anderson, C. R. (2018). Where are we? Critical race theory in education 20 years later. *Peabody Journal of Education*, *93*(1), 121–131. doi:10.1080/0161956X.2017.1403194

Dorado, J. S., Martinez, M., McArthur, L. E., & Leibovitz, T. (2016). Healthy environments and response to trauma in schools (HEARTS): A whole-school multi-level prevention and intervention program for creating trauma-informed, safe, and supportive schools. *School Mental Health, 8*(1), 164–176. doi:10.100712310-016-9177-0

Duane, A., Casimir, A. E., Mims, L. C., Kaler-Jones, C., & Simmons, D. (2021). Beyond deep breathing: A new vision for equitable, culturally responsive, and trauma-informed mindfulness practice. *Middle School Journal, 52*(3), 4–14. doi:10.1080/00940771.2021.1893593

El-Amin, A. (2022). Improving organizational commitment to diversity, equity, inclusion, and belonging. In *Social Justice Research Methods for Doctoral Research*. IGI Global. doi:10.4018/978-1-7998-8479-8.ch010

Fondren, K., Lawson, M., Speidel, R., McDonnell, C. G., & Valentino, K. (2020). Buffering the effects of childhood trauma within the school setting: A systematic review of trauma-informed and trauma-responsive interventions among trauma-affected youth. *Children and Services Review, 109*, 104691. Advance online publication. doi:10.1016/j.childyouth.2019.104691

Forber-Pratt, A. J., El Sheikh, A. J., Robinson, L. E., Espelage, D. L., Ingram, K. M., Valido, A., & Torgal, C. (2021). Trauma-informed care in schools: Perspectives from school resource officers and school security professionals during professional development training. *School Psychology Review, 50*(2-3), 344–359. doi:10.1080/2372966X.2020.1832863

Gay, G. (2018). *Culturally responsive teaching: Theory, research, and practice*. Teachers College Press.

Graham, D. L., Alvarez, A. J., Heck, D. I., Rand, J. K., & Milner, H. R. (2019). Race, violence, and teacher education. In K. Han & J. Laughter (Eds.), *Critical Race Theory in Teacher Education: Informing Classroom Cultural and Practice* (pp. 13–25). Teachers College Press.

Gray, D. L., Hope, E. C., & Matthews, J. S. (2018). Black and belonging at school: A case for interpersonal, instructional, and institutional opportunity structures. *Educational Psychologist, 53*(2), 97–113. doi:10.1080/00461520.2017.1421466

Grineski, S., Landsman, J., & Simmons, R. (Eds.). (2013). *Talking about race: Alleviating the fear*. Stylus.

Grooms, A. A., Mahatmya, D., & Johnson, E. T. (2021). The retention of educators of color amidst institutionalized racism. *Educational Policy*, *35*(2), 180–212. doi:10.1177/0895904820986765

Gutiérrez, K. D., & Arzubiaga, A. (2012). An ecological and activity theoretic approach to studying diasporic and nondominant communities. *Research on schools, neighborhoods, and communities: Toward civic responsibility*, 203-216.

Halberstadt, A. G., Castro, V. L., Chu, Q., Lozada, F. T., & Sims, C. (2018). Preservice teachers' racialized emotion recognition, anger bias, and hostility attributions. *Contemporary Educational Psychology*, *54*, 125–138. doi:10.1016/j.cedpsych.2018.06.004

Halberstadt, A. G., Cooke, A. N., Garner, P. W., Hughes, S. A., Oertwig, D., & Neupert, S. D. (2022). Racialized emotion recognition accuracy and anger bias of children's faces. *Emotion (Washington, D.C.)*, *22*(3), 403–417. doi:10.1037/emo0000756 PMID:32614194

Hammond, Z. (2014). *Culturally Responsive Teaching and the Brain: Promoting Authentic Engagement and Rigor among Culturally and Linguistically Diverse Students*. SAGE Publications.

Hooks, B. (2014). *Teaching to transgress*. Routledge. doi:10.4324/9780203700280

Hopkins, M., Ozimek, D., & Sweet, T. M. (2017). Mathematics coaching and instructional reform: Individual and collective change. *The Journal of Mathematical Behavior*, *46*, 215–230. doi:10.1016/j.jmathb.2016.11.003

Horsford, S. D. (2010). Mixed feelings about mixed schools: Superintendents on the complex legacy of school desegregation. *Educational Administration Quarterly*, *46*(3), 287–321. doi:10.1177/0013161X10365825

Johnson, T. R., Gold, E., & Zhao, A. (2022). How anti-critical race theory bills are taking aim at teachers. *FiveThirtyEight*. Retrieved from https://fivethirtyeight.com/features/how-anti-critical-race-theory-bills-are-taking-aim-at-teachers/

Kaczkurkin, A. N., & Foa, E. B. (2022). Cognitive-behavioral therapy for anxiety disorders: An update on the empirical evidence. *Dialogues in Clinical Neuroscience*, *17*(3), 337–346. doi:10.31887/DCNS.2015.17.3/akaczkurkin PMID:26487814

Khalifa, M. A., Gooden, M. A., & Davis, J. E. (2016). Culturally responsive school leadership: A synthesis of the literature. *Review of Educational Research*, *86*(4), 1272–1311. doi:10.3102/0034654316630383

King, J. (2016). The invisible tax on teachers of color. *The Washington Post*. Retrieved from https://www.washingtonpost.com/opinions/the-invisible-tax-on-black-teachers/2016/05/15/6b7bea06-16f7-11e6-aa55-670cabef46e0_story.html

Kohli, R. (2016). Behind school doors: The impact of hostile racial climates on urban teachers of color. *Urban Education, 53*(3), 307–333. doi:10.1177/0042085916636653

Ladson-Billings, G. (1995). "But that's just good teaching!" The case for culturally relevant teaching. *Theory into Practice, 34*(3), 159–165. doi:10.1080/00405849509543675

Ladson-Billings, G. (2009). *Dreamkeepers: Successful teachers of African American children*. John Wiley & Sons.

Ladson-Billings, G., & Tate, W. F. IV. (1995). Toward a critical race theory of education. *Teachers College Record, 97*(1), 47–68. doi:10.1177/016146819509700104

McCready, L., & Mosely, M. (2013). Making space for Black queer teachers: Pedagogic possibilities. In C. W. Lewis, Y. Sealey-Ruiz, & I. Toldson (Eds.), *Teacher education and Black communities: Implications for access, equity, and achievement* (pp. 43–58). Information Age Publishing.

McIntyre, E. M., Baker, C. N., & Overstreet, S. (2019). Evaluating foundational professional development training for trauma-informed approaches in schools. *Psychological Services, 16*(1), 95–102. doi:10.1037er0000312 PMID:30489111

Mellom, P. J., Straubhaar, R., Balderas, C., Ariail, M., & Portes, P. R. (2018). "They come with nothing:" How professional development in a culturally responsive pedagogy shapes teacher attitudes towards Latino/a English language learners. *Teaching and Teacher Education, 71*, 98–107. doi:10.1016/j.tate.2017.12.013

Milner, H. R. IV. (2007). Race, culture, and researcher positionality: Working through dangers seen, unseen, and unforeseen. *Educational Researcher, 36*(7), 388–400. doi:10.3102/0013189X07309471

Moore, B. A. (2018). Developing special educator cultural awareness through critically reflective professional learning community collaboration. *Teacher Education and Special Education: The Journal of the Teacher Education Division of the Council for Exceptional Children, 41*(3), 243–253. doi:10.1177/0888406418770714

Mosely, M. (2018). The Black teacher project: How racial affinity professional development sustains Black teachers. *The Urban Review, 50*(2), 267–283. doi:10.100711256-018-0450-4

Palmer, E. L., & Louis, K. S. (2017). Talking about race: Overcoming fear in the process of change. *Journal of School Leadership, 27*(4), 581–610. doi:10.1177/105268461702700405

Riehl, C. J. (2009). The principal's role in creating inclusive schools for diverse students: A review of normative, empirical, and critical literature on the practice of educational administration. *Review of Educational Research, 70*(1), 55–81. doi:10.3102/00346543070001055

Saleem, F. T., Anderson, R. E., & Williams, M. (2020). Addressing the "Myth" of Racial Trauma: Developmental and Ecological Considerations for Youth of Color. *Clinical Child and Family Psychology Review, 23*(1), 1–14. doi:10.100710567-019-00304-1 PMID:31641920

Sealey-Ruiz, Y. (2022). An Archaeology of Self for Our Times: Another Talk to Teachers. *English Journal, 111*(5), 21–26.

Singleton, G. (2015). *Courageous conversations about race: A Field Guide for Achieving Equity in Schools*. Corwin.

Sleeter, C. E. (2011). An agenda to strengthen culturally responsive pedagogy. *English Teaching, 10*(2), 7–23.

Supovitz, J. A., D'Auria, J., & Spillane, J. P. (2019). *Meaningful and sustainable school improvement with distributed leadership*. CPRE Research Reports. Retrieved from: https://repository.upenn.edu/cpre_researchreports/112

Tate, W. R., Hamilton, C., Jones, B. D., Robertson, W. B., & Macrander, A. Schultz, l., & Thorne-Washington, E. (2013). Serving vulnerable children and youth in the urban context. In H.R. Milner & K. Lomotey (Eds), Handbook of Urban Education (pp. 3-23). Routledge.

Uline, C., & Tschannen-Moran, M. (2008). The walls speak: The interplay of quality facilities, school climate, and student achievement. *Journal of Educational Administration, 46*(1), 55–73. doi:10.1108/09578230810849817

Ullucci, I., & Battey, D. (2011). Exposing color blindness/grounding color consciousness: Challenges for teacher education. *Urban Education, 46*(6), 1195–1225. doi:10.1177/0042085911413150

Venet, A. S. (2021). Equity-Centered Trauma-Informed Education (Equity and Social Justice in Education). WW Norton & Company.

Wang, T., Olivier, D. F., & Chen, P. (2020). Creating individual and organizational readiness for change: Conceptualization of system readiness for change in school education. *International Journal of Leadership in Education*, 1–25. Advance online publication. doi:10.1080/13603124.2020.1818131

Woodward, J. R. (2011). How busing burdened Blacks: Critical race theory and busing for desegregation in Nashville-Davidson County. *The Journal of Negro Education*, *80*(1), 22–32.

Yosso, T. J. (2005). Whose culture has capital? A critical race theory discussion of community cultural wealth. *Race, Ethnicity and Education*, *8*(1), 69–91. doi:10.1080/1361332052000341006

Young, B. L., Madsen, J., & Young, M. A. (2010). Implementing diversity plans: Principals' perception of their ability to address diversity in their schools. *NASSP Bulletin*, *94*(2), 135–157. doi:10.1177/0192636510379901

KEY TERMS AND DEFINITIONS

Collective Readiness: Collective readiness deals with the preparedness of the school at the systems-level to engage in discourse related to cultural responsiveness and trauma-informed practice.

Cultural Responsiveness: Cultural responsiveness centers students' lived experiences and cultural background into instruction and the school environment for the purposes of learning and achievement.

Individual Readiness: Individual readiness is concerned with how people connect to the local environment related to conversations about cultural responsiveness and trauma-informed practice.

Trauma-Informed Practice: Trauma-informed practice refers to the utilization of knowledge related to how trauma affects learning and behavior for use in the school environment.

Chapter 11
Using Positive Behavioral Interventions and Supports to Disrupt the School-to-Prison Pipeline:
Decriminalizing Childhood Adversity

Erin E. Neuman-Boone
Robert Morris University, USA

Patricia Kardambikis
Robert Morris University, USA

Vicki J. Donne
Robert Morris University, USA

ABSTRACT

Poverty and trauma risks need not create a criminal pathway or pipeline to prison. As the number of adverse childhood experiences (ACEs) increase, so does the risk of dropping out of school. The more often students are suspended, the more likely they are to be referred to the juvenile justice system and face jail or prison time. Once in the system, the likelihood of recidivism is great. One multifaceted intervention to disrupt the school-to-prison pipeline (STPP) is positive behavioral interventions and supports (PBIS). The aim of this model is to alter the school environment by creating improved systems involving discipline, reinforcement, and data management. These systematic changes may disrupt the STPP for students living in poverty and experiencing ACEs.

DOI: 10.4018/978-1-6684-5713-9.ch011

INTRODUCTION

The most recent statistics indicate that there are more than six million offenders under correctional supervision in the U.S., including those incarcerated, on probation, and on parole (Minton et al., 2021). Every day more than 48,000 youth under the age of 18 are held in detention centers, long term secure facilities, residential treatment, adult prisons and jails, group homes, and shelters (Rowe, 2020). Once released from incarceration facilities, less than half of these youth return to school while many others drop out or reoffend (Cavendish, 2014). Neither the schools nor the correctional facilities have addressed the underlying, adverse effects of trauma experienced in childhood. Researchers report that in the U.S., 90% or more of juvenile offenders have experienced childhood trauma (Baglivio et al., 2014; Dierkhising et al., 2013) with poverty concomitant with childhood trauma (Felitti et al., 1998). Poverty and trauma risk factors need not form a pathway or pipeline to prison; schools, rather than systemically criminalizing youth's reaction to trauma, can create proactive, protective policies and practices to divert the pathway. This chapter examines using positive behavioral interventions and supports to decriminalize childhood adversity and disrupt the school to prison pipeline.

Adverse Childhood Experiences and Poverty

To illustrate the pathway from trauma to prison, consider the fictitious case of Jane. Jane, a female in her mid thirties, was recently incarcerated for the second time as an adult. Jane has been involved with the criminal justice system since the age of 14 with multiple juvenile offenses. Her academic records are laced with truancy reports, failing grades, disciplinary reports, and suspensions. Eventually, Jane was placed in a residential treatment facility for a brief period and upon discharge dropped out of school. Jane's academic and criminal records give us a snapshot of her history and possibly some indication of her future; however, these records do not give us Jane's full story. Jane grew up in a home with her mother and stepfather, never knowing her birth father. Both her mother and stepfather struggled with substance abuse and had difficulty maintaining employment, barely earning enough to pay rent and put food on the table. Because of this, Jane never knew when she would have her next meal, wore unkempt clothing, and could not afford to participate in extracurricular activities. Jane's stepfather was in and out of jail; when he was around he was physically abusive towards Jane and her mother. Jane was often neglected, both physically and emotionally. Strangers frequented their apartment to get high with Jane's mother and stepfather. When Jane was 13, she was raped in her apartment while her mother was passed out in the next room. Jane's chaotic home life contributed to a chaotic academic life. As a result of the many traumatic experiences that Jane endured, her focus was on surviving rather than succeeding in school or forming healthy peer relationships. The trauma responses that helped Jane survive at home are the same behaviors that contributed to Jane's disciplinary reports and suspensions in school. Jane's history of trauma and abuse is devastating, but unfortunately, it is not uncommon among those who are incarcerated.

The traumatic events that Jane endured during her childhood are referred to as adverse childhood experiences (ACEs). The term ACE originated in the mid-nineties from a large, groundbreaking study by Dr. Vincent Felitti from Kaiser Permanente and Robert Anda from the Centers for Disease Control and Prevention (CDC). Through their research, they developed the ACE Survey which includes self-reports of items to assess abuse (physical, emotional, and sexual), neglect (physical and emotional), and household challenges (parent divorce, parental substance abuse, parental incarceration, parental mental illness, and spousal abuse) (Felitti et al., 1998). "Adverse childhood experiences are operationally defined as childhood events, varying in severity and often chronic, occurring in a family or social environment and causing harm or distress" (Kalmakis & Chandler, 2014, p. 1490).

ACEs have a detrimental impact on health and social outcomes. The negative health and social implications result from toxic stress (Sacks & Murphey, 2018; Shonkoff et al., 2012).

Childhood toxic stress is severe, prolonged, or repetitive adversity with a lack of the necessary nurturance or support of a caregiver to prevent an abnormal stress response. This abnormal stress response consists of a derangement of the neuro-endocrine-immune response resulting in prolonged cortisol activation and a persistent inflammatory state, with failure of the body to normalize these changes after the stressor is removed. Children who experience early life toxic stress are at risk of long-term adverse health effects that may not manifest until adulthood. These adverse health effects include maladaptive coping skills, poor stress management, unhealthy lifestyles, mental illness and physical disease. (Franke, 2014, p.391)

Nearly 61% of the general population report at least one ACE (Centers for Disease Control and Prevention [CDC], 2019). As the number of ACEs increases, so does the risk for adverse health and social outcomes. Individuals reporting four or more ACEs are at a much greater risk for developing toxic stress and the myriad of negative outcomes previously mentioned. Sixteen percent of the general population fall into this category; however, females, minority groups, those involved in the juvenile justice system, and incarcerated adults are at a greater risk of having experienced four or more (CDC, 2019; Stensrud et al., 2019). In fact, nearly two thirds of incarcerated females and male sex offenders, and 43% of non-violent offenders reported four or more ACEs (Stensrud et al., 2019). Additionally, ACEs are disproportionately reported among juvenile offenders, with 97% reporting at least one and 50% reporting four or more (Baglivio et al., 2014). These findings suggest that all individuals who interact with children in the juvenile and criminal justice systems and incarcerated adults should be aware of the impact of ACEs and provide trauma informed support.

Furthermore, ACEs disproportionately affect those living in poverty (Hughes & Tucker, 2018) with some assessments of ACEs including poverty or economic hardship as an ACE itself (Whiteside-Mansell et al., 2019). "Poverty is measured in the United States by comparing a person's or family's income to a set poverty threshold or minimum amount of income needed to cover basic needs. People whose income falls under their threshold are considered poor" (Institute for Research on Poverty, 2022, How is Poverty Measured section). According to the 2022 poverty guidelines, a family of four is considered to be living in poverty if they earn $27,750 or less per year (Assistant Secretary for Planning and Evaluation [ASPE], 2022). Income-based poverty measures are necessary for determining eligibility for safety net programs; however, the definition fails to capture the human experience of poverty. Poverty is more than lacking in resources and income.

Being poor is about not being able to partake in society on equal terms with others, and therefore in the long run being excluded by fellow citizens or withdrawing from social and civic life because of a lack of economic resources, typically in combination with the concomitant shame of not being able to live a life like them. (Mood & Jonsson, 2016, p. 634)

Poverty has a profound impact on children, with nearly 1 in 6 children living in poverty in the United States (Center on Poverty and Social Justice at Columbia University, 2022). It is well-documented that poverty affects children's physical, mental, emotional, and behavioral health and that the longer children live in poverty and stress, the greater the impact (Gitterman et al., 2016; Jensen, 2009; Yoshikawa et al., 2012). This impact is compounded when considering that there is a strong correlation between poverty and incarceration (Kenter et al., 2020). Those who are incarcerated are more likely to have experienced childhood poverty and poverty into adulthood prior to incarceration (Looney & Turner, 2018; Rabuy & Kopf, 2015). According to Rabuy and Kopf (2015), those who are incarcerated earned 41% less prior to incarceration compared to non-incarcerated individuals, suggesting that poverty may be a risk factor for incarceration. Additionally, those who are incarcerated are at a greater risk of poverty following imprisonment due to employment barriers (Looney & Turner, 2018).

When examining poverty and trauma, it is also essential to consider race. Particularly, racial minority youth experience poverty and trauma at disproportionate rates compared to white youth (Alvarez, 2020). According to the National Center for Education Statistics (2019), 89% of youth living in poverty are youth of color. Youth of color are at greater risk of poverty due to multigenerational poverty and less opportunities for income mobility resulting from racial oppression (Winship et al., 2022). Poverty not only increases the risk for experiencing ACEs, but poverty-related stress is an ACE in and of itself. The combination of poverty and ACEs is devastating for children, particularly children of color, and the implications are lasting and persist through adulthood.

IMPACT ON EDUCATION

Poverty and ACEs impact brain development and influence attitudes which ultimately effect a child's education. We see this effect in the areas of school engagement, behavior, and academics. Children with ACEs have lower rates of school engagement (Bethell et al., 2014). School engagement refers to the degree of attention and excitement students show toward learning and school-related activities. The level of student engagement is dependent on the quality of the student's relationship with the school community. It is often measured by school attendance and children with ACEs have higher rates of unexcused absences (Duke, 2020). Additionally, students of low socioeconomic status have lower rates of engagement than those not eligible for free and reduced lunch and students of color have lower rates of engagement than Caucasian students (Yazzie-Mintz, 2007). School engagement is important as there is a reciprocal relationship between school engagement and academic achievement (Marsh & O'Mara, 2008). Those who are engaged in school tend to do well academically and those that do well academically tend to be engaged in school.

Exposure to ACEs also increases the likelihood of children exhibiting socioemotional maladjustment such as the inability to regulate emotions, maintain positive peer relationships, and make age-appropriate decisions (Hughes et al., 2017; Oh et al., 2018). When students have difficulty regulating their emotions, they often exhibit what teachers and schools consider inappropriate behaviors. For example, there is an increased likelihood of children with ACEs to show externalizing behaviors (Hunt et al., 2017) such as hyperactivity, conduct problems, substance abuse, aggression, bullying, or general rule breaking. The schools' disciplinary responses to these external behaviors are often suspension or expulsion. Schools have adopted zero tolerance policies that mandate "the application of predetermined consequences, most often severe and punitive in nature, that are intended to be applied regardless of the gravity of behavior, mitigating circumstances, or situational context" (APA, 2008, p. 852). The consequence of these policies is that students experiencing three or more ACEs are two to three times more likely to experience suspensions or expulsions (Davis & Buchanan, 2020). Additionally, students from low socioeconomic homes and students of color are disproportionately suspended from school (APA, 2008; Skiba et al., 1997; Sprague, 2014). Theoretically, the goal of suspensions and expulsions is to maintain a safe environment for all students, however, for students experiencing poverty and ACEs, the consequence of these disciplinary responses place them at home or back in an environment that may have contributed to the origins of their disruptive behavior. Furthermore, students who are expelled or suspended have lower attendance, course completion rates, and academics and are more likely to drop out of school (Chu & Ready, 2018; Rausch & Skiba, 2004; Skiba et al., 1997). Thus, the measures in place to maintain the safe environment in which students can learn have unintended negative consequences for students experiencing ACEs.

ACEs impact academic achievement in several ways. ACEs and cumulative ACEs are predictive of academic failure (Hughes et al., 2017; Oh et al., 2018). For example, children with more than three ACEs by 5 years of age experience below average language, math, and social skills (Jimenez et al., 2016). Additionally, children with ACEs were more likely to repeat a grade in school (Bethell et al., 2014) and were at increased risk of dropping out of school (Dube et al., 2010; Giovanelli et al., 2016; Morrow & Villodas, 2018). Rates for repeating a grade are significantly higher for students of color and students living in poverty (Crouch et al., 2019). Students experiencing ACEs also present with fewer plans for high school graduation or for the development of skills past high school (Duke, 2020). As one might expect with the poor graduation and employment rates, children experiencing ACEs were also more likely to live in poverty as an adult (Metzler et al., 2017; Zielinski, 2009), thus perpetuating this cycle.

SCHOOL TO PRISON PIPELINE

The impact of poverty and ACEs is intertwined among many aspects within education related to successful high school completion. For example, students who were chronically absent were more likely to drop out of school (Utah Education Policy Center, 2012) and students with ACEs have higher rates of absences (Duke, 2020) and increased risk of dropping out of school (Dube et al., 2010; Giovanelli et al., 2016; Morrow & Villodas, 2018). Additionally, students who receive an out of school suspension (OSS) are more likely to experience academic difficulties (Rausch & Skiba, 2004) and are at an increased risk for dropping out of school (Skiba et al., 1997). These findings are problematic for students experiencing ACEs as accumulated ACEs are predictors of expulsion and suspension (Davis & Buchanan, 2020), with this pattern seen even at the preschool level (Zeng et al.,

2019). Additionally, low-income schools use school suspensions at significantly higher rates than other schools (Noltemeyer & Mcloughlin, 2010) and students of color are disproportionately suspended (APA, 2008). Suspension further excludes these students from the academic instruction necessary to successfully progress in school which in turn lowers school engagement and attendance.

School experiences for children experiencing poverty and ACEs become increasingly punitive and detached. Zero tolerance policies have resulted in increased referrals to the juvenile system for infractions that were previously not considered dangerous or threatening and would have been handled by the school (APA, 2008). Researchers found that the more often students were suspended and the earlier in their school career suspensions occurred, the more likely they were to be referred to the juvenile justice system and face jail or prison time (Heidelburg et al., 2021; Shollenberger, 2015). Consider that children suspended from school during an academic year were almost three times more likely to become involved with the juvenile and criminal justice system the next year (Novak, 2021). The concept that harsh disciplinary policies and actions in public schools decrease the probability of successful school outcomes, pushing children out of the classroom and into the juvenile and criminal justice system, has been referred to as the school to prison pipeline (STPP) (Wald & Losen, 2003). Once referred to the justice system, students have an increased likelihood of academic failures and dropping out of school (Wald & Losen, 2003) as schools lack the proper resources to support re-enrollment of adjudicated students. This makes it difficult for students to reverse the path down the pipeline to prison.

As described, the educational disadvantages of students experiencing ACEs, living in poverty, and of color are not independent, single-factored explanations but rather complex, cumulative intersections. These students are more apt to experience multiple forms of trauma and more likely to present traumatic reactions which in turn are more likely to be punished (Baumle, 2018). This intersectionality amplifies the marginalization of these students in school (McIntosh et al., 2019), increasing the probability of negative outcomes or participation in the STPP as demonstrated by the disproportionate representation of students of color, poverty, and ACEs in the juvenile system (Skiba et al., 2014). The systemic denial of access to educational opportunities and discrimination brings additional trauma to these students in the form of structural trauma (Baumle, 2018).

These systems ignore the risk factors, i.e. poverty, race, and ACEs, fail to take into account why the behaviors occurred, and do not teach children or educators the skills necessary to identify the risk factors or provide trauma-informed care in order to break the STPP. The association between risk factors such as school disengagement, school exclusion, dropout, and juvenile justice involvement have been well-documented. Thus, the existing school policies and practices essentially criminalize students experiencing ACEs (Baumle, 2018).

Better practices are needed to address the challenge of meeting the needs of students experiencing poverty and ACEs while maintaining a safe school environment for lower student aggression, disruptive behaviors, office discipline referrals (ODRs), and suspensions (Bradshaw et al., 2010; Bradshaw et al., 2012; Goodman-Scott et al., 2018; Luiselli et al., 2005; Simonsen et al., 2012). To support all. Researchers suggest that "focusing on any single risk factor (e.g., deviant peer association) is unlikely to adequately explain elevated dropout rates among high-risk adolescents" (Morrow & Villodas, 2018, p. 336). Therefore, a multifaceted approach to intervention is suggested to disrupt the STPP. One multifaceted intervention approach which may address the underlying contributing factors within the STPP, increase knowledge of ACEs, while integrating trauma informed practices is positive behavioral interventions and supports (PBIS) (APA, 2008).

Positive Behavioral Interventions and Supports (PBIS)

PBIS is a systems-level framework designed to improve school climate, reduce discriminatory discipline practices, and improve student outcomes for all students through use of evidence-based practices and data-driven decision making (Gage et al., 2020; Sugai & Horner, 2009; Sugai & Simonsen, 2012; Waasdorp et al., 2012). PBIS incorporates a positive, direct instructional approach to behavioral intervention. The framework allows schools to select evidence-based practices to meet the needs of students in their school, including the use of trauma informed practices. Trauma informed practice trains all school staff about trauma, its impact on education, and the importance of developing relationships with teachers and schools (Eber et al., 2020). These practices create a positive school climate where children who have experienced trauma can feel safe and more comfortable communicating with peers, staff, and teachers about academics and their traumatic experiences.

PBIS evidence-based framework focuses on multicomponent interventions that are preventive, proactive, and educative involving effective teaching strategies for all students in academic, social, and mental health areas (Keller-Bell & Short, 2019). PBIS is not designed to be scripted nor does it require the use of specific strategies or interventions. Rather, PBIS is developed through a core PBIS leadership team typically consisting of an interdisciplinary team of six to eight school staff, including at least one coach facilitating the team, who are responsible for leading, coordinating, and evaluating PBIS school-wide (Goodman-Scott et al., 2018). These teams work with administrators to provide the training, policy support, and organizational support needed for initial implementation, active application, and sustained use of the core elements (Horner et al., 2015; Sugai & Horner, 2009). A team problem-solving approach is used to select and apply a range of evidence-based interventions to meet the needs of their student population based upon continuous progress monitoring (Barrett et al., 2018; Keller-Bell & Short, 2019; Swain-Bradway et al., 2015). Resources are allocated to ensure that the systems and practices selected are implemented with fidelity over time (Sprague & Horner, 2006). Fidelity is the "extent to which the delivery of an intervention adheres to the protocol or program model originally developed" (Mowbray et al., 2003, p. 315). Fidelity of implementation is an essential variable in assessing the impact of PBIS on student performance (George & Childs, 2012) as there is a significant relationship between fidelity of implementation of PBIS and student academic and truancy outcomes (Childs et al., 2016; Pas & Bradshaw, 2012).

PBIS is a three-tiered intervention framework associated with team-based planning, behavioral interventions, and school-wide implementation. The core elements at each of the three tiers in the prevention model are defined in Table 1 (Horner et al., 2015, p. 2). According to the foundational premise of PBIS, all students receive Tier 1 prevention involving direct instruction in school-wide expectations, procedures, routines, and acknowledgements or rewards. Tier 1 supports serve as the foundation for behavior and academics (Center on Positive Behavioral Intervention and Supports, 2022b). Tier 1 interventions might include school wide instruction in and posting of rules (being respectful, walking in the halls, etc.), a school wide system of classroom management and rewards (students and classrooms are awarded points for positive behavior and cumulated points result in a class pizza party or lunch with the principal), and a curriculum or set of practices to address social emotional learning. Tier 1 supports strategies that successfully address the behavioral management needs of approximately 80% of students (Keller-Bell & Short, 2019).

Tier 2 is a more intensive support tier based on individual school data. Tier 2 data includes elevated behavioral needs based on office discipline referrals. Instruction in identified skills based on such data is provided to small groups of students with similar identified needs (Keller-Bell & Short, 2019). By providing small group support, students are provided additional opportunities for practice and feedback while keeping the interventions maximally productive and efficient. Examples of Tier 2 interventions can include social skills groups, school counseling programs, peer tutoring, and after-school homework clubs (Keller-Bell & Short, 2019; Walker et al., 2005). Approximately 15% of students are served in Tier 2.

Tier 3 interventions are provided individually only to students who exhibit intense problem behaviors or intense academic needs and are designed for approximately 1% - 5% of students (Center on Positive Behavioral Intervention and Supports, 2022a). These supports are the most resource intensive due to the individualized approach of developing and conducting interventions (Goodman-Scott et al., 2021). At this level, schools typically rely on data from formal assessments such as a functional behavior assessment (FBA) to determine a student's needs and to develop an individualized support plan (Keller-Bell & Short, 2019). A FBA "assesses the relationship between a behavior and the surrounding environment to create effective intervention plans" (Scott & Caron, 2005, p. 13). Examples of Tier 3 interventions might include individual counseling, Behavior Intervention Plans (BIP), individual behavior contracts, or wrap around support.

Table 1. Core elements of PBIS tiers (Horner et al., 2015, pg. 2)

Prevention Tier	Core Elements
Tier 1	• Behavioral expectations defined • Behavioral expectations taught • Reward system for appropriate behavior • Clearly defined consequences for problem behavior • Differentiated instruction for behavior • Continuous collection and use of data for decision-making • Universal screening for behavior support
Tier 2	• Progress monitoring for at risk students • System for increasing structure and predictability • System for increasing contingent adult feedback • System for linking academic and behavioral performance • System for increasing home/school communication • Collection and use of data for decision-making • Basic-level function-based support

Tier 3	• Functional Behavioral Assessment (full, complex)
	• Team-based comprehensive assessment
	• Linking of academic and behavior supports
	• Individualized intervention based on assessment information focusing on
	  (a) prevention of problem contexts,
	  (b) instruction on functionally equivalent skills, and instruction on desired performance skills,
	  (c) strategies for placing problem behavior on extinction,
	  (d) strategies for enhancing contingence reward of desired behavior, and
	  (e) use of negative or safety consequences if needed.
	• Collection and use of data for decision-making.

Data are reviewed to select, monitor, and evaluate practices, outcomes, and systems across all three tiers of PBIS. Data provide educators with an unbiased way to assess how well they are improving student outcomes (McIntosh et al., 2014). For example, to support a positive school culture, systematic procedural changes using data-based decision making in the collection of Office Discipline Referral (ODR) data promotes positive changes in student and teacher behaviors (Bradshaw et al., 2015). School teams will determine the data sources to track school-wide progress in reducing incidents and identifying students in need of additional support.

PBIS and Adverse Childhood Experiences

PBIS is recommended as an alternative approach to maintaining school safety while keeping students experiencing ACEs in school (APA, 2008). All tiers within PBIS can include trauma informed practices. Trauma informed practices focus on how teachers, staff and administration can recognize and respond effectively to the impact of trauma on students. As PBIS Tier 1 involves the instruction of expectations and skills, it can meet the needs of students experiencing ACEs on several fronts. First, it includes training staff and teachers on the widespread incidence of ACEs, recognition of signs, their impact, and possible interventions (Eber et al., 2020). Secondly, it includes instruction across PBIS tiers in social emotional skills, skills such as problem solving, anger management, and mindfulness (McIntosh et al., 2018). Thirdly, it involves teachers instructing on routines and appropriate behaviors through positive examples and providing reinforcement when behavior expectations are met. PBIS establishes a school environment that is consistent, positive, safe, and equitable, all of which are important to reduce anxiety and address the needs of students who have ACEs (Sugai & Horner, 2020).

Additional supports in Tiers 2 and 3 utilize trauma informed practices integrated within referrals, assessments, interventions, and data collection (Eber et al., 2020). For example, members of the implementation team are knowledgeable in trauma informed practices, use community data in evaluation of school needs, select interventions that are trauma informed practices, and schedule periodic professional development on ACEs and trauma informed care. To illustrate, if students in Tier 2 are taught a self-calming strategy or sensory breaks are utilized, teachers would be provided professional development on these strategies and data on use of the skill or strategy would be monitored and evaluated for effectiveness. An example of trauma informed care in Tier 3 might be the provision of school based mental health services as indicated by a FBA and mental health assessment. Again, professional development would be provided to teachers on the referral process and an overview of the school based mental health services. These structures assist schools in implementing practices throughout the PBIS tiers to meet the needs of students experiencing ACEs.

PBIS to Meet the Needs of Students in Poverty

There are many components of the PBIS framework which can support the needs of students in poverty who are experiencing ACEs. Teacher professional development on characteristics of specific school communities and specific problems experienced at a school can be elements of PBIS. As the number of schools with high numbers of students in mid to high poverty is increasing, it is very important that educators be aware of the effects of poverty on student behavior and learning in the classroom (McKenszie, 2019). Additional professional development found to be effective in high poverty schools was training on PBIS, data analysis, classroom management, and FBAs (McCurdy et al., 2003). The McCurdy and colleague study also reported that professional development positively impacted discipline and ODR. Lassen et al. (2006) also reported positive effects on ODR, suspensions, and academic performance when teachers in low income schools were trained in PBIS and behavior assessment techniques.

In addition to recognizing the signs of poverty, empowering students and altering the classroom environment can assist the academic achievement of students with ACEs living in poverty (McKenzie, 2019; Geitz & McIntosh, 2014; Jensen, 2013). Classroom suggestions to close the achievement gaps of students in low income schools include training teachers on developing strong relationships with their students, embodying respect in their interactions with students, embedding social skills in lessons, promoting inclusive classrooms, building core skills, providing accurate assessments, and recruiting caring and empathetic staff (Budge & Parrett, 2018; McKenzie, 2019).

PBIS helps to create and maintain a positive school climate and acknowledges students for their appropriate behavior (McKenzie, 2019). Some of the reward systems used in high poverty schools included awarding of tickets for good behavior with tickets entered in random drawings for keychains and books along with taking the picture of winners and displaying pictures in a trophy case (Lassen et al., 2006) and awarding of tickets in exchange for rewards and group activities such as movies and trips (McCurdy et al., 2003). Behavior reward systems are individualized by schools based on identified positive reinforcers.

The impact of poverty and how PBIS implementation impacts students living in poverty has been researched across diverse settings including urban schools (Bohannon et al., 2006; Goodman-Scott et al., 2018; Lassen et al., 2006; McCurdy et al., 2003; Netzel & Eber, 2003; Utley et al., 2002), rural schools (Oyen & Wollersheim-Shervey, 2019; Steed et al., 2013), and schools with diverse racial/ethnic student populations (McCurdy et al., 2003; McIntosh et al., 2018; Utley et al., 2002; Vincent & Tobin 2011). This research has provided specific recommendations for implementation of PBIS. For example, researchers have also examined school variables that may affect PBIS implementation and found that schools in areas of rural poverty tend to be in favor of implementing PBIS (McDaniel et al., 2018) and less likely to abandon PBIS implementation compared to urban schools in high poverty areas. Additionally, research in low-socioeconomic schools implementing PBIS revealed the need for local and external coaches, external resources, state and district training, sufficient time and support for implementation, and inclusion of culturally responsive training practices (Weiland et al., 2014). Additionally, challenges associated with poverty, such as mental health issues, transiency, single-parent homes, and low family income, must be addressed and evidence-based interventions for students in poverty integrated within PBIS (Heidelburg et al., 2021; McDaniel et al., 2018). For example, McCurdy et al. (2003) utilized consultants from a local behavioral health care agency to address behavioral concerns and to design their PBIS model.

When funding is tied to neighborhood income (i.e. urban low income schools) or small student population (i.e. rural low income schools), operational challenges exist (DeJarenett et al., 2022). In the United States, public schools are funded by state, local, and federal governments. This funding is reliant on income and property taxes, which poses a threat to poorer areas of the country and causes funding disparities. Wealthier districts are able to collect more in these taxes for school funding than poorer districts. This often results in low-income families with the highest needs receiving the least resources available, the least-qualified teachers, and substandard learning facilities (Watson, 2016). It also impacts student achievement as researchers have found a causal relationship between school spending and student outcomes (Jackson, 2020). This means that in public schools, the majority of children in low socioeconomic areas will enter their first year behind their more privileged peers, and they may never catch up. This also means that education policy and funding decisions must be adapted to help those children who come to school every day to learn (Watson, 2016). While PBIS cannot change the funding formulas, it can mitigate some of the inequities by creating positive school environments to keep students in school and improve student outcomes (Goodman-Scott et al., 2021; Sugui et al., 2012). Additionally, use of federal funds, i.e. Title I or grants, and collaboration with external institutions, i.e. universities or state departments of education, have been suggested to facilitate PBIS implementation in areas with less resources and funds (DeJarenett et al., 2022).

PBIS and Equity and Cultural Responsiveness

In dismantling the school to prison pipeline through PBIS, schools must look at the intersectionality of race, class, and ACEs and structural trauma in the design of processes and interventions. The design of PBIS components, implementation, and evaluation should incorporate input from culturally representative school stakeholders such as students, families, and community members (Goodman-Scott et al., 2021; Toney & Rodgers, 2011). The PBIS team members should reflect the student and community demographics. By acquiring the voices of various stakeholders and considering the school's culture, PBIS can be customized to represent and meet the specific needs of the school's demographics and community (Goodman-Scott et al., 2018).

As part of data collection and progress monitoring, data must be disaggregated by individual identities, i.e. ACE, and intersection of categories or identities, i.e. race and class (Carter et al., 2017; Toney & Rodgers, 2011). For example, data on attendance, ODR, and expulsions should be disaggregated. Data must be analyzed to identify areas of disproportionate discipline and justice referrals. Administrators and PBIS teams can facilitate professional development and discussions of race, poverty, ACEs and discipline to address identified areas of disproportionality. Additionally, data should be analyzed for trends in behavior so that additional teacher training can be provided at the systems level and direct instruction of replacement behaviors for students can occur. Then, PBIS teams can identify strategies to address any disparities. In identifying strategies, input from culturally representative school stakeholders should also be considered (Carter et al., 2017). This process creates culturally responsive data analysis.

To achieve social and academic success, school teams will need to create systems within PBIS that address equity and build cultural knowledge (Goodman-Scott et al., 2021; Sugai et al., 2012). Pedagogy that supports instruction which takes into consideration the culture and lived experiences of each child, particularly marginalized students, is culturally responsive teaching. Culturally responsive practices within PBIS involve staff and faculty self-awareness of culture, knowledge of and validation of the cultures of others, academic content (lesson plans, materials, and events) which is culturally relevant, and culturally valid practices. Culturally valid practices encompass using knowledge of students' circumstances and backgrounds to identify reasons for disengagement and/or sources of misbehavior for resolution and cultural equity in discipline referrals and consequences (Parsons, 2017). This begins with professional development for teachers on race, culture, and other social norms of the particular school community (Tier 1). An example of culturally responsive PBIS at Tier 2 includes analyzing screening instruments for cultural bias. Additionally, PBIS interventions at Tier 2 might include restorative circles where students check in, identify problems, brainstorm how to solve the problem, and come to agreement on a solution. Tier 3 culturally responsive PBIS might include ensuring that external agencies, i.e. mental health agencies, have the knowledge and ability to support diverse students and families in the community (Algozzine et al., 2014). These are just a few examples of how the PBIS model can be designed and implemented around culturally responsive pedagogy to provide equity in educational opportunities to interrupt the STPP.

PROMISES & LIMITATIONS

Exclusionary disciplinary practices, such as suspensions and expulsions, were originally intended to address school safety, but these practices led to a loss of academic instruction, truancy, increase in dropout rates, and entry into the juvenile justice system (Skiba & Sprague, 2008). Mathur and Nelson (2013) addressed the juvenile entry into the school to prison pipeline and the influence of individual characteristics and local factors highlighting the impact of school disciplinary policies and practices. The major common factor was the zero tolerance for child misbehavior (Boccanfuso & Kuhfeld, 2011; Mathur & Nelson, 2013). The exclusionary discipline practices became risk factors for engagement with the juvenile justice system. "Any effort to maintain safe and orderly school climates must take into account the clear and negative consequences of exclusionary discipline practices for young students, and especially young students of color, which last well into adulthood" (Bacher-Hicks et al., 2021, pg. 53). Disrupting the school to prison pipeline will be significantly influenced by the way that school leaders encourage their schools to adopt systems and practices for creating relationships with students and dealing with unwanted behaviors (Bornstien, 2017).

When implementing PBIS, the improvement of school climate and school discipline should be top improvement goals (Sprague & Horner, 2006). As more schools are finding that such comprehensive systemic programs can reduce school disruption and improve school climate without reducing students' opportunity to learn (Skiba & Sprague, 2008). The research of Heidelberg et al. (2021) highlighted that schools implementing PBIS with fidelity had fewer out-of-school suspensions for vulnerable groups of students, including Black students and students with disabilities. Multiple researchers have linked PBIS to a reduction in ODRs and exclusionary discipline practice (Bradshaw et al., 2010; Gage et al., 2020; Heidelburg et al., 2021; McIntosh et al., 2018). Addressing and integrating culturally responsive practices and trauma informed practices impacts effective implementation of PBIS in reducing ODRs and suspensions (Heidelberg et al., 2021; Johnson et al., 2018). It was recommended by Mathur and Nelson (2013) for schools that are implementing PBIS to compare data on rates of arrest, court involvement, and juvenile incarceration as part of the implementation assessment to ensure that the practices to support students with ACEs and students living in poverty are effective.

COVID-19 also presented a challenge in implementing PBIS with the abrupt school closures and a sudden transition to distance learning in the Spring of 2020. This disrupted student learning and engagement, resulting in lost learning time, and exacerbated pre-existing inequities in students' access to resources. With virtual or hybrid learning environments, implementing the tiered systems of support to meet students' academic and social emotional needs may be challenging.

Chow et al. (2020) developed resources for teachers and school administrators for implementing a tiered system of support, to continue the framework without interruption. Some of the resources included professional development webinars, materials for teaching appropriate behavior in an online environment (use of video, chat, etc.), and metacognitive behavior management matrices. These resources and recommendations can be applied to continue the work PBIS established in creating supportive educational environments.

In conclusion, the PBIS framework employs input from stakeholders and systematic student data to support decisions to improve program implementation and employs systematic interventions and assessments. The aim of this model is to alter the school environment by creating improved systems involving discipline, reinforcement, and data management. Researchers have found a relationship between PBIS implementation and numerous positive student and school outcomes, which includes a more positive school climate, and lower student aggression, disruptive behaviors, ODRs, and OSSs (Goodman-Scott et al., 2018). Numerous studies illustrate examples of PBIS models designed to provide teachers with the training, policies, and disaggregated data to address the needs of students experiencing poverty and ACEs. These systematic changes may disrupt the school to prison pipeline for students living in poverty and experiencing ACEs.

REFERENCES

Algozzine, B., Barrett, S., Eber, L., George, H., Horner, R., Lewis, T., Putnam, B., Swain-Bradway, J., McIntosh, K., & Sugai, G. (2014). *School-wide PBIS Tiered Fidelity Inventory*. OSEP Technical Assistance Center on Positive Behavioral Interventions and Supports. www.pbis.org/resource/tfi

Alvarez, A. (2020). Seeing race in the research on youth trauma and education: A critical review. *Review of Educational Research, 90*(5), 583–626. doi:10.3102/0034654320938131

American Psychological Association Zero Tolerance Task Force. (2008). Are zero tolerance policies effective in the schools? *American Psychological Association, 63*(9), 852-862. doi:10.1037/0003-066X.63.9.852

Assistant Secretary for Planning and Evaluation. (2022). *Poverty guidelines*. https://aspe.hhs.gov/topics/poverty-economic-mobility/poverty-guidelines

Bacher-Hicks, A., Billings, S. B., & Deming, D. J. (2021). Proving the school-to-prison pipeline: Stricter middle schools raise the risk of adult arrest. *Education Next*, *21*(4), 52–57.

Baglivio, M. T., Epps, N., Swartz, K., Huq, M. S., Sheer, A., & Hardt, N. S. (2014). The prevalence of adverse childhood experiences (ACE) in the lives of juvenile offenders. *Journal of Juvenile Justice*, *3*(2).

Barrett, S., Eber, L., McIntosh, K., Perales, K., & Romer, N. (2018). *Teaching social-emotional competencies within a PBIS framework*. OSEP Technical Assistance Center on Positive Behavioral Interventions and Supports. https://www.pbis.org/resource/teaching-social-emotional-competencies-within-a-pbis-framework

Baumle, D. (2018). Creating the trauma-to-prison pipeline: How the U.S. justice system criminalizes structural and interpersonal trauma experienced by girls of color. *Family Court Review*, *56*(4), 695–708. doi:10.1111/fcre.12384

Bethell, C. D., Newacheck, P., Hawes, E., & Halfon, N. (2014). Adverse childhood experiences: Assessing the impact on health and school engagement and the mitigating role of resilience. *Health Affairs*, *33*(12), 2106–2115. doi:10.1377/hlthaff.2014.0914 PMID:25489028

Boccanfuso, C., & Kuhfeld, M. (2011). Multiple responses, promising results: Evidence-based, nonpunitive alternatives to zero tolerance. *Child Trends*. Publication #2011-09. https://www.childtrends.org/publications/multiple-responses-promising-results-evidence-based-nonpunitive-alternatives-to-zero-tolerance

Bohannon, H., Fenning, P., Carney, K., Minnis-Kim, M., Anderson-Harris, S., Moroz, K., Hicks, K., Kasper, B., Culos, C., Sailor, W., & Pigott, T. (2006). Schoolwide application of positive behavior support in an urban high school: A case study. *Journal of Positive Behavior Interventions*, *8*(3), 131–145. doi:10.1177/10983007060080030201

Bornstein, J. (2017). Can PBIS build justice rather than merely restore order? In *The school to prison pipeline: The role of culture and discipline in school* (pp. 135–167). Emerald Publishing. doi:10.1108/S2051-231720160000004008

Bradshaw, C., Mitchell, M., & Leaf, P. (2010). Examining the effects of schoolwide positive behavioral interventions and supports on study outcomes: Results from a randomized controlled effectiveness trial in elementary schools. *Journal of Positive Behavior Interventions*, *12*(3), 133–148. doi:10.1177/1098300709334798

Bradshaw, C., Pas, E., Debnam, K., & Johnson, S. (2015). A focus on implementation of positive behavioral interventions and supports (PBIS) in high schools: Associations with bullying and other indicators of school disorder. *School Psychology Review*, *44*(4), 480–498. https://files.eric.ed.gov/fulltext/EJ1141556.pdf. doi:10.17105pr-15-0105.1

Bradshaw, C., Waasdrip, T., & Leaf, P. (2012). Effects of school-wide positive behavioral interventions and supports on child behavior problems. *Pediatrics*, *130*(5), 1136–1145. doi:10.1542/peds.2012-0243 PMID:23071207

Budge, N., & Parrett, W. (2018). *Disrupting poverty, five powerful classroom practices*. ASCD.

Carter, P. L., Skiba, R., Arrendondo, M. I., & Pollock, M. (2017). You can't fix what you don't look at: Acknowledging race in addressing racial disparities. *Urban Education*, *52*(2), 207–235. doi:10.1177/0042085916660350

Cavendish, W. (2014). Academic attainment during commitment and post release education-related outcomes of juvenile justice-involved youth with and without disabilities. *Journal of Emotional and Behavioral Disorders*, *22*(1), 41–52. doi:10.1177/1063426612470516

Center on PBIS. (2022a). *Tier 3 comprehensive functional behavior assessment (FBA) guide*. University of Oregon. https://www.pbis.org/resource/tier-3-comprehensive-functional-behavior-assessment-fba-guide

Center on PBIS. (2022b). *Tiered framework, positive behavioral interventions and supports (PBIS)*. University of Oregon. https://www.pbis.org

Center on Poverty and Social Justice at Columbia University. (2022). *3.7 million more children in poverty in Jan 2022 without monthly Child Tax Credit*. https://www.povertycenter.columbia.edu/news-internal/monthly-poverty-january-2022

Centers for Disease Control and Prevention. (2019, November 5). *Adverse childhood experiences (ACEs)*. https://www.cdc.gov/violenceprevention/aces/index.html

Childs, K., Kincaid, D., George, H., & Gage, N. (2016). The Relationship Between School-Wide Implementation of Positive Behavior Intervention and Supports and Student Discipline Outcomes. *Journal of Positive Behavior Interventions*, *18*(2), 88–89. doi:10.1177/1098300715590398

Chow, K., Ortiz, C., & Nakamura, J. (2020). *Resources for implementing tiered systems of support in virtual or hybrid learning environments.* Regional Education Laboratory Appalachia. https://ies.ed.gov/ncee/edlabs/regions/appalachia/blogs/blog34_resources-for-implementing-tiered-systems.asp

Chu, E. M., & Ready, D. D. (2018). Exclusion and urban public high schools: Short- and long-term consequences of school suspensions. *American Journal of Education, 124*(4), 479–509. doi:10.1086/698454

Crouch, E., Radcliff, E., Hung, P., & Bennett, K. (2019). Challenges to school success and the role of adverse childhood experiences. *Academic Pediatrics, 19*(8), 899–907. doi:10.1016/j.acap.2019.08.006 PMID:31401231

Davis, L., & Buchanan, R. (2020). Trauma-informed practices in rural education. *Theory & Practice in Rural Education, 10*(1), 24–41. doi:10.3776/tpre.v10n1p24-41

DeJarnett, G., McDaniel, S., Kern, L., & George, H. P. (2022, February). *Is tier 1 PBIS feasible and effective in rural, high poverty secondary schools? initial examination of a model demonstration.* Center on PBIS, University of Oregon. https://www.pbis.org/resource/is-tier-1-pbis-feasible-and-effective-in-rural-high-poverty-secondary-schools-initial-examination-of-a-model-demonstration

Dierkhising, C. B., Ko, S. J., Woods-Jaeger, B., Briggs, E. C., Lee, R., & Pynoos, R. S. (2013). Trauma histories among justice-involved youth: Findings from the National Child Traumatic Stress Network. *European Journal of Psychotraumatology, 4*(1), 1–12. doi:10.3402/ejpt.v4i0.20274 PMID:23869252

Dube, S. R., Cook, M. L., & Edwards, V. J. (2010). Peer reviewed: Health-related outcomes of adverse childhood experiences in Texas, 2002. *Preventing Chronic Disease, 7*(3), A52. PMID:20394691

Duke, N. (2020). Adolescent adversity, school attendance, and academic achievement: School connection and the potential for mitigating risk. *The Journal of School Health, 90*(8), 618–629. doi:10.1111/josh.12910 PMID:32557700

Eber, L., Barrett, S., Scheel, N., Flammini, A., & Pohlman, K. (2020). *Integrating a trauma-informed approach within a PBIS framework.* Center on PBIS, University of Oregon. https://www.pbis.org/resource/integrating-a-trauma-informed-approach-within-a-pbis-framework

Felitti, V., Anda, R., Nordenberg, D., Williamson, D., Spitz, A., Edwards, V., Koss, M., & Marks, J. (1998). Relationship of childhood abuse and household dysfunction to many of the leading causes of death in adults: The adverse childhood experiences (ACE) study. *American Journal of Preventive Medicine, 14*(4), 245–258. doi:10.1016/S0749-3797(98)00017-8 PMID:9635069

Franke, H. A. (2014). Toxic stress: Effects, prevention and treatment. *Children (Basel, Switzerland), 1*(3), 390–402. doi:10.3390/children1030390 PMID:27417486

Gage, N., Beahm, L., Kaplan, R., MacSuga-Gage, A., & Lee, A. (2020). Using positive behavioral interventions and supports to reduce school suspension. *Beyond Behavior, 29*(3), 132–140. doi:10.1177/1074295620950611

George, H., & Childs, K. (2012). Evaluating implementation of schoolwide behavior support. *Preventing School Failure, 56*(4), 197–20. doi:10.1080/1045988X.2011.645909

Gietz, C., & McIntosh, K. (2014). Relations between student perception of their school environment and academic achievement. *Canadian Journal of School Psychology, 29*(3), 161–176. doi:10.1177/0829573514540415

Giovanelli, A., Reynolds, A. J., Mondi, C. F., & Ou, S. R. (2016). Adverse childhood experiences and adult well-being in a low income, urban cohort. *Pediatrics, 137*(4), 1–20. doi:10.1542/peds.2015-4016 PMID:26966132

Gitterman, B. A., Flanagan, P. J., Cotton, W. H., Dilley, K. J., Duffee, J. H., Green, A. E., Kean, V. A., Krugman, S. D., Linton, J. M., McKelvey, C. D., & Nelson, J. L. (2016). Poverty and child health in the United States. *Pediatrics, 137*(4), e20160339. Advance online publication. doi:10.1542/peds.2016-0339 PMID:26962238

Goodman-Scott, E., Hayes, D., & Cholewa, B. (2018). It takes a village: A case study of positive behavioral interventions and supports implementation in an exemplary urban middle school. *The Urban Review, 50*(1), 97–122. doi:10.100711256-017-0431-z

Goodman-Scott, E., McMahon, G., Kalkbrenner, M., Smith-Durkin, S., Patel, S., Czack, A., & Weeks, N. (2021). An ex post facto study examining implementation of positive behavioral interventions and supports across school and community variables from an inclusive innovation perspective. *Journal of Positive Behavior Interventions, 24*(4), 1–11. doi:10.1177/10983007211013784

Heidelberg, K., Rutherford, L., & Parks, T. (2021). A preliminary analysis assessing SWPBIS implementation fidelity in relation to disciplinary outcomes of black students in urban schools. *The Urban Review, 54*(1), 138–154. doi:10.100711256-021-00609-y

Horner, R., Sugai, G., & Lewis, T. (2015). *Is school-wide positive behavioral interventions and supports (PBIS) an evidence-based practice?* Center on Positive Behavioral Intervention. University of Oregon. https://www.pbis.org/resource/is-school-wide-positive-behavior-support-an-evidence-based-practice

Hughes, K., Bellis, M. A., Hardcastle, K. A., Sethi, D., Butchart, A., Milton, C., Jones, L., & Dunne, M. P. (2017). The effect of multiple adverse childhood experiences on health: A systematic review and meta-analysis. *Lancet, 2*(8), e356–e366. doi:10.1016/S2468-2667(17)30118-4 PMID:29253477

Hughes, M., & Tucker, W. (2018). Poverty as an adverse childhood experience. *North Carolina Medical Journal, 79*(2), 124–126. doi:10.18043/ncm.79.2.124 PMID:29563312

Hunt, T. K. A., Berger, L. M., & Slack, K. S. (2017). Adverse childhood experiences and behavior problems in middle childhood. *Child Abuse & Neglect, 67*, 391–402. doi:10.1016/j.chiabu.2016.11.005 PMID:27884508

Institute for Research on Poverty. (2022). *Poverty faqs.* https://www.irp.wisc.edu/poverty-faqs/

Jackson, C. K. (2020). *Does school spending matter? The new literature on an old question.* American Psychological Association. doi:10.3386/w25368

Jensen, E. (2009). *Teaching with poverty in mind: What being poor does to kids' brains and what schools can do about it.* ASCD.

Jensen, E. (2013). *Engaging students with poverty in mind.* ASCD.

Jimenez, M. E., Wade, R. Jr, Lin, Y., Morrow, L. M., & Reichman, N. E. (2016). Adverse experiences in early childhood and kindergarten outcomes. *Pediatrics, 137*(2), e1–e9. doi:10.1542/peds.2015-1839 PMID:26768347

Johnson, A., Anhalt, K., & Cowan, R. (2018). Culturally responsive school-wide positive behavior interventions and supports: A practical approach to addressing disciplinary disproportionality with African American students. *Multicultural Learning and Teaching, 13*(2). Advance online publication. doi:10.1515/mlt-2017-0013

Kalmakis, K. A., & Chandler, G. E. (2014). Adverse childhood experiences: Towards a clear conceptual meaning. *Journal of Advanced Nursing*, *70*(7), 1489–1501. doi:10.1111/jan.12329 PMID:24329930

Keller-Bell, Y., & Short, M. (2019). Positive behavioral interventions and supports in schools: A tutorial. *Language, Speech, and Hearing Services in Schools*, *50*(1), 1–15. doi:10.1044/2018_LSHSS-17-0037 PMID:30950772

Kenter, R. C., Morris, J. C., Mayer, M. K., & Newton, J. M. (2020). Reconsidering state variation in incarceration rates. *Politics & Policy*, *48*(6), 1029–1061. doi:10.1111/polp.12371

Lassen, S., Steel, M., & Sailor, W. (2006). The relationship of school-wide positive behavior support of academic achievement in an urban middle school. *Psychology in the Schools*, *43*(6), 701–712. doi:10.1002/pits.20177

Looney, A., & Turner, N. (2018). *Work and opportunity before and after incarceration*. Brookings Institution. https://www.brookings.edu/research/work-and-opportunity-befo re-and-after-incarceration/

Luiselli, J., Puntnam, R., Handler, M., & Feinber, A. (2005). Whole-school positive behavior support: Effects on student discipline problems and academic performance. *Educational Psychology*, *25*(2-3), 183–198. doi:10.1080/0144341042000301265

Marsh, H. W., & O'Mara, A. (2008). Reciprocal effects between academic self-concept, self-esteem, achievement, and attainment over seven adolescent years: Uni-dimensional and multidimensional perspectives of self-concept. *Personality and Social Psychology Bulletin*, *34*(4), 542–552. doi:10.1177/0146167207312313 PMID:18340036

Mathur, S., & Nelson, C. (2013). PBIS as prevention for high-risk youth in restrictive settings: Where do we go from here? *Education & Treatment of Children*, *36*(3), 175–181. doi:10.1353/etc.2013.0025

McCurdy, B., Mannella, M., & Eldridge, N. (2003). Positive behavior support in urban schools: Can we prevent the escalation of antisocial behavior? *Journal of Positive Behavior Interventions*, *5*(3), 158–170. doi:10.1177/10983007030050030501

McDaniel, S., Sunyoung, K., Kwon, D., & Choi, Y. (2018). Stakeholder perceptions of contextual factors related to PBIS implementation in high needs schools. *Journal of Children & Poverty*, *24*(2), 109–122. doi:10.1080/10796126.2018.1518777

McIntosh, K., Barnes, A., Eliason, B., & Morris, K. (2014). *Using discipline data within SWPBIS to identify and address disproportionality: A guide for school teams*. OSEP Technical Assistance Center on Positive Behavioral Interventions and Supports. https://www.pbis.org/resource/using-discipline-data-within-swpbis-to-identify-and-address-disproportionality-a-guide-for-school-teams

McIntosh, K., Mercer, S., Nese, R., Strickland-Cohen, M., Kittelman, A., Hoselton, R., & Horner, R. (2018). Factors predicting sustained implementation of a universal behavior support framework. *Educational Researcher, 47*(5), 307–316. doi:10.3102/0013189X18776975

McKenzie, K. (2019). The Effects of Poverty on Academic Achievement. *BU Journal of Graduate Studies in Education., 99*(2), 21–25.

Metzler, M., Merrick, M. T., Klevens, J., Ports, K. A., & Ford, D. C. (2017). Adverse childhood experiences and life opportunities: Shifting the narrative. *Children and Youth Services Review, 72*, 141–149. doi:10.1016/j.childyouth.2016.10.021

Minton, T., Beatty, L., & Zeng, Z. (2021). *Correctional populations in the United States, 2019-statistical tables*. Bureau of Justice Statistics. https://bjs.ojp.gov/sites/g/files/xyckuh236/files/media/document/cpus19st.pdf

Mood, C., & Jonsson, J. O. (2016). The social consequences of poverty: An empirical test on longitudinal data. *Social Indicators Research, 127*(2), 633–652. doi:10.100711205-015-0983-9 PMID:27239091

Morrow, A. S., & Villodas, M. T. (2018). Direct and indirect pathways from adverse childhood experiences to high school dropout among high-risk adolescents. *Journal of Research on Adolescence, 28*(2), 327–341. doi:10.1111/jora.12332 PMID:28736884

Mowbray, C., Holter, M., Teague, G., & Bybee, D. (2003). Fidelity criteria: Development, measurement, and validation. *The American Journal of Evaluation, 24*(3), 315–340. doi:10.1177/109821400302400303

National Center for Education Statistics. (2019, February). *Indicator 4 Snapshot: Children Living in Poverty for Racial/Ethnic Subgroups*. Retrieved August 16, 2022, from https://nces.ed.gov/programs/raceindicators/indicator_rads.asp

Netzel, L., & Eber, L. (2003). Shifting from reactive to proactive discipline in an urban school district: A change of focus through PBIS implementation. *Journal of Positive Behavior Interventions, 5*(2), 71–79. doi:10.1177/10983007030050020201

Noltemeyer, A. L., & Mcloughlin, C. S. (2010). Changes in exclusionary discipline rates and disciplinary disproportionality over time. *International Journal of Special Education, 25*(1), 59–70.

Novak, A. (2021). Trajectories of exclusionary discipline: Risk factors and associated outcomes. *Journal of School Violence, 20*(2), 182–194. doi:10.1080/15388220.2021.1872028

Oh, D. L., Jerman, P., Silvério Marques, S., Koita, K., Purewal Boparai, S. K., Burke Harris, N., & Bucci, M. (2018). Systematic review of pediatric health outcomes associated with childhood adversity. *BioMed Central Pediatrics, 18*(1), 83. doi:10.118612887-018-1037-7 PMID:29475430

Oyen, K., & Wollersheim-Shervey, S. (2019). An examination of critical features of positive frameworks: Impact in rural environments for school-based practitioners. *Contemporary School Psychology, 23*(4), 388–400. doi:10.100740688-018-0198-6

Parsons, F. (2017). An intervention for the intervention: Integrating positive behavioral interventions and supports with culturally responsive practices. *Delta Kappa Gamma Bulletin, 83*(3), 52–57.

Pas, E., & Bradshaw, C. (2012). Examining the association between implementation and outcomes: State-wide scale-up of school-wide positive behavior interventions supports. *The Journal of Behavioral Health Services & Research, 39*(4), 417–433. doi:10.100711414-012-9290-2 PMID:22836758

Rabuy, B., & Kopf, D. (2015). Prisons of poverty: Uncovering the pre-incarceration incomes of the imprisoned. *Prison Policy Initiative, 9*.

Rausch, M. K., & Skiba, R. (2004). *Unplanned outcomes: Suspensions and expulsions in Indiana*. Indiana University, Center for Evaluation and Education Policy.

Rowe, W. (2020). COVID-19 and youth in detention. *Child and Youth Services, 41*(3), 310–312. doi:10.1080/0145935X.2020.1835184

Sacks, V., & Murphey, D. (2018, February 12). *The prevalence of adverse childhood experiences, nationally, by state, and by race or ethnicity*. Child Trends. https://www.childtrends.org/publications/prevalence-adverse-childhood-experiences-nationally-state-race-ethnicity

Scott, T. M., & Caron, D. B. (2005). Conceptualizing functional behavior assessment as prevention practice within positive behavior support systems. *Preventing School Failure, 50*(1), 13–20. doi:10.3200/PSFL.50.1.13-20

Shollenberger, T. (2015). Racial disparities in school suspension and subsequent outcomes: Evidence from the natural longitudinal survey of youth. In D. J. Losen (Ed.), *Closing the school discipline gap: Equitable remedies for excessive exclusion* (pp. 31–43). Teachers College Press.

Shonkoff, J. P., Garner, A. S., Siegel, B. S., Dobbins, M. I., Earls, M. F., Garner, A. S., McGuinn, L., Pascoe, J., & Wood, D. L. (2012). The lifelong effects of early childhood adversity and toxic stress. *Pediatrics*, *129*(1), e232–e246. doi:10.1542/peds.2011-2663 PMID:22201156

Simonsen, B., Eber, L., Black, A., Sugai, G., Lewandowski, H., Sims, B., & Myers, D. (2012). Illinois statewide positive behavioral interventions and supports: Evolution and impact on student outcomes across years. *Journal of Positive Behavior Interventions*, *14*(1), 5–16. doi:10.1177/1098300711412601

Skiba, R., & Sprague, J. (2008). Safety without suspensions. *Educational Leadership: Journal of the Department of Supervision and Curriculum Development*, *66*(1), 38–43.

Skiba, R. J., Chung, C. G., Trachok, M., Baker, T. L., Sheya, A., & Hughes, R. L. (2014). Parsing disciplinary disproportionality: Contributions of infraction, student, and school characteristics to out-of-school suspension and expulsion. *American Educational Research Journal*, *51*(4), 640–670. doi:10.3102/0002831214541670

Skiba, R. J., Peterson, R. L., & Williams, T. (1997). Office referrals and suspension: Disciplinary intervention in middle schools. *Education & Treatment of Children*, *20*(3), 295–313.

Sprague, J. (2014). Integrated PBIS and Restorative Discipline *The Special Edge. Student Behavior*, *3*(1), 11–16.

Sprague, J., & Horner, R. (2006). Schoolwide positive behavior support. In S. Jimerson & M. Furlong (Eds.), Handbook of school violence and school safety: From research to practice (pp. 413–427). Academic Press.

Steed, E., Pomerleau, T., Muscott, H., & Rohde, L. (2013). Program-wide positive behavioral interventions and support in rural preschools. *Rural Special Education Quarterly*, *32*(1), 38–46. doi:10.1177/875687051303200106

Stensrud, R. H., Gilbride, D. D., & Bruinekool, R. M. (2019). The childhood to prison pipeline: Early childhood trauma as reported by a prison population. *Rehabilitation Counseling Bulletin*, *62*(4), 195–208. doi:10.1177/0034355218774844

Sugai, G., & Horner, R. (2009). Responsiveness-to-intervention and school-wide positive behavior supports: Integration of multi-tiered systems approached. *Exceptionality, 17*(4), 223–237. doi:10.1080/09362830903235375

Sugai, G., & Horner, R. (2020). Sustaining and scaling positive behavioral intervention and supports: Implementation drivers, outcomes, and considerations. *Exceptional Children, 86*(2), 120–136. doi:10.1177/0014402919855331

Sugai, G., & Simonsen, B. (2012). *Positive behavior interventions and supports: History, defining features, and misconceptions* (No. 4). Center for PBIS, University of Connecticut. https://challengingbehavior.cbcs.usf.edu/docs/PBIS_revisited_June19_2012.pdf

Swain-Bradway, J., Pinkney, C., & Flannery, K. (2015). Implementing school-wide positive behavior interventions and supports in high schools: Contextual factors and stages of implementation. *Teaching Exceptional Children, 47*(5), 245–255. doi:10.1177/0040059915580030

Toney, J., & Rodgers, H. (2011). Racial equity policy brief: 16 solutions that deliver equity and excellence in education. [OAP]. *Organizing Apprenticeship Program, 2*, 1–20.

Utah Education Policy Center. (2012). *Research brief: Chronic absenteeism*. https://www.attendanceworks.org/wp-content/uploads/2017/09/UTAH-Chronic-AbsenteeismResearch-Brief-July-2012.pdf

Utley, C., Kozleski, E., Smith, A., & Draper, I. (2002). Positive behavior support: A proactive strategy for minimizing behavior problems in urban multicultural youth. *Journal of Positive Behavior Interventions, 4*(4), 192–207. doi:10.1177/10983007020040040301

Vincent, C., & Tobin, T. (2011). The relationship between implementation of school-wide positive behavior support (SWPBIS) and disciplinary exclusions of students from various ethnic backgrounds with and without disabilities. *Journal of Emotional and Behavioral Disorders, 19*(4), 217–232. doi:10.1177/1063426610377329

Waasdorp, T., Bradshaw, C., & Leaf, P. (2012). The impact of schoolwide positive behavioral interventions and supports on bullying and peer rejection. *Archives of Pediatrics & Adolescent Medicine, 166*(2), 149–156. doi:10.1001/archpediatrics.2011.755 PMID:22312173

Wald, J., & Losen, D. J. (2003, Autumn). Defining and redirecting a school-to-prison pipeline. *New Directions for Youth Development, 99*(99), 9–15. doi:10.1002/yd.51 PMID:14635431

Walker, B., Cheney, D., Stage, S., Blum, C., & Horner, R. (2005). Schoolwide screening and positive behavior supports: Identifying and supporting students at risk for school failure. *Journal of Positive Behavior Interventions*, *7*(4), 194–204. doi:10.1177/10983007050070040101

Watson, K. (2016). *Why Richer Areas Get More School Funding Than Poorer Ones*. Global Citizens. https://www.globalcitizen.org/en/content/cost-of-education-in-us/

Weiland, C., Murakami, E., Aguilera, E., & Richards, M. (2014). Advocates in odd places: Social justice for behaviorally challenged, minority students in large urban school districts. *Education, Citizenship and Social Justice*, *9*(2), 114–137. doi:10.1177/1746197914520647

Whiteside-Mansell, L., McKelvey, L., Saccente, J., & Selig, J. P. (2019). Adverse childhood experiences of urban and rural preschool children in poverty. *International Journal of Environmental Research and Public Health*, *16*(14), 2623. doi:10.3390/ijerph16142623 PMID:31340510

Winship, S., Pulliam, C., Shiro, A. G., Reeves, R. V., & Deambrosi, S. (2022, March 9). *Long shadows: The Black-white gap in multigenerational poverty*. Brookings. Retrieved August 16, 2022, from https://www.brookings.edu/research/long-shadows-the-black-white-gap-in-multigenerational-poverty/

Yazzie-Mintz, E. (2007). *Voices of students on engagement: A report on the 2006 high school survey of student engagement*. Center for Education & Evaluation Policy, Indiana University. https://files.eric.ed.gov/fulltext/ED495758.pdf

Yoshikawa, H., Aber, J. L., & Beardslee, W. R. (2012). The effects of poverty on the mental, emotional, and behavioral health of children and youth: Implications for prevention. *American Psychologist*, *67*(4), 272. https://psycnet.apa.org/doi/10.1037/a0028015

Zeng, S., Corr, C. P., O'Grady, C., & Guan, Y. (2019). Adverse childhood experiences and preschool suspension expulsion: A population study. *Child Abuse & Neglect*, *97*, 1–9. doi:10.1016/j.chiabu.2019.104149 PMID:31473382

Zielinski, D. S. (2009). Child abuse and neglect and adult socioeconomic well-being. *Child Abuse & Neglect*, *33*(10), 666–678. doi:10.1016/j.chiabu.2009.09.001 PMID:19811826

KEY TERMS AND DEFINITION

Adverse Childhood Experiences (ACEs): Experiences of children under the age of 18 that have a negative impact on their growth and physical, mental, and emotional development. These experiences are likely to have an impact into adulthood.

Culturally Responsive Teaching: Pedagogy that supports instruction which takes into consideration the culture and lived experiences of each child, particularly marginalized students.

Positive Behavioral Interventions and Supports (PBIS): A framework focusing on setting expectations for appropriate behavior, teaching those behaviors, and utilizing proactive interventions to prevent future behaviors. Framework centers on team leadership and decisions based on data.

Poverty: Poverty is based on a comparison of family income to a federally established minimum income level determined to cover basic needs, but which ultimately impacts an individual's ability to participate in social and civic life because of a lack of economic resources.

Social Emotional: Social emotional refers to the development of skills a person uses to respond to others and how they manage emotions to create relationships. It is constructed through cultural interactions as well.

Trauma: Trauma is the emotional or psychological response to a disturbing event such as death. It may involve a single event (i.e., death of a family member) or repeated exposure to disturbing events (i.e., physical abuse) or complex involving several types of events (i.e., substance abuse and physical abuse).

Trauma-Informed Practices: A strengths-based framework focusing on how teachers, staff and administration can recognize and respond effectively to the impact of trauma on students.

Zero Tolerance: School policies that mandate "the application of predetermined consequences, most often severe and punitive in nature, that are intended to be applied regardless of the gravity of behavior, mitigating circumstances, or situational context" (APA, 2008, p. 852).

Compilation of References

Abdullah, Y., Fruestleben, M., & Hampton, N. (2020). Open letter from Northside principals to MPS & MPD policymakers. *North News*.

Abramowitz, J. S. (2013). The practice of exposure therapy: Relevance of cognitive-behavioral theory and extinction theory. *Behavior Therapy*, *44*(4), 548–558. doi:10.1016/j.beth.2013.03.003 PMID:24094780

Adams, C. M., & Pierce, R. L. (2006). *Differentiating instruction: A practical guide to tiered lessons in the elementary grades*. Prufrock Press.

Adejumo, V. (2020). Beyond diversity, inclusion, and belonging. *Leadership*, *17*(1), 62–73. doi:10.1177/1742715020976202

Adichie, C. N. (2009, October 7). *The danger of a single story*. [Video] TED.

Afzal, A., Malik, N. I., & Atta, M. (2014). The moderating role of positive and negative emotions in relationship between positive psychological capital and subjective well-being among adolescents. *International Journal of Research Studies in Psychology*, *3*(3), 29–42. doi:10.5861/ijrsp.2014.687

Agorastos, A., Pervanidou, P., Chrousos, G. P., & Baker, D. G. (2019). Developmental trajectories of early life stress and trauma: A narrative review on neurobiological aspects beyond stress system dysregulation. *Frontiers in Psychiatry*, *10*, 118. doi:10.3389/fpsyt.2019.00118 PMID:30914979

Akbar, M. (2017). *Urban trauma: A legacy of racism*. Publish Your Purpose Press.

Alberty v. State, 1914 OK CR 48 (1914). https://law.justia.com/cases/oklahoma/court-of-appeals-criminal/1914/21571.html

Alexander, K. (2014). *The crossover* (D. Anyabwile, Illus.). Clarion Books.

Alexander, M. (2010). The war on drugs and the new Jim Crow. *Race, Poverty, & Environment*. https://www.reimaginerpe.org/files/Alexander.20th.17-1.pdf

Alexander, J. (2019). *Building trauma-sensitive schools: Your guide to create, safe, supportive learning environments for all students*. Brookes Publishing.

Alexander, M. (2012). *The new Jim Crow: Mass incarceration in the age of color blindness.* The New Press.

Algozzine, B., Barrett, S., Eber, L., George, H., Horner, R., Lewis, T., Putnam, B., Swain-Bradway, J., McIntosh, K., & Sugai, G. (2014). *School-wide PBIS Tiered Fidelity Inventory.* OSEP Technical Assistance Center on Positive Behavioral Interventions and Supports. www.pbis.org/resource/tfi

Alisic, E. (2012). Teachers' perspectives on providing support to children after trauma: A qualitative study. *School Psychology Quarterly*, 27(1), 51–59. doi:10.1037/a0028590 PMID:22582936

Allee-Herndon, K. A., Kaczmarczyk, A. B., & Buchanan, R. (2021). Is it "just" planning? Exploring the integration of social justice education in an elementary language arts methods course thematic unit. *Journal for Multicultural Education*, 15(1), 103–116. doi:10.1108/JME-07-2020-0071

Allee-Herndon, K. A., & Roberts, S. K. (2019). Poverty, self-regulation and executive function, and learning in K-2 classrooms: A systematic literature review of current empirical research. *Journal of Research in Childhood Education*, 33(3), 345–362. doi:10.1080/02568543.2019.1613273

Allee-Herndon, K. A., & Roberts, S. K. (2021). The power of purposeful play in primary grades: Adjusting pedagogy for children's needs and academic gains. *Journal of Education*, 201(1), 54–63. doi:10.1177/0022057420903272

Allee-Herndon, K. A., Roberts, S. K., Hu, B. Y., Clark, M. H., & Stewart, M. L. (2022). Let's talk play! Exploring the possible benefits of play-based pedagogy on language and literacy learning in Title I kindergarten classrooms. *Early Childhood Education Journal*, 50(1), 119–132. doi:10.100710643-020-01141-6

Allen, A., Scott, L. M., & Lewis, C. W. (2013). Racial microaggressions and African American and Hispanic students in urban schools: A call for culturally affirming education. *Interdisciplinary Journal of Teaching and Learning*, 3(2), 117–129.

Alston, J. A. (2005). Tempered radicals and servant leaders: Black females persevering in the superintendency. *Educational Administration Quarterly*, 41(4), 675–688. doi:10.1177/0013161X04274275

Alvarez, A. (2020). Seeing race in the research on youth trauma and education: A critical review. *Review of Educational Research*, 90(5), 583–626. doi:10.3102/0034654320938131

Alvarez, A., & Farinde-Wu, A. (2022). *Advancing a holistic trauma framework for collective healing from colonial abuses.* Sage Publications. doi:10.1177/23328584221083973

American Civil Liberties Union. (n.d.). *School-to-prison pipeline.* ACLU. https://www.aclu.org/issues/juvenile-justice/juvenile-justice-school-prison-pipeline

American Psychological Association Zero Tolerance Task Force. (2008). Are zero tolerance policies effective in the schools? *American Psychological Association*, 63(9), 852-862. doi:10.1037/0003-066X.63.9.852

American Psychological Association. (2019). *Trauma.* APA. https://www.apa.org/topics/trauma

Compilation of References

Anfara, V. A. Jr, Evans, K. R., & Lester, J. N. (2015). Restorative justice in education: What we know so far. *Middle School Journal, 44*(5), 57–63. doi:10.1080/00940771.2013.11461873

Annamma, S. A., Jackson, D. D., & Morrison, D. (2017). Conceptualizing color-evasiveness: Using dis/ability critical race theory to expand a color-blind racial ideology in education and society. *Race, Ethnicity and Education, 20*(2), 147–162. doi:10.1080/13613324.2016.1248837

Anti-Bullying Alliance. (n.d.). *The impact of bullying.* ABA. https://anti-bullyingalliance.org.uk/tools-information/all-about-bullying/prevalence-and-impact-bullying/impact-bullying

Antiri, K. O. (2016). Types of bullying in the senior high schools in Ghana. *Journal of Education and Practice, 7*(36), 131–138.

Arribas-Ayllon, M., & Walkerdine, V. (2008). Foucauldian discourse analysis. In The Sage Handbook of Qualitative Research in Psychology (pp. 91-108). Sage Publications. doi:10.4135/9781848607927.n6

Arseneault, L. (2017). The long-term impact of bullying victimization on mental health. *World Psychiatry; Official Journal of the World Psychiatric Association (WPA), 16*(1), 27–28. doi:10.1002/wps.20399 PMID:28127927

Assistant Secretary for Planning and Evaluation. (2022). *Poverty guidelines.* https://aspe.hhs.gov/topics/poverty-economic-mobility/poverty-guidelines

Atallah, D., Koslouski, J., Perkins, K., Marsico, C., & Porche, M. (2019). *An Evaluation of Trauma and Learning Policy Initiative's (TLPI) Inquiry-Based Process: Year Three.* Boston University, Wheelock College of Education and Human Development. https://traumasensitiveschools.org/wp-content/uploads/2020/07/Evaluation-Trauma-Learning-Policy-Initiative-Inquiry-Based-Process-Year-3-BU.pdf

Bacher-Hicks, A., Billings, S., & Deming, D. (2021). Proving the school-to-prison pipeline: Stricter middle schools raise the risk of adult arrest. *Education Next, 21*(4), 52–57.

Baglivio, M. T., Epps, N., Swartz, K., Huq, M. S., Sheer, A., & Hardt, N. S. (2014). The prevalence of adverse childhood experiences (ACE) in the lives of juvenile offenders. *Journal of Juvenile Justice, 3*(2).

Bailey, T. K. M., Yeh, C. J., & Madu, K. (2022). Exploring Black adolescent males' experiences with racism and internalized racial oppression. *Journal of Counseling Psychology, 69*(4), 375–388. https://psycnet.apa.org/doi/10.1037/cou0000591. doi:10.1037/cou0000591 PMID:34807669

Ball, A., Zhang, D., & Molloy, M. (2022). *'She looks like a baby': Why do kids as young as 5 or 6 still get arrested at schools?* The Center for Public Integrity. https://publicintegrity.org/education/criminalizing-kids/young-kids-arrested-at-schools/

Bandura, A. (1977). Self-efficacy: Toward a unifying theory of behavioral change. *Psychological Review, 84*(2), 191–215. doi:10.1037/0033-295X.84.2.191 PMID:847061

Bannister, T. (2019). *Teaching is a work of heart: A narrative inquiry on the impact of trauma-informed practice on teacher self-efficacy* [Master's thesis]. University of Victoria.

Baranyi, G., Cassidy, M., Fazel, S., Priebe, S., & Mundt, A. (2017). Prevalence of posttraumatic stress disorder in prisoners. *Epidemiologic Reviews, 40*(1), 134–145. doi:10.1093/epirev/mxx015 PMID:29596582

Barrett, S., Eber, L., McIntosh, K., Perales, K., & Romer, N. (2018). *Teaching social-emotional competencies within a PBIS framework*. OSEP Technical Assistance Center on Positive Behavioral Interventions and Supports. https://www.pbis.org/resource/teaching-social-emotional-competencies-within-a-pbis-framework

Bartlett, J. D., & Smith, S. (2019). The role of early care and education in addressing early childhood trauma. *American Journal of Community Psychology, 64*(1), 1–14. doi:10.1002/ajcp.12380 PMID:31449682

Basford, L., Lewis, J., & Trout, M. (2020). It can be done: How one charter school combats the school to prison pipeline. *The Urban Review*. doi:10.100711256-020-00583-x

Bath, H. (2017). The trouble with trauma. *Scottish Journal of Residential Child Care, 16*(1), 1–12. https://www.traumebevisst.no/program/etgodthjem/filer/Bath_H_The_Trouble_with_Trauma.pdf

Baumle, D. (2018). Creating the trauma-to-prison pipeline: How the U.S. justice system criminalizes structural and interpersonal trauma experienced by girls of color. *Family Court Review, 56*(4), 695–708. doi:10.1111/fcre.12384

Baweja, S., Santiago, C., Vona, P., Pears, G., Langley, A., & Kataoka, S. (2016). Improving implementation of a school-based program for traumatized students: Identifying factors that promote teacher support and collaboration. *School Mental Health, 8*(1), 120–131. doi:10.100712310-015-9170-z

Bellazaire, A. (2018, August). *Preventing and mitigating the effects of adverse childhood experiences*. National Conference of State Legislatures. https://www.ncsl.org/Portals/1/HTML_LargeReports/ACEs_2018_32691.pdf

Bell, D. (1987). *And we are not saved: The elusive quest for racial justice*. Basic Books.

Bell, H., Limberg, D., & Robinson, M. III. (2013). Recognizing trauma in the classroom: A practical guide for educators. *Childhood Education, 89*(3), 139–145. doi:10.1080/00094056.2013.792629

Bellis, M. A., Hughes, K., Ford, K., Hardcastle, K., Sharp, C., Wood, S., Homolova, L., & Davies, A. (2018). Adverse childhood experiences and sources of childhood resilience: A retrospective study of their combined relationships with child health and educational attendance. *BMC Public Health, 18*(1), 1–12. doi:10.118612889-018-5699-8 PMID:29940920

Bender, D., & Lösel, F. (2011). Bullying at school as a predictor of delinquency, violence and other anti-social behaviour in adulthood. *Criminal Behaviour and Mental Health*, *21*(2), 99–106. doi:10.1002/cbm.799 PMID:21370295

Berger, E., Bearsley, A., & Lever, M. (2021). Qualitative evaluation of teacher trauma knowledge and response in schools. *Journal of Aggression, Maltreatment & Trauma*, *30*(8), 1041–1057. doi:10.1080/10926771.2020.1806976

Berger, R., Abu-Raiya, H., & Benatov, J. (2016). Reducing primary and secondary traumatic stress symptoms among educators by training them to deliver a resiliency program (ERASE-stress) following the Christchurch earthquake in New Zealand. *The American Journal of Orthopsychiatry*, *86*(2), 236–251. doi:10.1037/ort0000153 PMID:26963188

Berlowitz, M., Frye, R., & Jette, K. (2014). Bullying and zero-tolerance policies: The school to prison pipeline. *Multicultural Learning and Teaching*, *12*(1), 7–25. doi:10.1515/mlt-2014-0004

Bertrand, M. (2014). Reciprocal dialogue between educational decision makers and students of color: Opportunities and obstacles. *Educational Administration Quarterly*, *50*(5), 812–843. doi:10.1177/0013161X14542582

Bertrand, M., & Rodela, K. C. (2018). A framework for rethinking educational leadership in the margins: Implications for social justice leadership preparation. *Journal of Research on Leadership Education*, *13*(1), 10–37. doi:10.1177/1942775117739414

Bethell, C. D., Davis, M. B., Gombojav, N., Stumbo, S., & Powers, K. (2017). *Issue Brief: A national and across state profile on adverse childhood experiences among children and possibilities to heal and thrive*. Johns Hopkins Bloomberg School of Public Health.

Bethell, C. D., Newacheck, P., Hawes, E., & Halfon, N. (2014). Adverse childhood experiences: Assessing the impact on health and school engagement and the mitigating role of resilience. *Health Affairs*, *33*(12), 2106–2115. doi:10.1377/hlthaff.2014.0914 PMID:25489028

Billups, F. D. (2020). *Qualitative data collection tools: Design, development, and applications*. SAGE Publications.

Bingham, C., & Sidorkin, A. M. (2004). *No Education Without Relation*. Peter Lang.

Black, P. J., Woodworth, M., Tremblay, M., & Carpenter, T. (2012). A review of trauma-informed treatment for adolescents. *Canadian Psychology*, *53*(3), 192–203. doi:10.1037/a0028441

Blake, P., & Louw, J. (2010). Exploring high school learners' perceptions of bullying. *Journal of Child and Adolescent Mental Health*, *22*(2), 111–118. doi:10.2989/17280583.2010.536657 PMID:25859768

Blaustein, M. E. (2013). Childhood trauma and a framework for intervention. In E. Rossen & R. Hull (Eds.), Supporting and educating traumatized students: A guide for school-based professionals (pp. 3–21). Oxford University Press.

Blaustein, M., & Kinniburgh, K. (2018). Treating traumatic stress in children and adolescents: How to foster resilience through attachment, self-regulation, and competency (2nd ed.). Guilford.

Blitz, L. V., Anderson, E. M., & Saastamoinen, M. (2016). Assessing perceptions of culture and trauma in an elementary school: Informing a model for culturally responsive trauma-informed schools. *The Urban Review*, *48*(4), 520–542. doi:10.100711256-016-0366-9

Blitz, L. V., Yull, D., & Clauhs, M. (2020). Bringing sanctuary to school: Assessing school climate as a foundation for culturally responsive trauma-informed approaches for urban schools. *Urban Education*, *55*(1), 95–124. doi:10.1177/0042085916651323

Boccanfuso, C., & Kuhfeld, M. (2011). Multiple responses, promising results: Evidence -based, nonpunitive alternatives to zero tolerance. *Child Trends*. Publication #2011-09. https://www.childtrends.org/publications/multiple-responses-promising-results-evidence-based-nonpunitive-alternatives-to-zero-tolerance

Bohannon, H., Fenning, P., Carney, K., Minnis-Kim, M., Anderson-Harris, S., Moroz, K., Hicks, K., Kasper, B., Culos, C., Sailor, W., & Pigott, T. (2006). Schoolwide application of positive behavior support in an urban high school: A case study. *Journal of Positive Behavior Interventions*, *8*(3), 131–145. doi:10.1177/10983007060080030201

Booth, C. (2015). *Kinda like brothers*. Scholastic.

Bornstein, J. (2017). Can PBIS build justice rather than merely restore order? In *The school to prison pipeline: The role of culture and discipline in school* (pp. 135–167). Emerald Publishing. doi:10.1108/S2051-231720160000004008

Borntrager, C., Caringi, J. C., van den Pol, R., Crosby, L., O'Connell, K., Trautman, A., & McDonald, M. (2012). Secondary traumatic stress in school personnel. *Advances in School Mental Health Promotion*, *5*(1), 38–50. doi:10.1080/1754730X.2012.664862

Borreno, N. E., Flores, E., & de la Cruz, G. (2016). Developing and enacting culturally relevant pedagogy: Voices of new teachers of color. *Equity & Excellence*, *49*(1), 27-40. https://eric.ed.gov/?id=EJ1095807

Botelho, M., & Rudman, M. (2010). *Critical multicultural analysis of children's literature: Mirrors, windows, and doors*. Routledge.

Bottero, W. (2015). Practicing family history: "Identity" as a category of social justice. *The British Journal of Sociology*, *66*(3), 534–556. doi:10.1111/1468-4446.12133 PMID:26173995

Bottiani, J. H., Larson, K. E., Debnam, K. J., Bischoff, C. M., & Bradshaw, C. P. (2018). Promoting educators' use of culturally responsive practices: A systematic review of inservice interventions. *Journal of Teacher Education*, *69*(4), 367–385. doi:10.1177/0022487117722553

Boutte, G., & Bryan, N. (2021). When will Black children be well? Interrupting anti-Black violence in early childhood classrooms and schools. *Contemporary Issues in Early Childhood*, *22*(3), 232–243. doi:10.1177/1463949119890598

Compilation of References

Boyd, M. (2019). *Incorporating SEL as a new teacher*. Edutopia. https://www.edutopia.org/article/incorporating-sel-new-teacher

Bradshaw, C., Mitchell, M., & Leaf, P. (2010). Examining the effects of schoolwide positive behavioral interventions and supports on study outcomes: Results from a randomized controlled effectiveness trial in elementary schools. *Journal of Positive Behavior Interventions, 12*(3), 133–148. doi:10.1177/1098300709334798

Bradshaw, C., Pas, E., Debnam, K., & Johnson, S. (2015). A focus on implementation of positive behavioral interventions and supports (PBIS) in high schools: Associations with bullying and other indicators of school disorder. *School Psychology Review, 44*(4), 480–498. https://files.eric.ed.gov/fulltext/EJ1141556.pdf. doi:10.17105pr-15-0105.1

Bradshaw, C., Waasdrip, T., & Leaf, P. (2012). Effects of school-wide positive behavioral interventions and supports on child behavior problems. *Pediatrics, 130*(5), 1136–1145. doi:10.1542/peds.2012-0243 PMID:23071207

Braveman, P., & Gottlieb, L. (2014). The social determinants of health: It's time to consider the causes of the causes. *Public Health Reports, 129*(1, suppl2), 19–31. doi:10.1177/00333549141291S206 PMID:24385661

Brennan, J. (Ed.). (2002). *The funding gap*. Education Trust.

Briere, J., & Scott, C. (2015). Complex trauma in adolescents and adults: Effects and treatment. *The Psychiatric Clinics of North America, 38*(3), 515–527. doi:10.1016/j.psc.2015.05.004 PMID:26300036

Brodsky, B. S., Oquendo, M., Ellis, S. P., Haas, G. L., Malone, K. M., & Mann, J. J. (2001). The relationship of childhood abuse is impulsivity and suicidal behavior in adults with major depression. *The American Journal of Psychiatry, 158*(11), 1871–1877. doi:10.1176/appi.ajp.158.11.1871 PMID:11691694

Brooks, M., Barclay, L., & Hooker, C. (2018). Trauma-informed care in general Practice: Findings from a women's health centre evaluation. *Australian Journal of General Practice, 47*(6), 370–375. doi:10.31128/AJGP-11-17-4406 PMID:29966183

Brooks, R. B., & Goldstein, S. (2008). The mindset of teachers capable of fostering resilience in students. *Canadian Journal of School Psychology, 23*(1), 114–126. doi:10.1177/0829573508316597

Brown, S. W., & King, F. B. (2000). Constructivist pedagogy and how we learn: Educational psychology meets international studies. *Oxford University Press, 1*(3), 245-254. https://www.jstor.org/stable/44218131

Brown, E. C., Freedle, A., Hurless, N. L., Miller, R. D., Martin, C., & Paul, Z. A. (2022). Preparing teacher candidates for trauma-informed practices. *Urban Education, 57*(4), 662–685. doi:10.1177/0042085920974084

Brown, S. J., Mears, D. P., Collier, N. L., Montes, A. N., Pesta, G. B., & Siennick, S. E. (2020). Education versus punishment? Silo effects and the school-to-prison pipeline. *Journal of Research in Crime and Delinquency*, *57*(4), 403–443. doi:10.1177/0022427819897932

Brunzell, T., Stokes, H., & Waters, L. (2019). Shifting teacher practice in trauma-affected classrooms: Practice pedagogy strategies within a trauma-informed positive education model. *School Mental Health*, *11*(3), 600–614. doi:10.100712310-018-09308-8

Brunzell, T., Waters, L., & Stokes, H. (2015). Teaching with strengths in trauma-affected students: A new approach to healing and growth in the classroom. *The American Journal of Orthopsychiatry*, *85*(1), 3–9. doi:10.1037/ort0000048 PMID:25642652

Bryan, N. (2017). White teachers' role in sustaining the school-to-prison pipeline: Recommendations for teacher education. *The Urban Review*, *49*(2), 326–345. doi:10.100711256-017-0403-3

Bryant-Davis, T., & Ocampo, C. (2005). The trauma of racism: Implications for counseling, research, and education. *The Counseling Psychologist*, *33*(4), 574–578. doi:10.1177/0011000005276581

Bryk, A., & Schneider, B. (2002). *Trust in schools: A core resource for improvement*. Russell Sage Foundation.

Budge, N., & Parrett, W. (2018). *Disrupting poverty, five powerful classroom practices*. ASCD.

Capper, C. A., Hafner, M. M., & Keyes, M. W. (2002). The role of community in spiritual centered leadership for justice. In G. Furman (Ed.), *School as community: From promise to practice* (pp. 77–94). State University of New York Press.

Capra, C., Haller, R., & Kennedy, K. (2019). *Introduction to the profession of horticulture therapy*. CRC Press.

Carey, K. (2020, March 13). Everybody ready for the big migration to online college? Actually, no. *New York Times*. https://www.nytimes.com/2020/03/13/upshot/coronavirus-online-college-classes-unprepared.html

Carter, P. L., Skiba, R., Arrendondo, M. I., & Pollock, M. (2017). You can't fix what you don't look at: Acknowledging race in addressing racial disparities. *Urban Education*, *52*(2), 207–235. doi:10.1177/0042085916660350

Carver-Thomas, D., & Darling-Hammond, L. (2017). *Teacher turnover: Why it matters and what we can do about it*. Learning Policy Institute., doi:10.54300/454.278

Case, A., & Ngo, B. (2017). Do we hae to call it that? The response to neoliberal multiculturalism to college antiracism efforts. *Multicultural Perspectives*, *19*(4), 215–222. doi:10.1080/15210960.2017.1366861

Cavendish, W. (2014). Academic attainment during commitment and post release education-related outcomes of juvenile justice-involved youth with and without disabilities. *Journal of Emotional and Behavioral Disorders*, *22*(1), 41–52. doi:10.1177/1063426612470516

Compilation of References

Center for Disease Control and Prevention. (1995). *Fast Facts: Preventing adverse childhood experiences*. Retrieved on July 21, 2022, from https://www.cdc.gov/violenceprevention/aces/fastfact.html

Center on PBIS. (2022a). T*ier 3 comprehensive functional behavior assessment (FBA) guide*. University of Oregon. https://www.pbis.org/resource/tier-3-comprehensive-functional-behavior-assessment-fba-guide

Center on PBIS. (2022b). *Tiered framework, positive behavioral interventions and supports (PBIS)*. University of Oregon. https://www.pbis.org

Center on Poverty and Social Justice at Columbia University. (2022). *3.7 million more children in poverty in Jan 2022 without monthly Child Tax Credit*. https://www.povertycenter.columbia.edu/news-internal/monthly-poverty-january-2022

Center on the Developing Child at Harvard University. (2020, October 30). *What are ACEs? And how do they relate to toxic stress?* Harvard University Press.https://developingchild.harvard.edu/resources/aces-and-toxic-stress-frequently-asked-questions/

Centers for Disease Control and Prevention. (2019, November 5). *Adverse childhood experiences (ACEs)*. https://www.cdc.gov/violenceprevention/aces/index.html

Centers for Disease Control and Prevention. (2022, January 18). *The social-ecological model: A framework for prevention*. https://www.cdc.gov/violenceprevention/about/social-ecologicalmodel.html

Centers for Disease Control and Prevention. (n.d.). *Social determinants of health*. Social Determinants of Health. https://www.cdc.gov/publichealthgateway/sdoh/index.html

Chai, L., Xue, J., & Han, Z. (2020). Excessive weight and academic performance among Chinese children and adolescents: Assessing the mediating effects of bullying victimization and self-rated health and life satisfaction. *Children and Youth Services Review*, *119*, 105586. doi:10.1016/j.childyouth.2020.105586

Champagne, T., & Stromberg, N. (2004). Sensory Approaches in inpatient Psychiatric settings: Innovative alternatives to seclusion & restraint. *Journal of Psychosocial Nursing and Mental Health Services*, *42*(9), 34–44. doi:10.3928/02793695-20040901-06 PMID:15493494

Chapman, D., Whitfield, C., Felitti, V., Dube, S., Edwards, V., & Anda, R. (2004). Adverse childhood experiences and the risk of depressive disorders in adulthood. *Journal of Affective Disorders*, *82*(2), 217–225. doi:10.1016/j.jad.2003.12.013 PMID:15488250

Chaturvedi, S., Purohit, S., & Verma, M. (2021). Effective teaching practices for success during Covid-19 pandemic: Toward phygital learning. *Frontiers in Education*, *6*, 1–10. doi:10.3389/feduc.2021.646557

Childs, K., Kincaid, D., George, H., & Gage, N. (2016). The Relationship Between School-Wide Implementation of Positive Behavior Intervention and Supports and Student Discipline Outcomes. *Journal of Positive Behavior Interventions*, *18*(2), 88–89. doi:10.1177/1098300715590398

Choi, B., & Park, S. (2021). Bullying perpetration, victimization, and low self-esteem: Examining their relationship over time. *Journal of Youth and Adolescence*, *50*(4), 739–742. doi:10.100710964-020-01379-8 PMID:33428081

Chow, K., Ortiz, C., & Nakamura, J. (2020). *Resources for implementing tiered systems of support in virtual or hybrid learning environments*. Regional Education Laboratory Appalachia. https://ies.ed.gov/ncee/edlabs/regions/appalachia/blogs/blog 34_resources-for-implementing-tiered-systems.asp

Christle, C., Jolivette, K., & Nelson, C. (2005). Breaking the school to prison pipeline: Identifying school risk and protective factors for youth delinquency. *Exceptionality*, *13*(2), 69–88. doi:10.120715327035ex1302_2

Chu, E. M., & Ready, D. D. (2018). Exclusion and urban public high schools: Short- and long-term consequences of school suspensions. *American Journal of Education*, *124*(4), 479–509. doi:10.1086/698454

Chung, Y. (2013). Trainee readiness for diversity training. *Journal of Diversity Management*, *8*(2), 77–84. doi:10.19030/jdm.v8i2.8234

Clark-Robinson, M. (2018). *Let the children march* (F. Morrison, Illus.). HMH Books for Young Readers.

Cohen, J. A., & Mannarino, A. P. (2011). Supporting children with traumatic grief: What educators need to know. *School Psychology International*, *32*(2), 117–131. doi:10.1177/0143034311400827

Cole, S. F., Eisner, A., Gregory, M., & Ristuccia, J. (2013). *Creating and advocating for trauma-sensitive schools*. Trauma and Learning Policy Initiative, partnership of Massachusetts Advocates for Children and Harvard Law School. https://www.traumasensitiveschools.org

Colich, N., Rosen, M., Williams, E., & McLaughlin, K. (2020). Biological aging in childhood and adolescence following experiences of threat and deprivation: A systematic review and meta-analysis. *Psychological Bulletin*, *146*(9), 721–764. doi:10.1037/bul0000270 PMID:32744840

Collaborative for Academic, Social, and Emotional Learning. (2022). *Fundamentals of SEL*. https://casel.org/fundamentals-of-sel/

Colosi, A. (2019). Teaching emotion coaching to teachers of toddlers. [Capstone Projects and Master's Theses, California State University, USA]. https://digitalcommons.csumb.edu/caps_thes_all/706

Combs, G. (2002). Meeting the leadership challenges of a diverse and pluralistic workplace: Implications of self-efficacy for diversity training. *Journal of Leadership & Organizational Studies*, *8*(4), 1–16. doi:10.1177/107179190200800401

Compilation of References

Conley, B. (2002). *Alternative schools: A reference book*. American Bibliographical Center and CLIO Press.

Conyne, R. K., & Cook, E. P. (2004). *Ecological Counseling: An innovative approach to conceptualizing person-environment interaction*. American Counseling Association.

Cook, A., Spinazzola, J., Ford, J., Lanktree, C., Blaustein, M., Cloitre, M., DeRosa, R., Hubbard, R., Kagan, R., Liautaud, J., Mallah, K., Olafson, E., & van der Kolk, B. (2005). Complex trauma in children and adolescents. *Psychiatric Annals*, *35*(5), 390–398. doi:10.3928/00485713-20050501-05

Cooperative Children's Book Center. (2021). *CCBC Diversity Statistics*. Cooperative Children's Book Center. https://ccbc.education.wisc.edu/

Cooper, K. (2013). Safe, affirming, and productive spaces: Classroom engagement among Latina high school students. *Urban Education*, *48*(4), 490–528. doi:10.1177/0042085912457164

Covey, H. C., Menard, S., & Franzese, R. J. (2013). Effects of adolescent physical abuse, exposure to neighborhood violence, and witnessing parental violence on adult socioeconomic status. *Child Maltreatment*, *18*(2), 85–97. doi:10.1177/1077559513477914 PMID:23420296

Cozolino, L. (2017). *The neuroscience of psychotherapy: Healing the social brain* (3rd ed.). Norton & Company.

Crabtree, L. M., Richardson, S. C., & Lewis, C. W. (2019). The gifted gap, STEM education, and economic immobility. *Journal of Advanced Academics*, *30*(2), 203–231. doi:10.1177/1932202X19829749

Craig, K., Bell, D., & Leschied, A. (2011). Pre-service teachers' knowledge and attitudes regarding school-based bullying. *Canadian Journal of Education*, *34*(2), 21–33.

Creswell, J. W. (2013). *Qualitative inquiry and research design: Choosing among five traditions* (3rd ed.). Sage.

Cronholm, P. F., Forke, C. M., Wade, R., Bair-Merritt, M. H., Davis, M., Harkins-Schwarz, M., Pachter, L. M., & Fein, J. A. (2015). Adverse childhood experiences: Expanding the concept of adversity. *American Journal of Preventive Medicine*, *49*(3), 354–361. doi:10.1016/j.amepre.2015.02.001 PMID:26296440

Cross, D., Lester, L., & Barnes, A. (2015). A longitudinal study of the social and emotional predictors and consequences of cyber and traditional bullying victimisation. *International Journal of Public Health*, *60*(2), 207–217. doi:10.100700038-015-0655-1 PMID:25645100

Crouch, E., Radcliff, E., Hung, P., & Bennett, K. (2019). Challenges to school success and the role of adverse childhood experiences. *Academic Pediatrics*, *19*(8), 899–907. doi:10.1016/j.acap.2019.08.006 PMID:31401231

Currie, J., & Widom, C. S. (2010). Long-term consequences of child abuse and neglect on adult economic well-being. *Child Maltreatment*, *15*(2), 111–120. doi:10.1177/1077559509355316 PMID:20425881

Curry, J. R. (2010). Addressing the spiritual needs of African American students: Implications for school counselors. *The Journal of Negro Education, 79*(3), 405–415.

Cuseo, J. (2000). Cooperative/collaborative structures explicitly designed to promote positive interdependence among group members. Illinois State University, Office of Academic Technologies, Center for Teaching, Learning, and Technology.

Dalenberg, C. J., Straus, E., & Carlson, E. B. (2017). Defining trauma. In S. N. Gold (Ed.), *APA handbook of trauma psychology: Foundations in knowledge* (pp. 15–33). American Psychological Association., doi:10.1037/0000019-002

Daniels, H. (2002). *Literature circles: Voice and choice in book clubs and reading groups*. Stenhouse.

Darling-Hammond, L. (2000). How teacher education matters. *Journal of Teacher Education, 51*(3), 166–173. doi:10.1177/0022487100051003002

Davis, M. (2013). Restorative justice: Resources for schools. *Edutopia*. https://www.edutopia.org/blog/restorative-justice-resources-matt-davis

Davis, J. (2001). American Indian boarding school experiences: Recent studies from Native perspectives. *Magazine of History, 15*(2), 20–22. doi:10.1093/maghis/15.2.20

Davis, L., & Buchanan, R. (2020). Trauma-informed practices in rural education. *Theory & Practice in Rural Education, 10*(1), 24–41. doi:10.3776/tpre.v10n1p24-41

Day-Vines, N. L., & Day-Hairston, B. O. (2005). Culturally congruent strategies for addressing the behavioral needs of urban, African American male adolescents. *Professional School Counseling, 8*(3), 236–243.

de Brey, C., Musu, L., McFarland, J., Wilkinson-Flicker, S., Diliberti, M., Zhang, A., Branstetter, C., & Wang, X. (2019, February). *Status and trends in the education of racial and ethnic groups 2018* (NCES 2019–038). National Center for Education Statistics and American Institutes for Research. https://nces.ed.gov/pubs2019/2019038.pdf

de Oliveira, W., Silva, M., de Mello, F., Porto, D., Yoshinaga, A., & Malta, D. (2015). The causes of bullying: Results from the National Survey of School Health (PeNSE). *Revista Latino-Americana de Enfermagem, 23*(2), 275–282. doi:10.1590/0104-1169.0022.2552 PMID:26039298

Deci, E., & Ryan, R. (1987). The support of autonomy and the control of behavior. *Journal of Personality and Social Psychology, 53*(6), 1024–1037. doi:10.1037/0022-3514.53.6.1024 PMID:3320334

DeJarnett, G., McDaniel, S., Kern, L., & George, H. P. (2022, February). *Is tier 1 PBIS feasible and effective in rural, high poverty secondary schools? initial examination of a model demonstration*. Center on PBIS, University of Oregon. https://www.pbis.org/resource/is-tier-1-pbis-feasible-and-effective-in-rural-high-poverty-secondary-schools-initial-examination-of-a-model-demonstration

Compilation of References

Delale-O'Connor, L. A., Alvarez, A. J., Murray, I. E., & Milner, H. R. IV. (2017). Self-efficacy beliefs, classroom management, and the cradle-to-prison pipeline. *Theory into Practice*, *56*(3), 178–186. doi:10.1080/00405841.2017.1336038

Delgado, R. (1989). Storytelling for oppositionists and others: A plea for narrative. *Michigan Law Review*, *87*(8), 2411–2441. doi:10.2307/1289308

Delgado, R., & Stefancic, J. (2017). *Critical race theory: An introduction* (Vol. 20). NYU Press.

Delgado, R., & Stefanic, J. (2000). *Critical Race Theory: The Cutting Edge* (2nd ed.). Temple University Press.

Delpit, L. (1988). The silenced dialogue: Power and pedagogy in education other people's children. *Harvard Educational Review*, *53*(3), 280–298. doi:10.17763/haer.58.3.c43481778r528qw4

Dewar, G. (2021). Emotion coaching: Helping kids cope with negative feelings. *Parenting Science*. https://parentingscience.com/emotion-coaching/

Dhaliwal, K. (2015). *Initial Conceptualization of ACE Effects*. RYSE Center Richmond. [Online image]. http://www.acesconnection.com/blog/adding-layers-to-the-aces-pyramid-what-do-you-think

Dias, B. G., Maddox, S., Klengel, T., & Ressler, K. J. (2015). Epigenetic mechanisms underlying learning and the inheritance of learned behaviors. *National Institute of Health*, *38*(2), 96–107. doi:10.1016/j.tins.2014.12.003

Diem, S., Carpenter, B. W., & Lewis-Durham, T. (2019). Preparing antiracist school leaders in a school choice context. *Urban Education*, *54*(5), 706–731. doi:10.1177/0042085918783812

Diem, S., & Welton, A. D. (2021). *Anti-racist educational leadership and policy: Addressing racism in public education*. Routledge.

Dierkhising, C. B., Ko, S. J., Woods-Jaeger, B., Briggs, E. C., Lee, R., & Pynoos, R. S. (2013). Trauma histories among justice-involved youth: Findings from the National Child Traumatic Stress Network. *European Journal of Psychotraumatology*, *4*(1), 1–12. doi:10.3402/ejpt.v4i0.20274 PMID:23869252

Diliberti, M. K., Schwartz, H. L., & Grant, D. (2021). *Stress topped the reasons why public school teachers quit, even before COVID-19*. RAND Corporation. doi:10.7249/RRA1121-2

Dixson, A. D., & Anderson, C. R. (2018). Where are we? Critical race theory in education 20 years later. *Peabody Journal of Education*, *93*(1), 121–131. doi:10.1080/0161956X.2017.1403194

Dobbie, W., & Fryer, R. G. Jr. (2011). Are high-quality schools enough to increase achievement among the poor? Evidence from the Harlem children's zone. *American Economic Journal. Applied Economics*, *3*(3), 158–187. https://www.jstor.org/stable/41288642. doi:10.1257/app.3.3.158

Doll, B., Brehm, K., & Zucker, S. (2014). *Resilient classrooms: Creating healthy environments for learning*. The Guilford Press.

Doney, P. A. (2013). Fostering Resilience: A Necessary Skill for Teacher Retention. *Journal of Science Teacher Education*, *24*(4), 645–664. doi:10.100710972-012-9324-x

Donovan, M. (2014). *1200 creative writing prompts (Adventures in writing)*. Swan Hatch Press.

Dorado, J. S., Martinez, M., McArthur, L. E., & Leibovitz, T. (2016). Healthy environments and response to trauma in schools (HEARTS): A whole-school multi-level prevention and intervention program for creating trauma-informed, safe, and supportive schools. *School Mental Health*, *8*(1), 164–176. doi:10.100712310-016-9177-0

Doucet, A., Netolicky, D., Timmers, K., & Tuscano, F. J. (2020, March 29). *Thinking about pedagogy in an unfolding pandemic: An independent report on approaches to distance learning during COVID-19 school closures*. https://issuu.com/educationinternational/docs/2020_research_covid-19_eng

Downey, D., & Pribesh, S. (2004). When race matters: Teachers' evaluations of students' classroom behavior. *Sociology of Education*, *77*(4), 267–282. doi:10.1177/003804070407700401

Duane, A., Casimir, A. E., Mims, L. C., Kaler-Jones, C., & Simmons, D. (2021). Beyond deep breathing: A new vision for equitable, culturally responsive, and trauma-informed mindfulness practice. *Middle School Journal*, *52*(3), 4–14. doi:10.1080/00940771.2021.1893593

Dube, S. R., Anda, R. F., Felitti, V. J., Chapman, D. P., Williamson, D. F., & Giles, W. H. (2001). Childhood abuse, household dysfunction, and the risk of attempted suicide throughout the life span: Findings from the adverse childhood experiences study. *Journal of the American Medical Association*, *286*(24), 3089–3096. doi:10.1001/jama.286.24.3089 PMID:11754674

Dube, S. R., Cook, M. L., & Edwards, V. J. (2010). Peer reviewed: Health-related outcomes of adverse childhood experiences in Texas, 2002. *Preventing Chronic Disease*, *7*(3), A52. PMID:20394691

Duke, N. (2020). Adolescent adversity, school attendance, and academic achievement: School connection and the potential for mitigating risk. *The Journal of School Health*, *90*(8), 618–629. doi:10.1111/josh.12910 PMID:32557700

Dunning-Lozano, J. L. (2018). School discipline, race, and the discursive construction of the "deficient" student. *Sociological Spectrum*, *38*(5), 326–345. doi:10.1080/02732173.2018.1532364

Durie, B. (2017). What is genealogy? Philosophy, education motivations, and future prospects. *Genealogy*, *1*(1), 1–4. doi:10.3390/genealogy1010004

Dye, H. (2018). The impact and long-term effects of childhood trauma. *Journal of Human Behavior in the Social Environment*, *28*(3), 381–392. doi:10.1080/10911359.2018.1435328

Eber, L., Barrett, S., Scheel, N., Flammini, A., & Pohlman, K. (2020). *Integrating a trauma-informed approach within a PBIS framework*. Center on PBIS, University of Oregon. https://www.pbis.org/resource/integrating-a-trauma-informed-approach-within-a-pbis-framework

Compilation of References

Education Staffing Space. (n.d.). *Best practices in teaching and learning elementary education.* https://ess.com/blog/articles-best-practices-in-teaching-and-learning-in-elementary-school/

Education Week Research Center. (2018). *School Policing: Results of a National Survey of School Resource Officers.* Editorial Projects in Education Inc.

El-Amin, A. (2022). Improving organizational commitment to diversity, equity, inclusion, and belonging. In Social Justice Research Methods for Doctoral Research. IGI Global. doi:10.4018/978-1-7998-8479-8.ch010

Ellis, W. R. (2020 October). *Healing communities to heal schools.* Educational Leadership, ACSD. https://www.ascd.org/el/articles/healing-communities-to-heal-schools

Emdin, C. (2016). *For white folks who teach in the hood...and the rest of y'all too.* Beacon Press.

Emotional Coaching, U. K. (2020). *Our emotions, brain, and stress: Emotion coaching to support health and wellbeing.* ECUK. https://www.emotioncoachinguk.com/_files/ugd/994674_d5e9463056a64632ac45298c5ab577a6.pdf

English, D., Lambert, S. F., Tynes, B. M., Bowleg, L., Zea, M. C., & Howard, L. C. (2020). Daily multidimensional racial discrimination among Black U.S. American adolescents. *Journal of Applied Developmental Psychology, 66*, 101068. Advance online publication. doi:10.1016/j.appdev.2019.101068 PMID:33994610

Espelage, D., & Swearer, S. (2009). Contributions of three social theories to understanding bullying perpetration and victimization among school-aged youth. In J. M. Harris (Ed.), *Bullying, rejection, and peer victimization: A social cognitive neuroscience perspective* (pp. 151–170). Springer Publishing Company.

Evans, M. L., Lindauer, M., & Farrell, M. E. (2020). A pandemic within a pandemic: Intimate partner violence during COVID-19. *The New England Journal of Medicine, 383*(24), 2302–2304. doi:10.1056/NEJMp2024046 PMID:32937063

Felitti, V. J., Anda, R. F., Nordenberg, D., Williamson, D. F., Spitz, A. M., Edwards, V., Koss, M. P., & Marks, J. S. (1998). Relationship of childhood abuse and household dysfunction to many of the leading causes of death in adults: The Adverse Childhood Experience (ACE) study. *American Journal of Preventive Medicine, 14*(4), 245–258. doi:10.1016/S0749-3797(98)00017-8 PMID:9635069

Fenning, P., & Rose, J. (2007). Overrepresentation of African American students in exclusionary discipline: The role of school policy. *Urban Education, 42*(6), 536–559. doi:10.1177/0042085907305039

Fetterman, D., Kaftarian, S. J., & Wandersman, A. (2014). *Empowerment evaluation: Knowledge and tools for self-assessment, evaluation capacity building, and accountability* (2nd ed.). Sage.

Flessa, J. (2009). Urban school principals, deficit frameworks, and implications for leadership. *Journal of School Leadership*, *19*(3), 334–373. doi:10.1177/105268460901900304

Flores, A. (2007). Examining disparities in mathematics education: Achievement gap or opportunity gap? *High School Journal*, *91*(1), 29–42. https://www.jstor.org/stable/40367921. doi:10.1353/hsj.2007.0022

Fondren, K., Lawson, M., Speidel, R., McDonnell, C. G., & Valentino, K. (2020). Buffering the effects of childhood trauma within the school setting: A systematic review of trauma-informed and trauma-responsive interventions among trauma-affected youth. *Children and Services Review*, *109*, 104691. Advance online publication. doi:10.1016/j.childyouth.2019.104691

Forber-Pratt, A. J., El Sheikh, A. J., Robinson, L. E., Espelage, D. L., Ingram, K. M., Valido, A., & Torgal, C. (2021). Trauma-informed care in schools: Perspectives from school resource officers and school security professionals during professional development training. *School Psychology Review*, *50*(2-3), 344–359. doi:10.1080/2372966X.2020.1832863

Ford, T., Reber, S., & Reeves, R. V. (2020, June 16). *Race gaps in COVID-19 deaths are even bigger than they appear*. Brookings Institute. https://www.brookings.edu/blog/up-front/2020/06/16/race-gaps-in-covid-19-deaths-are-even-bigger-than-they-appear/

Foulger, T. S., & Jimenez-Silva, M. (2007). Enhancing the writing development of English language learners: Teacher perceptions of common technology in project-based learning. *Journal of Research in Childhood Education*, *22*(2), 109–124. doi:10.1080/02568540709594616

Franke, H. (2014). Toxic stress: Effects, prevention and treatment. *Children (Basel, Switzerland)*, *1*(3), 390–402. doi:10.3390/children1030390 PMID:27417486

Franke, K. B., Huebner, E. S., & Hills, K. J. (2017). Cross-sectional and prospective associations between positive emotions and general life satisfaction in adolescents. *Journal of Happiness Studies: An Interdisciplinary Forum on Subjective Well-Being*, *18*(4), 1075–1093. doi:10.100710902-016-9763-8

Freeman, J., Simonsen, B., Briere, D. E., & MacSuga-Gage, A. S. (2014). Pre-service teacher training in classroom management: A review of state accreditation policy and teacher preparation programs. *Teacher Education and Special Education*, *37*(2), 106–120. doi:10.1177/0888406413507002

Fronius, T., Persson, H., Guckenburg, S., Hurley, N., & Petrosino, A. (2016). *Restorative justice in US schools: A research review*. WestEd. https://files.eric.ed.gov/fulltext/ED596786.pdf

Frothingham, M. (2021). Fight, flight, freeze, or fawn: What this response means. *Simply Psychology*. www.simplypsychology.org/fight-flight-freeze-fawn.html

Fulgencio, L., Corrêa-Faria, P., Lage, C., Paiva, S., Pordeus, I., & Serra-Negra, J. (2016). Diagnosis of sleep bruxism can assist in the detection of cases of verbal school bullying and measure the life satisfaction of adolescents. *International Journal of Paediatric Dentistry*, *27*(4), 293–301. doi:10.1111/ipd.12264 PMID:27598528

Gaffney, C. (2019). When schools cause trauma. *Learning for Justice, 62.* https://www.learningforjustice.org/magazine/summer-2019/when-schools-cause-trauma

Gage, N., Beahm, L., Kaplan, R., MacSuga-Gage, A., & Lee, A. (2020). Using positive behavioral interventions and supports to reduce school suspension. *Beyond Behavior, 29*(3), 132–140. doi:10.1177/1074295620950611

Gagnon, D. J., & Mattingly, M. J. (2016). *Most US school districts have low access to school counselors: Poor, diverse, and city school districts exhibit particularly high student-to-counselor ratios* (Report No. 108). Carsey School of Public Policy. doi:10.34051/p/2020.275

Galloway, M. K., & Ishimaru, A. M. (2015). Radical recentering: Equity in educational leadership standards. *Educational Administration Quarterly, 51*(3), 372–408. doi:10.1177/0013161X15590658

Garcia, S. N. (n.d.). *How SEL helps you as a teacher.* Understood. https://www.understood.org/en/articles/how-sel-helps-you-as-a-teacher

Gardiner, M. E., & Enomoto, E. (2006). Urban school principals and their role as multicultural leaders. *Urban Education, 41*(6), 560–584. doi:10.1177/0042085906294504

Gardner, R., & Stephens-Pisecco, T. L. (2019). Empowering educators to foster student resilience. *The Clearing House: A Journal of Educational Strategies, Issues and Ideas, 92*(4-5), 125–134. doi:10.1080/00098655.2019.1621258

Gay, G. (2000). *Culturally responsive teaching: Theory, research, and practice.* Teachers College Press.

Gay, G. (2002). Preparing for culturally responsive teaching. *Journal of Teacher Education, 53*(2), 106–116. doi:10.1177/0022487102053002003

Gelkopf, M., & Berger, R. (2009). A school-based, teacher-mediated prevention program (ERASE-Stress) for reducing terror-related traumatic reactions in Israeli youth: A quasi-randomized controlled trial. *Journal of Child Psychology and Psychiatry, and Allied Disciplines, 50*(8), 962–971. doi:10.1111/j.1469-7610.2008.02021.x PMID:19207621

George, H., & Childs, K. (2012). Evaluating implementation of schoolwide behavior support. *Preventing School Failure, 56*(4), 197–20. doi:10.1080/1045988X.2011.645909

Gietz, C., & McIntosh, K. (2014). Relations between student perception of their school environment and academic achievement. *Canadian Journal of School Psychology, 29*(3), 161–176. doi:10.1177/0829573514540415

Gilbert, J., & Graham, S. (2010). Teaching writing to elementary students in grades 4–6: A national survey. *The Elementary School Journal, 110*(4), 494–518. doi:10.1086/651193

Gillborn, D. (2005). Education policy as an act of white supremacy: Whiteness, critical race theory and education reform. *Journal of Education Policy, 20*(4), 485–505. doi:10.1080/02680930500132346

Giovanelli, A., Reynolds, A. J., Mondi, C. F., & Ou, S. R. (2016). Adverse childhood experiences and adult well-being in a low income, urban cohort. *Pediatrics, 137*(4), 1–20. doi:10.1542/peds.2015-4016 PMID:26966132

Gitterman, B. A., Flanagan, P. J., Cotton, W. H., Dilley, K. J., Duffee, J. H., Green, A. E., Kean, V. A., Krugman, S. D., Linton, J. M., McKelvey, C. D., & Nelson, J. L. (2016). Poverty and child health in the United States. *Pediatrics, 137*(4), e20160339. Advance online publication. doi:10.1542/peds.2016-0339 PMID:26962238

Glaser, B. G., & Strauss, A. L. (1967). *The discovery of grounded theory*. Aldine.

Godfrey, M. (2021). *Diversity in children's books from 2012 to 2020*. Jambo Books Blog. https://blog.jambobooks.com/diversity-in-childrens-books-from-2012-to-2020/

Goldman, M., & Rodriguez, N. (2021). Juvenile court in the school-prison nexus: Youth punishment, schooling and structures of inequity. *Journal of Crime and Justice, 45*(3), 270–284. doi:10.1080/0735648X.2021.1950562

Goldsmith, R. E., Martin, C. G., & Smith, C. P. (2014). Systemic trauma. *Journal of Trauma & Dissociation, 15*(2), 117–132. doi:10.1080/15299732.2014.871666 PMID:24617751

Goldsmith, R., & Freyd, J. (2005). Awareness for emotional abuse. *Journal of Emotional Abuse, 5*(1), 95–123. doi:10.1300/J135v05n01_04

Gonchar, M. (2021, October 14). Over 1,000 writing prompts for students. *The New York Times*. https://www.nytimes.com/2018/04/12/learning/over-1000-writing-prompts-for-students.html

Gonzalez, N., Moll, L., & Amanti, C. (2005). *Funds of knowledge: Theorizing practice in households, communities and classrooms*. Lawrence Erlbaum Associates.

Gonzalez, T. (2015). Socializing schools: Addressing racial disparities in discipline through restorative justice. In D. J. Losen (Ed.), *Closing the school discipline gap: Equitable remedies for excessive exclusion* (pp. 151–165). Teachers College Press.

Gooden, M. A. (2005). The role of an African American principal in an urban information technology high school. *Educational Administration Quarterly, 41*(4), 630–650. doi:10.1177/0013161X04274273

Gooden, M. A., & O'Doherty, A. (2015). Do you see what I see? Fostering aspiring leaders' racial awareness. *Urban Education, 50*(2), 225–255. doi:10.1177/0042085914534273

Goodman-Scott, E., Hayes, D., & Cholewa, B. (2018). It takes a village: A case study of positive behavioral interventions and supports implementation in an exemplary urban middle school. *The Urban Review, 50*(1), 97–122. doi:10.100711256-017-0431-z

Compilation of References

Goodman-Scott, E., McMahon, G., Kalkbrenner, M., Smith-Durkin, S., Patel, S., Czack, A., & Weeks, N. (2021). An ex post facto study examining implementation of positive behavioral interventions and supports across school and community variables from an inclusive innovation perspective. *Journal of Positive Behavior Interventions*, *24*(4), 1–11. doi:10.1177/10983007211013784

Goodman, W. (2001). Living (and teaching) in an unjust world. In W. Goodman (Ed.), *Living and teaching in an unjust world: New perspectives on multicultural education* (pp. 1–25). Heinemann.

Gopalakrishnan, A. (2010). Multicultural children's literature: A critical issues approach. *Sage (Atlanta, Ga.)*.

Gorski, P. (2013). *Reaching and teaching students in poverty: Strategies for erasing the opportunity gap*. Teachers College Press.

Grace, J. (2016). *Rerouting the school to prison pipeline: A phenomenological study of the educational experiences of African American males who have been expelled from public schools* [Doctoral dissertation, University of New Orleans, USA].

Grace, J. (2020). "They are scared of me": Black male perceptions of sense of belonging in U.S. public schools. *Journal of Contemporary Issues in Education*, *15*(2), 36–49. doi:10.20355/jcie29402

Grace, J. E., & Nelson, S. L. (2019). "Tryin' to survive": Black male students' understandings of the role of race and racism in the school-to-prison pipeline. *Leadership and Policy in Schools*, *18*(4), 664–680. doi:10.1080/15700763.2018.1513154

Graham, D. L., Alvarez, A. J., Heck, D. I., Rand, J. K., & Milner, H. R. (2019). Race, violence, and teacher education. In K. Han & J. Laughter (Eds.), *Critical Race Theory in Teacher Education: Informing Classroom Cultural and Practice* (pp. 13–25). Teachers College Press.

Graves, S. L. Jr, Phillips, S., Johnson, K., Jones, M. A. Jr, & Thornton, D. (2020). Pseudoscience, an emerging field, or just a framework without outcomes? A bibliometric analysis and case study presentation of social justice research. *Contemporary School Psychology*, *25*(3), 358–366. doi:10.100740688-020-00310-z

Gray, L., & Taie, S. (2015). *Public school teacher attrition and mobility in the first five years: Results from the first through fifth waves of the 2007-08 beginning teacher longitudinal study*. U.S. Department of Education. https://nces.ed.gov/pubs2015/2015337.pdf

Gray, D. L., Hope, E. C., & Matthews, J. S. (2018). Black and belonging at school: A case for interpersonal, instructional, and institutional opportunity structures. *Educational Psychologist*, *53*(2), 97–113. doi:10.1080/00461520.2017.1421466

Gregory, A., & Evans, K. (2020). The starts and stumbles of restorative justice in education: Where do we go from here? *Boulder, CO: National Education Policy Center*. https://nepc.colorado.edu/publication/restorative-justice

Gregory, A., & Fergus, E. (2017). Social and emotional learning and equity in school discipline. *The Future of Children*, *27*(1), 117–136. doi:10.1353/foc.2017.0006

Gregory, A., Skiba, R. J., & Noguera, P. (2010). The achievement gap and the discipline gap: Two sides of the same coin? *Educational Researcher, 39*(1), 59–68. doi:10.3102/0013189X09357621

Grineski, S., Landsman, J., & Simmons, R. (Eds.). (2013). *Talking about race: Alleviating the fear*. Stylus.

Grooms, A. A., Mahatmya, D., & Johnson, E. T. (2021). The retention of educators of color amidst institutionalized racism. *Educational Policy, 35*(2), 180–212. doi:10.1177/0895904820986765

Gross, B., Tuchman, S., & Yatsko, S. (2016). *Grappling with discipline in autonomous schools: New approaches from DC and New Orleans*. Center on Reinventing Public Education.

Guo, J., Zhu, Y., Fang, L., Zhang, B., Liu, D., Fu, M., & Wang, X. (2020). The relationship between being bullied and addictive internet use among Chinese rural adolescents: The mediating effect of adult attachment. *Journal of Interpersonal Violence, 37*(9-10), NP6466–NP6486. doi:10.1177/0886260520966681 PMID:33084482

Gus, L., Rose, J., Gilbert, L., & Kilby, R. (2017). The introduction of emotion coaching as a whole school approach in a primary specialist social emotional and mental health setting: Positive outcomes for all. *The Open Family Studies Journal, 9*(S1, M3), 95-110. doi:10.2174/1874922401709010095

Gutermann, J., Schreiber, F., Matulis, S., Schwartzkopff, L., Deppe, J., & Steil, R. (2016). Psychological treatments for symptoms of posttraumatic stress disorder in children, adolescents, and young adults: A meta-analysis. *Clinical Child and Family Psychology Review, 19*(2), 77–93. doi:10.100710567-016-0202-5 PMID:27059619

Gutiérrez, K. D., & Arzubiaga, A. (2012). An ecological and activity theoretic approach to studying diasporic and nondominant communities. *Research on schools, neighborhoods, and communities: Toward civic responsibility*, 203-216.

Gwinn, C., & Hellman, C. (2019). *Hope rising: How the science of hope can change your life*. Morgan James Publishing.

Halberstadt, A. G., Castro, V. L., Chu, Q., Lozada, F. T., & Sims, C. (2018). Preservice teachers' racialized emotion recognition, anger bias, and hostility attributions. *Contemporary Educational Psychology, 54*, 125–138. doi:10.1016/j.cedpsych.2018.06.004

Halberstadt, A. G., Cooke, A. N., Garner, P. W., Hughes, S. A., Oertwig, D., & Neupert, S. D. (2022). Racialized emotion recognition accuracy and anger bias of children's faces. *Emotion (Washington, D.C.), 22*(3), 403–417. doi:10.1037/emo0000756 PMID:32614194

Haller, R. L., & Capra, C. L. (Eds.). (2016). *Horticultural therapy methods: Connecting people and plants in health care, human services, and therapeutic programs*. CRC Press. doi:10.1201/9781315369563

Hammond, Z. (2014). *Culturally Responsive Teaching and the Brain: Promoting Authentic Engagement and Rigor among Culturally and Linguistically Diverse Students*. SAGE Publications.

Compilation of References

Hammond, Z. (2015). *Culturally responsive teaching and the brain: Promoting authentic engagement and rigor among culturally and linguistically diverse students*. Corwin.

Hansen, M. (2020, August 25). *Writing for justice*. Rethinking Schools. https://rethinkingschools.org/articles/writing-for-justice-persuasion-from-the-inside-out/

Harris, K., & Trauth, J. (2020). Horticulture therapy benefits: A report. *International Journal of Current Science and Multidisciplinary Research, 3*(4), 61–65.

Harvard Health. (2020, July 6). *Understanding the stress response*. Harvard University Press. https://www.health.harvard.edu/staying-healthy/understanding-the-stress-response

Hayes, T. O. (2020). *The economic costs of the U.S. Criminal Justice System*. American Action Forum. https://www.americanactionforum.org/research/the-economic-costs-of-the-u-s-criminal-justice-system/

Hayes, C., Bahruth, R., & Kessler, C. (1998). *Literacy con cariño: A story of migrant children's success* (9.8.1998 ed.). Heinemann.

Heidelberg, K., Rutherford, L., & Parks, T. (2021). A preliminary analysis assessing SWPBIS implementation fidelity in relation to disciplinary outcomes of black students in urban schools. *The Urban Review, 54*(1), 138–154. doi:10.100711256-021-00609-y

Heitzeg, N. A. (2009). *Education or incarceration: Zero tolerance policies and the school to prison pipeline*. Forum for Public Policy. https://files.eric.ed.gov/fulltext/EJ870076.pdf

Heitzeg, N. A. (2009). Education or incarceration: Zero tolerance policies and the school to prison pipeline. *Forum on Public Policy Online, 2009*(2), 1-21. https://eric.ed.gov/?id=EJ870076

Heitzeg, N. A. (2009). Education or incarceration: Zero tolerance policies and the school-to-prison pipeline. *Forum on Public Policy Online*. https://files.eric.ed.gov/fulltext/EJ870076.pdf

Hence, A. (2018). Bullying in grade school children and its connection to the school-to-prison pipeline. [Senior Honors Theses and Projects, EMU, USA]. https://commons.emich.edu/honors/596

Henderson, D. X., Walker, L., Barnes, R. R., Lundsford, A., Edwards, C., & Clark, C. (2019). A framework for race-related trauma in the public education system and implications on health for black youth. *The Journal of School Health, 89*(11), 926–933. doi:10.1111/josh.12832 PMID:31578726

Hicks, J., Jennings, L., Jennings, S., Berry, S., & Green, D. (2018). Middle school bullying: Student reported perceptions and prevalence. *Journal of Child and Adolescent Counseling, 4*(3), 195–208. doi:10.1080/23727810.2017.1422645

Hirschfield, P. J. (2008). Preparing for prison? The criminalization of school discipline in the USA. *Theoretical Criminology, 12*(1), 79–101. doi:10.1177/1362480607085795

Hollie, S. (2018). *Culturally and linguistically responsive teaching and learning* (2nd ed.). Shell Education.

Hooks, B. (2014). *Teaching to transgress*. Routledge. doi:10.4324/9780203700280

Hopkins, M., Ozimek, D., & Sweet, T. M. (2017). Mathematics coaching and instructional reform: Individual and collective change. *The Journal of Mathematical Behavior*, *46*, 215–230. doi:10.1016/j.jmathb.2016.11.003

Hopper, E. (2020a). *Maslow's hierarchy of needs explained*. https://www.christianworldmedia.com/client/docs/603_1585079540_17.pdf

Hopper, E. (2020b, July 6). *The psychology of hope: How to build hope and a better future*. https://healthypsych.com/psychology-of-hope

Hoppey, D., Mills, K., Reed, D., & Collinsworth, C. (2021). Teacher candidates' perspectives of infusing innovative pedagogical methods and trauma-informed practices into a teacher education program during the COVID-19 pandemic. *School-University Partnerships*, *14*(3), 43–69.

Horner, J. (2019, May 01). *Let's think about equity, equality, and justice*. Wisconsin Heights School Psychology. https://psychology.wisheights.org/2019/05/01/lets-think-about-equity-equality-justice/

Horner, J. (2019, May 1). *Let's think about equity, equality and justice*. https://psychology.wisheights.org/2019/05/01/lets-think-about-equity-equality-justice/

Horner, R., Sugai, G., & Lewis, T. (2015). *Is school-wide positive behavioral interventions and supports (PBIS) an evidence-based practice?* Center on Positive Behavioral Intervention. University of Oregon. https://www.pbis.org/resource/is-school-wide-positive-behavior-support-an-evidence-based-practice

Horsford, S. D. (2010). Mixed feelings about mixed schools: Superintendents on the complex legacy of school desegregation. *Educational Administration Quarterly*, *46*(3), 287–321. doi:10.1177/0013161X10365825

Hromek, R. (2007). Emotional coaching: A practical programme to support young people. *Psychology*.

Huang, F., Lewis, C., Cohen, D., Prewett, S., & Herman, K. (2018). Bullying involvement, teacher–student relationships, and psychosocial outcomes. *School Psychology Quarterly*, *33*(2), 223–234. doi:10.1037pq0000249 PMID:29878821

Hughes, D., Rodriguez, J., Smith, E. P., Johnson, D. J., Stevenson, H. J., & Spicer, P. (2006). Parents' ethnic-racial socialization practices: A review of research and direction for future study. *Developmental Psychology*, *42*(5), 747–770. doi:10.1037/0012-1649.42.5.747 PMID:16953684

Compilation of References

Hughes, K., Bellis, M. A., Hardcastle, K. A., Sethi, D., Butchart, A., Milton, C., Jones, L., & Dunne, M. P. (2017). The effect of multiple adverse childhood experiences on health: A systematic review and meta-analysis. *Lancet*, *2*(8), e356–e366. doi:10.1016/S2468-2667(17)30118-4 PMID:29253477

Hughes, M., & Tucker, W. (2018). Poverty as an adverse childhood experience. *North Carolina Medical Journal*, *79*(2), 124–126. doi:10.18043/ncm.79.2.124 PMID:29563312

Hulvershorn, K., & Mulholland, S. (2018). Restorative practices and the integration of social emotional learning as a path to positive school climates. *Journal of Research in Innovative Teaching &amp. Learning*, *11*(1), 110–123. doi:10.1108/JRIT-08-2017-0015

Hunt, T. K. A., Berger, L. M., & Slack, K. S. (2017). Adverse childhood experiences and behavior problems in middle childhood. *Child Abuse & Neglect*, *67*, 391–402. doi:10.1016/j.chiabu.2016.11.005 PMID:27884508

Hurley, B. (2021, December 15). *Adverse childhood events more common among adults in prison*. Interrogating Justice. https://interrogatingjustice.org/ending-mass-incarceration/adverse-childhood-events-more-common-among-adults-in-prison/

Hutchinson, M. (2012). Exploring the impact of bullying on young bystanders. *Educational Psychology in Practice*, *28*(4), 425–442. doi:10.1080/02667363.2012.727785

Imad, M. (2022). Trauma-informed education for wholeness: Strategies for faculty & advisors. *New Directions for Student Services*, *2022*(177), 39–47. doi:10.1002s.20413

Ingersoll, R., Merrill, L., & May, H. (2016). Do accountability policies push teachers out? *Educational Leadership*, *73*(8), 44–49. https://www.ascd.org/el/articles/do-accountability-policies-push-teachers-out

Iniguez, K. C., & Stankowski, R. V. (2016). Adverse childhood experiences and health in adulthood in a rural population-based sample. *Clinical Medicine & Research*, *14*(3-4), 126–137. doi:10.3121/cmr.2016.1306 PMID:27503793

Institute for Research on Poverty. (2022). *Poverty faqs*. https://www.irp.wisc.edu/poverty-faqs/

Institute of Education Sciences. (2008). *IES practical guide: Reducing behavior problems in the elementary classroom*. U.S. Department of Education. https://ies.ed.gov/ncee/wwc/Docs/PracticeGuide/behavior_pg_0 92308.pdf

International Schooling. (n.d.). *Six ways to minimize the effect of childhood trauma*. Retrieved August 15, 2022, from https://internationalschooling.org/blog/6-ways-to-minimize-the-effect-of-childhood-trauma/

International Schooling. (n.d.). Six ways to minimize the effects of childhood trauma. *International Schooling*. https://internationalschooling.org/blog/6-ways-to-minimize-the-effect-of-childhood-trauma/

Ireland, T., & Widom, C. S. (1994). Childhood victimization and risk for alcohol and drug arrests. *The International Journal of the Addictions*, *27*(2), 251–271. doi:10.3109/10826089409047380 PMID:8144278

Irvine, J. (2002). The common experience, In J. Irvine (Ed.), In search of wholeness: African American teachers and their culturally specific classroom practices (p.1-8). Palgrave Macmillan.

Jackson, C. K. (2020). *Does school spending matter? The new literature on an old question.* American Psychological Association. doi:10.3386/w25368

Jackson, R. (2021, October). After a year of trauma for all, how can we discipline more fairly? *Educational Leadership*, *79*(2), 45–49.

Jagannathan, M. (2021, February 22). *Teachers were already leaving the profession due to stress then covid-19 hit.* https://www.marketwatch.com/story/teachers-were-already-leaving-the-profession-due-to-stress-then-covid-19-hit-11614025213

Jaycox, L. H. (2006). *How schools can help students recover from traumatic experiences: A tool-kit for supporting long-term recovery (Technical Report).* RAND.

Jenkins, D. A. (2021). Unspoken grammar of place: Anti-Blackness as a spatial imaginary in education. *Journal of School Leadership*, *31*(1-2), 107–126. doi:10.1177/1052684621992768

Jensen, E. (2009). *Teaching with poverty in mind: What being poor does to kids' brains and what schools can do about it.* ASCD.

Jensen, E. (2013). *Engaging students with poverty in mind.* ASCD.

Jimenez, M. E., Wade, R. Jr, Lin, Y., Morrow, L. M., & Reichman, N. E. (2016). Adverse experiences in early childhood and kindergarten outcomes. *Pediatrics*, *137*(2), e1–e9. doi:10.1542/peds.2015-1839 PMID:26768347

Johnson, T. R., Gold, E., & Zhao, A. (2022). How anti-critical race theory bills are taking aim at teachers. *FiveThirtyEight*. Retrieved from https://fivethirtyeight.com/features/how-anti-critical-race-theory-bills-are-taking-aim-at-teachers/

Johnson, A., Anhalt, K., & Cowan, R. (2018). Culturally responsive school-wide positive behavior interventions and supports: A practical approach to addressing disciplinary disproportionality with African American students. *Multicultural Learning and Teaching*, *13*(2). Advance online publication. doi:10.1515/mlt-2017-0013

Johnson, L. S. (2006). "Making her community a better place to live": Culturally responsive urban school leadership in historical context. *Leadership and Policy in Schools*, *5*(1), 19–36. doi:10.1080/15700760500484019

Kaczkurkin, A. N., & Foa, E. B. (2022). Cognitive-behavioral therapy for anxiety disorders: An update on the empirical evidence. *Dialogues in Clinical Neuroscience*, *17*(3), 337–346. doi:10.31887/DCNS.2015.17.3/akaczkurkin PMID:26487814

Compilation of References

Kaczmarczyk, A., Allee-Herndon, K. A., & Roberts, S. K. (2018). Using literacy approaches to begin the conversation on racial illiteracy. *The Reading Teacher*, *72*(4), 523–528. doi:10.1002/trtr.1757

Kaka, S. J., & Tygret, J. A. (2020). 'You Can't Pour from an Empty Cup': 6 Things New Teachers Can Do to Promote Their Own Wellness. *Education Faculty Work*, 15. https://digitalcommons.owu.edu/educ_pubs/15

Kalmakis, K. A., & Chandler, G. E. (2014). Adverse childhood experiences: Towards a clear conceptual meaning. *Journal of Advanced Nursing*, *70*(7), 1489–1501. doi:10.1111/jan.12329 PMID:24329930

Kalmuss, D. S. (1984). The intergenerational transmission of marital aggression. *Journal of Marriage and Family*, *46*(1), 11–19. doi:10.2307/351858

Kanzler, K. E., & Ogbeide, S. (2020). Addressing trauma and stress in the COVID-19 pandemic: Challenges and the promise of integrated primary care. *Psychological Trauma: Theory, Research, Practice, and Policy*, *12*(S1), S177–S179. doi:10.1037/tra0000761 PMID:32584101

Kaufman, T., Huitsing, G., & Veenstra, R. (2020). Refining victims' self-reports on bullying: Assessing frequency, intensity, power imbalance, and goal-directedness. *Social Development*, *29*(2), 375–390. doi:10.1111ode.12441

Kearney, M. H., Harris, B. H., Jácome, E., & Parker, L. (2014). *Ten economic facts about crime and incarceration in the United States*. The Hamilton Project. https://www.brookings.edu/wp-content/uploads/2016/06/v8_THP_10CrimeFacts.pdf

Keller-Bell, Y., & Short, M. (2019). Positive behavioral interventions and supports in schools: A tutorial. *Language, Speech, and Hearing Services in Schools*, *50*(1), 1–15. doi:10.1044/2018_LSHSS-17-0037 PMID:30950772

Kenter, R. C., Morris, J. C., Mayer, M. K., & Newton, J. M. (2020). Reconsidering state variation in incarceration rates. *Politics & Policy*, *48*(6), 1029–1061. doi:10.1111/polp.12371

Kerssen-Griep, J., & Eifler, K. (2008). When cross-racial contact transforms intercultural communication competence: White novice teachers learn alongside their African American high school mentees. *Journal of Transformative Education*, *6*(4), 251–269. doi:10.1177/1541344608330125

Khalifa, M. A. (2011). Teacher expectations and principal behavior: Responding to teacher acquiescence. *The Urban Review*, *43*(5), 702–727. doi:10.100711256-011-0176-z

Khalifa, M. A. (2012). A re-new-ed paradigm in successful urban school leadership principal as community leader. *Educational Administration Quarterly*, *48*(3), 424–467. doi:10.1177/0013161X11432922

Khalifa, M. A., Gooden, M. A., & Davis, J. E. (2016). Culturally responsive school leadership: A synthesis of the literature. *Review of Educational Research*, *86*(4), 1272–1311. doi:10.3102/0034654316630383

Kim, C. Y., Losen, D. J., & Hewitt, D. T. (2010). *The school-to-prison pipeline: Structuring legal reform*. NYU Press.

King, J. (2016). The invisible tax on teachers of color. *The Washington Post*. Retrieved from https://www.washingtonpost.com/opinions/the-invisible-tax-on-black-teachers/2016/05/15/6b7bea06-16f7-11e6-aa55-670cabef46e0_story.html

Kohli, R. (2016). Behind school doors: The impact of hostile racial climates on urban teachers of color. *Urban Education*, *53*(3), 307–333. doi:10.1177/0042085916636653

Kozak, S., & Recchia, H. (2019). Reading and the development of social understanding: Implications for the literacy classroom. *The Reading Teacher*, *72*(5), 569–577. doi:10.1002/trtr.1760

Kramer, A. M. (2011). Kinship, affinity, and connectedness: Exploring the role of genealogy in personal lives. *Sociology*, *54*(3), 379–395. doi:10.1177/0038038511399622

Kris, D. F. (2018). *How to build a trauma-sensitive classroom where all learners feel safe*. https://www.kqed.org/mindshift/52566/how-to-build-a-trauma-Sensitiveclassroom-where-all-learners-feel-safe

Kshirsagar, V., Agarwal, R., & Bavdekar, S. (2007). Bullying in schools: Prevalence and short-term impact. *Indian Pediatrics*, *44*, 25–28. PMID:17277427

Kuban, C. (2015). Healing trauma through art. *Reclaiming Children and Youth*, *24*(2), 18.

Ladson-Billings, G. (1995). But that's just good teaching! The case for culturally relevant pedagogy. *Theory into Practice*, *34*(3), 159–165. doi:10.1080/00405849509543675

Ladson-Billings, G. (1998). Just what is critical race theory and what's it doing in a nice field like education? *International Journal of Qualitative Studies in Education: QSE*, *11*(1), 7–24. doi:10.1080/095183998236863

Ladson-Billings, G. (2009). *Dreamkeepers: Successful teachers of African American children*. John Wiley & Sons.

Ladson-Billings, G., & Tate, W. F. IV. (1995). Toward a critical race theory of education. *Teachers College Record*, *97*(1), 47–68. doi:10.1177/016146819509700104

Lassen, S., Steel, M., & Sailor, W. (2006). The relationship of school-wide positive behavior support of academic achievement in an urban middle school. *Psychology in the Schools*, *43*(6), 701–712. doi:10.1002/pits.20177

Lawson, H. A., Caringi, J. C., Gottfried, R., Bride, B. E., & Hydon, S. P. (2019). Educators' secondary traumatic stress, children's trauma, and the need for trauma literacy. *Harvard Educational Review*, *89*(3), 421–447. doi:10.17763/1943-5045-89.3.421

Learning for Justice. (2016). *Responding to trauma in your classroom*. Learning for Justice. https://www.learningforjustice.org/magazine/spring-2016/responding-to-trauma-in-your-classroom

Legette, K. B., Rogers, L. O., & Warren, C. A. (2020). Humanizing student–teacher relationships for Black children: Implications for teachers' social–emotional training. *Urban Education*, *57*(2), 278–288. doi:10.1177/0042085920933319

Leiter, J. (2007). School performance trajectories after the advent of reported maltreatment. *Children and Youth Services Review*, *29*(3), 363–382. doi:10.1016/j.childyouth.2006.09.002

Lewis, J., & Basford, L. (2020). One student at a time: How an innovative charter school succeeds with dropout recovery. *National Youth-at-Risk Journal*, *4*(1). doi:10.20429/nyarj.2020.040104

Liebenberg, L., Theron, L., Sanders, J., Munford, R., van Rensburg, A., Rothmann, S., & Ungar, M. (2016). Bolstering resilience through teacher-student interaction: Lessons from school psychologists. *School Psychology International*, *37*(2), 140–154. doi:10.1177/0143034315614689

Lincoln, Y. S., & Guba, E. G. (1985). *Naturalistic inquiry*. Sage Publications. doi:10.1016/0147-1767(85)90062-8

Lindsey, D. B., Martinez, R. S., Lindsey, R. B., & Myatt, K. (2020). *Culturally proficient coaching: Supporting educators to create equitable schools*. Corwin Press.

Lin, Y. N., & Chiu, Y. H. C. (2020). Applying integrated Horticultural Therapy and aromatherapy to assist undergraduates in Taiwan. *College Student Journal*, *54*(1), 8–12.

Looney, A., & Turner, N. (2018). *Work and opportunity before and after incarceration*. Brookings Institution. https://www.brookings.edu/research/work-and-opportunity-before-and-after-incarceration/

Losen, D. J., & Martinez, P. (2020). *Lost opportunities: How disparate school discipline continues to drive differences in the opportunity to learn*. Learning Policy Institute; Center for Civil Rights Remedies at the Civil Rights Project. https://learningpolicyinstitute.org/product/crdc-school-discipline-report

Love, B. L. (2014). "*I See* Trayvon Martin": What teachers can learn from the tragic death of a young Black male. *The Urban Review*, *46*(2), 292–306. doi:10.100711256-013-0260-7

Luca, L., Nocentini, A., & Menesini, E. (2019). The teacher's role in preventing bullying. *Frontiers in Psychology*, *10*, 1830. doi:10.3389/fpsyg.2019.01830 PMID:31474902

Lucio, R., & Nelson, T. L. (2016). Effective practices in the treatment of trauma in children and adolescents: From guidelines to organizational practices. *Journal of Evidence-Informed Social Work*, *13*(5), 469–478. doi:10.1080/23761407.2016.1166839 PMID:27104619

Luiselli, J., Puntnam, R., Handler, M., & Feinber, A. (2005). Whole-school positive behavior support: Effects on student discipline problems and academic performance. *Educational Psychology*, *25*(2-3), 183–198. doi:10.1080/0144341042000301265

Lustick, H. (2017). Making discipline relevant: Toward a theory of culturally responsive positive schoolwide discipline. *Race, Ethnicity and Education*, *20*(5), 681–695. doi:10.1080/13613324.2016.1150828

Madhlangobe, L., & Gordon, S. P. (2012). Culturally responsive leadership in a diverse school: A case study of a high school leader. *NASSP Bulletin*, *96*(3), 177–202. doi:10.1177/0192636512450909

Mallett, C. A. (2016). The school-to-prison pipeline: From school punishment to rehabilitative inclusion. *Preventing School Failure*, *60*(4), 296–304. doi:10.1080/1045988X.2016.1144554

Maniglio, R. (2009). The impact of child sexual abuse on health: A systematic review of reviews. *Clinical Psychology Review*, *29*(7), 647–657. doi:10.1016/j.cpr.2009.08.003 PMID:19733950

Mann, A., Whitaker, A., Torres-Gullien, S., Morton, M., Jordan, H., Coyle, S., & Sun, W. (2019). *Cops and no counselors: How the lack of school mental health staff is harming students*. American Civil Liberties Union. https://www.aclu.org/issues/juvenile-justice/school-prison-pipeline/cops-and-no-counselors

Mansfield, K. C., & Lambrinou, M. (2022). "This is Not Who We Are": Students Leading for Anti-Racist Policy Changes in Alexandria City Public Schools, Virginia. *Educational Policy*, *36*(1), 19–56. doi:10.1177/08959048211059214

Marsh, H. W., & O'Mara, A. (2008). Reciprocal effects between academic self-concept, self-esteem, achievement, and attainment over seven adolescent years: Uni-dimensional and multidimensional perspectives of self-concept. *Personality and Social Psychology Bulletin*, *34*(4), 542–552. doi:10.1177/0146167207312313 PMID:18340036

Martinez, S. (2009). A system gone berserk: How are zero-tolerance policies really affecting schools? *Preventing School Failure*, *53*(3), 153–158. doi:10.3200/PSFL.53.3.153-158

Massachusetts Advocates for Children & Harvard Law School. (2022). *Frequently asked questions about trauma-sensitive schools*. Trauma and Learning Policy Initiative. https://traumasensitiveschools.org/frequently-asked-questions/

Masten, A. S., Herbers, J. E., Cutuli, J. J., & Lafavor, T. L. (2008). Promoting competence and resilience in the school context. *Professional School Counseling*, *12*(2), 76–84. doi:10.5330/PSC.n.2010-12.76

Masten, A. S., Monn, A. R., & Supkoff, L. M. (2011). Resilience in children and adolescents. In S. M. Southwick, B. T. Litz, D. Charney, & M. J. Friedman (Eds.), *Resilience and mental health: Challenges across the lifespan*. Cambridge University Press. doi:10.1017/CBO9780511994791.009

Mathis, J. (2020). Global picture books to provide critical perspectives. *English Journal*, *109*(5), 102–104.

Mathur, S., & Nelson, C. (2013). PBIS as prevention for high-risk youth in restrictive settings: Where do we go from here? *Education & Treatment of Children*, *36*(3), 175–181. doi:10.1353/etc.2013.0025

Maynard, B. R., Farina, A., & Dell, N. A. (2017). Protocol: Effects of trauma-informed approaches in schools. *Campbell Systematic Reviews*, *13*(1), 1–32. doi:10.1002/CL2.177

McAllister, G., & Irvine, J. J. (2002). The role of empathy in teaching culturally diverse students: A qualitative study of teachers' beliefs. *Journal of Teacher Education*, *53*(5), 433–443. doi:10.1177/002248702237397

McCleary, J., & Figley, C. (2017). Resilience and trauma: Expanding definitions, uses, and contexts. *Traumatology*, *23*(1), 1–3. doi:10.1037/trm0000103 PMID:29755296

McCready, L., & Mosely, M. (2013). Making space for Black queer teachers: Pedagogic possibilities. In C. W. Lewis, Y. Sealey-Ruiz, & I. Toldson (Eds.), *Teacher education and Black communities: Implications for access, equity, and achievement* (pp. 43–58). Information Age Publishing.

McCurdy, B., Mannella, M., & Eldridge, N. (2003). Positive behavior support in urban schools: Can we prevent the escalation of antisocial behavior? *Journal of Positive Behavior Interventions*, *5*(3), 158–170. doi:10.1177/10983007030050030501

McDaniel, S., Sunyoung, K., Kwon, D., & Choi, Y. (2018). Stakeholder perceptions of contextual factors related to PBIS implementation in high needs schools. *Journal of Children & Poverty*, *24*(2), 109–122. doi:10.1080/10796126.2018.1518777

McInerney, M., & McKlindon, A. (2014). Unlocking the door to learning: Trauma-informed classrooms & transformational schools. *Education law center*, 1-24.

McIntosh, K., Barnes, A., Eliason, B., & Morris, K. (2014). *Using discipline data within SWPBIS to identify and address disproportionality: A guide for school teams*. OSEP Technical Assistance Center on Positive Behavioral Interventions and Supports. https://www.pbis.org/resource/using-discipline-data-within-swpbis-to-identify-and-address-disproportionality-a-guide-for-school-teams

McIntosh, K., Mercer, S., Nese, R., Strickland-Cohen, M., Kittelman, A., Hoselton, R., & Horner, R. (2018). Factors predicting sustained implementation of a universal behavior support framework. *Educational Researcher*, *47*(5), 307–316. doi:10.3102/0013189X18776975

McIntyre, E. M., Baker, C. N., & Overstreet, S. (2019). Evaluating foundational professional development training for trauma-informed approaches in schools. *Psychological Services*, *16*(1), 95–102. doi:10.1037er0000312 PMID:30489111

McKenzie, K. (2019). The Effects of Poverty on Academic Achievement. *BU Journal of Graduate Studies in Education.*, *99*(2), 21–25.

McLeod, S. (2022, April 4). *Maslow's hierarchy of needs*. https://www.simplypsychology.org/maslow.html

Meek, S. E., & Gilliam, W. S. (2016). *Expulsion and suspension in early education as matters of social justice and health equity: NAM Perspectives.* Discussion Paper, National Academy of Medicine. doi:10.31478/201610e

Meiklejohn, J., Phillips, C., Freedman, M. L., Griffin, M. L., Biegel, G., Roach, A., Frank, J., Burke, C., Pinger, L., Soloway, G., Isberg, R., Sibinga, E., Grossman, L., & Saltzman, A. (2012). Integrating mindfulness training into K-12 education: Fostering the resilience of teachers and students. *Mindfulness, 3*(4), 291–307. doi:10.100712671-012-0094-5

Mellom, P. J., Straubhaar, R., Balderas, C., Ariail, M., & Portes, P. R. (2018). "They come with nothing:" How professional development in a culturally responsive pedagogy shapes teacher attitudes towards Latino/a English language learners. *Teaching and Teacher Education, 71*, 98–107. doi:10.1016/j.tate.2017.12.013

Merriam, S. B., & Grenier, R. S. (Eds.). (2019). *Qualitative research in practice: Examples for discussion and analysis.* John Wiley & Sons.

Merriam-Webster. (n.d.). *Hope.* Retrieved May 31, 2022, from https://www.merriam-webster.com/dictionary/hope

Merriam-Webster. (n.d.). *Hope.* Retrieved on August 18, 2022, from https://www.merriam-webster.com/dictionary/hope

Merritt, M. B., Cronholm, P., Davis, M., Dempsey, S., Fein, J., Kuykendall, S. A., & Wade, R. (2013). *Findings from the Philadelphia Urban ACE Survey.* Institute for Safe Families. https://www.rwjf.org/en/library/research/2013/09/findings-from-the-philadelphia-urban-ace-survey.html

Metzler, M., Merrick, M. T., Klevens, J., Ports, K. A., & Ford, D. C. (2017). Adverse childhood experiences and life opportunities: Shifting the narrative. *Children and Youth Services Review, 72*, 141–149. doi:10.1016/j.childyouth.2016.10.021

Miles, M. B., Huberman, A. M., & Saldaña, J. (2020). *Qualitative data analysis: A methods sourcebook* (4th ed.). Sage.

Miller, L., & Harris, V. (2018). I can't be racist: I teach in an urban school, and I'm a nice white lady. *World Journal of Education, 8*(3). doi:10.5430/wje.v8n3p1

Miller, A., Gouley, K., Seifer, R., Zakriski, A., Eguia, M., & Vergnani, M. (2005). Emotion knowledge skills in low-income elementary school children: Associations with social status and peer experiences. *Social Development, 14*(4), 637–651. doi:10.1111/j.1467-9507.2005.00321.x

Mills, R., Kisely, S., Alati, R., Strahearn, L., & Naiman, J. M. (2019). Cognitive and educational outcomes of maltreated and non-maltreated youth: A birth cohort study. *The Australian and New Zealand Journal of Psychiatry, 53*(3), 248–255. doi:10.1177/0004867418768432 PMID:29696988

Milner, H. R. IV. (2007). Race, culture, and researcher positionality: Working through dangers seen, unseen, and unforeseen. *Educational Researcher, 36*(7), 388–400. doi:10.3102/0013189X07309471

Minahan, J. (2019, October). Trauma-informed teaching strategies. *Educational Leadership*, 30–35. https://www.ascd.org/el/articles/trauma-informed-teaching-strategies

Minton, T., Beatty, L., & Zeng, Z. (2021). *Correctional populations in the United States, 2019-statistical tables*. Bureau of Justice Statistics. https://bjs.ojp.gov/sites/g/files/xyckuh236/files/media/document/cpus19st.pdf

Mokuria, V., Williams, A., & Page, W. (2020). There has been no remorse over it: A narrative inquiry exploring enslaved ancestral roots through a critical family history project. *Genealogy*, *4*(26), 1–13. doi:10.3390/genealogy4010026

Moll, L., Amanti, C., Nef, D., & Gonzalez, N. (1992). Funds of knowledge for teaching: Using a qualitative approach to connect homes and classrooms. *Theory into Practice*, *31*(2), 132–141. doi:10.1080/00405849209543534

Mood, C., & Jonsson, J. O. (2016). The social consequences of poverty: An empirical test on longitudinal data. *Social Indicators Research*, *127*(2), 633–652. doi:10.100711205-015-0983-9 PMID:27239091

Moore, B. A. (2018). Developing special educator cultural awareness through critically reflective professional learning community collaboration. *Teacher Education and Special Education: The Journal of the Teacher Education Division of the Council for Exceptional Children*, *41*(3), 243–253. doi:10.1177/0888406418770714

Moore, S. M. (2022). How ancestor research affects self-understanding ad well-being: Introduction to the special issue. *Genealogy*, *6*(20), 1–6. doi:10.3390/genealogy6010020

Morgan, A., Pendergast, D., Brown, R., & Heck, D. (2015). Relational ways of being an educator: Trauma-informed practice supporting disenfranchised young people. *International Journal of Inclusive Education*, *19*(10), 1037–1051. doi:10.1080/13603116.2015.1035344

Morrison, K. A., Robbins, H. H., & Rose, D. G. (2008). Operationalizing culturally relevant pedagogy: A synthesis of classroom-based research. *Equity & Excellence in Education*, *41*(4), 433–452. doi:10.1080/10665680802400006

Morrow, A. S., & Villodas, M. T. (2018). Direct and indirect pathways from adverse childhood experiences to high school dropout among high-risk adolescents. *Journal of Research on Adolescence*, *28*(2), 327–341. doi:10.1111/jora.12332 PMID:28736884

Mortensen, J. A., & Barnett, M. A. (2016). The role of child care in supporting the emotional regulatory needs of maltreated infants and toddlers. *Children and Youth Services Review*, *64*, 73–81. doi:10.1016/j.childyouth.2016.03.004

Mosely, M. (2018). The Black teacher project: How racial affinity professional development sustains Black teachers. *The Urban Review*, *50*(2), 267–283. doi:10.100711256-018-0450-4

Motley, R., & Banks, A. (2018). Black males, trauma, and mental health service use: A systematic review. *Perspectives on social work: the journal of the doctoral students of the University of Houston Graduate School of Social Work, 14*(1), 3-19.

Moustakas, C. (1994). Phenomenological research methods. Sage.

Mowbray, C., Holter, M., Teague, G., & Bybee, D. (2003). Fidelity criteria: Development, measurement, and validation. *The American Journal of Evaluation, 24*(3), 315–340. doi:10.1177/109821400302400303

Muñiz, J. O. (2021). Exclusionary discipline policies, School–police partnerships, surveillance technologies and disproportionality: A review of the school to prison pipeline literature. *The Urban Review, 53*(5), 735–760. doi:10.100711256-021-00595-1

Muskogee Times-Democrat. (1913, February 15). *Death penalty for Negro.* https://www.newspapers.com/clip/50460331/february-15-1913-muskogee-times

Nagara, I. (2016). *A is for activist.* Seven Stories Press.

Najjar, A., Foroozandeah, E., & Gharneh, A. (2018). Horticulture therapy effects on memory and psycho-logical symptoms of depressed male outpatients. *Iranian Rehabilitation Journal, 16*(2), 147–154. doi:10.32598/irj.16.2.147

Nash, K., Howard, J., Miller, E., Boutte, G., Johnson, G., & Reid, L. (2018). Critical racial literacy in homes, schools, and communities: Propositions for early childhood contexts. *Contemporary Issues in Early Childhood, 19*(3), 256–273. doi:10.1177/1463949117717293

National Academies of Sciences, Engineering, and Medicine. (2016). *Preventing bullying through science, policy, and practice.* NASEM. doi:10.17226/23482

National Association of Schools Boards of Education. (2022, June 14). *States adopt trauma-informed teacher training, few consider secondary traumatic stress.* NASBE. https://www.nasbe.org/states-adopt-trauma-informed-teacher-training-few-consider-secondary-traumatic-stress/

National Bullying Prevention Center. (2019). *How is "direct bullying" different from "indirect bullying"?* Pacer. https://www.pacer.org/bullying/info/questions-answered/direct-vs-indirect.asp

National Center for Education Statistics. (2019, February). *Indicator 4 Snapshot: Children Living in Poverty for Racial/Ethnic Subgroups.* Retrieved August 16, 2022, from https://nces.ed.gov/programs/raceindicators/indicator_rads.asp

National Center for Education Statistics. (2022). *Racial/ethnic enrollment in public schools.* NCES. https://nces.ed.gov/programs/coe/indicator/cge/racial-ethnic-enrollment

Compilation of References

National Child Traumatic Stress Network Complex Trauma Taskforce. (2003). *Complex trauma in children and adolescents.* https://www.nctsn.org/resources/complex-trauma-children-and-adolescents

National Child Traumatic Stress Network. (2006). *Defining trauma and child traumatic stress.* https://www.nctsn.org/what-is-child-trauma/about-child-trauma

National Child Traumatic Stress Network. (2017). *Addressing race and trauma in the classroom: A resource for educators.*

National Child Traumatic Stress Network. (n.d.). *About child trauma.* NCTSN. https://www.nctsn.org/what-is-child-trauma/about-child-trauma

National Conference on State Legislatures. (2021, August 12). *Adverse childhood experiences.* NCSL. https://www.ncsl.org/research/health/adverse-childhood-experiences-aces.aspx

National Criminal Justice Reference Service. (2014). Beyond bullying: How hostile school climate perpetuates the school-to-prison pipeline for LGBT youth (NCJ Number 246129). Center for American Progress.

National Human Trafficking Training and Technical Assistance Center. (n.d.). *Adverse childhood experiences.* US Department of Health and Human Services. https://nhttac.acf.hhs.gov/soar/eguide/stop/adverse_childhood_experiences

National Human Trafficking Training and Technical Assistance Center. (n.d.). *Types of ACEs* [Online image]. US Department of Health and Human Services. https://nhttac.acf.hhs.gov/soar/eguide/stop/adverse_childhood_experiences

Netzel, L., & Eber, L. (2003). Shifting from reactive to proactive discipline in an urban school district: A change of focus through PBIS implementation. *Journal of Positive Behavior Interventions, 5*(2), 71–79. doi:10.1177/10983007030050020201

New York Civil Liberties Union. (n.d.). *School-to-prison pipeline.* NYCLU. https://www.nyclu.org/en/issues/racial-justice/school-prison-pipeline

Nobel, M. M. (2022a). Challenging deficit thinking in our schools: It starts during educator preparation. In R. D. Williams (Ed.), *Handbook of research on challenging deficit thinking for exceptional education improvement* (pp. 27–64). IGI Global. doi:10.4018/978-1-7998-8860-4.ch002

Nobel, M. M. (2022b). How a small, liberal arts university seeks to create socially conscious, resilient teachers. In O. S. Schepers, M. Brennan, & P. E. Bernhardt (Eds.), *Developing trauma-informed teachers: Creating classrooms that foster equity, resiliency, and asset-based approaches.* Information Age Publishing.

Nocella, A., Parmar, P., & Stovall, W. (2014). *From education to incarceration: Dismantling the school-to-prison pipeline* (2nd ed.). Peter Lang.

Noguera, P. (2008). What discipline is for: Connecting students to the benefits of learning. In M. Pollock (Ed.), *Everyday antiracism* (pp. 132–137). The New Press.

Noguera, P. A. (2017, April). Introduction to "racial inequality and education: Patterns and prospects for the future". [). Routledge.]. *The Educational Forum, 81*(2), 129–135.

Noltemeyer, A., & Robertson, J. (2015). *Project AWARE Ohio Brief No. 2*. Ohio Department of Education. https://education.ohio.gov/getattachment/Topics/Other-Resour ces/School-Safety/Building-Better-Learning-Environments/PBIS -Resources/Project-AWARE-Ohio/Project-AWARE-Ohio-Statewide-R esources/Fostering-Resilience-in-a-Tiered-System.pdf.aspx

Noltemeyer, A. L., & Mcloughlin, C. S. (2010). Changes in exclusionary discipline rates and disciplinary disproportionality over time. *International Journal of Special Education, 25*(1), 59–70.

Novak, A. (2019). The school-to-prison pipeline: An examination of the association between suspension and justice system involvement. *Criminal Justice and Behavior, 46*(8), 1165–1180. doi:10.1177/0093854819846917

Novak, A. (2021). Trajectories of exclusionary discipline: Risk factors and associated outcomes. *Journal of School Violence, 20*(2), 182–194. doi:10.1080/15388220.2021.1872028

Nunez-Eddy, E. (2020). *The coalescence of education and criminal justice in the United States: The school-to-prison nexus and the prison-industrial complex in a capitalist society.* Arizona State University. https://keep.lib.asu.edu/_flysystem/fedora/c7/224798/NunezEd dy_asu_0010N_20092.pdf

Nyumba, T. O., Wilson, K., Derrick, C. J., & Mukherjee, N. (2018). The use of focus group discussion methodology: Insights from two decades of application in conversation. *Qualitative Methods for Eliciting Judgements for Decision Making, 9*(1), 20–32. doi:10.1111/2041-210X.12860

O'Brien, N., Munn-Giddings, C., & Moules, T. (2018). The repercussions of reporting bullying: Some experiences of students at an independent secondary school. *Pastoral Care in Education, 36*(1), 29–43. doi:10.1080/02643944.2017.1422004

Oh, D. L., Jerman, P., Silvério Marques, S., Koita, K., Purewal Boparai, S. K., Burke Harris, N., & Bucci, M. (2018). Systematic review of pediatric health outcomes associated with childhood adversity. *BioMed Central Pediatrics, 18*(1), 83. doi:10.118612887-018-1037-7 PMID:29475430

Oliveira, F., de Menezes, T., Irffi, G., & Oliveira, G. (2018). Bullying effect on student's performance. *Economía, 19*(1), 57–73. doi:10.1016/j.econ.2017.10.001

Olweus, D. (1994). Bullying at School. In L. R. Huesmann (Ed.), *Aggressive Behavior* (pp. 97–130). Springer., doi:10.1007/978-1-4757-9116-7_5

Compilation of References

Openshaw, L. (2011). School-based support groups for traumatized students. *School Psychology International*, *32*(2), 163–178. doi:10.1177/0143034311400830

Opiola, K. K., Alston, D. M., & Copeland-Kamp, B. L. (2020). The effectiveness of training and supervising urban elementary school teachers in child–teacher relationship training: A trauma-informed approach. *Professional School Counseling*, *23*(1 part 2), 1–11. doi:10.1177/2156759X19899181

Osher, D., Coggshall, J., Colombi, G., Woodruff, D., Francios, S., & Osher, T. (2012). Building school and teacher capacity to eliminate the school-to-prison pipeline. *Teacher Education and Special Education*, *35*(4), 284–295. doi:10.1177/0888406412453930

Oster, E., Jack, R., Halloran, C., Schoof, J., McLeod, D., Yang, H., Roche, J., & Roche, D. (2021). Disparities in learning mode access among K–12 students during the COVID-19 pandemic, by race/ethnicity, geography, and grade level. *Morbidity, and Mortality Weekly Report*, *70*(26), 953–958. doi:10.15585/mmwr.mm7026e2 PMID:34197363

Overstreet, S., & Chafouleas, S. M. (2016). Trauma-informed schools: Introduction to the special issue. *School Mental Health*, *8*(1), 1–6. doi:10.100712310-016-9184-1

Oyen, K., & Wollersheim-Shervey, S. (2019). An examination of critical features of positive frameworks: Impact in rural environments for school-based practitioners. *Contemporary School Psychology*, *23*(4), 388–400. doi:10.100740688-018-0198-6

Palmer, E. L., & Louis, K. S. (2017). Talking about race: Overcoming fear in the process of change. *Journal of School Leadership*, *27*(4), 581–610. doi:10.1177/105268461702700405

Paris, D. (2012). Culturally sustaining pedagogy: A needed change in stance, terminology, and practice. *Educational Researcher*, *41*(3), 93–97. doi:10.3102/0013189X12441244

Paris, D., & Alim, H. S. (2017). *Culturally sustaining pedagogies: Teaching and learning for justice in a changing world*. Teachers College Press.

Parker-Drabble, H. (2022). How key psychological theories can enrich our understanding of our ancestors and help improve mental health for present and future generations: A family history perspective. *Genealogy*, *6*(1), 1–21. doi:10.3390/genealogy6010004

Parker, J., Olson, S., & Bunde, J. (2020). The impact of trauma-based training on educators. *Journal of Child & Adolescent Trauma*, *13*(2), 217–227. doi:10.100740653-019-00261-5 PMID:32549933

Parker, R., & Hodgson, D. (2020). "One size does not fit all": Engaging students who have experienced trauma. *Issues in Educational Research*, *30*(1), 245–259. https://search.informit.org/doi/abs/10.3316/ielapa.086214776638143

Park, N. (2004). The role of subjective well-being in positive youth development. *The Annals of the American Academy of Political and Social Science*, *591*(1), 25–29. doi:10.1177/0002716203260078

Parsons, F. (2017). An intervention for the intervention: Integrating positive behavioral interventions and supports with culturally responsive practices. *Delta Kappa Gamma Bulletin, 83*(3), 52–57.

Paschall, K. W., Gershoff, E. T., & Kuhfeld, M. (2018). A Two Decade Examination of Historical Race/Ethnicity Disparities in Academic Achievement by Poverty Status. *Journal of Youth and Adolescence, 47*(6), 1164–1177. doi:10.100710964-017-0800-7 PMID:29313249

Pas, E., & Bradshaw, C. (2012). Examining the association between implementation and outcomes: State-wide scale-up of school-wide positive behavior interventions supports. *The Journal of Behavioral Health Services & Research, 39*(4), 417–433. doi:10.100711414-012-9290-2 PMID:22836758

Pauls, E. P. (2021). Trail of tears. In *Encyclopædia Britannica*. Retrieved May 25, 2022, from https://www.britannica.com/event/Trail-of-Tears

Pawlo, E., Lorenzo, A., Eichert, B., & Elias, M. J. (2019). All SEL should be trauma-informed. *Kappan, 101*(3), 37–41. doi:10.1177/0031721719885919

Pember, M. A. (2016). *Intergenerational trauma: Understanding Natives' inherited pain*. Indian Country Today Media Network. https://amber-ic.org/wp-content/uploads/2017/01/ICMN-All-About-Generations-Trauma.pdf

Pemberton, J. V., & Edeburn, E. K. (2021). Becoming a trauma-informed educational community with underserved students of color: What educators need to know. *Curriculum and Teaching Dialogue, 23*(1-2), 181–196.

Perfect, M. M., Turley, M. R., Carlson, J. S., Yohanna, J., & Saint Gilles, M. P. (2016). School-related outcomes of traumatic event exposure and traumatic stress symptoms in students: A systematic review of research from 1990 to 2015. *School Mental Health, 8*(1), 7–43. doi:10.100712310-016-9175-2

Perry, B., & Szalavitz, M. (2006). *The boy who was raised as a dog*. Basic Books.

Peterson, R., & Eeds, M. (1987/2007). *Grand conversations: Literature groups in action*. Scholastic.

Pickens, I. B., & Tschopp, N. (2017). *Trauma-informed classrooms*. National Council of Juvenile and Family Court Judges. https://www.ncjfcj.org/wp-content/uploads/2017/10/NCJFCJ_SJP_Trauma_Informed_Classrooms_Final.pdf

Pickens, I. B., & Tschopp, N. (2017, October 24). *Trauma-informed classrooms*. Council of Juvenile and Family Court Judges. https://www.ncjfcj.org/publications/trauma-informed-classrooms/

Plexousakis, S., Kourkoutas, E., Giovazolias, T., Chatira, K., & Nikolopoulos, D. (2019). School bullying and post-traumatic stress disorder symptoms: The role of parental bonding. *Frontiers in Public Health, 7*, 75. doi:10.3389/fpubh.2019.00075 PMID:31024876

Pokhrel, S., & Chhetri, R. (2021). A literature review on impact of COVID-19 pandemic on teaching and learning. *Higher Education for the Future, 8*(1), 133–141. doi:10.1177/2347631120983481

Compilation of References

Portnoi, L. M., & Kwong, T. M. (2015). Employing resistance and resilience in pursuing K-12 schooling and higher education lived experiences of successful female first-generation students of color. *Urban Education*, *54*(3), 1–29. doi:10.1177/0042085915623333

Positive Behavioral Interventions and Supports. (2022). *What is PBIS?* https://pbis.org/pbis/what-is-pbis

Pouya, S. (2019). The importance of horticulture therapy and gardening for older adults in nursing home. *Anadolu University*, *8*(2), 146–166. doi:10.20488anattasarim.529734

Pulido, R., Banks, C., Ragan, K., Pang, D., Blake, J., & McKyer, E. (2019). The impact of school bullying on physical activity in overweight youth: Exploring race and ethnic differences. *The Journal of School Health*, *89*(4), 319–327. doi:10.1111/josh.12740 PMID:30843227

Pur, I. (2014). Emotion regulation intervention for complex developmental trauma: Working with street children. *Procedia: Social and Behavioral Sciences*, *159*, 697–701. doi:10.1016/j.sbspro.2014.12.471

Pynoos, R. S., Steinberg, A. M., & Goenjian, A. (1996). Traumatic stress in childhood and adolescence: Recent developments and current controversies. In B. A. van der Kolk, A. McFarlane, & L. Weisaeth (Eds.), *Traumatic stress: The effects of overwhelming experience on mind, body and society* (pp. 133–141). Guilford Press.

Rabuy, B., & Kopf, D. (2015). Prisons of poverty: Uncovering the pre-incarceration incomes of the imprisoned. *Prison Policy Initiative, 9*.

Raby, K. L., Roisman, G. I., Labella, M. H., Martin, J., Fraley, R. C., & Simpson, J. A. (2019). The legacy of early abuse and neglect for social and academic competence from childhood to adulthood. *Child Development*, *90*(5), 1684–1701. doi:10.1111/cdev.13033 PMID:29336018

Rashid, H. (2009). From brilliant baby to child placed at risk: The perilous path of African American boys in early childhood education. *The Journal of Negro Education*, *78*(3), 347–358.

Rausch, M. K., & Skiba, R. (2004). *Unplanned outcomes: Suspensions and expulsions in Indiana.* Indiana University, Center for Evaluation and Education Policy.

Recorvits, H. (2003). My name is Yoon (G. Swiatkowska, Illus.). Macmillan.

Reddig, N., & VanLone, J. (2022). Pre-service teacher preparation in trauma-informed pedagogy: A review of state competencies. *Leadership and Policy in Schools*, 1–12. Advance online publication. doi:10.1080/15700763.2022.2066547

Relojo-Howell, D. (2020). Book review of 'Wales High School: First Diagnosis'. Psychreg. *The Journal of Psychology*, *4*(2), 140–142.

Richmond, E. (2015). What happens when instead of suspensions, kids talk out their mistakes? *The Hechinger Report.* https://hechingerreport.org/happens-instead-suspensions-kids-talk-mistakes/

Riddle, T., & Sinclair, S. (2019). Racial disparities in school-based disciplinary actions are associated with county-level rates of racial bias. *Proceedings of the National Academy of Sciences of the United States of America*, *116*(17), 8255–8260. doi:10.1073/pnas.1808307116 PMID:30940747

Riehl, C. J. (2009). The principal's role in creating inclusive schools for diverse students: A review of normative, empirical, and critical literature on the practice of educational administration. *Review of Educational Research*, *70*(1), 55–81. doi:10.3102/00346543070001055

Roberson, K., & Carter, R. T. (2021). The relationship between race-based traumatic stress and the Trauma Symptom Checklist: Does racial trauma differ in symptom presentation? *Traumatology*, *28*(1), 120–128. doi:10.1037/trm0000306

Robertson, H., Goodall, K., & Kay, D. (2021). Teachers' attitudes toward trauma-informed practice: Associations with attachment and adverse childhood experiences (ACEs). *The Psychology of Education Review*, *45*(2), 62-74. https://www.research.ed.ac.uk/en/publications/teachers-attitudes-towards-trauma-informed-practice-associations-

Rocque, M., & Snellings, Q. (2018). The new disciplinology: Research, theory, and remaining puzzles on the school-to-prison pipeline. *Journal of Criminal Justice*, *59*, 3–11. doi:10.1016/j.jcrimjus.2017.05.002

Rodríguez, L. F., & Greer, W. (2017). (Un)expected scholars: Counter-narratives from two (boys) men of color across the educational pipeline. *Equity & Excellence in Education*, *50*(1), 108–120. doi:10.1080/10665684.2016.1256004

Rodriguez, S. (2001). *Giants among us: First generation college graduates who lead activist lives*. Vanderbilt University Press. doi:10.2307/j.ctv16h2nct

Rose, J., McGuire-Snieckus, R., & Gilbert, L. (2015). Emotion coaching - a strategy for promoting behavioural self-regulation in children/young people in schools: A pilot study. *The European Journal of Social and Behavioural Sciences*, *13*(2), 130–157. doi:10.15405/ejsbs.159

Rosenthal, R. (2012). Self-fulfilling prophecy. In *Encyclopedia of Human Behavior* (2nd ed., pp. 328–335). Elsevier. doi:10.1016/B978-0-12-375000-6.00314-1

Rowe, W. (2020). COVID-19 and youth in detention. *Child and Youth Services*, *41*(3), 310–312. doi:10.1080/0145935X.2020.1835184

Ruzek, E., Hafen, C., Allen, J., Gregory, A., Mikami, A., & Pianta, R. (2016). How teacher emotional support motivates students: The mediating roles of perceived peer relatedness, autonomy support, and competence. *Learning and Instruction*, *42*, 95–103. doi:10.1016/j.learninstruc.2016.01.004 PMID:28190936

Rychly, L., & Graves, E. (2012). Teacher characteristics for culturally responsive pedagogy. *Multicultural Perspectives*, *14*(1), 44–49. doi:10.1080/15210960.2012.646853

Rynders, D. (2019). Battling implicit bias in the idea to advocate for African American students with disabilities. *Touro Law Review*, *35*, 461.

RYSE. (2015). Trauma and social location [Online image]. RYSE. https://www.pacesconnection.com/fileSendAction/fcType/0/fcOi d/416618476901050324/filePointer/425769210363174323/fodoid/4 25769210363174317/RYSEACEsDisorderDistressSocialLocation2015 .pdf

Sacks, V. (2021, March 8). *The prevalence of adverse childhood experiences, nationally, by state, and by race or ethnicity*. Child Trends. https://www.childtrends.org/publications/prevalence-adverse-childhood-experiences-nationally-state-race-ethnicity

Sacks, V., & Murphey, D. (2018). *The prevalence of adverse childhood experiences, nationally, by state, and by race/ethnicity* (Research Brief #2018-03). Child Trends. https://www.childtrends.org/wp-content/uploads/2018/02/ACESB rief_ChildTrends_February2018.pdf

Sacks, V., & Murphey, D. (2018, February 12). *The prevalence of adverse childhood experiences, nationally, by state, and by race or ethnicity.* Child Trends. https://www.childtrends.org/publications/prevalence-adverse-childhood-experiences-nationally-state-race-ethnicity

Sahlberg, P. (2020). Does the pandemic help us make education more equitable? *Educational Research for Policy and Practice, 20*(1), 11–18. doi:10.100710671-020-09284-4

Saldaña, J. (2021). The Coding Manual for Qualitative Researchers. *Sage (Atlanta, Ga.).*

Saleem, F. T., Anderson, R. E., & Williams, M. (2020). Addressing the "Myth" of Racial Trauma: Developmental and Ecological Considerations for Youth of Color. *Clinical Child and Family Psychology Review, 23*(1), 1–14. doi:10.100710567-019-00304-1 PMID:31641920

Sampson, R., & Lauritsen, J. (1994). Violent victimization and offending: Individual, situational, and community level risk factors. In A. J. Reiss Jr & J. A. Roth (Eds.), *Understanding and preventing violence* (Vol. 3, pp. 1–114). National Academy Press.

Sandler, J. D. (2017). African American language and American linguistic cultures: An analysis of language policies in education. *Working Papers in Educational Linguistics, 22*(1), 105-134. Retrieved August 9, 2022, from https://repository.upenn.edu/wpel/vol22/iss1/6

Schonert-Reichl, K. (2017). Social and Emotional Learning and Teachers. *The Future of Children, 27*(1), 137–155. https://www.jstor.org/stable/44219025. doi:10.1353/foc.2017.0007

Schwartz, R. M., Sison, C., Kerath, S. M., Murphy, L., Breil, T., Sikavi, D., & Taioli, E. (2015). The impact of Hurricane Sandy on the mental health of New York area residents. *American Journal of Disaster Medicine, 10*(4), 339–346. doi:10.5055/ajdm.2015.0216 PMID:27149315

Schwieter, J. W. (2010). Developing second language writing through scaffolding in the ZPD: A magazine project for an authentic audience. *Journal of College Teaching and Learning, 7*(10), 31–46. doi:10.19030/tlc.v7i10.154

Scott, T. (2015). Horticultural therapy. In N. Pachana (Ed.), *Encyclopedia of Geropsychology* (pp. 1–5). Springer. doi:10.1007/978-981-287-080-3_268-1

Scott, T. M., & Caron, D. B. (2005). Conceptualizing functional behavior assessment as prevention practice within positive behavior support systems. *Preventing School Failure*, *50*(1), 13–20. doi:10.3200/PSFL.50.1.13-20

Sealey-Ruiz, Y. (2022). An Archaeology of Self for Our Times: Another Talk to Teachers. *English Journal*, *111*(5), 21–26.

Sealey-Ruiz, Y., & Greene, P. (2015). Popular visual images and the (mis) reading of black male youth: A case for racial literacy in urban preservice teacher education. *Teaching Education*, *26*(1), 55–76. doi:10.1080/10476210.2014.997702

Sellers, R. M., Copeland-Linder, N., Martin, P. P., & Lewis, R. H. (2006). Racial identity matters: The relationship between racial discrimination and psychological functioning in African American adolescents. *Journal of Research on Adolescence*, *16*(2), 187–216. doi:10.1111/j.1532-7795.2006.00128.x

Serlin, I. A. (2020). Dance/movement therapy: A whole person approach to working with trauma and building resilience. *American Journal of Dance Therapy*, *42*(2), 176–193. doi:10.100710465-020-09335-6 PMID:33250545

Shaw, E. (2020). "Who we are and why we do it": A demographic overview and the cited motivations of Australian family historians. *Journal of Family History*, *45*(1), 109–124. doi:10.1177/0363199019880238

Shaw, E. L., & Donnelly, D. J. (2021). Rediscovering the familial past and its impact on historical consciousness. *Genealogy*, *5*(102), 102. Advance online publication. doi:10.3390/genealogy5040102

Sherblom, S. A., Marshall, J. C., & Sherblom, J. C. (2006). The relationship between school climate and math and reading achievement. *Journal of Research in Character Education*, *4*(1–2), 19–31.

Shields, C. M. (2010). Transformative leadership: Working for equity in diverse contexts. *Educational Administration Quarterly*, *46*(4), 558–589. doi:10.1177/0013161X10375609

Shollenberger, T. (2015). Racial disparities in school suspension and subsequent outcomes: Evidence from the natural longitudinal survey of youth. In D. J. Losen (Ed.), *Closing the school discipline gap: Equitable remedies for excessive exclusion* (pp. 31–43). Teachers College Press.

Shonkoff, J. P., Garner, A. S., Siegel, B. S., Dobbins, M. I., Earls, M. F., Garner, A. S., McGuinn, L., Pascoe, J., & Wood, D. L. (2012). The lifelong effects of early childhood adversity and toxic stress. *Pediatrics*, *129*(1), e232–e246. doi:10.1542/peds.2011-2663 PMID:22201156

Shonkoff, J. P., Slopen, N., & Williams, D. R. (2021). Early childhood adversity, Toxic stress, and the impacts of racism on the foundations of health. *Annual Review of Public Health*, *42*(1), 115–134. doi:10.1146/annurev-publhealth-090419-101940 PMID:33497247

Siegel, D. J. (2015). *The developing mind: How relationships and the brain interact to shape who we are* (2nd, rev. ed). The Guilford Press.

Siegel, D. (2009). Mindful awareness, mindsight, and neural integration. *The Humanistic Psychologist, 37*(2), 137–158. doi:10.1080/08873260902892220

Simonsen, B., Eber, L., Black, A., Sugai, G., Lewandowski, H., Sims, B., & Myers, D. (2012). Illinois statewide positive behavioral interventions and supports: Evolution and impact on student outcomes across years. *Journal of Positive Behavior Interventions, 14*(1), 5–16. doi:10.1177/1098300711412601

Simpson, V. (2020 September 14). *Incarceration rates by country.* World Atlas. https://www.worldatlas.com/articles/largest-prison-population-rates-in-the-world.html

Simpson, V. (2020, September 14). *Incarceration rates by country.* World Atlas. https://www.worldatlas.com/articles/largest-prison-population-rates-in-the-world.html

Singleton, G. (2015). *Courageous conversations about race: A Field Guide for Achieving Equity in Schools.* Corwin.

Singleton, G. E. (2021). *Courageous Conversations About Race: A Field Guide for Achieving Equity in Schools and Beyond.* Corwin Press.

Siregar, S., & Suparno, S. (2018). *Understanding child's emotions and responses to the food using words and emojis fat and thin child.* Proceedings of the International Conference on Special and Inclusive Education (ICSIE 2018), 296, 315-319. 10.2991/icsie-18.2019.57

Skiba, R. J., Arredondo, M. I., & Williams, N. T. (2014). More than a metaphor: The contribution of exclusionary discipline to a school-to-prison pipeline. *Equity & Excellence in Education, 47*(4), 546–564. doi:10.1080/10665684.2014.958965

Skiba, R. J., Chung, C. G., Trachok, M., Baker, T. L., Sheya, A., & Hughes, R. L. (2014). Parsing disciplinary disproportionality: Contributions of infraction, student, and school characteristics to out-of-school suspension and expulsion. *American Educational Research Journal, 51*(4), 640–670. doi:10.3102/0002831214541670

Skiba, R. J., Horner, R. H., Chung, C. G., Rausch, M. K., May, S. L., & Tobin, T. (2011). Race is not neutral: A national investigation of African American and Latino disproportionality in school discipline. *School Psychology Review, 40*(1), 85–107. doi:10.1080/02796015.2011.12087730

Skiba, R. J., Peterson, R. L., & Williams, T. (1997). Office referrals and suspension: Disciplinary intervention in middle schools. *Education & Treatment of Children, 20*(3), 295–313.

Skiba, R., & Sprague, J. (2008). Safety without suspensions. *Educational Leadership: Journal of the Department of Supervision and Curriculum Development, 66*(1), 38–43.

Skinner, E. A., & Pitzer, J. R. (2012). Developmental dynamics of student engagement, coping, and everyday resilience. In S. L. Christenson, A. L. Reschly, & C. Wylie (Eds.), *Handbook of research on student engagement*. Springer. doi:10.1007/978-1-4614-2018-7_2

Skrla, L., Scheurich, J. J., Garcia, J., & Nolly, G. (2004). Equity audits: A practical leadership tool for developing equitable and excellent schools. *Educational Administration Quarterly, 40*(1), 133–161. doi:10.1177/0013161X03259148

Sleeter, C. (2015). *White Bread: Weaving cultural past into the present*. Sense Publishers. doi:10.1007/978-94-6300-067-3

Sleeter, C. E. (2001). Preparing teachers for culturally diverse schools: Research and the overwhelming presence of Whiteness. *Journal of Teacher Education, 52*(2), 94–106. doi:10.1177/0022487101052002002

Sleeter, C. E. (2011). An agenda to strengthen culturally responsive pedagogy. *English Teaching, 10*(2), 7–23.

Smith, D. (2015). *Better Than carrots or sticks: Restorative practices for positive classroom management*. Association for Supervision and Curriculum Development.

Smyth, J. (2006). *When students have 'relational' power: The school as a site for identity formation around engagement and school retention*. Paper presented at the Australian Association for Research in Education, Adelaide, Australia.

Snyder, C. R. (1996). To hope, to lose, and to hope again. *Journal of Personal and Interpersonal Loss, 1*(1), 1–16. doi:10.1080/15325029608415455

Snyder, C. R. (1998). To hope, to lose, and hope again. In J. H. Harvey, J. Omarzu, & E. Miller (Eds.), *Perspectives on loss: A sourcebook* (pp. 63–79). Taylor and Francis.

Snyder, C. R., Feldman, B. D., Shorey, H. S., & Rand, K. L. (2002). Hopeful choices: A school counselor's guide to hope theory. *Professional School Counseling, 5*(5), 298–307. https://eric.ed.gov/?q=l&pg=808&id=EJ655195

Solomon, R. (2004). Schooling in Babylon, Babylon in school: When racial profiling and zero tolerance converge. *Canadian Journal of Educational Administration and Policy, 33*, http://search.proquest.com/docview/61859546?accountid=28109

Solórzano, D. G., & Delgado Bernal, D. (2001). Examining transformational resistance through a critical race and LatCrit theory framework—Chicana and Chicano students in an urban context. *Urban Education, 36*(3), 308–324. doi:10.1177/0042085901363002

Solórzano, D. G., & Yosso, T. J. (2001). Maintaining social justice hopes within academic realities: A Freirean approach to critical race/LatCrit pedagogy. *Denver Law Review, 78*(4), 595–612.

Souers, K., & Hall, P. (2016). *Fostering resilient learners: Strategies for creating a trauma-sensitive classroom*. ASCD.

Compilation of References

Souers, K., & Hall, P. (2020, October). Trauma is a word–not a sentence. *Educational Leadership*, *78*(2), 34–39.

Spanke, J., & Paul, K. A. (2015). From the pens of babes: Authentic audiences for talented, young writers. *Gifted Child Today*, *38*(3), 177–186. doi:10.1177/1076217515583743

Spence, R., Kagan, L., Kljakovic, M., & Bifulco, A. (2021). Understanding trauma in children and young people in the school setting. *Educational and Child Psychology*, *38*(1), 87–98.

Sprague, J., & Horner, R. (2006). Schoolwide positive behavior support. In S. Jimerson & M. Furlong (Eds.), Handbook of school violence and school safety: From research to practice (pp. 413–427). Academic Press.

Sprague, J. (2014). Integrated PBIS and Restorative Discipline *The Special Edge. Student Behavior*, *3*(1), 11–16.

Springer, K., Sheridan, J., Kuo, D., & Carnes, M. (2007). Long-term physical and mental health consequences of childhood physical abuse: Results from a large population-based sample of men and women. *Child Abuse & Neglect*, *31*(5), 517–530. doi:10.1016/j.chiabu.2007.01.003 PMID:17532465

Stahl, G. (2019). Critiquing the corporeal curriculum: Body pedagogies in 'no excuses' charter schools. *Journal of Youth Studies*, *7*, 1–17.

Standards & Testing Agency. (2020). The engagement model. *Assets*. https://assets.publishing.service.gov.uk/government/uploads/system/uploads/attachment_data/file/903458/Engagement_Model_Guidance_2020.pdf

Stavrianos, C., Stavrianou, P., Vasiliadis, L., Karamouzi, A., Mihailidou, D., & Mihail, G. (2011). Emotional maltreatment of children. *Social Sciences*, *6*(6), 441–446.

Steed, E., Pomerleau, T., Muscott, H., & Rohde, L. (2013). Program-wide positive behavioral interventions and support in rural preschools. *Rural Special Education Quarterly*, *32*(1), 38–46. doi:10.1177/875687051303200106

Steele, W., & Kuban, C. (2013). *Working with grieving and traumatized children and adolescents: Discovering what matters most through evidence-based, sensory interventions*. Wiley.

Stein, J. A., Golding, J. M., Siegel, J. M., Burnam, M. A., & Sorenson, S. B. (1988). Long-term psychological sequelae of child sexual abuse: The Los Angeles epidemiologic catchment area study. In F. Sage, G. E. Wyatt, & Y. G. J. Powell (Eds.), *Lasting effects of child sexual abuse* (Vol. 100, pp. 135–154). Sage Publications.

Stensrud, R. H., Gilbride, D. D., & Bruinekool, R. M. (2019). The childhood to prison pipeline: Early childhood trauma as reported by a prison population. *Rehabilitation Counseling Bulletin*, *62*(4), 195–208. doi:10.1177/0034355218774844

StopBullying.gov. (2021, May 21). *Effects of bullying*. Stopbullying. https://www.stopbullying.gov/bullying/effects

Stovall, D. (2018). Are we ready for 'school' abolition?: Thoughts and practices of radical imaginary in education. *Taboo: The Journal of Culture and Education*, *17*(1), 6. doi:10.31390/taboo.17.1.06

Straus, M. A., Gelles, R. J., & Steinmetz, S. (1980). Behind closed doors: Violence in the American family. Anchor Press.

Subedi, K. (2020). Theoretical perspective of bullying. *International Journal of Health Sciences and Research*, *10*(8), 83–89.

Substance Abuse and Mental Health Services Administration. (2014). *SAMHSA's concept of trauma and guidance for a trauma-informed approach.* https://ncsacw.acf.hhs.gov/userfiles/files/SAMHSA_Trauma.pdf

Substance Abuse and Mental Health Services Administration. (2014). *SAMHSA's concept of trauma and guidance for a trauma-informed approach.* Substance Abuse and Mental Health Services Administration. https://store.samhsa.gov/sites/default/files/d7/priv/sma14-4884.pdf

Substance Abuse and Mental Health Services Administration. (2014). Understanding the Impact of Trauma. In *Trauma-Informed Care in Behavioral Health Services* (pp. 59–89). HHS Publication.

Substance Abuse and Mental Health Services Administration. (2022). *Trauma and Violence.* SAMHSA. https://www.samhsa.gov/trauma-violence

Substance Abuse and Mental Health Services Administration. (2022). *Understanding child trauma.* SAMHSA. https://www.samhsa.gov/child-trauma/understanding-child-trauma

Sue, D. W., Capodilupo, C. M., Torino, G. C., Bucceri, J. M., Holder, A. M. B., Nadal, K. L., & Esquilin, M. (2007). Racial microaggressions in everyday life: Implications for clinical practice. *The American Psychologist*, *62*(4), 271–286. doi:10.1037/0003-066X.62.4.271 PMID:17516773

Sugai, G., & Simonsen, B. (2012). *Positive behavior interventions and supports: History, defining features, and misconceptions* (No. 4). Center for PBIS, University of Connecticut. https://challengingbehavior.cbcs.usf.edu/docs/PBIS_revisited_June19_2012.pdf

Sugai, G., & Horner, R. (2009). Responsiveness-to-intervention and school-wide positive behavior supports: Integration of multi-tiered systems approached. *Exceptionality*, *17*(4), 223–237. doi:10.1080/09362830903235375

Sugai, G., & Horner, R. (2020). Sustaining and scaling positive behavioral intervention and supports: Implementation drivers, outcomes, and considerations. *Exceptional Children*, *86*(2), 120–136. doi:10.1177/0014402919855331

Sun, W. (2022). *Finding alternative pathways beyond the rhetoric of the racial disparities in disciplinary practices: Racialized politics of principals' reasonings of disciplinary practices* [Manuscript submitted for publication].

Compilation of References

Supovitz, J. A., D'Auria, J., & Spillane, J. P. (2019). *Meaningful and sustainable school improvement with distributed leadership*. CPRE Research Reports. Retrieved from: https://repository.upenn.edu/cpre_researchreports/112

Sutcher, L., Darling-Hammond, L., & Carver-Thomas, D. (2016). *A coming crisis in teaching? Teacher supply, demand, and shortages in the U.S.* Learning Policy Institute. https://learningpolicyinstitute.org/product/coming-crisis-teaching

Swain-Bradway, J., Pinkney, C., & Flannery, K. (2015). Implementing school-wide positive behavior interventions and supports in high schools: Contextual factors and stages of implementation. *Teaching Exceptional Children*, *47*(5), 245–255. doi:10.1177/0040059915580030

Swedo, E., Idaikkadar, N., Leemis, R., Dias, T., Radhakrishnan, L., Stein, Z., Chen, M., Agathis, N., & Holland, K. (2020). Trends in U.S. emergency department visits related to suspected or confirmed child abuse and neglect among children and adolescents age < 18 years before and during the COVID-19 pandemic: United States, January 2019 – September 2020. *MMWR. Morbidity and Mortality Weekly Report*, *69*(49), 1841–1847. doi:10.15585/mmwr.mm6949a1 PMID:33301436

Swindler Boutte, G., & Johnson, G. L. (2014). Community and family involvement in urban schools. In R. H. Milner & K. Lomotey (Eds.), *Handbook of urban education* (1st ed., pp. 167–187). Routledge.

Tate, W. R., Hamilton, C., Jones, B. D., Robertson, W. B., & Macrander, A. Schultz, l., & Thorne-Washington, E. (2013). Serving vulnerable children and youth in the urban context. In H.R. Milner & K. Lomotey (Eds), Handbook of Urban Education (pp. 3-23). Routledge.

Taub, A. (2020). A new COVID-19 crisis: Domestic abuse rises worldwide. *The New York Times*. https://www.nytimes.com/2020/04/06/world/coronavirus-domestic-violence.html

Taylor, R., Oberle, E., Durlak, J., & Weissberg, R. (2017). Promoting positive youth development through schoolbased social and emotional learning interventions: A meta-analysis of follow-up effects. *Child Development*, *88*(4), 1156–1171. doi:10.1111/cdev.12864 PMID:28685826

Telef, B. B. (2020). Hope and life satisfaction in elementary students: Mediation role of affective experiences. *Journal of Positive School Psychology*, *4*(2), 176–186. doi:10.47602/jpsp.v4i2.232

The National Child Traumatic Stress Network. (n.d.). *About child trauma*. NCTSN. https://www.nctsn.org/what-is-child-trauma/about-child-trauma

The World Bank. (2018). *World development report 2018: Learning to realize education's promise*. https://www.worldbank.org/en/publication/wdr2018

Thomas, M. S., Crosby, S., & Vanderhaar, J. (2019). Trauma-informed practices in schools across two decades: An interdisciplinary review of research. *Review of Research in Education*, *43*(1), 422–452. doi:10.3102/0091732X18821123

Thompkins-Bigelow, J. (2020). *Your name is a song* (L. Uribe, Illus.). The Innovation Press.

Todd, R. (2021). *Recognizing the signs of trauma*. Edutopia. https://www.edutopia.org/article/recognizing-signs-trauma#:~:text=Some%20classroom%20signs%20of%20trauma,%2C%20excessive%20crying%2C%20etc)

Tompkins, G. E. (2022). *Literacy for the 21st century: A balanced approach* (5th ed.). Pearson.

Tonatiuh, D. (2014). *Separate is never equal: Sylvia Mendez and her family's fight for desegregation*. Harry N. Abrams.

Toney, J., & Rodgers, H. (2011). Racial equity policy brief: 16 solutions that deliver equity and excellence in education. [OAP]. *Organizing Apprenticeship Program, 2*, 1–20.

Trauma and Learning Policy Initiative. (2022). *Frequently asked questions about trauma-sensitive schools*. https://traumasensitiveschools.org/frequently-asked-questions/

Trauth, J. (2017). Lighthouse community school: A case study of a school for behaviorally challenged youth. *Journal of Therapeutic Horticulture, 27*(1), 60–65.

Trauth, J., & Harris, K. (2019). Lighthouse community school: An in-depth look at successful strategies used with at-risk students. *Multicultural Education, 27*(1), 24–28.

Tsoi-A-Fatt Bryant, R. (2015). *College preparation for African American students: Gaps in the high school educational experience*. CLASP. https://vtechworks.lib.vt.edu/handle/10919/83649

Ttofi, M., Farrington, D., & Losel, F. (2011). Health consequences of school bullying. *Journal of Aggression, Conflict and Peace Research, 3*(2). doi:10.1108/jacpr.2011.55003baa.002

Tulsa City-County Library. (2022, May 17). *Tulsa Race Massacre*. https://www.tulsalibrary.org/tulsa-race-riot-1921

Ukpokodu, O. N. (2007). Preparing socially conscious teachers: A social-justice oriented teacher education. *Multicultural Education, 15*(1), 8–15.

Uline, C., & Tschannen-Moran, M. (2008). The walls speak: The interplay of quality facilities, school climate, and student achievement. *Journal of Educational Administration, 46*(1), 55–73. doi:10.1108/09578230810849817

Ullucci, I., & Battey, D. (2011). Exposing color blindness/grounding color consciousness: Challenges for teacher education. *Urban Education, 46*(6), 1195–1225. doi:10.1177/0042085911413150

United Nations Educational, Scientific, and Cultural Organization. (2019). *Behind the numbers: Ending school violence and bullying*. UNESCO. https://unesdoc.unesco.org/ark:/48223/pf0000366483

Compilation of References

United Nations Educational, Scientific, and Cultural Organization. (2020). *International conference on school bullying: Recommendations by the scientific committee on preventing and addressing school bullying and cyberbullying*. UNESCO. https://unesdoc.unesco.org/ark:/48223/pf0000374794.locale=en

United Nations. (2015). *Transforming our world: The 2030 agenda for sustainable development*. https://sdgs.un.org/2030agenda

United Nations. (2020, August 22). *Policy brief: Education during covid-19 and beyond*. https://unsdg.un.org/resources/policy-brief-education-during-covid-19-and-beyond

United Nations. (2020, August). *Policy Brief: Education during COVID-19 and beyond*. Retrieved from United Nations: https://unsdg.un.org/resources/policy-brief-education-during-covid-19-and-beyond

US Department of Education. (1997). *America's teachers: Profile of a profession, 1993-94*. National Center for Educational Statistics. https://nces.ed.gov/pubs97/97460.pdf

Usher, K., Bhullar, N., Durkin, J., Gyamfi, N., & Jackson, D. (2020). Family violence and COVID-19: Increased vulnerability and reduced options for support. *International Journal of Mental Health Nursing*, *29*(4), 549–552. doi:10.1111/inm.12735 PMID:32314526

Utah Education Policy Center. (2012). *Research brief: Chronic absenteeism*. https://www.attendanceworks.org/wp-content/uploads/2017/09/UTAH-Chronic-AbsenteeismResearch-Brief-July-2012.pdf

Utley, C., Kozleski, E., Smith, A., & Draper, I. (2002). Positive behavior support: A proactive strategy for minimizing behavior problems in urban multicultural youth. *Journal of Positive Behavior Interventions*, *4*(4), 192–207. doi:10.1177/10983007020040040301

Valle, M. F., Huebner, E. S., & Suldo, S. M. (2006). An analysis of hope as a psychological strength. *Journal of School Psychology*, *44*(5), 393–406. doi:10.1016/j.jsp.2006.03.005

van der Kolk, B. A., Pynoos, R. S., Cicchetti, D., Cloitre, M., D'Andrea, W., Ford, J. D., Lieberman, A. F., Putnam, F. W., Saxe, G., Spinazzola, J., Stolbach, B. C., & Teicher, M. (2009). *Proposal to include Developmental Trauma Disorder diagnosis for children and adolescents in DSM-V*. https://www.cttntraumatraining.org/uploads/4/6/2/3/46231093/dsm-v_proposal-dtd_taskforce.pdf

van der Kolk, B. A. (2003). The neurobiology of childhood trauma and abuse. *Child and Adolescent Psychiatric Clinics of North America*, *12*(2), 293–317. doi:10.1016/S1056-4993(03)00003-8 PMID:12725013

van der Kolk, B. A. (2005). Developmental trauma disorder: Toward a rational diagnosis for children with complex trauma histories. *Psychiatric Annals*, *35*(5), 401–408. doi:10.3928/00485713-20050501-06

Van der Kolk, B. A., Pelcovitz, D., Roth, S., Mandel, F. S., McFarlane, A., & Herman, J. L. (1996). Dissociation, somatization, and affect dysregulation: The complexity of adaptation of trauma. *The American Journal of Psychiatry*, *153*(7), 83–93. doi:10.1176/ajp.153.7.83 PMID:8659645

van der Kolk, B. A., Roth, S., Pelcovitz, D., Sunday, S., & Spinazzola, J. (2005). Disorders of extreme stress: The empirical foundation of a complex adaptation to trauma. *Journal of Traumatic Stress*, *18*(5), 389–399. doi:10.1002/jts.20047 PMID:16281237

Vander Ark, T. (2019). Eleven alternative schools that are real alternatives. *Forbes*. https://www.forbes.com/sites/tomvanderark/2019/10/07/11-alternative-schools-thatare-real-alternatives/#5d7fa6351c1c

Venet, A. S. (2021). Equity-Centered Trauma-Informed Education (Equity and Social Justice in Education). WW Norton & Company.

Venet, A. S. (2019). Role-clarity and boundaries for trauma-informed teachers. *Educational Considerations*, *44*(2), 1–9. doi:10.4148/0146-9282.2175

Venet, A. S. (2021). *Equity-Centered Trauma-Informed Education*. W. W. Norton & Company.

Vincent, C., & Tobin, T. (2011). The relationship between implementation of school-wide positive behavior support (SWPBIS) and disciplinary exclusions of students from various ethnic backgrounds with and without disabilities. *Journal of Emotional and Behavioral Disorders*, *19*(4), 217–232. doi:10.1177/1063426610377329

Volk, A., Dane, A., & Marini, Z. (2014). What is bullying? A theoretical redefinition. *Developmental Review*, *34*(4), 327–343. doi:10.1016/j.dr.2014.09.001

Waasdorp, T., Bradshaw, C., & Leaf, P. (2012). The impact of schoolwide positive behavioral interventions and supports on bullying and peer rejection. *Archives of Pediatrics & Adolescent Medicine*, *166*(2), 149–156. doi:10.1001/archpediatrics.2011.755 PMID:22312173

Wald, J., & Losen, D. J. (2003). Defining and redirecting a school-to-prison pipeline. *New Directions for Youth Development*, *2003*(99), 9–15. doi:10.1002/yd.51 PMID:14635431

Waliski, A., & Carlson, L. (2008). Group work with preschool children: Effect on emotional awareness and behavior. *Journal for Specialists in Group Work*, *33*(1), 3–21. doi:10.1080/01933920701476714

Walker, B., Cheney, D., Stage, S., Blum, C., & Horner, R. (2005). Schoolwide screening and positive behavior supports: Identifying and supporting students at risk for school failure. *Journal of Positive Behavior Interventions*, *7*(4), 194–204. doi:10.1177/10983007050070040101

Walker, V. S. (2001). African American teaching in the South: 1940–1960. *American Educational Research Journal*, *38*(4), 751–799. doi:10.3102/00028312038004751

Walmsley, R. (2016). *World prison population list* (11th ed.). Institute for Criminal Policy Research. https://www.prisonstudies.org/sites/default/files/resources/downloads/world_prison_population_list_11th_edition_0.pdf

Compilation of References

Wang, G., Han, A., Zhang, G., Xu, N., Xie, G., Chen, L., Yuan, M., & Su, P. (2020). Sensitive periods for the effect of bullying victimization on suicidal behaviors among university students in China: The roles of timing and chronicity. *Journal of Affective Disorders*, *268*, 12–19. doi:10.1016/j.jad.2020.02.049 PMID:32158002

Wang, H., Wang, Y., Wang, G., Wilson, A., Jin, T., Zhu, L., Yu, R., Wang, S., Yin, W., Song, H., Li, S., Jia, Q., Zhang, X., & Yang, Y. (2021). Structural family factors and bullying at school: A large scale investigation based on a Chinese adolescent sample. *BMC Public Health*, *21*(1), 2249. doi:10.118612889-021-12367-3 PMID:34895204

Wang, T., Olivier, D. F., & Chen, P. (2020). Creating individual and organizational readiness for change: Conceptualization of system readiness for change in school education. *International Journal of Leadership in Education*, 1–25. Advance online publication. doi:10.1080/13603124.2020.1818131

Ward, M. E., Shelley, K., Kaase, K., & Pane, J. F. (2008). Hurricane Katrina: A longitudinal study of the achievement and behavior of displaced students. *Journal of Education for Students Placed at Risk*, *13*(2–3), 297–317. doi:10.1080/10824660802350391

Wastvedt, S. (2017). St. Paul schools see hope in 'restorative' discipline. *MPR News*. https://www.mprnews.org/story/2017/11/20/stpaul-schools-see-hope-in-restorative-discipline

Watson, K. (2016). *Why Richer Areas Get More School Funding Than Poorer Ones*. Global Citizens. https://www.globalcitizen.org/en/content/cost-of-education-in-us/

Way, N., Reddy, R., & Rhodes, J. (2008). Students' perceptions of school climate during the middle school years: Associations with trajectories of psychological and behavioral adjustment. *American Journal of Community Psychology*, *40*(3-4), 194–213. doi:10.100710464-007-9143-y PMID:17968655

Weiland, C., Murakami, E., Aguilera, E., & Richards, M. (2014). Advocates in odd places: Social justice for behaviorally challenged, minority students in large urban school districts. *Education, Citizenship and Social Justice*, *9*(2), 114–137. doi:10.1177/1746197914520647

Weinhold, B. (2000). Uncovering the hidden causes of bullying and school violence. *Counseling and Human Development*, *32*(6), 1–18.

Welsh, R., & Little, S. (2018). The School Discipline Dilemma: A Comprehensive Review of Disparities and Alternative Approaches. *Review of Educational Research*, *88*(5), 752–794. doi:10.3102/0034654318791582

Welton, A. D., Mansfield, K. C., & Salisbury, J. D. (2022). The Politics of Student Voice: The Power and Potential of Students as Policy Actors. *Educational Policy*, *36*(1), 3–18. doi:10.1177/08959048211059718

Welton, A. D., Owens, D. R., & Zamani-Gallaher, E. M. (2018). Anti-racist change: A conceptual framework for educational institutions to take systemic action. *Teachers College Record*, *120*(14), 1–22. doi:10.1177/016146811812001402

Whiteside-Mansell, L., McKelvey, L., Saccente, J., & Selig, J. P. (2019). Adverse childhood experiences of urban and rural preschool children in poverty. *International Journal of Environmental Research and Public Health*, *16*(14), 2623. doi:10.3390/ijerph16142623 PMID:31340510

Widom, C. S., & Maxfield, M. G. (2001, February). *An update on the "Cycle of Violence"* (NCJ 184894). National Institute of Justice. https://www.ojp.gov/pdffiles1/nij/184894.pdf

Widom, C. S. (1989). Child abuse, neglect, and violent criminal behavior. *Criminology*, *27*(2), 251–271. doi:10.1111/j.1745-9125.1989.tb01032.x

Wiest-Stevenson, C., & Lee, C. (2016). Trauma-informed schools. *Journal of Evidence-Informed Social Work*, *13*(5), 498–503. doi:10.1080/23761407.2016.1166855 PMID:27210273

Williams, P. J. (1991). *The alchemy of race and rights*. Harvard University Press.

Winninghoff, A. (2020). Trauma by numbers: Warnings against the use of ACE scores in trauma-informed schools. *Occasional Paper Series*, *2020*(43), 4.

Winship, S., Pulliam, C., Shiro, A. G., Reeves, R. V., & Deambrosi, S. (2022, March 9). *Long shadows: The Black-white gap in multigenerational poverty*. Brookings. Retrieved August 16, 2022, from https://www.brookings.edu/research/long-shadows-the-black-white-gap-in-multigenerational-poverty/

Wisner, W. (2022, February 24). What are adverse childhood experiences? *Very Well Mind*. https://www.verywellmind.com/what-are-aces-adverse-childhood-experiences-5219030

Wolff, N., & Shi, J. (2012). Childhood and adult trauma experiences of incarcerated persons and their relationship to adult behavioral health problems and treatment. *International Journal of Environmental Research and Public Health*, *9*(5), 1908–1926. doi:10.3390/ijerph9051908 PMID:22754481

Wolke, D., & Lereya, S. (2015). Long-term effects of bullying. *Archives of Disease in Childhood*, *100*(9), 879–885. doi:10.1136/archdischild-2014-306667 PMID:25670406

Wong, C., Cheng, Y., & Chen, L. (2013). Multiple perspectives on the targets and causes of school bullying. *Educational Psychology in Practice*, *29*(3), 278–292. doi:10.1080/02667363.2013.837030

Wong, S. S., & Lim, T. (2009). Hope versus optimism in Singaporean adolescents: Contributions to depression and life satisfactions. *Personality and Individual Differences*, *45*(5-6), 648–652. doi:10.1016/j.paid.2009.01.009

Woodward, J. R. (2011). How busing burdened Blacks: Critical race theory and busing for desegregation in Nashville-Davidson County. *The Journal of Negro Education*, *80*(1), 22–32.

Compilation of References

World Health Organization. (n.d.). *Coronavirus disease (COVID-19)*. WHO. https://www.who.int/health-topics/coronavirus#tab=tab_1

Wu, N., Hou, Y., Zeng, Q., Cai, H., & You, J. (2021). Bullying experiences and nonsuicidal self-injury among Chinese adolescents: A longitudinal moderated mediation model. *Journal of Youth and Adolescence*, *50*(4), 753–766. doi:10.100710964-020-01380-1 PMID:33428080

Wyman, P., Cross, W., Brown, C., Yu, Q., Tu, X., & Eberly, S. (2010). Intervention to strengthen emotional self-regulation in children with emerging mental health problems: Proximal impact on school behavior. *Journal of Abnormal Child Psychology*, *38*(5), 707–720. doi:10.100710802-010-9398-x PMID:20180009

Xiao, J. (2021). From equality to equity to justice: Should online education be the new normal in education? In A. Bozkurt (Ed.), *Emerging pedagogies for the future of education: Trauma-Informed, Care, and Pandemic Pedagogy* (pp. 1–15). IGI Global. doi:10.4018/978-1-7998-7275-7.ch001

Yang, A., & Salmivalli, C. (2015). Effectiveness of the KiVa antibullying programme on bully-victims, bullies and victims. *Educational Research*, *57*(1), 80–90. doi:10.1080/00131881.2014.983724

Yazzie-Mintz, E. (2007). *Voices of students on engagement: A report on the 2006 high school survey of student engagement.* Center for Education & Evaluation Policy, Indiana University. https://files.eric.ed.gov/fulltext/ED495758.pdf

Yehuda, R., & Lehrner, A. (2018). Intergenerational transmission of trauma effects: Putative role of epigenetic mechanisms. *World Psychiatry; Official Journal of the World Psychiatric Association (WPA)*, *17*(3), 243–257. doi:10.1002/wps.20568 PMID:30192087

Yin, R. (2017). *Case study research and applications: Design and methods* (6th ed.). SAGE Publications.

Yoshikawa, H., Aber, J. L., & Beardslee, W. R. (2012). The effects of poverty on the mental, emotional, and behavioral health of children and youth: Implications for prevention. *American Psychologist*, *67*(4), 272. https://psycnet.apa.org/doi/10.1037/a0028015

Yosso, T. J. (2005). Whose culture has capital? A critical race theory discussion of community cultural wealth. *Race, Ethnicity and Education*, *8*(1), 69–91. doi:10.1080/1361332052000341006

Young, B. L., Madsen, J., & Young, M. A. (2010). Implementing diversity plans: Principals' perception of their ability to address diversity in their schools. *NASSP Bulletin*, *94*(2), 135–157. doi:10.1177/0192636510379901

Zacarian, D., Alvarez-Ortiz, L., & Haynes, J. (2020, October). Meeting trauma with an asset-based approach. *Educational Leadership*, 69–73.

Zarate, M. E., & Mendoza, Y. (2020). Reflections on race and privilege in an educational leadership course. *Journal of research on leadership education*, *15*(1), 56-80. doi:10.1177/1942775118771666

Zawilinski, L. M. (2016). Primary grade students create science eBooks on iPads: Authentic audiences, purposes and technologies for writing. *New England Reading Association Journal*, *51*(2), 81.

Zeng, S., Corr, C. P., O'Grady, C., & Guan, Y. (2019). Adverse childhood experiences and preschool suspension expulsion: A population study. *Child Abuse & Neglect*, *97*, 1–9. doi:10.1016/j.chiabu.2019.104149 PMID:31473382

Zhang, G., & Zeller, N. (2016, Spring). A longitudinal investigation of the relationship between teacher preparation and teacher. *Teacher Education Quarterly*, 73–92.

Zielinski, D. S. (2009). Child abuse and neglect and adult socioeconomic well-being. *Child Abuse & Neglect*, *33*(10), 666–678. doi:10.1016/j.chiabu.2009.09.001 PMID:19811826

About the Contributors

Belinda Alexander-Ashley, Ph.D., is an independent researcher, editor, author, genealogist, and consultant. After serving more than 22 years in various positions within the U.S. Probation system in three districts, she advocated for underrepresented and underserved populations gaining insight from their multifaceted perspectives. During her tenure, the author acquired insight on the impact of mass incarceration in relationship to trauma and the school-to-prison pipeline (STPP). Additionally, a need was identified to broaden integration of social justice into the educational framework and interject hope and personalized family history to enhance the historical tapestry, strengthen personal identity, and promote healthy dialogues. Subsequently, the first chapter titled, "Reducing Mass Incarceration through Trauma-Informed Pedagogy" was published in 2021. Committed to personal excellence and community, she graduated from Leadership Tulsa (OK), Leadership Cape Girardeau (MO), and Leadership Pittsburgh (PA) to enhance her service to the citizenry, educational system, and global community.

* * *

Karyn Allee earned a PhD in Elementary Education from the University of Central Florida, and her professional experiences include teaching at high-need schools, working in a large urban district as a coach and PD facilitator, and working corporately to facilitate customized PD, support large-scale district implementations and school improvement efforts, to evaluate programs, and to develop early childhood curriculum. Dr. Allee's responsibilities as an Assistant Professor of Elementary Education at Mercer University include working primarily with elementary MAT initial teacher certification candidates and PhD students in the Curriculum & Instruction track. Currently, Dr. Allee's research focuses on how poverty affects cognitive development, executive function/self-regulation as predictors of school readiness and achievement, and instructional strategies (including play and physical activity) to reduce academic achievement gaps. Dr. Allee has been published in multiple journals including the Early Childhood Education Journal, The Reading Teacher, and the Journal of Research in Childhood Education.

Letitia Basford is a professor at Hamline University's School of Education & Leadership. Her teaching and research interests focus on inclusive instructional practices, student access to equitable education, and restorative school-wide practices. She has studied the experiences of a family's experience in the school-to-prison pipeline, how schools are working to prevent that pipeline and the experiences of Somali and Hmong youth in ethnocentric charter schools. Letitia's work has been published in journals such as The Urban Review, Review of Research in Education, and in books such as Six Lenses for Anti-Oppressive Education and From Education to Incarceration: Dismantling the School-to-Prison Pipeline.

Vicki Donne is a University Professor in the Education department at Robert Morris University. She has more than 15 years of experience as a deaf educator in the public schools and 15 years of experience in special education teacher preparation. Her research interests focus on reading instruction for students who are deaf/hard of hearing, interventions and technology use among students with disabilities, and special education teacher preparation. This research has been published and presented at the national and international levels.

Jennifer Grace is an Assistant Professor of Educational Leadership at the University of Houston-Clear Lake. She earned a Ph.D. in Education Administration from the University of New Orleans (2016). She is an experienced K-12 educational leader in both urban and rural districts. Dr. Grace's research areas include the school to prison pipeline, race and racism in education, and equity-focused leadership. She has developed courses in social justice leadership for school leaders presented research on disproportionate discipline and equity-focused leadership at national and international conferences and workshops.

Karleah Harris has a Ph.D. in Educational Psychology and a Masters degree in Curriculum and Instruction from Purdue University and a Bachelors degree in Agricultural Education from North Carolina Agricultural and Technical State University. Dr. Harris has taught several undergraduate and graduate students. Her research interests include using inquiry-based science learning to study kindergarten students' explanations, the types of discourse strategies teachers use during classroom science discourse, children with learning disabilities, grandparenting, gardening, technology in education, and adolescence development.

About the Contributors

Elan C. Hope, PhD, is the Program Area Director for Research and Evaluation at Policy Research Associates. Dr. Hope takes an assets-based approach to understanding individual and community factors that promote well-being for adolescents and young adults, particularly structural barriers to wellness. She uses qualitative and quantitative methods to examine factors related to behavioral health, educational attainment, and well-being, including racial identity, critical consciousness, socialization, and activism.

Nikkita Jackson has a master's degree in Social Work from Wright State University and a bachelor's degree in Social Work from Central State University. Nikkita is a licensed social worker in the state of Ohio with over 12 years of experience in many facets pertaining to social work. Nikkita has worked in many settings, using her social work skill set in areas such as: community mental health, child protective services, home health services, crisis intervention, and working with at risk populations. Her research interests include childhood, youth, and family, mental health, student retention, health, and social care.

Annemarie Kaczmarczyk is an Assistant Professor of Elementary Education at Mercer University's Tift College of Education in Atlanta, GA. Her courses taught at the collegiate level focus on enhancing teachers' knowledge of working with culturally and linguistically diverse learners, as well as teaching strategies and classroom management. Dr. Kaczmarczyk has a passion for integrating picture books and other literature across content areas to discuss issues related to social justice and advocacy. She has co-published several journal articles related to using literature to engage children in conversations around these topics. Dr. Kaczmarczyk's current research focuses on teacher preparation for culturally and linguistically diverse student populations, examinations of preservice teacher identity and understanding of critical issues in education, and how to aid preservice teachers in becoming advocates for their students.

Patty Kardambikis is the Coordinator for both the Principal Certification Program and the Supervision of Curriculum and Instruction Certification at Robert Morris University. Dr. Kardambikis has worked in educational administration in every capacity since 2007. She began her administrative journey as the Director of e-CADEMY (now Waterfront Learning) at the Allegheny Intermediate Unit #3. She then journeyed to Aliquippa School District as the Director of Curriculum and Student Achievement. The changing economy brought her to Peters Township School District as the Assistant Superintendent. Her last stop in her public education journey was Slippery Rock School District where she was the Assistant Superintendent in the District. Dr. Kardambikis began her undergraduate work at Carlow University where she earned a Bachelor of Science in Nursing degree. She then utilized this career to springboard her counseling degree from Slippery Rock University. Dr. Kardambikis has her second master's degree in Health Education and is a Certified Health Educator Specialist (CHES). Dr. Kardambikis earned her doctorate from Kent State University in Curriculum and Instruction. After completing her Ph.D., Dr. Kardambikis received her Principal's and Superintendent's Letter of Eligibility from Westminster College. Prior to teaching at RMU, Dr. Kardambikis was an Adjunct Professor at Westminster College in both the Undergraduate and Graduate programs in Education. Outside of the world of academia, Dr. Kardambikis spends her time with her husband, three children and seven grandchildren.

Jerica Knox, PhD, is a Postdoctoral Fellow at the National Center for School Mental Health at the University of Maryland, Baltimore. Dr. Knox explores systems-level school contextual factors that promote well-being in children and adolescents. She specifically uses mixed methods to examine the effectiveness of culturally responsive and trauma-informed approaches.

Joe Lewis is an Associate Professor of Education, Chair, and Administrative Head of the School of Education and Leadership at Hamline University. His area of teaching expertise is Communication Arts and Literature / English Language Arts. His research interests focus on cross-cultural language and literacy practices, student access to equitable education, and dismantling the school-to-prison pipeline through "institutional and pedagogical plasticity." His work has been published in journals such as The Urban Review, Multicultural Education, and the National Youth-at-Risk Journal, and in books such as Six Lenses for Anti-Oppressive Education and From Education to Incarceration: Dismantling the School-to-Prison Pipeline.

Erin E. Neuman-Boone, Ph.D., is a licensed professional counselor (LPC) and Assistant Professor in the Department of Psychology at Robert Morris University. Dr. Neuman-Boone teaches courses in the Master's in Counseling Psychology Program and the undergraduate psychology program. Dr. Neuman-Boone has nearly 20 years of experience in community mental health in various clinical, supervisory, and administrative roles. She also provides independent consulting and licensure supervision. She holds degrees from Duquesne University, University of Pittsburgh, and Florida State University.

Michele McMahon Nobel is an Assistant Professor at Ohio Wesleyan University. She has worked in the field of special education for over 25 years as an advocate, teacher, and professor. She started her career as a public school teacher in Central Ohio teaching K-8 students with disabilities in inclusive and self-contained classrooms. After earning her Ph.D. from The Ohio State University in Applied Behavior Analysis and Special Education, she shifted her focus to academia and has prepared and supervised preservice Intervention Specialists since 2005. She has published in peer-reviewed journals, has written book chapters, and has presented at regional, national, and international conferences. Her research includes peer-mediated interventions for students with exceptionalities, educational technology, and educator preparation, particularly regarding trauma-informed education, equity, and developing antiracist educators.

Vijaya R. is currently working as Assistant Professor in CHRIST (Deemed to be University). She has worked as a Human Resource Professional for eight years, as part of her Ph.D. work she researched the topic on Downsizing employees. She has authored a few articles and book chapters on Organizational behaviour and continues her research work in the area of downsizing organizations, retrenched employees, entrepreneurship, leadership and management. She has presented her research papers at various international and national conferences. She has conducted various workshops, lectures and training programmes in schools, colleges and on a need-base for some Government organizations. She is actively engaged in various research projects in the field of Human Resource, specifically on employee retention and well-being. She passionately integrates the academics and the corporate world adding research components with the strong belief that collaboration is essential for the growth and sustenance of today's organization. She is a certified Lean six sigma green belt, Lumina Spark Practitioner, and Lean expert. Her clientele includes the Luxury Segment sector, Manufacturing industry, hospitality sector and education sector. Some of her projects include Leadership, Organisational change, Employee involvement, and Personality development.

Wei-Ling Sun is an assistant professor in the Department of Educational Leadership and Foundations. She received a Ph.D. from the Department of Educational Leadership and Policy at The University of Texas at Austin, with a graduate portfolio in women and gender studies. Her research examines the social and political dimensions of discipline policy reforms and culturally responsive school leadership. She is currently studying sociopolitical contexts of the school-to-prison pipeline from high school principals' perspectives and the impact of COVID-19 in borderland schools. In the summer of 2016, she was a Bill Archer Graduate Fellow with the University of Texas System, where she spent the summer working as a policy analyst with a leading civil rights organization, Advancement Project, in Washington, D.C. In the summer of 2019, American Educational Research Association (AERA) named her as a congressional fellow for 2019-20. She worked as a legislative fellow for a member of Congress and used her education research expertise to inform public policy.

Sruthi Suresh is a doctoral research scholar in Psychology at CHRIST (Deemed to be University). In 2018, she completed her M.Sc. in Counseling Psychology and worked as an IB DP Psychology Faculty for the next two years. After joining the Ph.D. program in 2020, she has been an active scholar and engaged with the department as a Research Assistant, Teaching Assistant, Impact Assessment Research Team Lead, and Department Magazine Editor. She writes and presents widely on issues related to child and adolescent mental health, teacher education, and social emotional learning.

Jonathan Trauth is Assistant professor in the Social Work Department. the last few years he was a lecturer in the Department of Counseling, Social Work & Leadership at Northern Kentucky University and Miami University. In the 1990s while working for the affordable housing coalition and serving special needs populations, Jonathan studied psychology and theology leading to a dual Degree from Xavier University. In 2001, Dr. Trauth began working in substance abuse dependency counseling in inner city Lexington, KY, while working on his MSW at the University of Kentucky. He completed his Doctorate in Counseling at the University of Cincinnati in 2016. Dr. Trauth traveled to El Salvador and to Nicaragua to help build water filtration systems and malaria-proofing latrines while also being introduced to permaculture techniques for third-world country applications. Dr. Trauth worked three years at the Clermont Recovery Center in Batavia, Ohio, with adolescents incorporating therapy through gardening. He then brought the ideas learned in horticulture therapy to clients and families at Lighthouse Youth Services where he worked as a social worker and clinical supervisor. Last year he completed his 72 hour permaculture certification. More recently at St. Leo the Great parish, Dr. Trauth began working with the Burundian refugee population. These refugees requested his help in obtaining land for farming so they could grow their own food. Observable outcomes that have had a significant impact on these refugees include community integration, self-efficacy, self-sufficiency, increase in business knowledge, opportunities for physical exercise for all ages, and a collaboration with different organizations focused on the creation and sustainability of a refugee garden.

Boas Yu is an associate professor at School of Nursing and Allied Health, Fairleigh Dickinson University, Teaneck, NJ. She is a researcher who studies meditation effects and have published in many research journals. She is a gerontological clinical nurse specialist, certified as nurse educator; also a licensed psychiatric nurse practitioner and family nurse practitioner.

Index

A

Adolescents 42-43, 64, 66, 78-81, 91, 104-105, 109, 147, 161-162, 165, 191, 218, 220, 223-224, 227, 268, 283
Adverse Childhood Experiences (ACEs) 84, 109, 115-119, 122, 125, 129-130, 132-134, 136-137, 139, 145, 148, 161, 169-170, 179, 187, 203-204, 225, 261, 263-268, 271-278, 280, 288
Alternative Education 7, 28, 46
Ambassadors of Hope 141, 156-157, 160
Anti-Racism 33, 36, 39, 46
At-Risk Students 72, 81

C

Challenging Behavior 194, 196, 205, 212, 216
Childhood Trauma 5, 50, 53, 57, 59-60, 69, 72, 74, 77-79, 81, 83-85, 105, 109, 126, 141-145, 148, 151, 153-154, 156-157, 161, 163, 168-172, 177-179, 182, 184-186, 189, 203, 205, 218, 227, 230, 256, 262, 285
Children's Literature 111, 128, 133, 135, 139
Collective Readiness 231, 235-238, 242-246, 253, 260
Constructivist Learning Theory 146, 148, 166, 168, 193
Coronavirus Pandemic 69, 77
COVID-19 11, 48-53, 59-61, 63-64, 67, 81, 112, 141-142, 149, 158, 162-163, 165, 169, 174, 187-188, 190, 202, 206, 220-221, 275, 284
Cultural Responsiveness 38-39, 229-233, 235, 237-241, 245-247, 250-251, 253-254, 260, 273
Culturally Responsive Pedagogy 191, 202, 209, 229, 233, 258-259, 274
Culturally Responsive School Leadership 44, 48, 51, 57, 60, 62, 257
Culturally Responsive Teaching 123, 135, 188, 256-257, 274, 288
culturally sustaining pedagogies 1, 7, 16, 18

D

DAEP 20, 28, 30, 41, 46
Direct Bullying 86, 106, 109
Dropout Prevention 66
Dropout Recovery 1-2, 8, 16, 18

E

Education 1-2, 5, 7, 12, 14, 16-18, 21-22, 26-28, 32, 37, 39, 42-46, 48, 50-51, 59, 61-64, 69, 72, 81, 87, 90-91, 95, 103-104, 106-107, 113-114, 118-120, 125, 131-140, 142-144, 150-151, 155, 157-159, 161-163, 165-166, 169, 172, 177, 179, 183-192, 195, 197, 200, 204, 207-208, 210, 212, 217-227, 230, 232-234, 238-239, 244, 253-256, 258-260, 265-266, 268, 273, 276-279, 282-287
Educational Equity 20, 38, 40-41, 46, 199, 235
Elementary Education 139, 162, 188
Elementary School 55, 57, 65, 106, 111,

134, 139, 168-169, 172, 176, 183, 185, 218, 224, 255
Emotional Coaching 83-85, 91-93, 95-97, 100, 102-103, 105, 109
Epigenetics 139-140, 174, 177, 193
Equality 7, 128, 143-144, 163, 166, 184, 189, 192
Equity 20, 34, 36, 38-41, 43, 45-47, 51, 63-64, 128, 143-144, 160, 163, 166, 184, 186, 189-190, 192, 199, 201, 221, 223-224, 229, 233, 235-236, 239-240, 243, 246, 256, 258-259, 273-274, 286

F

Family History 163, 168-173, 175-185, 187, 189-191, 193
Fixed Mindset 193

G

Gardening 80, 82
Genealogy 163, 168, 171, 174-177, 180, 183-185, 188-191, 193
Growth Mindset 183, 193

H

Higher Hope 141-142, 146-148, 150-152, 154-155, 157-160, 166
Historically Marginalized Students 114, 130-131, 140
Holistic Approach 75-76, 82, 148, 183
Hope 17, 19, 31-32, 42, 141-142, 145-152, 154-160, 162-168, 181, 184-185, 188-189, 229, 256
Hopelessness 26, 141, 147, 167
Horticulture Therapy 66-70, 72, 76-80

I

Indirect Bullying 86, 106, 110
Individual Readiness 229, 231-235, 245-249, 251-253, 260
Inherited Trauma 113, 118, 140
Institutional Anti-Racist Change 38-41, 47
Instructional Strategies 111-112, 131, 140

Interventions 7, 70-73, 76, 78, 80-81, 114-115, 138, 140, 194, 196, 198-199, 201, 204, 225, 255-256, 261-262, 268-271, 273-274, 276-278, 280-288
Introspection 131, 168, 171-172, 176, 178, 184-185

M

Maslow's Hierarchy of Needs 152-153, 155, 162-163, 193

N

Narratives 32, 40, 51, 60, 171, 173, 176, 184, 186, 244

O

Opportunity Gap 22, 43, 47, 135

P

Pedagogical and Institutional Plasticity 1-2, 16
Positive Behavioral Intervention and Supports 269, 286
Positive Behavioral Interventions and Supports (PBIS) 196, 198, 261, 268, 278, 281, 288
Poverty 45, 56-57, 68, 114, 126, 132, 135, 144, 168-169, 186, 195, 204, 261-262, 264-268, 271, 273-276, 278-284, 287-288

R

Race-Based Trauma 20-22, 41, 47
Reflection 7, 34-35, 41, 126, 131, 168, 178, 185, 202, 209, 216, 242, 245-246, 249, 253
Restorative Practices 7, 16, 19, 60, 135, 208

S

School Bullying 83-87, 89, 91, 105, 107-110
School Discipline 6, 18-19, 29, 43-44, 46,

Index

64, 158, 196, 221, 226, 275, 285
School Pushout 22, 47
School to Prison Pipeline 17, 20, 43, 63, 103, 135, 162, 262, 266-267, 273, 275-277
Schools 1-5, 7-9, 11-14, 16-24, 28, 33, 37-38, 41-46, 48-51, 53, 55, 59-60, 62, 65-66, 68-69, 71-72, 76-77, 85-86, 89-90, 103, 106-107, 111-114, 118-120, 125, 128, 130-132, 135-139, 160, 170, 172, 178, 180-184, 188, 196-200, 202, 204-205, 208-209, 214-216, 218, 220-225, 227, 230-233, 235-239, 243-244, 246, 248-250, 252-260, 262, 265, 267-269, 271-273, 275-279, 281-282, 285-286
School-to-Prison Nexus 114, 130, 140-146, 148, 150-151, 153, 159, 169-172, 174-175, 177, 181, 183, 185, 190
School-to-Prison Pipeline 1-3, 8, 16-17, 21-23, 33, 41, 43-45, 48-49, 51-53, 60, 62-64, 67-69, 78, 83-85, 89-90, 102-103, 105-106, 110, 112, 114, 130, 139, 142, 144, 156-158, 161, 163, 165, 167, 169, 184, 186, 190, 192-199, 201, 203, 205, 214-217, 219, 222, 230-231, 261, 277, 286
Science of Hope 142, 146-148, 151, 154, 159, 162, 166-167, 188
Social Determinants 114, 133, 140
Social Emotional 105, 135, 269, 271, 275, 288
Social Emotional Learning 135, 269
Social Justice (in Education) 140
Storytelling 61, 126, 169, 181, 183, 248
Strategies 10, 12, 21, 33-36, 38, 40, 42, 48-53, 56-57, 59, 66, 72, 78, 81, 83, 85, 93-94, 97, 99-100, 103, 111-112, 122-123, 126-129, 131, 135-136, 140-142, 144-146, 148, 150, 153, 156, 160, 168-169, 173, 175, 177, 184-185, 196-197, 199, 205, 209-211, 213, 215-216, 219, 221, 223, 226, 228-229, 231, 243, 252-254, 268-269, 271, 274
Students 1, 3-18, 21-22, 25, 27, 30, 33, 35-60, 63-78, 81, 83, 85-91, 93-100, 102, 106-108, 110-112, 114, 118-132, 134-135, 137, 139-142, 144-146, 148-155, 157-160, 165, 167-186, 189, 192-193, 195-221, 223-226, 230-232, 236-239, 242, 244, 246, 248-250, 253-255, 257, 259-261, 265-276, 281, 286-288
Systemic Trauma 113, 117-119, 131, 134, 140

T

Teacher Preparation 201-202, 207, 209, 214-216, 220, 225, 227
Teachers 2, 4-7, 9-13, 15, 17-18, 21-22, 27, 30-31, 33, 35, 37, 39, 41, 44, 46, 49, 51-52, 54-59, 66, 68-69, 83, 85, 89-100, 102-104, 111-112, 119-125, 127-131, 134-136, 138, 140, 142, 148-151, 153-155, 157-160, 163, 172-178, 180-184, 186, 188-189, 194-209, 212-217, 219-227, 232, 235-236, 238, 242-246, 250, 256-259, 265, 268, 271-274, 276, 285, 288
Toxic Stress 117-118, 122, 129, 133-134, 138, 140, 263, 280, 285
Trauma 1-2, 5, 8, 10, 12-14, 16, 20-23, 25-26, 31, 33, 41-42, 44-45, 47-50, 52-54, 56-60, 67-72, 74, 76-82, 84-85, 92, 103, 105, 107-109, 111-115, 117-127, 129-134, 136-151, 154, 156-161, 163-179, 181-186, 188-190, 192-194, 196-209, 211-218, 220-222, 224-227, 229-232, 244, 249, 254-256, 259-264, 267-268, 271, 273, 275-277, 279, 285, 288
Trauma Informed Care 70, 72, 76, 271
Trauma Responses 123-124, 130, 140, 208-209, 212, 263
Trauma-Informed 44, 66-71, 75-78, 108, 125, 130-131, 136, 139-140, 148, 153-155, 157, 159, 163-164, 166, 169, 172, 174, 181, 183-184, 190, 192, 194, 196, 199-204, 207-209, 212, 215-219, 221, 223-227, 229-235, 237-251, 253-256, 258-260, 267, 279, 288
Trauma-Informed Approach 68, 77, 164, 194, 224, 226, 232-233, 248, 279
Trauma-Informed Education 130, 136, 140, 204, 208, 212, 227, 259

Trauma-Informed Practices 148, 172, 174, 181, 196, 200-202, 204, 207-209, 212, 216-217, 219, 221, 227, 229, 239, 245, 247, 253, 279, 288

Y

Young Adults 79, 82, 196, 202

Z

Zero Tolerance 4-5, 16, 19, 62, 135, 141, 162, 168-169, 265, 267, 275-277, 288

Recommended Reference Books

IGI Global's reference books can now be purchased from three unique pricing formats:
Print Only, E-Book Only, or Print + E-Book.
Shipping fees may apply.
www.igi-global.com

Participatory Pedagogy
Emerging Research and Opportunities

ISBN: 9781522589648
EISBN: 9781522589655
© 2021; 156 pp.
List Price: US$ 155

Transformative Pedagogical Perspectives on Home Language Use in Classrooms

ISBN: 9781799840756
EISBN: 9781799840763
© 2021; 282 pp.
List Price: US$ 185

Advancing Online Course Design and Pedagogy for the 21st Century Learning Environment

ISBN: 9781799855989
EISBN: 9781799856009
© 2021; 382 pp.
List Price: US$ 195

Deep Fakes, Fake News, and Misinformation in Online Teaching and Learning Technologies

ISBN: 9781799864745
EISBN: 9781799864752
© 2021; 271 pp.
List Price: US$ 195

Enhancing Higher Education Accessibility Through Open Education and Prior Learning

ISBN: 9781799875710
EISBN: 9781799875734
© 2021; 252 pp.
List Price: US$ 195

Connecting Disciplinary Literacy and Digital Storytelling in K-12 Education

ISBN: 9781799857709
EISBN: 9781799857716
© 2021; 378 pp.
List Price: US$ 195

Do you want to stay current on the latest research trends, product announcements, news, and special offers?
Join IGI Global's mailing list to receive customized recommendations, exclusive discounts, and more.
Sign up at: **www.igi-global.com/newsletters**.

Publisher of Timely, Peer-Reviewed Inclusive Research Since 1988

IGI Global
PUBLISHER of TIMELY KNOWLEDGE

www.igi-global.com   Sign up at www.igi-global.com/newsletters   facebook.com/igiglobal   twitter.com/igiglobal

Ensure Quality Research is Introduced to the Academic Community

Become an Evaluator for IGI Global Authored Book Projects

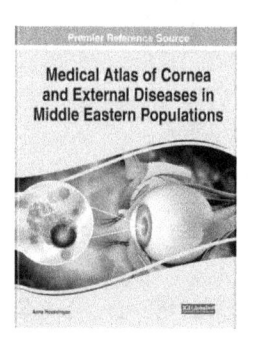

The overall success of an authored book project is dependent on quality and timely manuscript evaluations.

Applications and Inquiries may be sent to:
development@igi-global.com

Applicants must have a doctorate (or equivalent degree) as well as publishing, research, and reviewing experience. Authored Book Evaluators are appointed for one-year terms and are expected to complete at least three evaluations per term. Upon successful completion of this term, evaluators can be considered for an additional term.

If you have a colleague that may be interested in this opportunity, we encourage you to share this information with them.

Easily Identify, Acquire, and Utilize Published
Peer-Reviewed Findings in Support of Your Current Research

IGI Global OnDemand

Purchase Individual IGI Global OnDemand Book Chapters and Journal Articles

For More Information:
www.igi-global.com/e-resources/ondemand/

Browse through 150,000+ Articles and Chapters!

Find specific research related to your current studies and projects that have been contributed by international researchers from prestigious institutions, including:

MIT Massachusetts Institute of Technology • HARVARD UNIVERSITY • COLUMBIA UNIVERSITY IN THE CITY OF NEW YORK • Australian National University

- Accurate and Advanced Search
- Affordably Acquire Research
- Instantly Access Your Content
- Benefit from the InfoSci Platform Features

It really provides an excellent entry into the research literature of the field. It presents a manageable number of highly relevant sources on topics of interest to a wide range of researchers. The sources are scholarly, but also accessible to 'practitioners'.

- Ms. Lisa Stimatz, MLS, University of North Carolina at Chapel Hill, USA

Interested in Additional Savings?

Subscribe to
IGI Global OnDemand Plus

Learn More

Acquire content from over 128,000+ research-focused book chapters and 33,000+ scholarly journal articles for as low as US$ 5 per article/chapter (original retail price for an article/chapter: US$ 37.50).

6,600+ E-BOOKS.
ADVANCED RESEARCH.
INCLUSIVE & ACCESSIBLE.
IGI Global e-Book Collection

- **Flexible Purchasing Options** (Perpetual, Subscription, EBA, etc.)
- Multi-Year Agreements with **No Price Increases** Guaranteed
- **No Additional Charge** for Multi-User Licensing
- No Maintenance, Hosting, or Archiving Fees
- Transformative **Open Access Options** Available

Request More Information, or Recommend the IGI Global e-Book Collection to Your Institution's Librarian

Among Titles Included in the IGI Global e-Book Collection

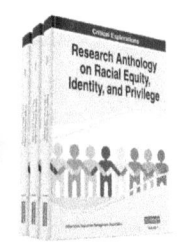

Research Anthology on Racial Equity, Identity, and Privilege (3 Vols.)
EISBN: 9781668445082
Price: US$ 895

Handbook of Research on Remote Work and Worker Well-Being in the Post-COVID-19 Era
EISBN: 9781799867562
Price: US$ 265

Research Anthology on Big Data Analytics, Architectures, and Applications (4 Vols.)
EISBN: 9781668436639
Price: US$ 1,950

Handbook of Research on Challenging Deficit Thinking for Exceptional Education Improvement
EISBN: 9781799888628
Price: US$ 265

Acquire & Open

When your library acquires an IGI Global e-Book and/or e-Journal Collection, your faculty's published work will be considered for immediate conversion to Open Access *(CC BY License)*, at no additional cost to the library or its faculty *(cost only applies to the e-Collection content being acquired)*, through our popular **Transformative Open Access (Read & Publish) Initiative**.

For More Information or to Request a Free Trial, Contact IGI Global's e-Collections Team: eresources@igi-global.com | 1-866-342-6657 ext. 100 | 717-533-8845 ext. 100

Open Access Publishing

Have Your Work Published and Freely Accessible

With the industry shifting from the more traditional publication models to an open access (OA) publication model, publishers are finding that OA publishing has many benefits that are awarded to authors and editors of published work.

- Freely Share Your Research
- Higher Discoverability & Citation Impact
- Rigorous & Expedited Publishing Process
- Increased Advancement & Collaboration

Acquire & Open

When your library acquires an IGI Global e-Book and/or e-Journal Collection, your faculty's published work will be considered for immediate conversion to Open Access *(CC BY License)*, at no additional cost to the library or its faculty *(cost only applies to the e-Collection content being acquired)*, through our popular **Transformative Open Access (Read & Publish) Initiative**.

- Provide Up To **100%** OA APC or CPC Funding
- Funding to Convert or Start a Journal to **Platinum OA**
- Support for Funding an **OA Reference Book**

IGI Global publications are found in a number of prestigious indices, including Web of Science™, Scopus®, Compendex, and PsycINFO®. The selection criteria is very strict and to ensure that journals and books are accepted into the major indexes, IGI Global closely monitors publications against the criteria that the indexes provide to publishers.

WEB OF SCIENCE™ **Compendex** **Scopus**
PsycINFO® **IET Inspec**

Learn More Here:

For Questions, Contact IGI Global's Open Access Team at openaccessadmin@igi-global.com

IGI Global
PUBLISHER of TIMELY KNOWLEDGE
www.igi-global.com